SEA TROUT FISHING

Plate 1

Waiting for Dusk

SEA TROUT FISHING

A GUIDE TO SUCCESS

by

HUGH FALKUS

Illustrated with numerous
photographs and diagrams
and five colour plates

CASSELLPAPERBACKS

First published in the United Kingdom in 1962 by
H. F. & G. Witherby Ltd.

Reprinted 1971
Second edition (much enlarged) 1975
Impression with minor corrections, January 1976
Reprinted with some revision, 1977
Reprinted, January 1978
Reprinted, July 1978
Reprinted, August 1979
Revised second edition with new colour plates, 1981
Reprinted, January 1982
Reprinted with minor corrections, February 1983
Reprinted, April 1984
Reprinted, March 1985
Reprinted, February 1986
Reprinted, September 1986
Reprinted, December 1987
Reprinted, January 1989
Reprinted, December 1990
Reprinted, January 1995
Reprinted, February 1997
Reprinted 1998

This paperback edition first published in 2002 by
Cassell Paperbacks, Cassell & Co
Wellington House, 125 Strand
London, WC2R 0BB

A CIP catalogue record for this book is available
from the British Library

ISBN 1-84188-184-8

Printed and bound in Great Britain by
MPG Books Ltd. Bodmin, Cornwall

For
Kathleen

Preparing for dusk. "Trusties" tackle-up together with the author on the lawn at Cragg. *Far right:* Arthur Oglesby. *Second from right:* Peter Lewars. *Third from right:* Eric Horsfall Turner. *Far left:* Bill Bruxby.

The picture was taken in August, 1966. That year had a wonderful sea trout season with great runs of fish. Alas, they were devastated in late September by UDN.

Preface

My motive in writing the first edition of this book was twofold. First, I knew I had something original to say. Secondly, I wanted to try to repay a debt; to give something back to the sport of angling in return for the lifetime of enjoyment it had given me.

In doing so I did not anticipate much profit—royalties from angling books are not high in the list of literary rewards, and I am after all a professional writer. But although in one sense I was right, in another and much more important sense I was wrong. The friendships which formed directly or indirectly because of what I had written proved a "royalty" vastly more valuable than mere sales.

Over the years, Cragg Cottage became a kind of "club". To it came Antony Witherby, most delightful of fishing companions. Eric Horsfall Turner and Arthur Oglesby, successive editors of *Angler's Annual* and fishermen extraordinary. Fred Buller, of *Pike* fame (with whom I now have a happy partnership in several sporting books). Those hardy annuals, F. J. Taylor and his brother Ken, two of the best all-rounders in the country. Jimmy Skene, of Windermere—who as an angler needs no introduction from me in the north. And Richard Walker—who needs none in the south. The surgeon "Peters", Lewars and Cook (as skilled with skillet as scalpel). The schoolmaster "Peters", Stansfield and Dams—although the latter, like "Briggy" Wilson, Eric Dawson, Frank Plum, Joe Hatton, John Sanders, Jimmy Brown, Tommy Duggan and Bill Wareing—together with the "Michaels" Heaton and Hordern, belongs to earlier days. Frank Chamberlain, John Stamp and Edgar Freshman are old lags. So is that gifted sportsman, Denis Bridge (to whom all things are ever fresh). Jimmy Deterding, John Wilson, Henry Musgrave and "Mad" Ned Minihan are short-term men. Anne and Conrad Voss Bark, David Burnett, John Griffiths and "Tim" Rickett have been recently sentenced. Peter Thomas has served a longer stretch. So has George Weston and his troupe. And Bill Bruxby longer still. So, too, has that thoughtful angler Tom Rawling, who wrote with such deep understanding of my methods in *Trout and Salmon* and to whom credit for a demand for this second edition is undoubtedly due. For many years that fine angler Justin Lewars has served with distinction. And latterly, Ron Harrison, whose enthusiasm has never reflected the diminishing runs of fish. Finally, we have Jonathan and Adam Price—last in name, but among the first in skill and dedication.

No angler can fish in company with others without learning something new about the sport—and about himself. So—to all these "Trusties" and to the many other friends who over the years have stayed with me, I offer my thanks. I shall always remember with delight the excitement of those days and nights gone by, when we fished the hours away and watched the sky catch fire behind Scawfell.

Hugh Falkus

Cragg Cottage, January 1981

Special acknowledgement and thanks are due to Fred Buller, the late William Fowler, Anne and Krov Menuhin, Tom Rawling, Niko Tinbergen, 'Briggy' Wilson and Arthur Oglesby for their photography, and Macdonald and Jane's (Publishers) Ltd., for permission to reprint material originally published in *Falkus and Buller's Freshwater Fishing* (1975). The photograph of Walter Caddy on page 434 is reproduced by kind permission of his grandson Allan Caddy.

The flies and lures photographed by Alan C. Parker on the colour plates were tied under my direction. I wish to thank my old friend Richard Barnes Woodall for tying all the traditional sea trout flies and dapping flies (except for the Kingsmill and Claret Bumble kindly supplied by David Burnett), and for the others I am indebted to the Riding Brothers of 135 Church Street, Preston from whom sets of all lures can be obtained.

8

Contents

Colour Plates

And first and most essential whereof, is that a skilful angler ought to be a general scholar, and seen in all the liberal sciences; as a grammarian, to know how either to write or discourse of his art in true and fitting terms, either without affectation or rudeness; and he should have sweetness of speech to persuade others, and engage others, to delight in an exercise so much laudable.

Gervase Markham, *The Whole Art of Angling* (fifth edition), 1633.

Introduction

It was a dark mid-August night with a heavy tumble of cloud and a hint of rain; the little river at summer low, running crystal clear over its pale blue-grey stones. A brown owl hooting from the wooded fellside; another from a spinney at my back. No other sound—except a whisper of wind in the leaves and a faint chuckle of water from the run-in at the head of the pool.

Two o'clock in the morning. I was alone, sitting on the bank smoking a cigarette, rod propped against a bush. In the fish-bag hanging from a branch, five sea trout; all caught between dusk and midnight. Since then, nothing. Not an offer. Not even the *movement* of a fish.

There was an early morning chill. The kitchen light at Cragg winked invitingly from the distant fell. I thought of hot coffee and whisky and debated whether to pack up and go home.

Then, with dramatic suddenness, a heavy splash—somewhere out in the darkness to my left, up near the head of the pool. "Splosh" would fit it better: the sound a big fish makes when it lunges on the surface before sinking back to its lie. I could guess to a foot where it had risen: by a sunken rock under some sycamore branches on the far bank. An age-old lie for a big sea trout.

Ripples lapped the shingle at my feet. I took my rod and retired behind the bushes. Torch in mouth I cut off the fly I had been using—a size four Mallard and Silver—and tied on the big Sunk Lure: a slender, tenuous thing of peacock herl and blue, three inches long.

To attack at once when a big fish moves late at night is always a great temptation—and a great mistake. I sucked the lure, tested the knot, then sat down and lit another cigarette.

When the cigarette had burned down I stubbed it out and walked softly up the shingle to the neck of the pool. Well upstream, clear of the "Sycamore" lie, I started to cast. Not for the big chap. Not yet. Just practice, to make sure everything was working as it should.

When all was going smoothly I moved downstream. The line hissed in the air. The lure went out into the bushy darkness, touched down, sank and started to swing.

The big fish took it at once.

A feeling of . . . not surprise—I had caught other big sea trout in low water late at night after hearing them move, some of them in that very lie. A sense, rather, of wonderment. Once again the trick had actually worked.

Anyway, there was the fish, seemingly well hooked and rushing about. No snags in that pool, so it was just a matter of time. The fish kept on the go and did most of the work. In about fifteen minutes it was ready to land.

It felt a mighty fine fish, well into the teens of pounds, so I didn't take any risks. I walked it to some deep, slack water, sank the big net, the handle held between my knees, and waited for the gleam of a silver flank before drawing it gently in. . . .

Beside the fishing shelter behind the bushes I stretched the fish out on the grass and shone the light. I nearly dropped the torch. It wasn't a sea trout. It was a salmon!

*   *   *

That happened a long time ago. The first salmon I had ever caught with "fly" on a dark night. Intriguing. I had been told that salmon wouldn't take on dark nights.

Now I am not going to argue the definition of a "dark" night. It was dark. Pitch dark, if you like. But when I write "fly" you will understand what I mean. It wasn't a fly that hooked the salmon, it was a lure, in this case a big Sunk Lure—three inches of it.

It was all very exciting. But it is not about salmon fishing that I want to write at the moment. Of catching salmon on Sunk Lure at night, more in a later chapter. The point I make here is simply that when the fish moved I didn't think it was a salmon. What I thought I was after; what I expected to hook, and what I thought I had hooked was a big sea trout.

Well, if you are one of those fishermen who believe that, like those of brown trout, sea trout "taking" times in a river correspond to actual feeding times—and it is surprising how many people do—you will be wondering why I was fishing for sea trout at two o'clock in the morning in a small, low, clear river, with a three-inch Sunk Lure.

The answer is that (for reasons given in the following chapters) it seemed the logical size of lure to use. Experience had taught me that sea trout frequently took well late at night, and I didn't believe that many of them took because they were "on the feed".

It is important to remember that I refer specifically to sea trout with a sea life of 1 year+ *not* to the young fish (herling, whitling, finnock, smelt, sprod, scurf, truff or what-have-you) a certain number of which continue to feed in freshwater as avidly as the food supply permits. During their river life following their return from sea, most sea trout (like salmon) have no need of food. The supply of nourishment in their tissues is sufficient to sustain them during a long fast and to provide for the developing ova and milt.

As G. H. Nall says in *The Life of the Sea Trout* (1930), the greatest work on the sea trout ever written:

"... they lose not only their brightness, but their condition also, in fresh water. Their weight in relation to their length depreciates week by week, as they consume the stores of fat, which they have accumulated on their muscles and internal organs."

That this is undoubtedly true is obvious to anybody who has compared the table qualities of a silver-bright fresh-run early summer sea trout with a dark, lack-lustre fish that has spent three months in the river. The flesh of the former; firm, pink, of unrivalled flavour, contrasts dramatically with that of the latter—which is pale and tasteless.

This is not to suggest that sea trout take no food at all while in freshwater. Many sea trout swallow items of food from time to time. But then, so do salmon. And yet salmon are commonly regarded as non-feeders. Salmon are caught on worms and maggots with great frequency. Do people really suppose that a salmon sucks down only the worm or maggot that is fastened to a hook?

Young salmon, like young sea trout—the "grilse"of the species—often interest themselves in food items of one sort or another. And although the elderly fish are less inclined to do so, there are always exceptions. David Jacques told me of a 10 lb. salmon that he rose, hooked and landed on a dry fly on the River Test. In a letter to *The Field*, Sir Richard Levinge describes an experience on the River Boyne, where the mayfly hatch happened to coincide with the end of the spring run of salmon:

"An apparently great trout was rising steadily to mayfly all of one day, just out of casting reach from the bank. The following afternoon I came back to the river, equipped with breast waders to find the fish still sucking down mayflies.

"I waded out close enough to cover it and was, I remember, disappointed to find it was only a salmon of 6 lb. Not only was its stomach packed full, enough to fill two cupped hands, with mayfly nymph and dun, but it also had a broken cast and a bedraggled mayfly in its gullet.

"In a previous year, an eminent Dublin surgeon enjoyed a great evening with the mayfly on the same beat, taking two trout of 8 lb. and 4 lb. and a salmon of 12 lb. The following year on the Deel, a tributary of the Boyne, I saw a large salmon, 15 lb. or more, sucking down mayfly as hard as it could go."

I, too, have observed salmon taking surface fly, and many people have had similar experiences. But such examples do not turn the salmon into an active freshwater feeder any more than the taking of a caterpillar or a sedge at dusk turns the sea trout into a "feeding" fish. There is, I submit, a great difference between "the taking of occasional food items" and "feeding". If "feeding" is defined as: *the taking of nourishment for the maintenance of life*, then like the returning salmon most sea trout are non-feeders.

This point is of the utmost importance to the fisherman, in particular to the fly fisherman.

There are two completely different forms of approach to sea trout fishing:

1. That the fish on their return from sea remain active feeders.
2. That the fish do *not* remain active feeders (in the sense already defined).

The fisherman who favours the first will take a bag of sea trout only at certain times and under certain conditions. He will be fishing a fly that is intended to simulate a natural insect. When fish have "gone down", he will lose hope, believing that sport is finished.

The fisherman who adopts the second approach has always a chance of catching fish. While taking advantage of any hatch that may materialize, he will know this to be merely a passing phase. When the fish are down he will change his technique—and continue fishing with every hope of success.

Nevertheless, it is quite likely that some of my readers who fish waters that provide a considerable hatch of fly, and where the sea trout indulge in occasional orgies, still firmly believe that sea trout are regular feeders and should be treated as such.

Although, technically, they may be exceptionally skilful anglers, I doubt whether their results really do them justice.

To offer sea trout an imitation of an insect they are seen to be taking is, in the circumstances, a very sensible approach and (for a time at any rate) the anglers concerned should catch fish. But the question I pose is this: how do these anglers behave when there is no hatch of fly; when the evening turns cold and the river seems empty and the ground mist swirls round their legs like smoke? What do they do then—take their rods to pieces and go home?

You think this a *reductio ad absurdum*?

Listen.

In an article not long ago a fellow traveller stated categorically:

"The only time worth fishing for sea trout is when the fish are on the feed. Otherwise . . ." as he put it, "you might as well pack up."

Other gems mined from the angling press include the following:

"Sea trout . . . feed regularly while visiting freshwaters to spawn."

"The food situation is the decidedly dominant influence in the habits of the sea trout."

"The sea trout's life as an adult fish in fresh water is not at all difficult to understand. He is, in fact, quite an uncomplicated fish. He has a big appetite, is an aggressive feeder, and is extremely fond of flies. . . . If the flies do not materialise, the river eventually goes dead and fishing is pretty useless."

"If there are no flies excepting around dusk, no amount of skill makes very much difference and catches will not be heavy."

Well—I'm sorry, but all this is nonsense, and anyone believing it need not feel surprised when catches are light. I assure you that if your approach to sea trout fishing in freshwater is based on the idea of satisfying the hunger of a feeding fish you will be denying yourself all but occasional chances of success—especially with big fish.

Of course, not all sea trout waters present the same picture. Sea trout behaviour does not conform to a similar pattern all over Great Britain and Ireland. Far from it. The behaviour of many species of animals depends largely on environment, and the sea trout is no exception. For generation after generation fish return mainly to the rivers that bred them. This is so consistent that populations of fish (sometimes in rivers only a few miles apart) undoubtedly follow slightly separate lines of evolution. It is noticeable in some of the rivers and lakes of North West Britain, where night fly-fishing is seldom attempted. In some food-rich river and lake systems, sea trout certainly take more interest in food than sea trout found in spate rivers. But I suggest that the reason for this interest in a food item (or, for that matter, an angler's lure) is similar to that well-known mountaineer's interest in his mountain— *because it is there*!

If it is not there, most sea trout make little or no effort to search for it. Like the salmon they are equipped to endure a long fast while in freshwater, and although their behaviour may vary according to their environment few can (by the terms of our definition) be called feeding fish.

This is the similarity between the behaviour of sea trout and salmon and the difference between the behaviour of sea trout and brown trout. The difference between sea trout and salmon is that whereas the salmon tends to take a lure mainly by day, the sea trout (with certain exceptions, notably those of the western lakes) does so mainly by night.

Catching sea trout in stillwater is studied in Chapter XIII. The earlier part of the book relates to catching river sea trout, and for this the concept of a fish that takes a lure or bait because of habit rather than hunger and is more active by night than by day is a very sound basis from which to start.

Much of our river fishing takes place during the hours of darkness, and I urge you to remember that provided fish are present and the river not in flood (in which case daylight fishing will be in operation) the absence of a hatch of fly, or any surface movement of sea trout, need have no effect whatever on your chances, however low the water.

There are very few nights of the season when sea trout cannot be caught.

The methods described in this book are the result of my own experience and observations on many waters throughout Great Britain and Ireland. They have worked very well for me, and for my friends. I am sure that if you accept them not word for word but as a *guide*: to be adapted to the various conditions of weather and water you meet, they will work as well for you.

COLOUR PLATE OPPOSITE
Notwithstanding its credited title, the fly at the left end of row 5 is really a *Woodcock* and Green. The idiosyncratic nomenclature dates from an old Irish companion long ago who confided that he always tied a Teal and Green with woodcock because he thought it looked more natural! Here for posterity is his dressing.

The Claret Bumble and the Kingsmill are both comparatively recent additions to the 'traditional' list—splendid inventions of the late T. C. Kingsmill Moore. All the patterns shown on lines 7 and 8 are good 'bob' flies for Irish loughs, but those on line 8 are my favourites.

Sea Trout Flies — Historical

Unlike the brown trout and to a lesser degree the salmon, about both of which angling history has much to relate, the sea trout is a very 'modern' fish. Until a comparatively short time ago almost nothing was known about it. Even as recently as 1916, in his book: *The Sea Trout, A study in Natural History*, Henry Lamond asks: 'What is a sea-trout?' And continues: 'It is, one must admit, a question which has not yet been very satisfactorily answered by anybody, nor can I pretend to give a very satisfactory answer myself.'

In view of this it is not surprising that, like the salmon fly, the sea trout fly got off to a rather poor start.

Many traditional salmon flies resemble over-grown trout flies — because they are a hang-over from the days when people believed that salmon fed regularly on flies, like trout did, and so tied things like big trout flies to catch them with. And much the same happened with the sea trout fly. Despite the observations of an enlightened few, most anglers clung to the notion that sea trout behaved like brown trout and should, therefore, be approached in a similar manner. Hence the traditional sea trout fly, with an insect's wings and legs and tail.

Colour Plate 2 offers a fairly comprehensive selection of what are mainly traditional sea trout flies, used for fishing wet or on the bob. Colour Plate 5 shows a few of the patterns used for dapping. Although opinion will differ as to which are best for any particular water, all of these standard patterns are still in use and all will catch fish — I have at some time or other caught sea trout on every one of them.

Like modern salmon flies, however, many sea trout flies being fished today no longer resemble natural insects. They are mostly lures, designed not to satisfy a hungry fish but to entice one that has for the most part lost the desire to feed.

Colour Plates 3 and 4 show *inter alia*, a selection of my own creations. The reasoning behind these lures together with some notes on their construction and use will be found in my first three chapters.

Rivers and the inhabitants of the watery elements are made for wise men to contemplate and for fools to pass by without consideration.

Izaak Walton, *The Compleat Angler* (1653).

I
The Fish

It is tempting to start a fishing book by discussing rods, tackle, strategy or tactics; but such an approach is surely illogical. All fishing methods and accessories depend on what is to be offered to the fish; in other words—the lure; and not until that is chosen can we decide how or with what to present it. For reasons soon obvious, we shall not select our lure straight away from a list of traditional flies or baits, but try to construct one from reasoning based on what is known of the sea trout's habits. To do so, we must first consider the fish we intend to catch.

The sea trout is a fish of the same species as the brown trout. It is, in fact, a migratory brown trout—or, if you like, the brown trout is a non-migratory sea trout. According to the biologists there is no physical distinction, and the reason why some trout should migrate, while others of the same species should not, is shrouded in mystery.

> *Note.* It was once the custom to refer to the sea trout as *Salmo trutta*, and the brown trout as *Salmo fario*. This, although seemingly unscientific, had the merit of clarity. Today, on the grounds that there is no discernible anatomical difference, taxonomists use *Salmo trutta* to classify both sea trout *and* brown trout. This is a case of putting bones before behaviour which, although satisfying to the scientist, is irritating to the angler. Although there may be no difference in the way non-migratory and migratory trout are built, there is an enormous difference in the way they behave. This difference is of paramount importance, and it demands separate identification. To discuss the behaviour of "*Salmo trutta*" meaning either brown trout or sea trout (or both) is absurd. Above all else, it is essential that a writer should make his meaning clear. The use of the terms: *Salmo trutta fario* for the brown trout, and *Salmo trutta trutta* for the sea trout, avoids confusion.

A sea trout is a migratory brown trout; but there its likeness to a brown trout ends. It is similar in appearance to a salmon, but has very different habits. And before going any further it is necessary for the fisherman to appreciate that sea trout fishing is neither a branch of brown trout nor of salmon fishing: *it is a sport entirely of its own.*

Sea trout have acquired the reputation of being fickle and unpredictable. This is easily understood; few other fish are so sensitive to changes in weather and water. Nevertheless, a forecast of their reaction to these changes is far from impossible, and it is a point of fundamental importance—on which our fishing philosophy should be based—that sea trout, while in the river on their return from sea, conform to a distinct pattern of behaviour. Failure to understand and take advantage of this pattern is to deny ourselves any real hope of successful fishing. Without understanding, we cannot fish with confidence—and confidence is the finger-post to success.

The sea trout's life cycle is well known to most fishermen, but for the benefit of those to whom it is unfamiliar I will recount it very briefly.

At some time during the winter months, but usually in November or December, the female sea trout deposits her eggs in a spawning bed—or redd—often high in some moorland feeder-stream. The eggs are fertilized by milt from a male fish and hatch out after a period of between one and three months: the product being known as an alevin—a tiny, translucent, pinkish creature with an umbilical sac hanging below its throat. The time taken for the eggs to hatch depends on the water temperature; incubation being retarded until the water is warm enough to contain a supply of food. The yolk-sac attached to the alevin is a further insurance against starvation, for it contains upwards of a month's rations.

During the alevin stage our little creature lives on the contents of its yolk-sac and when that is exhausted the alevin becomes a fry.

It is now forced to fend for itself and, in company with other fry, hunts actively for food, gradually acquiring a form of camouflage in the shape of a row of dark "finger-marks" along its sides. At this stage of its development it becomes known as a parr, and in looks is very similar to a small brown trout.

As a parr it remains in the river for an average of three years. During this time it feeds on small flies, nymphs, insect larvae, crustacea and other forms of life depending on the food supply available. It lurks underneath stones in the winter, but seizes every opportunity to feed during spells of warm weather.

At the end of this time when, among other changes, salt-secreting cells have developed in the gills, it assumes a silver coat, becomes known as a smolt and goes to sea. It is then about six inches long and may be

The author fishing his Cumbrian river.

anything from two to five or six years old. And it migrates to the rich feeding grounds of the sea in order to grow.

This seaward migration takes place in the early summer, and after two or three months of sea life our little fish returns to the river—as a herling, whitling, finnock, sprod, smelt, scurf or truff, according to the locality. It now weighs anything between a few ounces and about $1\frac{1}{4}$ lb.— a weight which relates to the length of time it has spent at sea and the amount of food available during that period (wildlife food supplies fluctuate from year to year in the sea as they do on land). It is estimated that the survival rate so far represents less than ·5 per cent of the ova originally deposited.

This behaviour is by no means uniform. Smolts may behave in any of the following five ways:

1. Return to the river in the same summer as they migrated seawards, returning to sea later the same year either (a) having spawned, or (b) without spawning.

2. Return to the river in the same summer as they migrated seawards, spend the winter in the river and return to the sea in the early months of the following year either (a) having spawned, or (b) without spawning.

3. Return to the river in the winter of the same year as they migrated seawards, returning to sea the same winter or during the early spring either (a) having spawned, or (b) without spawning.

4. Return to the river in the spring of the year following that of their seaward migration.

5. Return to the river after an absence of 1–4 years at sea.

It is important to remember that only 25–30 per cent of the smolts spawn after their first brief migration. The majority do so after a sea life of 1 year+.

A sea trout upwards of one and a half pounds has reached its second summer after first migrating. It no longer has the herring-shaped herling tail; the sharp points are more rounded and, as the fish grows larger, the trailing edge of the tail becomes straighter until, on a big fish, the edge becomes convex. It is primarily the shape of the tail that enables a fisherman to distinguish at a glance between sea trout and salmon of similar size. The main points of difference between the two species are shown in the illustrations which follow on the next four pages.

Salmon (grilse) 6 lb. Note the forked tail.

Sea trout 6 lb. Note the square tail.

Tail of 11¼ lb. sea trout.   Tail of 13½ lb. salmon.

Although the trailing edge of a small sea trout's tail is forked, this fork becomes less and less pronounced as the fish increases in weight. At 4—5 lb. the tail becomes square. Upwards of about 8 lb., the tail is convex. A salmon's tail is invariably concave.

The finger points to the outermost ray of a sea trout's anal fin.

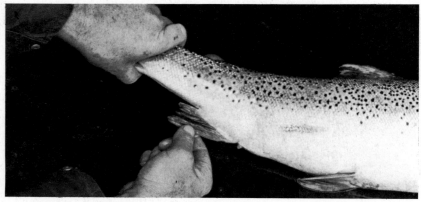

When the fin is closed, the tip of the outermost ray lies nearer to the tail than the innermost ray. Not so with salmon.

24

A salmon. Scale count from the hind edge of the adipose fin forwards and downwards obliquely to the lateral line: 9–13, usually 11. (Note also position of innermost ray of anal fin (arrowed) and compare with that of the sea trout pictured below.)

A sea trout. Scale count: 13–16, usually 14.

25

Grilse with mouth open. Note position of the maxillary in relation to the eye. When mouth is closed the extreme end of the bone is on a level with the hindmost edge of the eye. The head is usually more pointed than that of the sea trout—which has a blunter snout; a less receding forehead.

Sea trout. The extreme end of the maxillary extends beyond a vertical line drawn from the hindmost edge of the eye.

26

The significance of the "wrist" on the salmon's tail is referred to in Scandinavian tradition, as quoted by William Radcliffe, in that classic book: *Fishing from the Earliest Times* (1921).

> "Loki, fleeing from the pursuit of the gods whose anger he had provoked, had the wit and the time to transform himself into a salmon. Then and in this guise would he have surely escaped, had not Thor caught him by the tail."

Unfortunately for Loki he chose the wrong species! Had he turned himself into a sea trout, he would almost certainly have escaped. The sea trout's tail would have slipped through a grasp even as mighty as Thor's.

Apart from herling, most of the sea trout we catch weigh between $1\frac{1}{2}$ lb.

The "wrist" on the sea trout's broader-based tail is not nearly so pronounced as that of the salmon. Hence, a sea trout should be netted or beached, never tailed by hand.

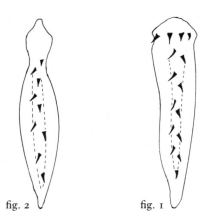

fig. 2   fig. 1

For trout, Alwyne Wheeler in his fine book *The Fishes of the British Isles and North West Europe*, lists up to eighteen teeth on the shaft of the vomerine bone (in the centre of the palate) with two to six on the *head* of the vomer (fig. 1). The salmon has a staggered single row of vomerine teeth, but none on the vomer head (fig. 2).

Note. Vomerine teeth become fewer with age.

The difference in tail structure of salmon and trout is illustrated by the angler's ability to tail a salmon by hand.

The tail is *not* gripped in the fist—as one grips a rope. Pressure is exerted only by the grip between thumb and index finger, the back of the hand pointing towards the fish's head. The other fingers play no part, but merely curl loosely round the tail.

28

and $2\frac{1}{2}$ lb. Anything over 3 lb. is a good fish; anything in double figures the fish of a lifetime. A sea trout of $22\frac{1}{2}$ lb., thought to have been the British rod-caught record, is no longer accepted. The present record is a River Tweed fish of 20 lb., hooked on a tube-fly, 7th November, 1983, by Mr G. Leavy of Peebles.

It has been said that the age limit of a sea trout is thirteen years. A hen fish of $12\frac{1}{2}$ lb., caught by a friend, Mr W. M. W. Fowler, had, according to scale readings, migrated as a two-year-old smolt and spent a little over a year at sea before returning to spawn for the first time. Altogether, it spawned in eight successive winters, with an interval of a few months in the sea each spring and summer between spawning visits. At the time of capture, the fish was back in the river for the ninth time. This fish had, therefore, spawned eight times and was eleven years old. On the other hand, a Loch Maree fish of $12\frac{1}{2}$ lb. had, according to a published report, spawned eleven times and was nineteen years old.

It was once thought that sea trout travel little further to sea than the vicinity of the estuary. Scientific investigations, however, have disproved this. For instance, of a number of sea trout kelts tagged at the experimental fish trap in the River Axe, south Devon, one was recaptured, 266 days after liberation, in the estuary of the River Tweed. The minimum distance this fish must have travelled (via the Straits of Dover) was approximately 580 miles. Via the Irish Sea, the distance would have been approximately 1,130 miles.

The minimum distance covered in the case of another recapture was 244 miles (in 174 days).

My own opinion is that whereas the smolt probably travels no great distance before its comparatively speedy return as a herling, many older sea trout undoubtedly do. Furthermore, that the object of this travel is to follow shoals of small fish which, I think, form the major part of their diet. As we shall see, their subsequent behaviour in the river would seem to indicate a sea-life of this nature.

There are two main sea trout runs each season: the summer run, which starts as early as April or May in some rivers but not until late June or early July in others, and the autumn or "harvest" run, which comes up during the early part of September. The biggest fish run early and late in the season, and the herling shoals begin to appear in the bottom pools some time towards the end of July.

A moderate spate encourages a run of sea trout and salmon, especially when it coincides with a period of spring tides. But contrary to general belief, both species show a preference for running at night, and will do so when the river is fairly low. Salmon, however, will not run when the river has dropped below a certain level; whereas sea trout can find their way up river in very low water. Some fish will, in fact, run at night in water so shallow that, between pools, they are sometimes unable to swim and force themselves on their sides over what is little more than a trickle in a series of convulsive flops. I have watched them doing this on many a June night during spells of dry weather.

At such times it is commonplace to hear fish after fish come splashing up the shallows below a pool as soon as darkness falls. The bulge of these fish can be plainly seen as they come up over the sill at the tail of the pool, followed by the long "V" of their wake as they swim on into deeper water. Such fish, fresh from the sea, often take a fly very readily soon after entering a pool.

But sea trout that run direct from salt water in this manner form only a small proportion of the total number entering the river each season. This proportion varies considerably from year to year. Very probably, the reason for this variation is simply—rainfall. If few fish are heard splashing through the shallows during a dry June night, rain can be expected.

Sea trout seem well aware of any impending change in weather, and this apparent prescience may account for much of their behaviour while in the river. For instance, the manner in which they sometimes take a fly enables us to forecast rain quite accurately. Their distinctive "nibbling" of the fly on these occasions may be a reaction due to changes in metabolism or to slight variation in the quantity of dissolved oxygen in the water— on which their lives depend.

Fish respire by drawing water into their mouths and expelling it through the gills. The minute blood vessels in the red gill filaments absorb the oxygen which is dissolved in the water, in return for carbon dioxide and other waste products. This oxygen is then distributed throughout the fish's body. The amount of dissolved oxygen available to the fish varies from different causes. It is a complex subject about which I do not pretend to have any advanced scientific knowledge, and I will do no more than summarize these causes very briefly.

Cold water is capable of containing more dissolved oxygen than warm water. As the temperature rises, so oxygen is driven off.

An increase of atmospheric pressure will cause more oxygen to dissolve. Conversely, when the pressure decreases, oxygen will tend to be driven off. This change due to variation in barometric pressure is probably very slight.

At dusk the "V"s of running sea trout can be seen in the smooth shallow water above the sill of the ford where the author and his dogs are crossing.
It was here that running sea trout were filmed, both in daylight and at dusk, for the author's World About Us documentary *Salmo the Leaper*.

As I know to my cost, many attempts at making "lies" for sea trout and salmon end in failure. All too often the fish ignore our efforts, having their own mysterious preferences. The picture shows a rare success. A simple groyne (and all the more gratifying because it *was* so simple) constructed of boulders against which shingle could build up, was extended for two thirds of the way across the river. As a result the current was set off hard against the left bank. This created a little "run" which now holds sea trout. It is significant that the densely wooded left bank, under which the fish lie, is on the eastern side of the river—the side on which the moon appears. This means that owing to heavy shadow thrown by the foliage the water is fishable in bright moonlight. An added triumph, since a stretch of "moonlight water" is a most welcome addition to any sea trout night fly-fishing beat (see also p. 276).

TRADITIONAL SEA TROUT FLIES

PLATE
2

1	Alexandra	Silver March Brown	Black and Silver	Peter Ross	Blae and Black
2		Kingsmill		Bloody Butcher	Butcher
3		Dunkeld	Fiery Brown	Thunder and Lightning	Cinnamon and Gold
4		Connemara Black	Snipe and Purple	Grouse and Claret	Mallard and Claret
5		Teal and Green	Teal and Red	Blae and Blue	Teal and Silver
6		Brown Turkey	Invicta	Woodcock Teal and Yellow	Pheasant and Yellow
7		Black Zulu		Blue Zulu	Black Pennell
8		Claret Bumble		Donegal Blue	Claret Pennell

PLATE
3

SUNK LURES AND SURFACE LURES

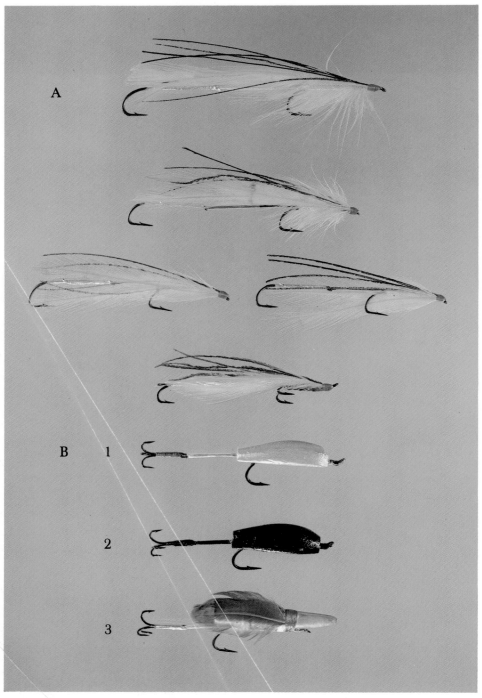

A SUNK LURES
  Various sizes

B SURFACE LURES
1 The Silver Cork
2 The All Black
3 The Dressed Quill

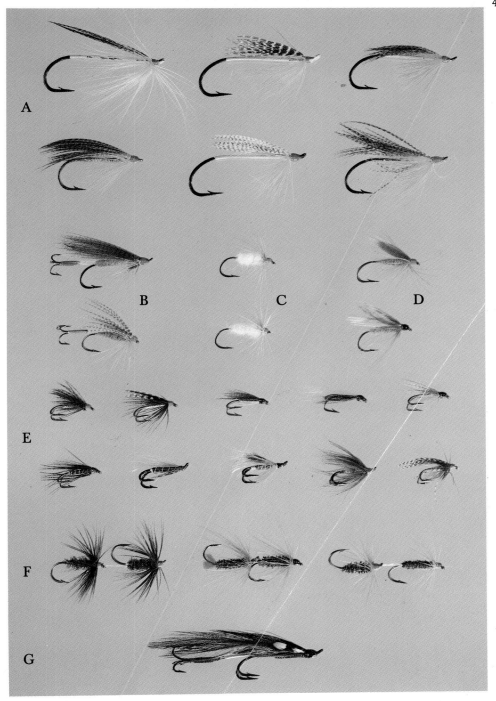

A MEDICINES
B SECRET WEAPONS   C MAGGOT FLIES   D MOTHS
E TWO ROWS OF SMALL DOUBLES
F WORM FLIES
G THE DEMON

PLATE
5

A SELECTION OF DAPPING FLIES

The colours of a dapping fly seem to be of secondary importance to the manner
of its presentation. Each of the flies shown has caught me fish

Sunlight induces a photosynthetic reaction in chlorophyll-bearing aquatic plants. Thus, by day, these plants will assist the water to become oxygenated, but by night they will absorb oxygen from the water in return for carbon dioxide.

A wind produces evaporation and cools the surface of the water, allowing it to take up oxygen from the air. In the same way, broken water will absorb more oxygen than still water. An increase in atmospheric pressure—assuming no temperature change—will, perhaps contrary to expectation, cause water to evaporate; but this is an extremely small effect and can probably be neglected.

River pollution, such as sewage disposal for example, will absorb the oxygen content of the water, and in extreme cases—of which, unfortunately, there are many—the river becomes unfit for any form of fish life.

Sea trout give every appearance of being exceedingly alert to any variation in their oxygen supply. Being cold-blooded, the rate at which their metabolism can function is largely determined by the water temperature. It is probable that much of a sea trout's differing behaviour when offered a lure may be accounted for by sudden changes in air and water temperature which, in turn, affect the fish's metabolism and cause its supply of oxygen to fluctuate.

There is little doubt that all fish spend a certain amount of time in a state of suspended animation which, for all intents and purposes, may be called sleep. A favourite position for a sea trout in this condition is underneath or half underneath a rock in the deep, slack part of a pool; often athwart the current which, where the fish is lying, will not be strong. Sometimes fish will be seen lying partly on their sides; sometimes completely so—indeed, I have occasionally mistaken these seemingly moribund fish for casualties, only realizing my error when attempting to net them out for examination.

As many anglers have discovered to their cost, sea trout are extremely shy. Whether they have a sense of taste is arguable, but there is little doubt that, like salmon, they have a highly developed sense of smell. Each river has its own particular odour, and experiments have shown that salmon returning from the sea select their home rivers—the rivers of their birth—by smell. There seems no reason to suppose that sea trout do otherwise. It also seems likely that the odours from the skin of an injured fish can produce a fright reaction among a shoal.

So far as I know, no one is certain over what range of the spectrum their eyes are sensitive to colour, although they are certainly colour

33

conscious. There is no doubt that their vision is unusually acute and that, being sensitive to vibration both from movement on the bank and in the water, they are easily frightened.

All fish possess otoliths, or earstones, which are located at the back of the brain. These not only assist a sense of balance but, as they are able to register vibration, form part of the warning system that transmits danger signals to the brain. Sea trout respond readily to the very low frequencies, but not to the high frequencies. They will remain unaffected by your conversation, but may become alarmed if you tread too heavily on the bank.

From my own experiments, sea trout remain unmoving and apparently unconcerned when a gun is fired on the river bank, nor do they react to the sound of the human voice. Nevertheless, although conversation may not affect the fish, it will certainly affect the fisherman. Nothing interferes so much with concentration as chatter, and concentration is vitally important to successful fishing, especially at night.

It is thought by some fishermen that sea trout take better during certain stages of the tide, irrespective of their distance from the sea. I have noticed no correlation myself, but do not deny its possibility. Many creatures possess powers that we find difficult to explain: the seemingly supernatural senses of dogs; the ability of certain coastal birds to behave in accordance with a (presumably in-built) "tidal-clock". Many wildfowlers must, like myself, have been impressed by the beautifully timed curlew flights that arrive on the salt marshes almost to the minute as the mud flats uncover with the ebb tide—although the birds may have come from fields several miles inland. And of course there are many other examples. Whether the tide does indeed influence sea trout when they are in fresh water I am unable to say. I can affirm, however, that they seem to take well in a sea pool just before the tide reaches it.

With the exception of the early and late seasonal runs, sea trout are not inclined to move very far at any one time, and certainly not at night. As an example, I observed a five pounder—easily recognized by the most distinctive mark on its back, probably a scar caused by some enemy at sea—in six different holding pools over a period of approximately a month. And during this time there were several heavy spates. So far as I could judge, he changed his ground every five or six days and swam an average of two-thirds of a mile each time, the intervening spates making no difference to his rate of progress or distance covered. It may be of interest that a salmon was timed by a friend of mine over fifteen miles. This fish, which also had most distinctive marking, moved only in spate water—roughly once every three weeks—and covered a distance of between three and four miles each time. He took three months to reach his final resting pool, where he remained until spawning in a near-by feeder. By comparison, I have caught salmon fifty miles from salt water with female sea lice on them.

When observing the inhabitants of a pool during daylight in conditions of low water, I frequently recognize individual sea trout that have come up the previous night from the pool below. This pool to pool night movement in low water is commonplace during June and early July.

Unlike sea trout, salmon seldom run in conditions of very low water. Although they frequently run at night, they need a greater depth of water than sea trout. I have known a disturbed salmon to leave a pool and run itself aground, but such a fish is exceptional. Usually, when frightened, salmon will swim round and round a pool, eventually attempting to hide—sometimes with only their heads under cover. This characteristic is well-known to the poacher who, when salmon are lying out of reach, will disturb the water and drive the fish to seek shelter. From these positions they are easily taken with snatch-hook or leister. Sea trout react differently. Acute disturbance will empty a pool even in broad daylight. I have watched a shoal of several hundreds leave *en masse* in bright sunshine and swim on up river through only a few inches of water.

Fish that reach their selected pools during a spate seek shelter for a time from the turbulence and force of the current in the slacker water beside and underneath banks; in little bays, or on the edges of some back-eddy. As the level of the water falls, they swing out into the stream and lie in shoals—the larger fish in front—on beds of firm gravel or small shingle (where this is possible), usually about two-thirds of the way down a pool, in a smooth, unbroken flow of water which ensures a steady supply of oxygen.

Fresh-run fish often carry sea lice on their bodies for several days. These lice usually drop off after forty-eight hours, or less, in fresh water; but in some instances may stay on for as long as five days. The female lice carry two long string-like "tails", or egg-sacs. These fall off very quickly after entry into fresh water, so that lice with "tails" intact give evidence of a fish being very fresh-run indeed.

Although the flesh hardens rapidly in fresh water, the mouth of a sea trout newly arrived from sea is very soft. Many fish hooked early in the season are lost not because they are poorly hooked, but because of this tenderness of the flesh. Normally, the best hold is in the "scissors" at the angle of the jaw. With many early fish hooked in this position, however, pressure on the hook while a fish is being played causes a slit to be torn in the thin flesh at the corner of the mouth. A momentary slackening of the line, especially when a fish is jumping, allows the hook to lose its hold. It is said that the hook tears out. Sometimes it probably does. More often than not, I think, it simply drops out. Examination of a fish from whose mouth the hook has come away on landing frequently gives evidence of this.

This softness of the mouth is far more noticeable among fresh-run fish early in the season than fish equally fresh-run later in the season. (Freshness judged by presence of sea-lice. Softness of mouth judged by proportion of fish lost, and condition of mouth in those landed.)

Unless very fine tackle is being used, it is a good rule when playing a sea trout never to drop the rod point as the fish jumps. Instead, it is better to *increase* the pressure as he leaves the water. This is not always successful in maintaining contact, but I am convinced that it helps to land many fish that would otherwise be lost.

But of course a lot of early season fish come off not during a jump but while playing deep. For no apparent reason the hook just comes away.

I wish I could be more helpful over the landing of these fish. But (apart from the suggestions made on p. 273) it is a problem I have never completely solved. The loss of a fish—after what seems to be a firm and determined "take"—is particularly irritating at the time, since there are few sea trout in the river and one has to work hard to get an offer. Over the years my fishing diary has become riddled with early season entries such as:

"June 17th. Height 7 in. Landed: 1. $2\frac{3}{4}$ lb. Lost: 3. (All seemingly well hooked. One a whopper!)"

Compare that with an entry a month later.

"July 20th. Height 8 in. Landed: 20 (average 3 lb.). Lost: 2. (Had caught enough, so stopped fishing soon after midnight.)"

Irrespective of the armament employed: single hooks, doubles, trebles, I have suffered a high proportion of lost fish at the start of a season for over forty years, and I am now resigned to it. (But see also the account of "a remarkable night" on p. 262. Also, advantages of using Sunk Lure for early season fish, p. 66.)

Hooking an early season fish

1. Angler at A casts a fly to B. A fish fresh from sea intercepts and takes the fly. He turns away. As he does so the fly hooks him at the back of the jaw in the "scissors" on the right hand side.

2. The fish runs hard downstream for a short distance.

3. The shank of the hook works to and fro against the fish's jaw as he turns from side to side.

4. The fish swings round towards the opposite bank.

5. Now he starts to come back upstream, keeping close to the opposite bank.

6. He swims steadily past the angler. This is where the angler wants him. But by now there is a big slit torn in the soft flesh at the corner of the mouth. If the fish suddenly turns towards the rod and jumps on a slack line he is very likely to come off; the hook will simply fall out of the torn slit.

5(b) and 6(b) show in close-up how the angle of pull on the hook-shank works the hook to and fro in the fish's jaw.

Note. When a fish jumps *don't drop the rod point and allow the line to go slack.* Unless it is a big fish and likely to break the leader, *raise the rod and keep a tight line.*

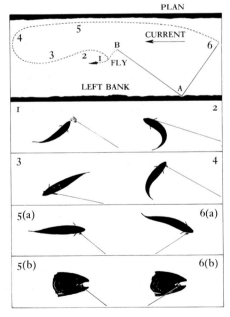

Sea lice attached
above anal fin.

Female sea louse
(enlarged).

Gill-maggots attached to gill.

Gill-maggot (enlarged).

The presence of gill-maggots on a fish would seem to offer another point of identification. According to Nall, gill-maggots do not infest sea trout (and I have certainly never found any on sea trout myself). They are often found on salmon that have spawned in previous years or ". . . in maiden salmon which have been some while in fresh water."

38

Some sea trout stay in a pool for only a few days before running further up river. Others remain in the same pool for most of the summer. From observations of marked fish that have reappeared in the same places after a succession of spates, I am of the opinion that every pool has its resident population, most of which "belong" to that pool for the greater part of the season—moving out only when spawning time approaches— the numbers varying from day to day or week to week as other fish move in and rest awhile before continuing towards their destined pools.

I have noticed that if a pool is disturbed after the first main run has come up—badly disturbed, so that fish are forced to leave that water— the pool will take a long time to recover. Indeed, it is unlikely to hold many sea trout until the autumn run has appeared; and even then it never seems to fish well nor hold its customary numbers. It is almost as though that particular pool has the "Indian Sign" on it and that, in some mystical way, subsequent fish sense disaster and press on to safer places higher up river. I am in no doubt at all that the harmful effects of poaching are more far-reaching than the actual numbers of fish killed. Remove, or drive, the "residents" from a pool, and that water will fish badly for weeks.

Many fishermen have observed that sea trout fresh from the sea take a lure much more readily than fish which have been for some time in the river. Various theories have been advanced in explanation of this, and while hesitating to disagree—after all, there is probably truth in all of them—I find none totally convincing. I suggest that the reason why a sea-trout becomes steadily more difficult to hook is because the longer it lies in the river the less susceptible it becomes to the sensation of hunger.

While in fresh water waiting to spawn most sea trout eat very little— for the very good reason that there is very little for them to eat. Many sea trout rivers are clear, rocky, acid, barren spate rivers that hold only a tiny proportion of the food necessary to support a sea trout population with normal appetites. While in the sea the fish feed greedily. Few rivers can provide such meals.

A moment's thought will put this beyond reasonable doubt. Consider a typical sea trout pool—there is an excellent example not very far from where I am writing—which at any time during the three main fishing months, in a good season, holds between a hundred and three hundred fish ranging in size from three or four ounces to ten or more pounds. If these fish retained their normal appetites their food requirements for one day would exceed what the river can supply in a year, and that is only one of many pools.

Nall makes a similar comment* (which I had not read when the previous paragraph was written):

"Though Sea-trout taken in the sea or in brackish tidal waters, are at times gorged with food, in fresh water they feed more intermittently and with a less robust appetite than fresh water Trout.

"A moment's reflection should convince us that if they did feed regularly, the food in our rivers and lochs would be quite inadequate to supply the needs of the shoals of Sea-trout, which run up during summer and autumn, to say nothing of the requirements of the permanent stock of fresh water Trout and other fish."

Precisely similar conditions apply to any salmon river. Where sea trout differ from salmon is that whereas salmon lose their appetites and cease feeding long before their return to the spawning rivers, sea trout, in some cases, continue to feed until very shortly before they run.

I write "in some cases" advisedly. By no means all sea trout feed in the sea right up to the last moment before running. In some estuaries, sea trout accept a lure readily; in others (mine included) very rarely. Like most salmon, many sea trout stop feeding some time before their return to fresh water. On the other hand, others that enter rivers containing a greater supply of food—such as fresh-water shrimp, or a good hatch of fly—may continue to feed not only in the estuary, but in the river. But even so, in a reduced capacity.

My little river is ideally suitable for observing the behaviour of sea trout and salmon. The water, when low, is crystal clear; the bottom is clean—mainly stones, gravel and small shingle—and there is very little weed. During many seasons it has been my custom (and delight) to lie on the bank of a pool during some of the daylight hours and watch the reactions of fish to various lures and baits presented by friends on the opposite bank. If my reader has the appropriate water and the opportunity, I recommend him to do the same. It is utterly fascinating, and very, very instructive.

I have seen fish give some peculiar performances—a few of which will be discussed in later chapters—but seldom have I seen them searching for food. And apart from the occasional "taking" fish—which is, after all, the fish that is prepared at a particular moment to accept our lure— seldom do they show much interest in food items that are drifted down to them. (But see also effect of maggots, p. 339). Regular exceptions to this are the young "first year" fish that I have already mentioned, and

40

* *The Life of the Sea Trout*, 1930.

about which I have a sort of notion. It has been computed that only twenty-five to thirty per cent of these fish spawn during the winter following their first return from sea, and a correlation seems possible between non-spawning and feeding; spawning and non-feeding. In other words, the *non-spawners* continue to feed, and to search for food, while the fish that are due to spawn *do not*.

This is pure conjecture, but it seems logical—and it would explain the large catches of small sea trout that are often made in daylight by bait anglers. At any rate it is an original concept, which I pass on to the fish biologists with my compliments.

It is in the stomach that evidence of a sea trout's feeding habits will be found.

Results published by *The Salmon Research Trust of Ireland* (1967) give evidence of sea trout night feeding in some Irish fresh-waters, it being estimated that approximately 20% of the adult fish examined continued to grow. This is for an area rich in natural food. Even so, approximately 80% had *not* continued to grow, a figure which scarcely indicates a lot of feeding activity. And I suggest that in many British rivers the proportion is far less.

Several hundreds of adult sea trout used to come into my cottage every summer. The stomachs of many of these fish were examined. They held very little. For instance, a sample of 300 fish (each upwards of 1¼lb.) produced five food items: three fly larvae; one caterpillar, and the remains of an unidentified creepy-crawly. No fish contained more than one item. This is fairly representative of the amount of food we have found in our sea trout over the years. So, while conceding that each of those five fish had enjoyed a tiny meal, I feel it is going a little too far to claim that they were *feeding*. The toad-eater (see p. 77) was an exception. But there are *always* exceptions. (For food taken by sea trout in stillwater, see p. 367.)

The majority of sea trout on their return from sea are prepared for an enforced fast, and nature has made provision for this. During their river life the fish live mainly on the store of energy accumulated in their tissues during their time at sea.

Indeed, it would be extraordinary if it were otherwise, for if the fish did not quickly lose the desire to feed, the little spate rivers would become denuded of everything that moved and the returning fry-devouring sea trout shoals would speedily exterminate themselves. In fact, they would have done so many thousands of years ago.

As it is, the fish lie quietly in the pools and "runs" for the time when they will nose up the tiny moorland streams to satisfy the sexual urge which has brought them back. And while they wait, the sensation of hunger dwindles.

"The life of the Sea trout, I suggest, is in fact a series of alternating phases, first feeding and growth, then abstinence and cessation of growth."   (Nall)

Why then, does a sea trout take a lure?

I feel certain that the answer is quite simply—habit. The habit of feeding it has acquired during its life at sea and also, as we shall see later, very probably during its earlier life in the river.

But even if they accept this theory, few sea trout fishermen seem to take advantage of it. They regard the sea trout as a regular feeder, treating it as though it were a brown trout and offering it much the same sort of lure in much the same way. In consequence of this the sea trout has acquired a reputation for being unpredictable and hard to catch. And I am not surprised.

I have suggested that by the very law of supply and demand the desire of most sea trout to continue feeding must quickly diminish shortly after, if not before, they enter the river. Whether this does, in fact, occur can easily be put to the test. Consider what happens when we fish for sea trout during the nights following a spate. At first the fresh-run fish take well and the fishing is good. Then, as night follows night, the fishing deteriorates; the fish show more and more reluctance to take, until the fishing becomes comparatively poor—apart from those nights, usually during a period of spring tides, when fish enter the river and run irrespective of the height of water. With the exception of those evenings, the fishing will remain poor until another spate brings a further quantity of fresh fish from the sea.

This is what actually happens, and this is what we should *expect* to happen if the sea trout's desire for food diminishes and the habit of feeding becomes less and less pronounced.

Let us go a stage further. Every experienced sea trout fisherman knows that, in other than spate conditions, although it is possible to catch sea trout at any hour of the day or night, night fishing is usually better than day fishing, and the early part of the night is the best time of all.

Again, the answer is surely—habit. According to my own experience the hour after sunset is the time when sea trout feed most avidly when in the sea. That they do so then is probably because at the time of changing light they can most easily catch their prey. Fish undoubtedly

SEA TROUT TAKING BEHAVIOUR

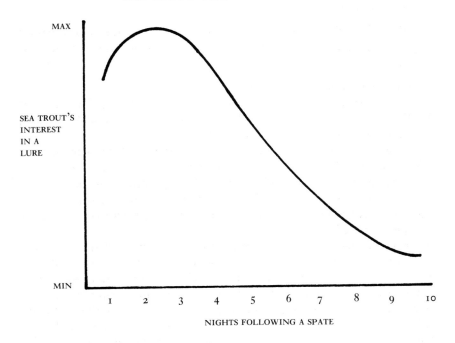

possess night vision, but dusk is the time when most sea fish come on to feed.

Night after night I have watched and fished for sea trout along a shore, or in a channel between sea loughs far from a river mouth. During the earlier part of the evening there has been little sign of sea trout activity. With the darkening sky, however, the water has become alive with fish, the surface "boiling" as sea trout turned with swirl after swirl to seize the small fish they were feeding on. So ravenously would they eat that nearly every sea trout caught had its throat stuffed with fish; but still they took my fly, so eager were they to snap up everything in sight. On one occasion, a two-pounder, its jaws jammed open by a big sparling that protruded from its mouth, was quite unable to take hold of the fly—which hooked on to the outside of its lip. I landed this combination . . . and ate them both!

(The last sentence, which was written in 1960 for the first edition of

43

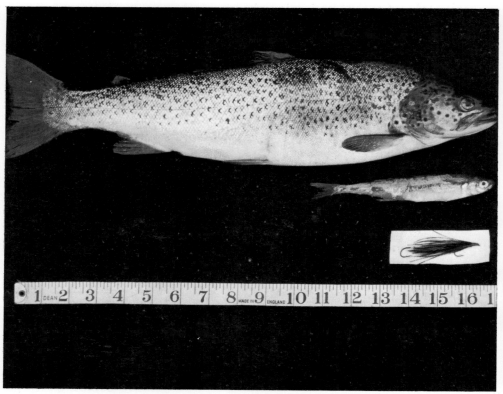

Sea trout: 2½ lb., caught at night by the author while fishing in company with Fred Buller in an Irish sea lough, June, 1970. The sparling underneath was taken from the sea trout's throat immediately after capture. In spite of having its mouth full, the sea trout took the Sunk Lure (see p. 63) pictured below. A graphic example of sea trout behaviour when feeding in salt water. (Like those quoted in the text, both fish were eaten for breakfast.)

this book, referred to an incident that occurred in 1952. The photograph shows the result of a repeat performance in exactly the same place eighteen years later!)

After such a period of gluttony, the sea trout seemed to reach a state of satiety and would "go down" for a time. Later in the night they would start feeding again, and it was noticeable that although this "second dinner" was attended by fewer fish it seemed mostly to comprise the larger sea trout. Dawn was sometimes the signal for a further snack, usually involving the smaller fish; the larger sea trout, it seemed, having gone into deeper water.

It is, I suggest, the habit formed by such feeding sessions that causes the "taking" periods in fresh-water; for it is a similar pattern of behaviour that in certain circumstances we experience when fishing a sea trout river at night.

We shall return to this in a later chapter, when considering our strategy. Until then, a more detailed analysis must wait. Having discussed the fish we wish to catch, we are now in a position to determine the next item in order of importance—which is, quite obviously, the lure with which to catch it.

A fish caught on a home-made fly is a greater satisfaction to the fisherman than one which has been tricked by a fly bought in a shop. Why? Because it better satisfies the fisherman's instinctive desire to re-create conditions in which he depends on himself alone in his voluntary contest with nature.

Arthur Ransome, *Mainly about Fishing* (1959)

II
The Underwater Lure

From what has been discussed in the previous chapter I hope you will agree that the most probable reason why a sea trout takes a lure on his return to freshwater is the feeding habit acquired so far during his lifetime. This being so, the sixty-four dollar question is: what has he been feeding on mostly, while in the sea? For, if we know the answer to that, and if the original premise is correct, it shouldn't be difficult to form a good idea of what to offer him when first he arrives in the river.

> *Note.* Henceforth to avoid confusion in grammatical construction, a fish is frequently referred to by the masculine pronoun rather than the more usual neuter pronoun "it". I am aware of the irony involved, since in a season's catch my females outnumber the males by at least 2:1. Early in the season the proportion is more like 20:1. Nevertheless, for the sake of clarity they are all masculine here!

Doubtless, the sea trout's tastes are catholic and he will eat anything he can get hold of: prawns, shrimps, shellfish, sand-eels, soft crab and so on (indeed, I once caught a $1\frac{1}{2}$ lb. sea trout on soft crab while fishing for bass in the estuary of the River Exe—oddly enough, a river which seems to produce a very poor run of sea trout). Nevertheless, it is likely that his main diet consists of small fish of the type that travel in shoals. This is in part confirmed by scientific research, which gives evidence of young herrings and sprats being eaten. Also by my own experience. As already mentioned, I have on many occasions watched sea trout feeding voraciously on sparling, and made splendid catches while they were doing so.

In which case, what sort of lure should sea trout be most likely to take when they come up-river? Surely, something that resembles the food they have most recently been eating. In other words, a little fish. If sea trout have been feeding mainly on small fish, they might reasonably be expected to take a lure ranging in size from, say, an inch and a quarter to three inches long. And they do.

Of course, there is nothing categorical about this. Sea trout will accept a variety of shapes and sizes of lure; but I am in no doubt whatsoever that the flies most commonly used for sea trout fishing are much too small. In fact, to generalize, I will go so far as to suggest to any sea trout fisherman who is not aware of it that if he doubles the size of his fly he will go a long way towards doubling the size of his bag. My experience is that a big fly catches many more fish than a small fly used at the same time in the same water.

Most of my sea trout are caught on large, finely dressed lures that are designed to simulate small fish. They are considerably larger than the traditional size of sea trout fly, but this seems entirely logical. If sea trout have recently been feeding on something like herring fry they should, more readily than taking anything else, take a lure which represents a tiny fish.

Is this, then, the only type of lure to use?

By no means. Let us take the theory a stage further and apply it to a fish that has been lying for some time in the river. He has become "absorbed" by his river surroundings; the memory of those hunting nights during his pelagic wandering are fading in sympathy with this new environment—which may more strongly evoke memories of his early life as a parr. In which case, we might expect him to show interest in nymph, or small fly. And again, broadly speaking, he does.

Naturally, I am not implying that all fresh-run fish take only one sort of fly and that all stale fish take only another; but my experience is that early in the season a big fly not only catches more fish than a standard size, it accounts for over ninety per cent of the fish caught on *anything.*

Later, however, this percentage begins to fall as more and more fish tend to take a smaller fly: perhaps a nymph, or the fly/maggot, or a size 12 or 14 double (which we shall discuss later in this chapter). To generalize, the big fly is good the season through, but as July turns to August and August to September, a smaller fly can also be used and with increasing advantage.

After all, the stale fish (whether sea trout or salmon) is never very easy to catch. The feeding habit persists less strongly; he has been in the river for some weeks, perhaps months, and has long lost the pangs of hunger. Nevertheless, the habit (it seems) will occasionally assert itself and, when it does, is it not reasonable to suppose that if the fish refuses a "sea-food" type of fly there is a good chance that he might be tempted by something more closely resembling the river-food he was eating when a parr?

The efficacy of any particular pattern of this type of fly varies from one river to another. A reason for this may be the different food contained by these rivers which was available to the sea trout when in the parr stage. For instance, the dry-fly though successful on some rivers catches comparatively few fish on others.

The hours of darkness provide the best opportunity to get on terms with our quarry, and usually the hour or so following dusk is the best time of all. There are seemingly good fishing evenings, however, when sea trout take no interest in a fly. The experienced fisherman, realizing there is a reason for this lack of enthusiasm—although not always a very obvious one—is confident that his chance will come later in the night, and is content to wait for it. But in these circumstances many a novice, taken with the desire to catch a sea trout but disheartened by failure during what he understood to be the most likely "taking" period, abandons his fly and turns to bait fishing. And it may be that on occasions he will catch fish by doing so.

Such moments give the bait an appearance of infallibility; but I advise the beginner not to be misled by this. There are, it is true, successful methods of fishing a worm at night that are both skilful and exciting (especially on a fly rod); but these are esoteric rites that we will deal with in due course. The point just now is that if the newcomer to the sport turns to bait whenever fish seem hard to catch on fly he will, in the long run, be denying himself his greatest chance of success. Over a period the fly will catch more fish than any other method.

I say this not as a fly "purist"—I am nothing of the sort—but as a practical fisherman who has fished spinner and bait in addition to fly for very many years. I still do. There is pleasure to be had from all methods of angling. But apart from the herling and small sea trout that continue to feed and will take bait avidly when they can get it, more of my fish are caught on fly than on anything else. There are times to spin and times to fish the bait; but however well they do on occasions, neither method provides a short-cut to success. Considerable skill is needed to fish the fly well at night. But if the beginner perseveres he will derive both a deep sense of satisfaction from his fishing and a suitable reward in the number (and size) of fish he catches. But I digress.

If small fish form the greater proportion of a sea trout's diet at sea, and if his acceptance of a lure in the river is force of habit, then it follows that our best chance of encouraging that habit is to offer him a lure resembling a small fish. *But* what must be remembered is that the sea

49

trout is not concerned about his stomach; he is neither hungry nor in need of food. So that, if he is to be tempted it must be with something rather tantalizing; something tenuous; not so much a lure that resembles a fish as a lure that represents the *impression* of a fish.

This being so, our lure should be dressed with economy, for it must appear not as a solid but as a shadowy, ethereal creature; a lure intended not to satisfy a non-existent hunger, but to entice our quarry to "go through the motions"; to indulge his habit—the habit acquired when those gargantuan meals of fry were gorged during many a recent dusk.

Having decided that our lure should represent the impression of a little fish, the next thought to present itself is that a much more convincing impression can be fashioned out of hair and feathers than from tin or plastic, or any other hard, unyielding material.

There is, needless to say, an exception to this (as there is to almost every other angling statement): the Mepps spinner—whose whirling action is most impressionistic! But of this, more later.

It is unnecessary to spend large sums of money on the gaudy and expensive feathered creations displayed so seductively in every catalogue and glass-topped tackle counter. Indeed, every fisherman—certainly every fisherman who intends to fish at night—should learn to tie his own flies without delay. The number he is destined to lose once he starts night fishing is formidable, and money spent on a fly vice and the few necessary tools and materials will prove a sound investment.

Apart from the economic benefit, the thrill and satisfaction accompanying the first fish hooked on a fly of his own manufacture will more than compensate for the small discipline entailed. Besides which, fly-tying opens up a new creative field providing almost limitless scope for experiment. During the long winter nights when the wind raves in the chimney, it keeps the keen fisherman in spiritual contact with those enchanted dusk-shadowed pools that seem an age away. A profitable and welcome relief from watching television.

With a little practice, the beginner will soon tie a more successful fly than most that are offered for sale. For some mysterious reason the professional fly-makers, with few exceptions, turn out an article that is pretty and beautifully finished, but hopelessly over-dressed and lacking in "life". I have seldom used one whose fishing qualities were not improved by pruning and a thorough rubbing in the dirt.

It is difficult to understand why this should be so in an otherwise enlightened age; although perhaps on one occasion I approached the truth. Appalled by the dressing of some flies with which a friend turned

50

The logical size of lure . . . With a square-tailed four-pounder fresh from the sea.

A lure for all sizes. Three sea trout and five herling.

up to fish, I offered a dozen or so proved sea trout "killers" to the tackle dealer, an old acquaintance. He refused them with regret.

"I like them", he said simply. "But they won't sell. There's not enough stuff on them. People won't think they're getting their money's worth!"

He was right. There are fishermen who regard flies primarily as *objets d'art*. They collect them; hoard them; gloat over them, admiring the pretty colours; listing them in rows, each with its name alongside. Their fly boxes are show cases, produced for admiring inspection. It is as much as they can bear, sometimes, to tie one of the precious contents on a leader and get it wet.

Fish have a different sense of beauty. They think little of colour, less of neatness and a polished finish and nothing at all of names, preferring something straggly and thoroughly well chewed. Some fishermen never seem to understand this. They gaze in awe at a successful fly and remark in hushed tones:

"Fish after fish takes it, although it's bitten to blazes with hardly any dressing left on the hook!"

That is precisely why the fish take it. That is the sort of fly we should start with.

Many years ago, the standard type of sea trout fly in general use — stubby, tail-bewhisked, in size little more than an overgrown brown trout wet fly—seemed to me an illogical form of lure for sea trout. I came to the conclusion that the majority of these flies were too small and, often, the wrong shape. Finally, as the result of much experiment on the river, night after night the seasons through, with every size and pattern available, including everything which a lifelong friend and I could devise on our fly vices, I decided that for all practical purposes the lures for night fishing could be reduced to half a dozen or so— each a different pattern designed for certain conditions. Nowadays, I use nothing else.

One point must be made clear: no fly, whatever its reputation, will kill fish if it is not fishing correctly. Presentation is very important, and I am convinced that fish move to and refuse a fly far more frequently than many fishermen realize. By day, such refusals are often seen. It is difficult to prove the point at night, but I am quite satisfied in my own mind, for I have often seen the surface bulge as fish have turned away from a fly, especially when I have been wading deep and fish have approached within a few yards. The obvious conclusion is that the fish are interested but not convinced; the reason being a poorly dressed or badly behaved fly—or both.

Faulty behaviour is due either to the way in which the fly is controlled, or to the way in which it is attached to the leader.

Great care should be taken when tying on a fly to ensure that it forms a direct continuation of the leader and doesn't stick out at an angle. Never start fishing until you have tested your fly. *Always* do this, both by day and by night. Go to some piece of fast, shallow water—naturally, well clear of the stretch you are going to fish—and watch the fly swimming. If you are in darkness you will, of course, need to use a flashlamp; but this will do no harm providing you don't wave it about. Stand in the river facing upstream with the rod straight in front of you and parallel to the water. Move the rod tip from side to side, with a rod's length of line out, and watch the fly as it swims to and fro in front of you across the current. If it isn't swimming straight or with the back of the dressing uppermost, cut it off and re-tie it. Then test again, and go on re-tying the fly until it does behave properly. In the case of a tube fly, make sure that the treble is not sticking off at an angle to the tube, a common fault with tubes. This drill is of the utmost importance. More fish are missed because of the fly's imperfect action than for any other reason.

Another common cause of a fish's refusal is the sudden change of speed when a fly moves out of a current into slack water. The fisherman should know the position of his fly at every moment of the cast. As it comes into slack water he must keep it moving on an even keel, otherwise it will suddenly lose its lifelike appearance and begin to sag. Any fish that might have been on the point of taking will refuse a lure that behaves so unnaturally.

Yet another fault is to fish the fly too fast. People who fish a fly fast near to the surface are right—up to a point. That point depends on the size of the fly and the strength of the current, if any. What is fast for a small fly may be comparatively slow for a large one. And what is fast for a large fly is much too fast for a small one. Most flies in general service are too small to be fished very fast, except upstream in a strong current; also, most of them are quite the wrong shape. A great many sea trout flies look rather like drowned moths and no fish is going to take a drowned moth that goes whizzing through the water at a speed considerably greater than it could attain even when airborne!

I say "no" fish, but this is not strictly true. (As Hamlet said: "We must speak by the card, or an equivocation will undo us.") An occasional fish *does* take a fly that is moving unnaturally fast. Quite recently a demented salmon came racing across a pool tail, with its back half out of the water, to take a size 10 fly over which I had lost control and which was skidding round doing everything it shouldn't. It is unwise to use the absolute in relation to animal behaviour any more than to our own. Fish, like other creatures, sometimes do strange things.

The use of a dark fly is often recommended for night fishing. Such a fly is not ineffective, especially late on in the season. Nevertheless, although after a certain stage of darkness colours are of little importance in themselves, they are important for their *tonal* value and I would not care to restrict myself too much. I once invented a special fly for the darkness called the "Nightmare". It had (I thought) a very attractive straggly body of black seal's fur. It caught a lot of fish in bright sunlight in a Donegal sea lough, but for the purpose intended was never an outstanding success.

There are few rivers that do not produce some special fly patterns which, it is claimed, hold magic properties. Sometimes they may. And if other people catch fish on them, so should you. But don't regard them as being the only flies worth trying. Some local anglers are inclined to be rather conservative, both in their choice of flies and methods of fishing. When conditions are poor and fish difficult to move, don't hesitate to put on something unusual—indeed startling. It is surprising what a big fish will take at times. I remember a big brown trout that was rising underneath an ancient bridge one hot, sunny afternoon, when I was a boy. He seemed a very perverse fish and declined fly after fly until, as a joke, I tied on a huge white moth. He took it at once! Big sea trout are like that, sometimes.

Well, the lures I fish with have proved their success many times in the face of general failure. Doubtless you will give preference to your own fancies—*and it is better you should, for confidence in a lure is (nearly) everything*. Nevertheless, I propose to give a description of the things I use, together with some notes on their construction, so that you may have the opportunity of trying them if you wish. They have the merit of being easy to tie.

> *Note.* Since the thickness of the leader, or leader "point" in the case of a tapered leader, depends to a certain extent on the size of lure being fished, suggested night-fishing leader sizes have been given in pounds breaking-strain standard "Platil" monofilament nylon.

The Medicine

This big silver-blue is called the "Medicine" in honour of that magnificent fisherman Brigadier G. H. N. Wilson, who christened it so. It can be used all through the season, on either floating or sunk line, and is the best all-round sea trout fly I have come across. A general purpose fly, it is good both at night in clear water and during the day when the river is in spate and coloured. (It is also a very good grilse fly—ideal for fishing the streamy, broken water at the neck of a pool.)

It should be tied in sizes: 2, 4, 6, on the lightest low-water salmon hook procurable. Contrary to general belief, it is *not* a heavy hook that fishes best on a sunk line, but a light one. A heavy iron, or the use of lead merely to get the fly down deep (when required) defeats the object of sunk line fishing. As we shall see in a later chapter, it is on the way in which the *line* is fished that the behaviour of a fly depends.

The features of a good sea trout fly of this type are simplicity and slimness since it is the tenuous impression of a little fish that we wish to create, not a solid facsimile. A slim-line dressing on a low-water hook with a silver painted shank provides just that.

Wigeon and brown mallard are the best wing dressings; mallard tending to be more successful from mid-August onwards. Sea trout seem to prefer a dark-winged fly late in the season. For the body, a coat of silver paint is preferable to tinsel—although even this is by no means essential. Even the addition of a hackle may be questioned; but the fly does not fish so well without one. Hackle fibres, like the wing fibres "work" slightly in the water when the fly is swimming, and so tend to create an impression of "life".

The Medicine can be fished effectively all night, although generally speaking the night fisherman will get better results *after midnight* by using Sunk Lure, Surface Lure or fly/maggot—especially if conditions become difficult. But in my experience when sea trout are active at dusk in fairly streamy water, there is nothing to beat it.

A tube-fly often gives good results, particularly in streamy water, but the wide bend of the low-water hook seems to lose fewer fish than the smaller treble of the tube-fly. When a lure larger than a size 2 Medicine is required late at night for sunk line fishing, a tube is undoubtedly better than a larger single hook. Years ago, I did well with a lure called the "Twin-Set": this was a tube-fly, the body dressing of

55

which was repeated on the shank of the treble. The articulated, or double fly effect, seemed more attractive to fish than an orthodox model dressed only on the tube. I fished it in various sizes, according to the state of the water, from half an inch to two inches or more, and once tied some with dark mink tail. These were good for both sea trout and salmon—but no better than common stoat! I mention the "Twin-Set" in case you care to try it. For reasons to be given, my preference nowadays is for the Sunk Lure.

Before

A "Medicine" in the hand before and after it has been fished. Like any other wet fly, it looks lifeless and bedraggled when it leaves the water. It will not, of course, look like this when immersed. If held stationary underwater, the fly will be fluffed-out just as it is in the open air when dry. As soon as it begins to move through the water it becomes "alive", with an action that is very attractive to sea trout. The separate movements of wing and hackle fibres, which seem to flicker with life, undoubtedly add to this attractiveness.

After

The respective merits of tube-fly, and Medicine dressed on single low-water hook are as follows:

TUBE
Advantages:

The treble provides a good hooking factor, since it is effective no matter what the position of the body may be. Great for salmon; but it doesn't hold on to a sea trout as well as the low-water hook.

If a hook point is snapped off against rock or shingle, it is only necessary to replace the treble.

Disadvantages:

Thickness of the body. Fewer "offers".

Inclination to hook back on the leader in much of a wind; a serious disadvantage at night.

Treble is inclined to stick out at an angle.

LOW-WATER HOOK
Advantages:

Very slender body. Gets more "offers".

Although its hooking factor is not so good as a treble, it holds on to a fish well.

Not so inclined to hook back on the leader.

Disadvantages:

Sometimes swims on its side, which may result in a fish being missed, or poorly hooked.

If the hook is broken the fly is destroyed.

Use the largest size of Medicine on the night following a spate; or by day when the water is dark. The next night, come down a size. I seldom go below a size 4, even in very low water. A size 4 can be used by day when the water is clearing after a spate and has assumed the colour of bitter beer. A size 6 serves well enough at night for fly maggot fishing; although usually, when deep-lying sea trout decline an unadorned fly but show interest in maggot, it is better to use a smaller fly, such as the "Maggot-Fly".

The photographs on the next two pages show the various stages in tying the Medicine.

A low-water salmon-hook size 2, 4, or 6, with silver-painted shank (alternatively, a straight-eyed size 4 Carp Hook). A few turns of red tying-silk have been wound round the head of the hook to make a seating. Now, the stalk of a dyed-blue cock's hackle is tied in.

The hackle feather has been wound round and round the seating. Hackle pliers hold it in place while turns of tying silk are worked down between the fibres to stop it unwinding.

The end of the feather is nipped off.

With wetted finger-tips the left forefinger and thumb drag the fibres back along the hook shank, while the hackle is tied in at the desired angle.

A section of fibres is cut from one of the brown flank-feathers of a mallard drake.

The section is folded in two.

Re-folded, then folded again.

The resulting bundle of fibres, or "wing" is held along the hook shank with right forefinger and thumb so that the length can be gauged.

The wing is taken by finger and thumb of the left hand and its head secured with three or four turns of tying silk.

The ends are trimmed short. The head is completed with a whipping. Then given two coats of quick-drying, clear varnish.

The finished fly. Of all sea trout flies the "Medicine" is one of the most successful. It is also one of the easiest to tie.

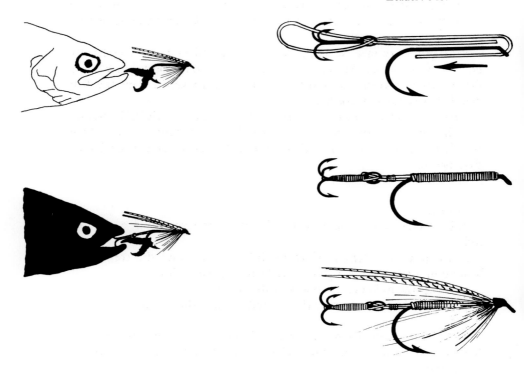

The Sea Trout Secret Weapon

This device was conceived during a frustrating night's fishing in August, 1962: sixteen offers, three fish landed. The prototype was tied the following afternoon and fished later that night. Result: eleven offers, nine fish landed. A dramatic improvement.

And so it has been ever since. Now, when a sea trout tweaks a maggot it finds itself lip-hooked by the tiny treble, which lies astern of the main hook.

Fishing the Secret Weapon often provides good sport late at night when sea trout have "gone down". At such times, fish are not inclined to race about in pursuit of a lure. It must, therefore, be placed right in front of their noses. To achieve this, it is fished very slowly on a smooth-shooting sunk line. It is delicate work and very exciting. To avoid damaging

60

the maggots, a special form of casting action should be developed. It is quite impossible to describe this cast other than to say that it should be as "soft" as possible, without jerkiness, all slack line being shot first time with no false casting.

When they are in a tweaking mood, fish are likely to be very lightly hooked through the skin of the lip. Great care must be taken when a fish is being played; the tension of the reel slackened, and the fish handled as though on cotton.

There is another reason for careful playing of fish. Suitable trebles are difficult to obtain; many have an unhappy tendency to straighten out. If this can be overcome, there is no better arrangement for fishing fly/maggot.

Construction

1. Lay a seating of fine tying silk along the shank of a size 16 treble.

2. Loop a short length of 12 lb. B.S. nylon round the treble and bring both ends out through the eye from opposite sides.

3. Whip the nylon to the shank of the treble.

4. Whip the strands of nylon together just above the eye of the treble.

5. Bring one strand of nylon through the eye of a size 8 Hardy "Perfect" hook and back along the shank. Cut off the other strand level with the eye of the hook.

> *Note.* It is very important that the distance between treble and hook is not too great. As a guide, the eye of the treble should be level with, or even slightly inside, the bend of the hook.

6. Whip the nylon mount to the hook shank, taking care to maintain equal tension in the two strands. Put extra turns of tying silk round the hook at the end nearest the treble, to provide maximum strength at this point.

7. Varnish mount.

8. Apply dressing. Body: brown dubbing. Hackle: natural red hen fluffed out. A sparse "wing" of brown mallard.

9. Varnish head of lure.

Avoid neatness in the dressing. The overall effect should be a small brown straggly-looking creature. It is a fiddly thing to make, but gloriously rewarding on the river in the small hours of a summer night.

The "Maggot-Fly"

Hackle: Brown hen.
Body: White dubbing; ridged.
Hook: Short-shanked, snecked hook, sizes: 8, 10.

This simple little fly with two or three maggots on the bend of the hook is deadly at times. It hooks more fish than a larger fly because, if given the opportunity, a fish will usually take it well back.

It has been said that the maggot alone of the fly/maggot combination attracts fish. This is not always so. I have often caught fish on fly/maggot that have declined either fly or maggot by itself. The use of a single hook, however, is not always effective.

When a sea trout takes with gusto a single hook is quite satisfactory, since (together with the maggots) the hook is taken inside the fish's mouth. But there are nights when sea trout do not take in such an obliging manner. Sometimes, using the very front of the mouth, a fish will give the maggots a little tweak and let them go again (rather in the same way that a salmon will sometimes nip a prawn). It usually occurs when rain is imminent, or when the night turns cold in the small hours. A fish behaving like this cannot be hooked on conventional tackle because the hook is never inside its mouth. All the angler feels is a series of infuriating little tugs. He may strike until his arm aches, but his only reward is a slack line.

The sea trout Secret Weapon puts an end to all this.

Small Double

Dressing: Black hen hackle. Silver body. Teal or Mallard wing.
Length: $\frac{1}{2} - \frac{5}{8}$ inch.
Hook: Size 12 or 14 double-iron.
Leader: 5–6 lb.

This little fly will sometimes work wonders when sea trout are in a tweaking mood and being finicky. It is difficult for a fish to tweak such a tiny fly without getting hooked (although some manage to do it!).

When the angler has no opportunity, or inclination, to fish with maggots the little double provides a good substitute for the Secret Weapon. The double iron is very effective. Fish taking it properly are usually well hooked. It is very much a summer, low-water lure.

> *Note.* This size of double iron, suitably dressed, is just right for a salmon late on a summer evening (or in the early morning) in dead low water.

Worm-Fly

Dressing: Brown or black hen hackles.
Body: Peacock herl.
Length: $1\frac{1}{4}$ – $1\frac{1}{2}$ inches.
Leader: 7–9 lb.

Of standard flies, the worm-fly is by far the best. A good lure for a sea trout fairly late in the season, say on a late August night. A very worthwhile alternative to the Medicine, fished in low water. The drill is to let it drift slowly round a pool tail on a sunk line. I like to think that a twist or two of green fluorescent silk underneath and just showing through the body dressing of peacock herl makes it more attractive; but, to be practical, I doubt whether its inclusion really makes any difference.

The Sunk Lure

The Sunk Lure seldom fails to catch fish. An excellent saltwater lure, it is also a most effective river, clear-water, night fly-fishing lure for sea trout of all sizes—and especially good for hooking the really big fish. I have taken a number of sea trout of over 10 lb. on it at night, in addition to the occasional salmon. Indeed, it is the only lure I know that will sometimes catch salmon late on dark nights. (So far, it has done so on at least ten different rivers.) It is also a successful daytime salmon lure for sunk line spring and early summer fishing.

Construction:
1. Put a seating of tying silk half-way along the shank of a sneck bend hook.
2. Loop the nylon (22–24 lb. B.S.) round the hook and bring both ends out through the eye. I suggest 22–24 lb. nylon as a rough guide; the thickness of the nylon used depends on the weight of the tail hook and the length of the mount. It should be stiff enough to support the tail hook without drooping, but flexible enough to bend double.

   Note. The length of a Sunk Lure can be from two to three inches. The standard length recommended for sea trout night fly-fishing is $2\frac{1}{2}$ in.

3. Whip the nylon to the shank of the hook.
4. Bring the longer strand "B" through the eye of the top hook and back along the shank. Cut off strand "A" level with the eye of the hook.

5. Whip the nylon to the shank of the hook, taking care to maintain equal tension in the two strands. Put extra turns of tying silk round the hook at "D" to provide additional strength at this point.

6. Whip part of the link at "C".

7. Varnish mount.

8. Coat with silver paint.

9. Apply dressing: two blue hackle feathers, one tied either side, with a few strands of peacock herl on top. This dressing provides good results with both salmon and sea trout. It is important that the tail of the dressing should not extend past the point of the tail hook.

10. Touch off the head of the lure with red varnish.

11. Method of replacing tail hook.

Having read my instructions for tying the Sunk Lure, Tom Rawling made the following comment:

"I think you could add a point or two that in my experience make a lot of difference.

"Nylon whipped to tail hook. Put hook round stem of vice. Pull on nylon to make sure all is tight. When Strand B is brought back through eye, put half a dozen turns of silk round the doubled B strand at the eye, then pull hard on both ends to make sure the eye of the hook will be clear for the leader, and that the nylon will not draw. Pull evenly, or you will alter the length of the lure. Make sure that leader nylon will go through the eye of the hook. Now whip Strand B only, cutting off spare end about two thirds of the way along the hook shank. Lay A on top of the front hook and whip forward to eye. Cut off surplus nylon. Make sure hook points are in line: both should touch an even surface when the mount is laid on its side. Varnish *twice*—with a day's interval. Silver paint is slow to dry. Two days."

Except on those occasions when the river is in spate and coloured, the fisherman armed with a Sunk Lure should experience few blank nights. Its particular merit is to attract fish late on—usually after midnight—when so often the fish have "gone down" and are refusing more conventional lures. It will even take fish when the river is at dead summer low, and when the water is running high but clear after two or more successive spates—never good conditions for catching sea trout.

At least, it has done so on the various rivers I have fished.

As its name implies, the Sunk Lure should be fished slowly on a sunk

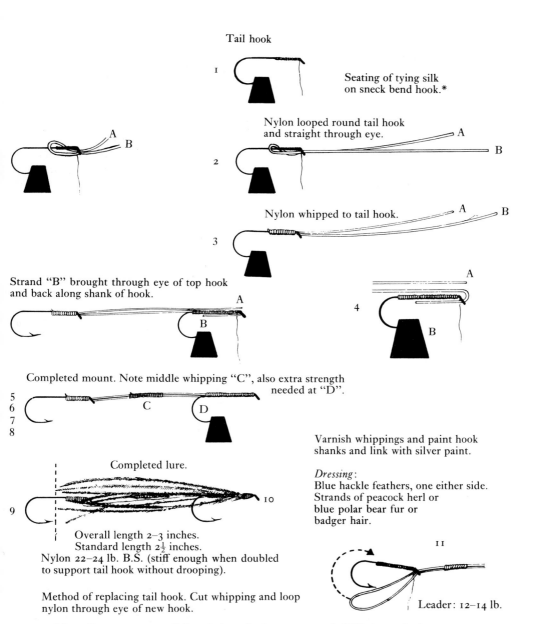

Tail hook

I

Seating of tying silk on sneck bend hook.*

Nylon looped round tail hook and straight through eye.

A

B

2

A

B

Nylon whipped to tail hook.

A

B

3

A

B

Strand "B" brought through eye of top hook and back along shank of hook.

A

B

4

A

B

Completed mount. Note middle whipping "C", also extra strength needed at "D".

5
6
7
8

C   D

Varnish whippings and paint hook shanks and link with silver paint.

Dressing:
Blue hackle feathers, one either side.
Strands of peacock herl or blue polar bear fur or badger hair.

Completed lure.

IO

9

Overall length 2–3 inches.
Standard length 2½ inches.
Nylon 22–24 lb. B.S. (stiff enough when doubled to support tail hook without drooping).

Method of replacing tail hook. Cut whipping and loop nylon through eye of new hook.

II

Leader: 12–14 lb.

Note. On no account fail to bring the longer strand "B" through the eye of the top hook and back along the shank. This method makes it almost impossible for the mount to "draw".

*Nowadays, I understand, this is called a "reversed" hook.

65

Two "posed" photographs showing hook holds typical of the Sunk Lure.

1. Fish hooked on tail hook. Top hook pulled firmly into the outside of the mouth when fish turned and ran.

2. Fish held on top hook only. Many early season fish are landed in this way; fish which, on a one-hook lure, would be lost—owing to the way in which early fish take a lure, or to the tenderness of the mouth (or both).

66

line. Late at night, it is always wise to try it over a big fish that has recently splashed, especially when this happens near the head of a pool (see Introduction).

A fish is usually hooked on the tail hook. The advantage of having two hooks set well apart in tandem on a *flexible* mount is that when the fish turns and runs, the top hook often secures a hold in the underside of the fish's jaw—effecting a double hold. If the tail hook subsequently comes away (which frequently happens with a big fish early in the season, probably owing to the way in which it takes a lure at this time of the year and to the tenderness of the mouth) the fish is still held by the top hook. For this reason, *use short-shanked hooks.* The long shanks so often found on a professionally tied lure prevent its flexibility.

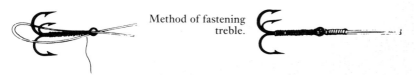

Method of fastening treble.

For salmon fishing, a small treble is recommended at the tail, but the single hook is better for hooking sea trout.

> *Note.* I have found that two light-ironed double hooks are well worth trying. The lure tends to swim on an even keel and the doubles secure a good hold. I have had great success in low water with a two inch lure of this nature, using size 8 doubles. But I am still of the opinion that a mount with single hooks gets more offers—perhaps because it is less bulky.

As with most lures, a variety of exotic feathers and other materials may be added, and if your confidence in the lure depends on their addition they should, of course, be included. But simplicity is the keynote of success. The purpose of a lure is to entice, and a simple, sparsely-dressed lure will entice more effectively than one which is heavily dressed. And in this context, all sea trout flies are simply—lures.

It is easy to allow fly-dressing to become a complicated and esoteric ritual. The novice, faced with a list of fly dressings, may well despair not only of the mechanics of construction but the cost and difficulty of obtaining the supposedly vital materials. It is all nonsense. Forget the name a fly has been given. Think merely of what you want your lure to look like, and use the most practical materials at your disposal. It is largely the shape, size and presentation of a lure that matter— certainly at night. A long, slender body, with some hair from your shaving brush, or your wife, or the tail of your dog will suffice.

Damage to a Sunk Lure caused by a big sea trout. The pictures illustrate two points:

1. The importance of bringing one strand of the nylon mount through the hook's eye and back along the shank—as shown in the diagram on p. 65. Had this not been done the fish would have been lost: the tail hook would undoubtedly have drawn.

2. The need to put extra turns of tying silk at the point of weakness near the bend of the top hook. The whipping on this mount was simply not strong enough.

68

The lures I have listed provide the newcomer to sea trout fishing with something to be going on with. Each is simple enough to tie and the materials are readily obtainable. Few fishermen, however, can resist filling their cases with flies. And for those who can't, two or three sizes of each of the following standard patterns should prove a reasonable investment: Peter Ross, Mallard and Claret, Black Pennell, Alexandra. If bought they are likely to be overdressed. Trim them with a pair of scissors. Thin out the hackle and wing and lop off the whiskers that stick out behind.

Owing to the tendency of sea trout to "nip" the dressing of a fly during certain weather conditions—particularly when rain or thunder is imminent—the less there is protruding beyond the hook the better. These tail whisks seem vaguely intended to represent some portion of an insect, a sort of hang-over from brown trout fishing. They serve no useful purpose, however, and are out of place on a sea trout fly. Some "bodied" flies, such as Mallard and Claret, or Teal and Green, for instance, are improved by the removal of the wing. This turns them into a kind of nymph, which can be effective at times; but the hackle may need trimming.

With this assortment of flies and lures at his disposal, the sea trout river fisherman should be equipped to tackle—and, if he fishes properly, defeat—almost any conditions, however unfavourable they may be. There is, however, one big omission from the list. This is a lure of the utmost importance, without which no night fisherman should ever go to the river—the Wake, or Surface Lure.

But this demands a chapter to itself.

The day has never dawned, nor will it ever dawn, on which the gillie will fail to find an excuse, as distinct from a convincing or even plausible explanation, of why the fish are not taking.
Hamish Stuart, *The Book of the Sea Trout* (*c*. 1917)

III
The Surface Lure

It is necessary to state clearly right at the start that Surface Lure fishing is quite hopeless during the hours of daylight. The principle underlying the attraction of this lure is different from that of any other type of fly or lure, either wet or dry—indeed, the way in which it is fished is the antithesis of all customary methods of fly fishing.

When we are fishing in daylight, the drag caused by a fly skidding across the water—either through the force of the current or faulty manipulation of rod and line—is something we try to avoid. But when fishing at night with a big dry fly, or a Surface Lure, it is precisely this drag we wish to create.

If a dry fly is cast on a straight line across a river at an angle of, say, forty-five degrees downstream, it will start immediately to swing round and drag against the current leaving a "V"-shaped wake and, unless line is payed out quickly, will continue to do so until it reaches the slack water close to the fisherman's bank. A wet fly will do the same if the current is too strong to allow the fly to sink below the surface. That the path of the fly will be along an "S"-shaped curve can for the moment be ignored.

Provided the night is dark enough, this drag, or wake, caused by a floating lure that is skimmed across the surface—either by the force of the current or through action on the part of the angler—can provide a deadly attraction for sea trout. And, incidentally, for brown trout, too.

It is clear that in order to produce this drag the lure must be kept moving over the surface of the water. If, when fished across a current, the line is allowed to go slack, the lure will begin to drift—and so lose its wake. The same thing will happen if the line becomes waterlogged and drowns the lure; the wake will vanish as the lure goes under. Similarly, if in conditions of still water the angler ceases to draw in line, the lure will remain motionless, without drag, without "life", and therefore without attraction. It is the wake of the lure and not the lure itself that attracts the fish.

Construction:

1. Trim a wine cork to the desired size and shape, or cut and plug a length of goose quill.

2. Prepare a mount in exactly the same way as described for the Sunk Lure, using either an eyed or an eyeless treble on the tail.

3. Whip the mount to the body (see arrows), and varnish.

4. Colour is unimportant; but, if desired, the whole thing can be given a coat of silver paint.

5. Dressing, too, is unimportant. But, although by no means essential for catching fish, the addition of two "wings" has the merit of increasing the angler's confidence in the lure as well as making it more stable in the water. So, *when the silver paint is dry*, add two wings as shown in the diagram. Any small dark feathers will do: grouse, owl, turkey, pheasant, etc. My preference is for grouse.

> *Note.* Overall length: 2–3 inches. (Standard length: 2½ inches.) Standard body length: 1½ in. Leader: 12–14 lb.

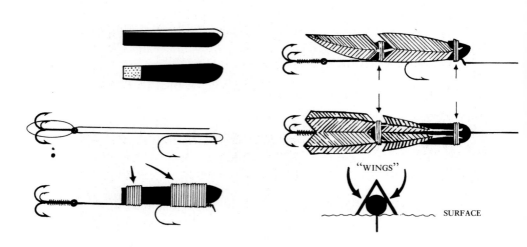

Shape, colour and dressing are relatively unimportant. What the lure *must* do is—float. Provided it does so, and is causing a suitable wake, almost anything will at times catch fish. Once, when no other materials were available, I caught some fine sea trout in the sea by means of an ordinary beer cork with a hook lashed to it. Later that night, having clumsily lost the cork in a bed of seaweed, I continued to catch fish on a piece of stick.

A form of Surface Lure can, of course, be fished with a fixed-spool reel. Over twenty years ago I designed a wooden lure called the "Swimming Mouse", which was fished in this way. It was particularly effective during the period of slack water at the top of the tide in Irish sea loughs— thrown out into the darkness and wound in again. Not very exciting fishing, but it caught some big fish.

For "fly" fishing, the body of a Surface Lure can be made either of quill plugged with cork, or entirely of cork. I prefer the latter because, being heavier than quill, it is easier to cast into wind—a not unimportant point when fishing a west coast river where the prevailing wind is upstream.

An unadorned Surface Lure, similar to that which accounted for the fish portrayed on p. 75.

A large well-oiled dry fly is effective at times in the half-light or when there is a moon behind the clouds. So too is a "dry-fly" lure consisting of two hooks tied in tandem with thin segments of cork whipped to the hook shanks and a dressing of dark, fuzzy hackles. If a dry fly is used, *Permaflote* (which makes a fly unsinkable, see p. 126) will be found a blessing.

When a cork or quill lure is used the leader should be attached underneath the body a short distance from the nose. This keeps the lure cocked up slightly as it moves across the water and helps to prevent it from being dragged under by a sodden line. If the lure dips beneath the surface, drag ceases immediately and the lure becomes ineffective. This often happened when grease wore off a silk line. Not so with the modern "floater".

A magnificent sea trout pool. The fish lie in a steady current under the far bank. Darkened by the trees at night, this water is perfect for Surface Lure.

> *Note.* The Surface Lure has a double function. It not only hooks you fish, it tells you where fish are lying. Many fish will splash at the lure without taking it. Knowing their position you can, if they continue to refuse the Surface Lure, go to work on them with a fly.

From the pool opposite: 14 lb. sea trout (H.F. Surface Lure).

Fish will sometimes "stalk" the lure, just as they will a fly, and it is not unusual for them to follow close behind for some distance suddenly seizing the lure just as it leaves the water. But if, once it has started to drag, the lure falters and loses "life", fish will have nothing more to do with it during that cast. From this it is obvious that the lure must be kept skimming across the surface right up to the moment of recovery.

Used on a fly rod the Surface Lure can provide most exciting fishing. It is especially good for hooking big fish, and some of the best sea trout I have ever caught were taken on bits of cork fished in this way. But it is not an infallible method of catching fish, even when conditions seem perfect; and, strangely enough, its success varies from season to season, more so than any other form of lure. Some years it catches a great number of sea trout, on others very few. Nevertheless, when conditions are suitable, it is *always* worth trying. It can hook you a whopper when all other methods fail.

Sea trout will take the lure at any time during the hours of darkness, provided the night is dark enough. As a result, the most likely period is usually between one and three o'clock in the morning. Small wonder that I view with pity the fisherman who packs up at midnight.

The best places to fish Surface Lure are unbroken runs and pool tails where the water flows in a smooth, steady glide. But all holding water is worth a try so long as the surface is calm enough for the lure to leave a wake.

The ideal position to cast from is that which allows the lure to swing round on the current and finish up, still causing drag, straight downstream of the rod in water deep enough to hold fish. Sea trout that follow the lure are then quite likely to take just at the moment of recovery. So—wade deep wherever possible. Wading reduces the casting distance— a great advantage when fishing into wind—and, if silk is being used, reduces the length of line that can become waterlogged. *But* be stealthy. To splash about in a still, unrippled sea trout pool is an angling crime.

A downstream wind, irrespective of direction, is preferable to an upstream wind. The latter makes casting difficult and also tends to increase the surface ripple. Better, no wind at all.

Bright moonlight is not suitable. But if there is sufficient shadow, fish may occasionally be taken beneath high banks, or bushes, or overhanging branches. Wherever it is dark enough. Darkness is the important factor.

A still, warm, cloudy night is best, without moon or stars. Provided it is dark enough, however, no conditions are hopeless—even the chill damp mist that creeps over the water meadows with such depressing effect on both fish and fishermen; or the approach of thunder, when lightning flickers and the river seems suddenly empty. Such conditions, needless to say, are rarely conducive to a large bag. Nevertheless, fish will sometimes take a Surface Lure in circumstances that defeat even a well-fished sunk fly.

Sea trout react to the lure in five different ways.

The first is tremendously exciting: they come with a rush and a splash, take like tigers and nearly pull the rod out of your hand. Obviously, no strike is necessary when they take like this.

Secondly, they take very, very gently, with scarcely any surface disturbance. Although seemingly impossible, this remarkable feat is accomplished with maddening frequency. Such a gentle form of "take" is a strange, almost uncanny sensation. It is all so quiet, and darkness lends an air of mystery. The lure suddenly stops. There is no tug; it just stops dead as though snagged on some trailing branch or tree root. One's automatic reaction is to drop the rod point and slacken line. Too late, the mistake is realised. There is a swirl on the surface . . . and the fish has gone—as mysteriously as he came.

Toad, 1¾ inches, taken from the stomach of a 1½ lb. sea trout. The fish was heard to swirl in the darkness; a Surface Lure was cast—and immediately accepted.

What happens, I think, is that a fish "formates" on the lure and then nips it very softly by the head, only the mouth breaking surface. I have sometimes found teeth marks on the body of a recently painted lure after such an encounter. It is inclined to happen when the lure is fishing rather too slowly in slack or slackish water. To avoid this form of "take", keep the lure moving faster. To hook the fish, tighten instantly (but as those of my readers who have experienced it will know, this is much more easily said than done!).

Thirdly, they come with a splash, give the lure a firm, decided tweak, and let it go again. How they manage to do this time after time without hooking themselves is both mysterious and irritating. But they do. And if there is any certain method of hooking the fish that behaves like this I have never discovered it.

Fourthly, they try to drown the lure, either by striking it with their tails or, more frequently, by heaving themselves up out of the water and coming down on it with a closed mouth. Fish are sometimes foul-hooked under the chin when they come at a lure in this manner. I don't think much can be done about it. They happen to be in that sort of mood and that's all there is to it. Usually, this behaviour indicates a falling barometer, with subsequent change of weather.

Lastly, they will splash at the lure without touching it. This occurs very frequently. For every fish that takes the lure, a dozen will splash at it. This happens in all conditions; but mostly on moonlit or starlit nights that are not sufficiently dark. I am sure that fish are attracted by the surface "V", and only pay attention to the lure itself at the very last moment of their attack. Perhaps, if there is too much light and the lure is not moving fast enough, they see it for what it is and turn aside with a splash of their tails—almost, one might think, derisively—without touching it. To rise fish after fish in this way without feeling one of them is not unusual and I think that the only course of action is to cast patiently away across the same piece of water time and time again. The fish either go down for good, or seem to lose their tempers and come at the lure with a rush.

Once, late at night, waist deep in a pool, I cast for well over an hour across some fish that had started by splashing at the lure and then gone down and, apparently, sulked. I decided as an experiment to stay where I was until dawn; and so, without moving my position or altering the length of line, continued to fish the lure cast after cast round exactly the same arc. After it had swung across that shoal of sea trout I don't know how many times, a fish suddenly took it. No splashing; no messing about; a sudden, decided take. I played and landed the fish well upstream of the shoal, then went back and fished in the same place. Fifteen other sea trout quickly followed suit.

The reason? I don't know. Was it curiosity? Or irritation? Possibly, but I rather doubt it. A more probable answer, it seems to me, was some subtle change of conditions—perhaps a tiny rise in temperature—too slight for me to sense, but sufficient to bring the fish "on". Whatever the reason, those fish, after a long period of refusal, suddenly started to take eagerly and continued to do so until daybreak.

That incident happened many years ago. Subsequent experience suggests that during such a sudden period of activity, some other lure might have been equally effective. Only by experiment does one learn these things. At such a time it is both interesting and instructive to have two anglers fishing the same piece of water with different lures.

A Surface Lure is not the easiest of objects to cast. This, I suggest, is worth bearing in mind when selecting a rod for sea trout fishing; but we shall deal with that in the next chapter. At the moment we are concerned only with tactics.

Once any casting difficulties are overcome, Surface Lure tactics are simple enough. When fishing down an unbroken "run", or glide, or the smooth run-off of a pool tail, start well above the fish and cast a loose line across the river and as far downstream as possible. The moment the cast has been made, shoot a little more slack line. Allow the lure to drift with the current for three or four yards. As the line tightens, the lure will start to drag and, leaving a "V" on the surface, begin to swing round towards your own bank. Let it continue to do so until it approaches slack water, then work it quickly and steadily upstream towards you. Fish will usually take as the lure first begins to swing, but sometimes they will follow it and take only at the moment of recovery. Its speed, therefore, should not decrease as it moves out of a current.

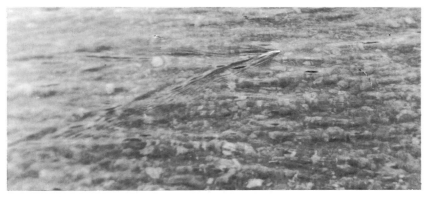

Lure in action.

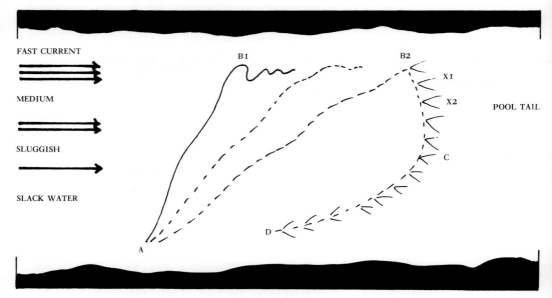

When fishing the Surface Lure in streamy water, cast a loose line from A to B1, and then flick out a little more slack. Allow the lure to drift downstream with the current for three or four yards. At B2, the slack will take up, and the line tighten on the lure—which will immediately begin to drag and swing round on the arc B2,C. Let the lure continue to fish to C, then work it quickly and steadily towards you to D. Fish will take anywhere between B2 and D, usually at X1 and X2. Sometimes, however, a fish will make a dash at the lure just as it is about to be recovered, so it is essential that the speed of the lure should not decrease between C and D. If anything, it should *increase*.

80

ELEVATION

B1   SURFACE   B2   LURE "COMES TO LIFE"

PATH OF DRIFT

PLAN

B1   B2   DRAG
                                                                            SUDDENLY
                                                                            STARTS

PATH OF DRIFT

Note. The idea of "inducing" a fish to take a bait or lure by giving it sudden
movement is, of course, by no means new. It is used in many different
ways in many forms of angling.   One example is the ploy of the stillwater
dry fly fisherman casting, say, a big sedge. In between periods during
which his fly remains motionless, he often finds it profitable to give it
little bursts of "life" and make it scutter—a yard or so at a time—across
the surface.

81

It is important to remember that a fish will ignore a drifting lure. Only when the lure "comes to life" and begins to drag across the stream are a fish's predatory instincts aroused. To take advantage of this is the reason for casting a loose line and then shooting more slack. The sudden action of the lure after a short, innocuous drift, seems most attractive. This little ruse may sometimes be employed successfully over the known lie of a big fish, or to induce a fish to take after he has already risen to but refused the lure at some other point of the cast.

Position yourself so that the lure can be placed just beyond and a few yards upstream of the fish. Check the lure after a short drift so that it suddenly "comes to life" and starts to drag just over the fish's nose. It will often be taken savagely—one of the most exciting of all fishing moments.

As already mentioned, fish tend to splash at a lure that is moving too slowly. The lure should never hesi ate as it comes into slack water. Since a fish may follow the lure for some distance before taking, the lure should speed-up slightly as it comes out of the current. This speeding-up is quite natural, and what one would expect of any living creature— whether a small fish breaking surface, or anything else—that is swimming across a river. The creature's ground speed will increase as the strength of the current diminishes; and the lure should behave in a similar manner.

This realistic action may sometimes entice a hesitant fish that is interested enough to follow but would otherwise türn away without taking. Such fish are rarely seen in the darkness, but that they *do* follow is indisputable. I have seen the surface movement of fish as they came towards me; indeed, on occasions when wading very deep, I have had them actually seize the lure within a couple of yards—splashing me when they did so!

The principle when fishing a pool is exactly the same. Should there be insufficient stream to work the lure, create the necessary drag by drawing in line with the non-casting hand; either by stripping and letting it fall, or gathering the slack by means of "Finger-Ring" Figure-of-Eight coils.

"Check the lure . . ." The line runs from the reel over the forefinger of the casting hand (to prevent line being drawn off the reel) and thence to the wetted tips of the first two fingers of the left (or non-casting) hand. For short distance retrieves at the end of a cast, the left hand is moved steadily away from the rod to arm's length. The same method is used for short distance retrieves with fly.

Note. Butt-spike hard against body. Reel handle clear of clothing and free to run, if required. (See p. 100.) Rod: Hardy "Houghton" 10½ ft. Reel: Hardy "Perfect" 3⅞ in.

Stripping-in line. Here the line is drawn by the non-casting hand from under the forefinger of the casting hand, and allowed to fall.

When a cast has been fished out, the last yard of line is brought in quite quickly while, at the same time, the rod is raised with a smooth but rapidly accelerating movement. If a lot of line has been stripped-in, a false cast may be necessary in order to shoot it all. But this should be avoided whenever possible.

Sea trout, 13 lb 10 oz. This magnificent fish came to the Surface Lure late at night in almost pitch darkness with the river at summer low. I had finished stripping-in line and was just starting my back-cast when the fish took with a tremendous splash. The lure must have been grabbed just as it was leaving the water!

The fish, which had evidently followed the lure across the pool, fought furiously and was unlucky not to escape, being only lightly hooked in the very tip of the neb.

The "Finger-Ring" Figure-of-Eight Retrieve

There are various methods of "working" and recovering a fly. The most common method—when more than an arm's length of line has to be recovered—is to strip the line in and let it fall. There are times, however, when this technique is unsuitable:

1. In a strong wind.
2. When the angler is wading in a current.
3. When the slack line may become entangled with undergrowth.

In these cases, the line is gathered in tight coils inside the non-casting hand by what is known as the "Figure-of-Eight" retrieve.

The conventional method is to draw the line straight from the butt ring, as shown in fig. 1. A far better method is shown in fig. 2. Here, the line is drawn *not* from the butt ring direct, but from a ring made by thumb and forefinger of the casting hand.

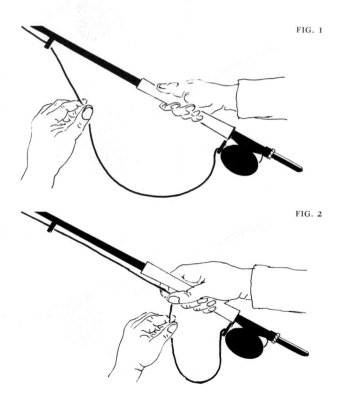

FIG. 1

FIG. 2

Having made a cast, grasp the rod only by the 3rd, 4th and 5th fingers of the right (or casting) hand and pass the line over the crook of the index finger (fig. 3). Drop the thumb until it touches the ball of the index finger. Thumb and index finger now perform the role of an extra rod ring.

Take hold of the fly line *behind* the thumb with thumb and index finger of the left hand (fig. 4) and draw about 4 inches of line through the "finger ring".

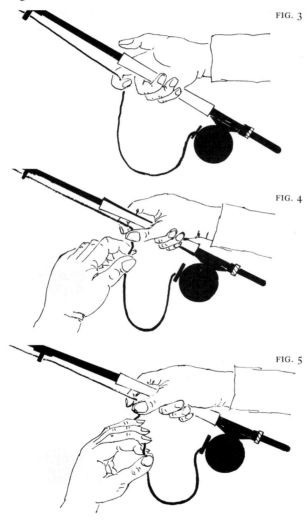

FIG. 3

FIG. 4

FIG. 5

FIG. 6

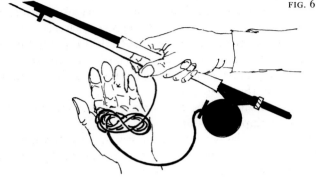

Grab the line with the remaining fingers of the left hand (fig. 5). Allow the loop that has formed over the tip of the left forefinger to slip off into the palm as the hand moves back to its former position.

Repeat the procedure over and over again, with the wrist pivoting in a smooth figure-of-eight movement. It is important to keep the hands very close together; indeed, the angler should be conscious of his left little finger brushing his right thumb with each backward stroke.

Gradually, as the fly is worked in towards the angler, coils of line are gathered up in the left hand. The gathered line is shown in fig. 6, with the hand displayed in an open position. This has been done purposely to reveal the coiled line. In practice, the hand merely opens sufficiently to grab each succeeding "bite" of line.

The advantages of the "Finger-Ring" Figure-of-Eight over the conventional method are considerable.

1. It is much easier to perform.

2. It is faster, and thus permits greater variation of fly speed during recovery.

3. When a fish is hooked, the line is under immediate control. One has simply to exert pressure with the right forefinger and trap the line against the rod butt.

> *Note.* The Figure-of-Eight retrieve is made much easier (as indeed are all methods of retrieve) if the rod butt is kept anchored firmly against the groin. For this reason, it is advisable to fish with a rod that has a short extension below the reel (as shown in the diagrams).

88

Not infrequently one is faced with a piece of good holding water that is beyond casting range and impossible to cover by normal methods: an overgrown "run" or glide where depth of water; trees, bushes or other obstructions, prevent the fisherman from going further downstream. Such water may, however, be fished satisfactorily by carrying out the following procedure, with a floating line and a much longer leader than usual. (See diagram.)

Wade out to A and let the lure drift downstream along the edge of the current by stripping off line.

Work the lure in zig-zags across the stream—as shown by the dotted lines in the diagram—by holding the rod parallel to the water on either side of you, at arm's length if necessary.

Try "hanging" the lure in the stronger parts of the current, and vary its path, sometimes, by drawing it upstream in the slacker water by the bank, underneath overhanging branches.

The length of line is controlled by means of a coil in the non–casting hand. The "Finger-Loop" Figure-of-Eight method of retrieve is just right for this.

PLAN VIEW

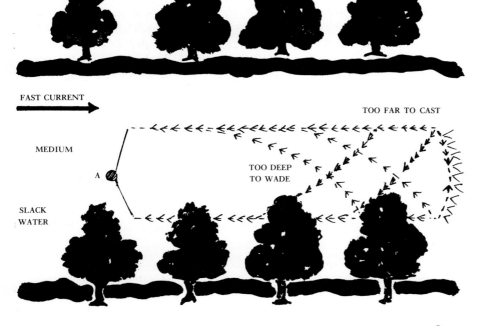

FAST CURRENT

TOO FAR TO CAST

MEDIUM

TOO DEEP
TO WADE

A

SLACK
WATER

89

A few general points:

When fishing disturbed water, put on a tubby lure that will cause sufficient drag to overcome the surface ripple. Use a larger lure on a "run" than when fishing the flat, unruffled tail of a pool.

On a windless evening use a leader of eight or nine feet; but if there is anything of a head wind, put on a heavier, shorter leader of not more than five or six feet.

In moonlight, or at dawn, fish fine. Sometimes sea trout will take a Surface Lure in the half-light, but only if a slender lure is fished on a fairly fine leader. But never fish *too* fine. To hook a fish merely to get broken is both pointless and unsporting.

In moonlight, contrive to fish with the moon in front or downstream of you. A moon that is shining straight down a pool, or from behind the rod, is a great handicap irrespective of what bait or lure is being used. A moon behind your shoulder provides the least favourable of all fishing conditions.

The Surface Lure should be a part of every night fisherman's armoury. This matched pair of sea trout came from a catch made by Tom Rawling during a night when no other type of lure was accepted.

The Steeple Cast

Since overhead, double-haul, Spey, roll and switch casting methods have been dealt with in detail in a host of publications I will not waste space by covering such well-beaten ground. The steeple cast is another matter. I have never come across an adequate description of this cast. Doubtless, somebody *has* dealt with it—probably better than I can do it—and if so I offer him my apologies. In the meantime, however, here are some notes on the subject together with a photographic sequence of the complete cast, shown on this page and the next two pages. The pictures show an angler fishing with a line of bushes at his back.

Of all ways of throwing a fly—whether on floating or sinking line—the steeple cast is the most practical for night fishing. It avoids so much trouble, especially when there are obstructions behind the rod.

Success in making this cast depends on four things:

1. Cocking the right wrist downwards and not "breaking" it.
2. Keeping the right arm straight throughout and not letting it go beyond the vertical.
3. Keeping the line tight and not letting the left hand wander about.
4. Releasing the line from the left hand at exactly the right moment.

It looks an awkward sort of cast. And so it is. But it is very, very effective.

1   2   3

1–3. The previous cast has been fished out, and now the left hand (holding the line) starts to move away from the rod.

4

5

6

7

8

9

10

11

12

4. The rod point dips slightly as the right wrist cocks downwards.
5. Ready to start the back cast. (There is no pause. The cast is made in one continuous movement.)
6. Start of the back cast. As the rod is raised it begins to lift the line from the water. (Note how the right wrist remains cocked downwards and is kept in that position.)
7–9. As the rod goes up, the left arm straightens to its full extent.
10. The top of the back cast. The right arm stays vertical and moves no further back.
11. The rod is bent slightly backwards by the line—which has shot up into the air high overhead above the bushes. (Note: the right wrist does not "break" but remains in the cocked position.)
12. The forward stroke. The lure is "dragged downwards out of the sky". The left hand, holding the line, is kept at full extent of its reach.

13. The left hand releases the line . . .
14. . . . which shoots out as the rod is lowered . . .
15. . . . and brought down towards the surface in sympathy with the falling line.
16–20. The left hand comes in towards the rod to take the line and bring it under
    control by means of "Finger-Loop Figure-of-Eight" (see p. 86). The rod point
    is raised towards the fishing position.
21. Rod in fishing position. Angler starts to fish the cast.

"Throw it back as high in the air as possible." The top of the steeple cast seen from a different angle: right arm vertical, stripped line taken down to full extent of left arm. *Note*: If on the forward stroke the line is not shooting satisfactorily, cast with the reel facing sideways—as shown above.

Any attempt to fish the Surface Lure with a sticky line is a waste of time and effort. A considerable amount of slack line has to be shot at every cast and this is impossible unless the line runs smoothly through the rod rings. To use a slightly heavier line than usual will help carry the lure out against a wind and to shoot the five or six yards of slack that accumulate during the final "work-in". Much more will have to be shot on still water.

When recovering the lure preparatory to casting again, speed it up over the last few yards and then, with a continuous and quickening movement, lift if off the surface. Throw it back as high in the air as possible. Imagine you are trying to hook the stars above and behind your back; and when making the forward stroke try to pull them down from the sky—so that the line is pushed out in front with plenty of punch. This form of steeple cast applies equally well to fishing any other type of fly or lure at night, especially when you are casting into wind, or have a high bank or bushes behind the rod.

The lure is easily pulled under by a waterlogged line, or one with a sinking tip, so on no account let it slow down or stop after a cast has been fished out. To snatch at the lure—especially a "drowned" lure with a quick jerk of the rod is usually to receive it straight in the face! Make absolutely sure it is on the surface before making the back-cast.

Lastly, a word of warning. The Surface Lure is a dangerous weapon on a dark night with a gusty wind blowing. It should be treated with respect. No matter how experienced an angler, if you have never fished this lure before, practice casting it in daylight. Observe its behaviour in various types of water and strengths of current, so that you will know what is happening to it when you fish it in the darkness. Time spent in practice and observation is never wasted. Besides, casting practice may well prevent a painful injury—the Surface Lure is no pleasant thing to have twirled around your neck!

Now—tackle.

How many rods of evil structure have been fab-
ricated. How many wheels have been constructed
on foolish and vicious principles; how many lines
badly prepared; how many casting-lines odiously
knotted; how many hooks ill-turned and round-
shanked, to the evident discomfort of the fly tier,
ill formed appearance of the fly, and missing of the
fish!
O'Gorman, *The Practice of Angling* (Vol. 1, 1845)

IV
Tackle, Angling Safety and Culinary Matters

TACKLE

The Rod

A rod is an extension of the angler's arm and is, primarily, a tool with which to present a bait or lure. Its value when playing a fish is of secondary importance. Admittedly, it acts as a spring and sometimes prevents breakage, or the hook being torn away from a soft hold, and (simply because it is longer than one's arm) it helps to keep the line out of the water and to control the fish. But its main function is to put a lure where it will attract and hook a fish.

The choice of a rod seldom depends on the size of the fish. If leader and line are strong enough, the biggest salmon can be landed on the smallest trout rod (curiously enough, a light rod seems to tire a big fish more quickly than a heavy rod). Conversely, the smallest trout can be landed on the biggest salmon rod. Nevertheless, it would be as foolish to use a small trout rod for spring salmon fishing as it would be pointless to use a big salmon rod for trout fishing.

What governs the choice of a rod is the angling method for which it is to be used; the weight of the baits and lures it is going to fish, and the distance they have to be cast. A salmon "fly" fisherman, for instance, casting in early spring with a sunk line and a 4 inch leaded tube needs a powerful 14–16 foot double-handed rod to present and control his lure. But by May/June the world has turned, the season has changed and so has the behaviour of the fish. When the water was cold the salmon hugged the bottom and were tempted only by large lures; but now that the water has warmed up they are tempted by small lures fished close to the surface. And, of course, the approach of the fisherman changes in accordance with this. He no longer needs a sunk line and powerful rod but an outfit resembling that of the trout fisherman—since his size of lure is going to be much the same. From May onwards, until the autumn, he can fish the same water for salmon of the same size with a $\frac{3}{4}$ inch tube fly on floating line, for which on a small river he need use nothing longer than a 10 ft. 6 in. single-handed rod.

Again, casting distance is not the only factor that dictates the choice of a rod. For example using a shooting-head the reservoir trout angler, standing out in the water with no obstructions behind him, can cast 30–40 yards with an $8\frac{1}{2}$–$9\frac{1}{2}$ foot rod. But although the water to be covered may be no more than 15–20 yards, the sea trout night fly fisherman steeple-casting a Sunk Lure with rhythm down a heavily bushed "run" will find a 10–11 foot rod a much better tool for the job.

It is fallacious to suppose that simply because the average sizes of sea trout and brown trout are similar, a short brown trout rod will do. It won't! Sea trout fishing differs considerably from orthodox brown trout fishing. At times you will need to cast and control some large and cumbersome lures, in difficult water, and you may well find yourself trying to fish all night into an upstream wind.

So, don't be misled by the delightful feel of a short rod when you have it in your hand in the shop. It may be useful for flicking a fly under the branches of some overgrown trout stream, but that technique is going to form only a very small part of your sea trout fishing.

A long rod is very useful for keeping the line out of the water and controlling the fish— particularly when it is close to the angler's bank or the other side of a line of bushes along which the fish must be "walked" to a landing place.

The American cult of the ultra-short rod for salmon fishing is in all but the most exceptional case an affectation and offers no practical advantage whatsoever. (All that can be said for it is that it does no harm to the fish, unlike the iniquitous American system of assessing the merit of a catch in terms of tackle breaking-strain. This is examined in detail on p. 252.)

Whatever angling method you employ; spinning, bait fishing, fly fishing; don't use a cheap rod, don't use a short rod. The stronger the rod, the longer the rod, the more line can be kept out of the water and clear of obstructions when a fish is being played. Use the longest rod you can handle conveniently with one hand. It is of no importance who made it, or what it is called, so long as it will do its job. I see no point in fishing for sea trout with a fly rod of less than ten feet. Ten feet six inches is better, and a good strong rod at that. The lightness of modern rod-making materials has removed any physical hardship from a rod of this length.

Makeshift but practical butt-extension: a plastic, 12 bore cartridge case. It was fitted in haste some years ago, intended only for one night's use. It is still firmly in place! (Reel: Hardy *St. George*. Line: DT7S.)

The 10′ 6″ Bruce and Walker carbon *Salmon and Sea Trout* will cope with all river requirements. To anyone who fancies cane, I recommend the Sharpe's 10′ 2″ *Sea Trout Special*. Another of my favourite rods is the old 10′ 6″ Hardy *Houghton* (not to be confused with the 10′ *Crown Houghton*). Built-cane, of course. It went out of production many years ago. A pity. (I get nothing for these advertisements, by the way.)

One other thing: most rod makers nowadays have a habit of placing the reel right at the very end of the butt. This is a mistake. The place for the butt when you are playing a fish is against the body, and there should be a few inches of clearance to prevent the reel handle from catching in loose clothing when a fish is running; or (as we shall see later) when you are "walking" a fish. Some rods contain a detachable spike—which slots into the butt—for sticking into the ground and holding the rod upright. For the purpose intended, this spike is a comparative failure; but, as an extension of the rod while you are fishing, it is very useful. If your rod incorporates a spike always use it. If the rod has no such extension, push a few inches of light tubing on to the butt. One day it may prevent the loss of a big fish.

> I must say that I totally detest, abhor, and repudiate all click wheels, lock wheels, and multiplying wheels . . . A multiplying wheel is not worth a farthing for anything but small fish. You cannot get up a weight without breaking your machinery, or dropping your rod to the water. I have had sad experience of this kind of wheel, of which I may hereafter speak—having spoiled the work and lost an immense salmon through its means.
>
> O'Gorman, *The Practice of Angling* (Vol. 1, 1845)

The Reel
A reel is simply a revolving drum that holds as much spare line as you think any fish is likely to take out. Nevertheless, it is a very important piece of tackle—as the novice appreciates when his first big fish sets off at speed. At such a moment only the best is good enough.

There are some very cheap reels on the market. Avoid them. You get what you pay for. Like all other cheap items of fishing tackle a cheap reel is false economy. Sooner or later it will let you down and what you lose will be worth considerably more than the extra price of a good reel. There may be some reliable rods, reels, lines and hooks going for a song—but I don't know about them.

Get the best. Look after it and it will last a lifetime. It should be wide in diameter (not less than $3\frac{3}{4}$ in.), fairly narrow in the drum, the check neither too heavy nor too light. What line a fish demands should run out smoothly, without snatch or the danger of an over-run.

In my opinion there was never a fly reel as good as the Hardy *Perfect* (never did anything so deserve its name). My own model—a $3\frac{7}{8}$ in., ideal for sea trout and summer salmon fishing alike—has been in constant action for well over thirty years. And has served without complaint. Although the *Perfect* accompanied the incomparable *Houghton* rod into obsolescence, there are still a few about. Most people who own one realize what they have got, but if you ever find one up for sale—grab it!

> *Note.* Hardy's now make a multiplier-type fly reel having a smaller diameter. I haven't tried it, so can offer no further comment. But I can certainly recommend the $3\frac{3}{4}$ in. Hardy Marquis 10, with exposed polished rim.

The Line
It is important that rod and line should be in balance. When choosing the right line for any fly rod, it is the *weight* of the line not its thickness that matters. From the American Association of Fishing Manufacturers has come an excellent system of describing a fly line with letters and numbers. This is known as the AFTM system.

The key is as follows:

WF = Weight forward (or forward-tapered).
DT = Double-tapered.
S   = Sinking.
F   = Floating.
1–12 = Weight of the first 10 yards of the taper.

Consider the following line: DT7S
The first two letters (DT) mean that it is a double-tapered line.
The number (7) refers to the weight of the first 10 yards.
The last letter (S) shows that it is a sinking line.
A line marked: DT7F is a double-tapered, Number 7, floating line.
If the line number for your rod is 7, then both lines will fit that rod. It must be remembered, however, that the floating line will be a good deal *thicker* than the sinking line—although the weight will be the same.

Suppose that the line number for a rod is 5, then a double-tapered floating line (DT5F) will be the same thickness as a double-tapered sinker (DT7S), but the sinker will be heavier than the floater. Thus since the floater is the right weight (5), the rod will be badly overloaded if the No. 7 sinker (same thickness but much heavier) is fitted to it. For that rod to be balanced, the sinking line must have the same number

Like doing anything else, there is a right way and a wrong way to thread a line through rod rings. The wrong way is to place the rod butt on the ground and poke the line upwards through the rings, reaching ever upwards as you go along. If you let go of the line it slips down through the rings and falls in a heap at your feet. There is also a danger of dirt getting into the reel mechanism. The right way is to place the butt on a bench or rock or on your fishing bag—*with the handle of the reel uppermost*—and work your way along with the rod horizontal. This method also helps to avoid missing a ring.

Wherever the reel is placed, whether on tackle bag or rock, make sure that the handle of the reel is uppermost.

as the floating line (5), or in full (DT5S), but this line will be a good deal thinner than the floater (DT5F).

Most good rod manufacturers nowadays give a fly rod a line number. As we have seen, this number specifies what *weight* of line suits the rod best. But since the AFTM number refers to the first 10 yards of the taper, this information about line suitability is based on the assumption that the angler will be doing most of his false casting with 10 yards of line out beyond the rod top. Sometimes an angler may want to use a greater or a lesser amount of line beyond the top ring. For example, if he is regularly fishing a small river he may do most of his casting with only about 10 yards in the air. But if he is fishing a large river he may aerialize 12 or 14 yards.

Each step in the AFTM numbers is equivalent to about 2 yards of line. This means that 10 yards of No. 7 weighs the same as 8 yards of No. 8, and the same as 12 yards of No. 6, or 14 yards of No. 5. For best casting results, therefore, you should choose a fly line of an AFTM number that suits your rod when you have got out the amount of line you do most of your casting with in practical fishing.

You can switch from one line to another, with the same rod, if you fish a number of different waters. You may, for example, choose a No. 7 for your rod when you are fishing a small brook and change to a No. 5 if you use the same rod to fish a wide river, because in the latter case you are likely to be false casting more line than you would in the former. In both cases, the weight of line that you will do most of your casting with will be about the same.

What is important to remember is that once you have found which AFTM number suits a rod, whatever kind of line you want—be it floater, sink-tip, slow sinker or high density—you can ask for it with the same number in the tackle shop and be sure of getting a line that the rod will handle successfully.

As a rough guide, for my own fishing I use a double-tapered floater, a double-tapered sink-tip (also ideal for summer salmon fishing) and a double-tapered high density. No. 7. On small rivers a certain amount of roll or switch casting creeps in, and to do this satisfactorily with a level or a forward-tapered line is almost impossible. At least, it is for me. A double-tapered line—which for this form of cast has the weight in the required position, i.e. close to the rod—is obligatory.

Backing
Backing is an extension of the casting line, forming a reserve of line that

is available for playing a fish. Monofilament nylon is rot-proof and makes very satisfactory backing. For years I have used nothing else. Depending on the diameter of your reel drum, put on about 150 yards of 25–30 lb. B.S. (I have had a big sea trout take out well over 100 yards on more than one occasion. It isn't often you need a hundred yards or more of backing, but when you do you need it badly!).

Nylon is slippery stuff. When fastening monofilament to the reel drum use the knot shown, and make sure you tie a safety knot in the end (at A).

Reel knot for monofilament nylon backing.

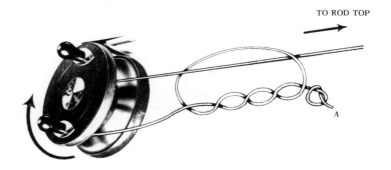

TO ROD TOP

A

Arrow indicates the direction in which the reel turns to wind up line. Pull both knots tight and trim at A, leaving a short stub.

Fly-Line/Backing Splice

A knot is a very personal matter. When buying a new fly line never let anyone splice on the backing for you (or, for that matter, tie the backing to the reel). If the splice draws you will lose not only a big fish but the line as well.

WARNING Wax changes with age, so that monofil will tend to draw from a two-or-three-year-old splice. Test all splices every season. *Note*: if diameters of fly-line and monofil backing are suitable, don't make a splice. The Needle-Knot shown on p. 110 is more reliable.

Crimp end of nylon with pliers. Tease out end (last ¾ in.) of fly line with needle point.

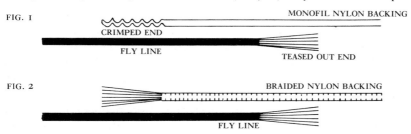

FIG. 1
CRIMPED END
MONOFIL NYLON BACKING
FLY LINE
TEASED OUT END

FIG. 2
BRAIDED NYLON BACKING
FLY LINE

FIG. 3

Splice tied at A leaving double lengths of tying silk (well waxed) whipped from A to B and back to A then A to C and back to A (Fig. 3). Or, with single length of tying silk, whip splice A to B to C and then back to A (Fig. 4).

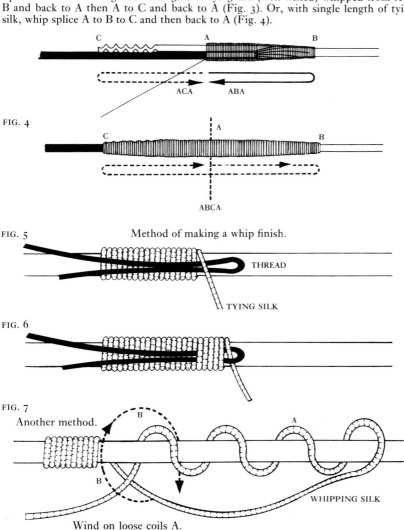

C   A   B
ACA   ABA

FIG. 4

C   A   B
ABCA

FIG. 5   Method of making a whip finish.

THREAD
TYING SILK

FIG. 6

FIG. 7
Another method.
B
A
B
WHIPPING SILK

Wind on loose coils A.
Wind whipping silk on fairly tightly in direction B.

Leaders

Nowadays in addition to spinning lines and fly-line backing most leaders are made of monofilament nylon. Although there are many different "brands", nylon is produced by a few large chemical combines and many of these brands are in fact the same "make". Since I cannot classify all these, my advice is to find a brand you like and stick to it. Compare the relative strengths of various brands by testing them for yourself on a spring balance—using the same knots and making sure that all samples have the same diameter.

(Strength in relation to diameter although important is not the only quality to look for in a line. Limpness is preferred for spinning reels. Limp nylon can be laid neatly and tightly on a small diameter drum and is less likely to spring off and cause over-runs.)

For fly-fishing leaders, stiffness is an advantage. It helps the leader to go down in a straight continuation of the line. A nylon less elastic than other nylons is useful in the hands of an expert angler, since limited elasticity transmits the action of a strike with greater speed. This lack of stretch, however, reduces the safety margin, so that a novice may suffer more frequent breaks when striking.

If you wish to take advantage of "strong" as opposed to "standard" nylon for any particular style of fishing, choose the *diameter* that you normally use, *not* the breaking strain. *Don't* replace a leader of 6 lb. B.S. "standard" with a 6 lb. B.S. "strong". It will not absorb the strike to the extent that you have come to expect from the standard nylon. If you normally use, say, 6 lb. "standard" you would choose 9 lb. "strong". Both have the same diameter.

From time to time you will need to tie two lengths of nylon together—often, lengths of different thickness—for instance, when making-up a tapered leader, or leader with one or more droppers. For this purpose you have, I suggest, the choice of Water Knot or Double-Grinner Knot. Both are more reliable than the Blood Knot.

Many wet-fly fishermen miss chances of catching fish because they fail to change the thickness of leader point when they change the size of fly. A small fly tied to thick nylon will attract few fish—even though the size of the fly is right for the prevailing conditions. Usually, this is not because the fish is afraid of the nylon, but because the fly is not "working" attractively. If the "greased-line" salmon fisherman goes down from, say, a size 6 iron to a size 8, or a size 10 iron, he *must* go down in nylon thickness if the smaller fly is to appear attractive. The same principle applies to the sea trout fisherman.

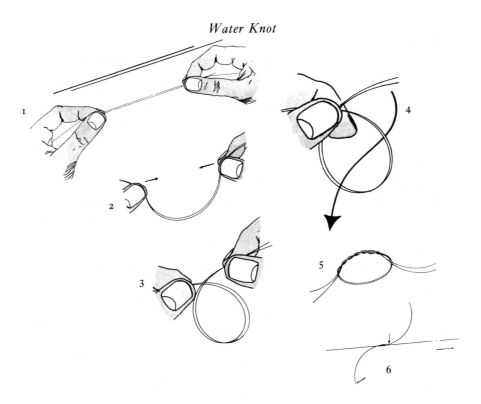

Hold the ends of the nylon together so that they overlap about ten inches (six inches if a dropper is not required) as shown in fig. 1.

Bring the paired thumbs and index fingers together (fig. 2) until a loop springs into place (fig. 3).

Grip the loop with the left thumb and forefinger (fig. 4).

Make an overhand knot by pulling the right-hand end through the loop from behind (see arrow, fig. 4). Make two more turns. At this point, the picture in fig. 5 will emerge.

Suck the circle of nylon, then pull tight. The resultant knot is shown in fig. 6.

Tied with two turns, the Water Knot was first recommended in *A Treatyse of Fysshynge wyth an Angle* (1496) for tying horsehairs together. Nylon, a slippery material, requires an extra turn.

When the knot is used for making a dropper, the fly is fastened to the stalk running away from the rod. It is true that if tied on the other stalk the fly will stand out better from the leader, but this method is not so strong.

Double-Grinner Knot

The Double-Grinner is a very good knot, especially useful for joining long lengths of nylon—which is difficult with the Water Knot. It was discovered by my old friend Richard Walker; or perhaps I should say "re-discovered", for it is in fact the traditional Fisherman's Knot, but made with four turns. However, his, rightly, is the credit for its present-day popularity.

As with the Water Knot, the stalk pointing away from the rod is used as a dropper.

For the Single Grinner Knot (joining fly to leader) see p. 117.

Note. Always lubricate nylon, by moistening in your mouth, just before you tighten a knot. This helps to overcome friction and to "set" the knot.

Needle Knot

Over the years, various methods of attaching a leader to a fly-line have been devised. None has been completely satisfactory. Shortcomings in traditional methods become acute when an angler uses a leader which is longer than the rod. The join of leader and line tends to catch in the top ring—sometimes with disastrous results when a fish is being landed. The Needle Knot has these advantages:

1. It passes more easily through the rod rings and allows the use of a leader which is much longer than the rod.

2. It is very strong.

3. Unlike a bulky knot, it causes no wake on the surface when the fly is retrieved on floating or "greased" line.

4. The centres of leader and fly-line are exactly in line.

With a needle that is slightly thicker than the nylon used (say, 24 lb. B.S.) perforate the end of the fly-line so that the point comes out at the side of the line about $\frac{1}{8}$ in. to $\frac{3}{16}$ in. from the end. Leave the needle stuck in the line with about a quarter of an inch of the point emerging.

Apply the flame of a match or cigarette lighter to the eye end of the needle, until the line starts to bend.

Take the flame away and blow the needle cool.

Remove the needle.

Take just over a yard of 24 lb. B.S. nylon and point one end. This is done by cutting the nylon obliquely with a razor blade. Pass this end into the hole at the end of the fly-line and out at the side. Pull a length of it through, then take five or six turns round the line. Bring the end back and lay parallel (fig. 1). See next page for diagram.

Take a turn in the opposite direction to the turns already made (fig. 2).

Lay on the other turns—taut, but not too tight. Continue until all original turns are uncoiled (fig. 3).

Snug down and tighten the knot. Cut off loose end of nylon (fig. 4).

Varnish knot, and also apply varnish to the end of the fly-line where the nylon emerges.

As a refinement, a taper can be built-up with tying silk, and then varnished (fig. 5). This is not strictly necessary, but it allows a smoother passage of the knot through the rod rings. Alternatively, the end of the line can be frayed in advance to create a smooth taper, and finished off with tying silk.

Now that a yard of heavy nylon has been attached to the end of the fly-line, a suitable tapered leader can be added, either with a Water Knot or a Double-Grinner.

Naturally, a leader so attached "lives" with the fly-line on the reel.

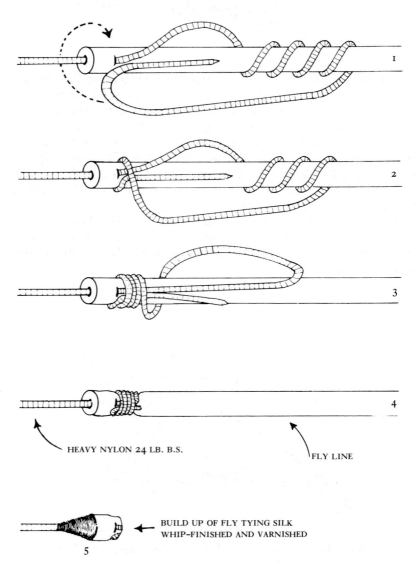

HEAVY NYLON 24 LB. B.S.

FLY LINE

BUILD UP OF FLY TYING SILK
WHIP-FINISHED AND VARNISHED

Although the Needle Knot is the neatest knot for joining fly-line and leader, the old fashioned Figure-of-Eight is sometimes preferable. This is when the angler wishes to make a number of leader changes to suit changes in size of fly or lure. Such changes can, of course, be made simply by replacing the point in a made-up tapered leader with one of different thickness, using a Double-Grinner or a Water Knot. But some anglers, wishing to avoid leader knots—especially when fishing at night—prefer either a knotless tapered leader or a length of level nylon in which a Blood-Bight Loop has been tied.

For joining line to loop in leader, the Figure-of-Eight knot is better than any other; simple both to tie and untie. The very end of the line does not stick out at an angle but lies in the same plane as the leader, thus reducing drag.

Blood-Bight Loop

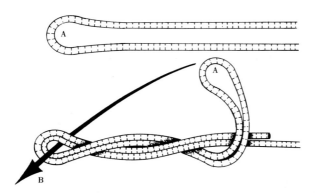

The loop for a level nylon fly-leader; the line being attached with a

Figure-of-Eight knot.

1. Bend end of leader back on itself to form loop A.
2. Twist loop A round leader to form loop B.
3. Pass loop A through loop B.
4. Suck the knot, then pull tight and trim the end.

Note. When tying knots in nylon don't economize. Give yourself plenty of
ends to play with.

Two Loops

A very simple, neat method of joining fly-line and leader. Useful for the
night fly-fisherman, since it facilitates the changing of a leader in the
darkness. The loop whipped in the end of the line should be renewed
at the start of each season. Better; loop the leader to a loop in a short
length of stout nylon needle-knotted to the line.

Tangles

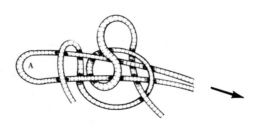

The simplified diagram shows a corner of a tangle. Tangles are the curse
of angling and darken the lives of all anglers from time to time. Don't
despair. Most tangles are easy to unravel once you know the secret. It is
this: almost all tangles are caused by loops of line getting caught up.
(See loop marked A.) Work round the tangle, freeing these loops.
Provided the line is not pulled too tight, there is no tangle that will not

unravel in a few minutes. The golden rules are:

1. Patience.
2. Don't pull.
3. Find the loops and free them one by one.

When you have freed all the loops the tangle will be undone.

OF A NEWLY INVENTED HOOK

This is a hook with an eye in the shank. It is another Scotch invention, and as to its usefulness may be placed on a par with the newly invented mode of breeding salmon.

O'Gorman, *The Practice of Angling* (Vol. 2, 1845)

Hooks

No matter how expensive and reliable our rod, reel, line and leader, what really matters is what we tie on the end of it all. Apart from our own incompetence, it is the hook we can blame for most of the fish we lose. Much is written about the various patterns of flies and lures, but what of the hooks they are tied on?

The eyed-hook was one of the great inventions of angling history. It was in use thousands of years ago but, as can be seen in the British Museum, the basic design has never changed. It seems, however, that after a time the eye got forgotten and was not re-discovered until the nineteenth century.

The Victorians made good hooks. Better than some of today's. And it is a sobering thought that in an age which boasts a "scientific" approach to angling, many of the hooks cast by the modern fly fisherman are inferior to those in use a hundred years ago. Some are disgraceful, and tackle dealers who stock them should hang their heads. To be fair, some of them do—confessing that they find it difficult to get good hooks.

But this doesn't help us much. To fish all day or all night to hook a fish—only to lose it is, to say the least, frustrating. Although in the case of a fresh-run sea trout the loss may be due to the softness of the fish's mouth, all too often it is due to the softness of the hook.

But even well-tempered hooks will lose their hold, and with irritating frequency. Are anglers doomed to this sort of disappointment? What really happens when a fish takes a hook and we put pressure on it?

Consider the hook in this drawing.

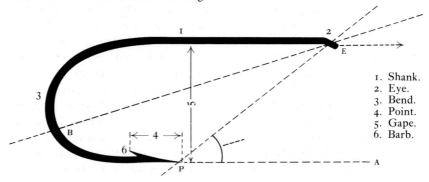

1. Shank.
2. Eye.
3. Bend.
4. Point.
5. Gape.
6. Barb.

Directly the point P starts to penetrate, the line of pull is in the direction of P–E. It is not, as one might suppose, in line with the hook-shank, no matter what form of attachment of line to hook is used.

EPA is the angle at which the hook starts its penetration. As the hook penetrates, this angle decreases until, at B (the furthest point from E), the maximum penetration is achieved.

The greater the angle of penetration (EPA) the more force is required to make the hook penetrate. This angle can be reduced by lengthening the shank in relation to the gape, but the longer the shank the greater the leverage against a fish's jaw, and the greater the tendency for the shank to bend. The thickness of the wire can be increased, but the thicker the wire, the greater the force needed to make the hook penetrate and (for sea trout anglers, most important of all) the heavier the hook.

Judging by the hooks on offer, experience seems to indicate that a hook whose total length is from 2 to $2\frac{1}{2}$ times its gape, and whose point is parallel to its shank is a reasonable compromise. But is this really so in the case of a sea trout fly-hook—and that, after all, is what concerns us here?

We will return to this in a moment. There is another aspect of a fly hook I want to discuss, one that has received scant attention: its degree of sharpness.

A sea trout has a very bony mouth. I am sure that the loss of some of the fish that seem to take well, run for a short distance, jump, and then depart, is due to a long-pointed, over-sharp hook, which sticks for a few seconds in a bony part of the mouth—before being shaken loose as soon as the fish jumps, if not sooner. I believe that a fly-hook can be too sharp; that the practice of honing it with a carborundum until it sticks in your thumbnail is all wrong. A carborundum should be used to take some of the sharpness off, not put it on. (With a bait hook we have to compromise. A bait hook needs to be very sharp, otherwise the bait may become damaged and so lose its attractiveness. So too does the hook used for fly/maggot fishing—e.g. the single hook of the *Secret Weapon* mount on which the maggots are impaled. But these are the exceptions.) I long ago stopped honing my fly hooks beyond a certain sharpness, and although no dramatic results can be claimed I am sure it has landed me the odd fish that would otherwise have been lost.

A hook should be short-pointed, sharp enough to penetrate gristle easily, but not so "sticky" sharp that it will prick into a bony surface. It should be able to slide across the bone until it comes to gristle, as it may if given the chance. Of course all this takes place in a fraction of a second, but what happens in that instant may make all the difference between a good and a poor hold.

This view has confirmation of a sort in *The Compleat Angler* (1653). For me, Izaak's greatness lies in his charming and evocative writing, his *feeling* for the sport of angling, but in this technical passage he has surely scored a bull's-eye:

". . . a Pike, a Perch, or Trout, and so some other fish, which have not their teeth in their throats, but in their mouths, which you shall observe to be very full of bones, and the skin very thin, and little of it. I say, of these fish the hook never takes so sure hold but you often lose your fish, unless he have gorged it."

And how often does a sea trout "gorge" our fly?

But to return to our hook design. If a fish swallows a bait, the design features of the hook and its sharpness are of comparatively little importance. A fly is seldom swallowed. The hook gets a hold somewhere inside the fish's mouth, usually in the "scissors", or around the bony jaw. If the hook gets a good hold in the "scissors" and comes adrift because of torn flesh (see p. 37), there is not much that design or sharpness can do to prevent it. But as practical anglers we can, at least, give ourselves the best chance of holding on to a fish. And I suggest the following:

1. Test a hook thoroughly before using it. This will sort out the soft hook or the over-brittle hook.

2. If a fly is tied on a single hook, make sure the hook has a pronounced barb; a big gape (to go round the bony jaw); a fairly long shank (total length, three times the width of the gape); a slightly in-turned, *short*,

but not over-sharp point.

3. Tie your Sunk Lures on flexible mounts, using two *short-shanked* single hooks—or combinations of singles, doubles and trebles—so that the top hook has a chance of securing the secondary hold shown on page 66.

Knots for tying Fly-Hook to Leader

Turle Knot

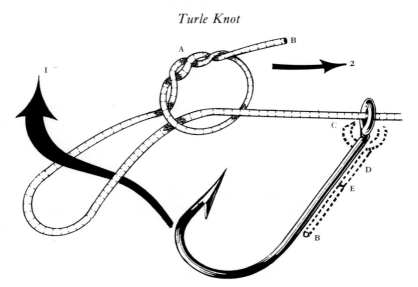

The Turle is a secure knot that grips the shank of the hook and is first choice for tying on a dry fly. It is not so good, however, for "wet" fly or lure. Unless the hook eye—whether up or down—is at right angles to the shank, the hook will stand out at an angle to the leader. In this case either Grinner or Tucked Half-Blood is better.

Tying instructions:

1. Tighten knot A.
2. Pass hook/fly through loop in direction of arrow 1.
3. Draw loop up to eye of knot in direction of arrow 2.
4. Hold end B inside loop, parallel to shank of hook, and draw loop tight round hook just below eye (dotted line, C). The end of the nylon (B) should now lie along hook (dotted line, D).
5. Cut off end, leaving short stub (at E).

116

Tucked Half-Blood Knot

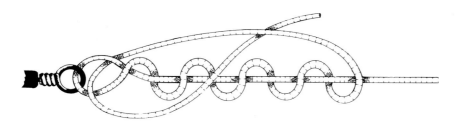

Grinner Knot

Good knots, to paraphrase Brutus, "must, of force, give way to better"! For many years I have used a variation of the standard Half-Blood Knot for attaching a fly. It has never let me down. But it has let others down. Clearly, therefore, it is not entirely safe and I shall no longer recommend it. The Tucked Half-Blood *is* a safe knot. So is the Grinner Knot, which is slightly stronger and even easier to tie. This is the knot I use myself nowadays.

For the Double-Grinner Knot, see p. 108.

Wading Staff

In many rivers a wading staff is an essential piece of equipment. If heavy enough in the butt a staff is a blessing. If too light it is a curse. The purchased article is seldom heavy enough.

Make your own.

The pictures explain all that is necessary—except the weight of the lead. This should be at least 12 oz.

A homemade but thoroughly practical wading-staff.

A light bamboo stick, heavily weighted with a length of thick lead sheeting wrapped round and tacked on to the butt—which is tipped with a rubber "shoe" from a three-legged shooting stick.

Most wading-staffs lack weight at the "business" end. As a result, they tend to float in anything of a current and become entangled with loose line. The pictures show the author's wading-staff "anchored" against the current and ready to hand during every moment of the cast.

A wader full of water never helped anyone to concentrate! Barbed wire, that curse of the countryside, ruins the pleasure of many a sportsman who fails to take his fences—all too easily done in the darkness. With a three inch rip in his boot he is faced with the choice of fishing "wet" or going home! A piece of piping, or an empty fertilizer bag, wrapped round the top strand will protect waders, clothing and vital parts. A simple stile is an added protection.

The Landing Net

A small net will accommodate only a small fish. Trying to land a whopper from a steep bank with one of those absurd (but expensive) little folding nets which plausible tackle vendors sometimes sell to novices is hair-raising. Don't let it happen. Get something simple and strong, with a great big wide mouth—and if it can be used as a wading staff as well, so much the better.

Do-it-yourself enthusiasts can construct frame and handle with laughable ease from a length of thick fencing wire, and a stout stick. Its diameter should be about twenty-two inches, and if the rim and upper part of the handle are covered with a coat of silver paint it will show up nicely in the darkness. A small piece of lead tied to the bottom of the net (or a pebble tossed into it before fishing starts) will prevent the meshes from bulging up when dipped into the water.

Method of Attachment

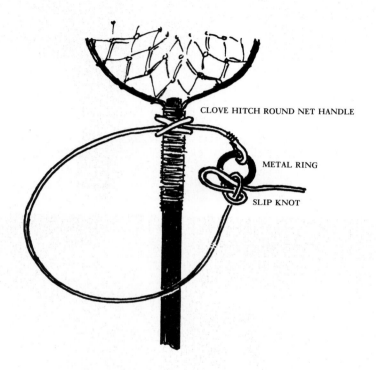

CLOVE HITCH ROUND NET HANDLE

METAL RING

SLIP KNOT

Slung loosely, the net makes a serviceable wading-staff—either while you are fishing or fording the river. For this purpose, a piece of lead sheeting should be tacked round the end of the handle. A rubber butt-pad helps to reduce noise. (See wading-staff, p. 118.) A net such as this can offer a ten or twelve pound fish the most comfortable accommodation. Indeed, this one has done so on a number of occasions. There is nothing that can nip the leader, and the wide mouth is a great blessing when landing any size of sea trout, especially at night.

A landing net is a trap. It must not be seen. While a fish is being played, the angler should stand well back from the water's edge. Only when the fish is tired and ready to land does he creep forward, kneel down and *sink the net in readiness*. Some sort of weight in a dry net—a pebble or piece of lead—is essential. A bulging net will frighten a fish and prolong the fight.

When the fish is exhausted and lying on its side—and not before—it is drawn steadily in over the waiting net.

124

The net is then raised to encompass it. If the fish is a heavy one, the grip on the handle will need to be foreshortened, with the butt braced against the angler's groin.

Ancillary Equipment.

It is aggravating to arrive at the waterside on time only to find that some necessary item has been left behind—fly case, perhaps, or reel. Fishermen as forgetful as myself should use a mnemonic to remind them of their basic needs. I use the following: "RR, NN, MM, SS, F, T, P"— which reminds me of rods, reels, net, nylon, midge-repellent, maggots (if I need them), scissors, spectacles, fly-case, torch, priest. It has saved much frustration.

If you prefer, write out a check-list and keep it in your tackle-bag.

The following photographs show some of the stuff that is needed on the river. Most of it can be carried in your pockets.

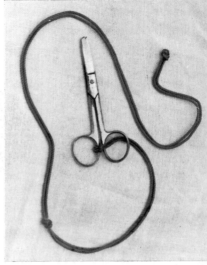

Don't forget your fly case. And if it has a compartment for carrying spare leaders, so much the better. An elastic band prevents it from coming open in your pocket. (The same safety precaution should be taken with a tin of maggots!)

Polaroid glasses are essential for daylight reconnaissance. This pair shows the value of carrying a reel of adhesive tape for waterside repairs!

Scissors, too, are essential. To avoid dropping them in the river or in long grass, fasten them with the method shown and hang them round your neck. Allow them to hang down inside your fishing coat. Blunt-ended scissors prevent any danger of injury.

During the late 1960s, conscious of the shortcomings of the various waterproofing liquids sold for dry-fly fishing, Richard Walker and Arnold Neave, of Hitchen, produced a formula whose waterproofing qualities are greatly superior to anything previously tried. A fly dressed with Permaflote is unsinkable. When the water is low or on still nights when there is no ripple, a large fly dressed with Permaflote makes an effective Surface Lure.

A spare reel of nylon lurking in the tackle bag ensures that you will never be caught short when leader carriers have been forgotten.

Adhesive tape should also live permanently in the tackle bag. Invaluable for making repairs at the waterside.

Harman loops. Marvellous for tying flies; or changing a fly—especially at night. They, too, can hang down inside the fishing coat if fastened with the attachment shown.

Bait fishermen should never be without this type of hook disgorger. A description of its use will be found in Chapter XI.

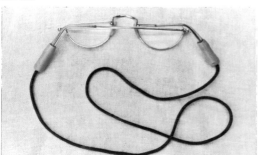

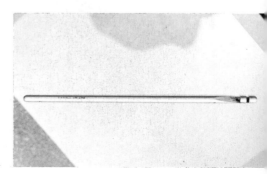

Midges can make evening fishing misery. *Always* carry some insect repellent, irrespective of what weather conditions are like when you set out. I should warn anglers intending to travel north, that the border country breeds a ferocious midge.

Always dress the part of the hunter. This will help you to feel like one. And perhaps even behave like one. So—every item of clothing and accessories should be of a suitable colour: preferably a drab olive green—even neck-cloth or hand-towel.

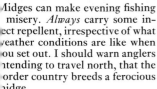

Tackle dealers offer a range of priests at not inconsiderable prices. This piece of chair-leg is equal to any of them and has served the author very well for many years.

Some sort of torch is essential at night. Needless to say, it should never be flashed on the water you are fishing. When you re-tie a fly or unravel a tangle in leader or line, keep well back from the river.

The best place for a flashlamp when you wish to use it is in your mouth. This leaves both hands free and the light can be directed exactly where you want; so that a lightweight, slender-bodied torch is the best. To enable the teeth to maintain a grip, wrap a piece of adhesive tape round the base of the torch. A red filter on the end of the torch protects your night vision.

Some fishermen prefer to carry spare leaders with flies attached. Serviceable carriers can be made for nothing from old Christmas and Invitation Cards. Eight cuts are made in the card, which is trimmed to the appropriate size. It can just as easily be cut in circular shape to fit inside a tobacco tin.

Pipe-cleaner Safety-Catch.

A piece of pipe-cleaner twisted round rod and leader just above the hook prevents fly (or spinner) from coming adrift and getting caught in bushes or the angler's clothing. By avoiding loss of time and temper (especially at night) it will, therefore, help to catch fish.

> *Note.* A large rigid fly-ring is very much more practical than the small floppy ring provided by most rod-makers—that is, when they provide one at all. There is a certain type of brassiere that contains just the right sort of ring for this purpose. Or there *was*.

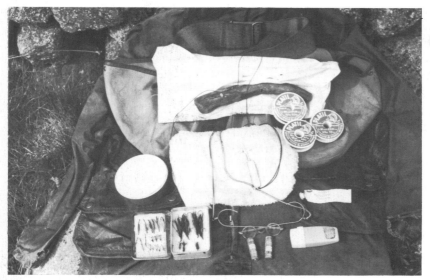

Ready for a night's fly-fishing. "Kit inspection" by Tom Rawling.

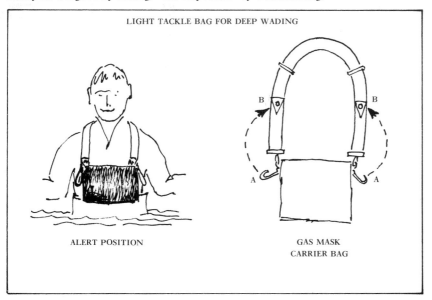

A handy bag for use when wading deep can be fashioned from any small haversack on the principle of the war-time gas-mask carrier bag, pictured above. Hooks AA fasten into eyelets BB, thus keeping the bag and its contents: fly-case, spare nylon etc., clear of the water.

The Wilson Fly-Retriever

This little gadget, invented by "Briggy" Wilson, should live permanently in the tackle bag. It consists of a crook that can be lifted on the rod point to obtain a hold on a branch in which one's hook or fly is caught.

The crook is strapped on to an empty cigar cylinder with adhesive tape. A suitable length of light, strong cord is tied to the crook, with which to pull down the branch. A piece of parachute cord is ideal.

1. Put the little cylinder with crook attached on to the rod tip.

2. Reach up with your rod and place the crook over the offending branch.

3. Remove the rod and put it safely out of the way, stripping line off the reel in order to do so.

4. Take hold of the cord and pull down the branch.

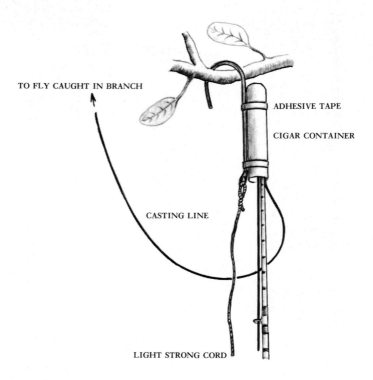

TO FLY CAUGHT IN BRANCH

ADHESIVE TAPE

CIGAR CONTAINER

CASTING LINE

LIGHT STRONG CORD

It is surprising how easily a fly can be retrieved from seemingly inaccessible branches.

The crook should be light enough to be lifted vertically on the rod tip, but strong enough to take the strain of pulling down the branch. Friction is increased by winding some adhesive tape round the bend of the crook. This prevents the crook from sliding down a branch when pressure is applied. This tendency to slip can, of course, be countered by intelligent selection of the place where the crook is put over the branch. If possible, place it just above the junction of a lateral (see diagram).

This equipment can also be used to retrieve a hook, fly or spinner from certain underwater snags, when clarity of water, strength of current and other circumstances permit.

Brigadier G. H. N. Wilson.

Wading

The ability to wade deep is an asset to every fly fisherman. But rivers vary enormously. Some are gay, uncomplicated little streams with easily-waded gravel runs and glides. Others are awkward and treacherous with slimy rocks and deep, sullen pools where a single false step may take the unsuspecting non-swimmer straight over a shallow, sunken ledge—into eternity.

On the river, wading is the most common cause of fishing accidents, and it is probable that those accidents involving the use of body waders form the highest proportion. No denigration of body waders is intended; the point is simply that the higher his waders the deeper the fisherman is tempted to wade, until sooner or later the fatal step is taken. When this happens the water is not up to his knees or thighs, but his chest, and in all probability he is swept off his feet by the current. An experienced fisherman who knows his river can tell at a glance where he can wade safely and where he can't. Even so, it is easy to make mistakes. A place quite safe to wade when the river is, say, nine inches above summer level may be impossible after a further rise of two inches. In a lake, a two-inch rise means that your effective wading depth is reduced by exactly that amount; but in the river there are two other factors involved. Two extra inches in the river mean not only two inches of extra depth, but a stronger current.

This added pressure of water against your body increases the water level against your back, or side, and also causes you to lean over at a greater angle against the current in order to maintain a footing—thus further reducing the safety margin of your waders. The combination of these two factors results in a loss of considerably more than two inches.

When wading for any distance downstream always be sure of the depth of water between the bank and wherever you happen to be. Your path may be along an underwater ridge with deep water on either side, in which case the only possible retreat is straight back upstream. Wading against even a weak current is a great deal more difficult than wading with it. Your return will be even more difficult if, while you have been wading downstream, the river has begun to rise.

Such a rise may be entirely unexpected. It is not by any means unusual for a downpour further up the valley to affect the river, although not a drop of rain has fallen in your locality. The early stages of such a rise are not immediately evident to anyone intent on his fishing. The water level may well creep up unnoticed—until the margin of safety is passed.

Wading upstream against a fast current. The net (or wading-staff) is used as a strut which the angler presses against as he leans into the current. It also probes in advance for rocks and holes.

Crossing a fast stream. The staff is now used on the downstream side of the angler, both to support him and to explore the nature of the bottom, as he edges across the river on a downstream diagonal.

133

When standing in a current remember that the water is piled higher against your back than your front, thus allowing a smaller margin of safety than you may think by a casual glance down. As soon as you begin to wade against that current the water will pile higher still, not only from the added pressure, but the greater angle at which it is necessary to lean.

When wading in a current *never* step up on top of a submerged rock. It is very difficult to keep your footing when trying to step down again.

When wading against the current *don't* turn round and face it. Go upstream backwards; or sideways, like a crab.

Don't cross your legs when fording fast water. Take a step with the upstream foot and then edge the downstream foot slowly level with it keeping the legs well apart. Provided the depth of water permits, cross over on a long downstream diagonal.

Always move with great care and avoid the slightest risk of getting a foot jammed between rocks. There is the tragic case of a fisherman drowning within a few yards of helpless and horrified friends when trapped in a rapidly rising river.

Finally, remember this: wading is seldom without danger, and it is sensible to give some thought both to wading techniques and to the correct action in event of emergency. Some of the accidents described may happen only rarely, but for the unprepared fisherman the first time may (in its more unfortunate sense) be the last! Wading is an aid to successful fishing. But compared with a fisherman's safety the catching of fish is of no account. *Never* take a chance. If you don't know the water well enough; if you don't know the ways of a river—stay out of it.

Emergency

Most fishing accidents result in little more than a wetting. A fisherman gets his boots full, or stumbles and falls unhurt in shallow water. But every so often comes news of a fishing fatality. Someone has lost his balance or been swept off his feet while wading; a loose rock has toppled over; a piece of river bank has collapsed; a boat has capsized . . . a fisherman has drowned.

Accidents such as these can happen very suddenly; indeed they usually do. Within seconds of being safe and sound, the unlucky man finds himself floundering out of his depth. Terrified, he throws up his arms and screams. Two involuntary actions. Both fatal.

Many lives would be saved if people would only think *beforehand* of the correct action to take in the event of emergency.

It is the unexpectedness of most accidents that carries the greatest threat to safety; the shock of a sudden plunge into cold water, followed immediately by panic—panic caused by the thought of being heavily clothed and shod, and out of one's depth. It has been said—and the number of people who believe it is surprising—that if a fisherman wearing waders falls into deep water, his boots will drag him down.

They will do nothing of the sort.

It is quite a simple matter to swim for short distances fully clothed and wearing waders; their weight when submerged is negligible, and although they don't make swimming any easier they certainly don't make it impossible. It is not too difficult to swim fully clothed while carrying a fishing rod. Provided you can swim, no great danger need accompany a tumble into deep water.

In order to enjoy a feeling of security on or beside water—whether river or lake—you should be able to paddle about fully clothed when out of your depth. If you can't, practice until you can, paying particular attention to the back-stroke. Most emergency swimming of this nature is (or should be) carried out on the back.

There is nothing difficult about it. On the contrary, it is really very easy. And it is very, very important, for once you are able to swim on your back you will be armed with confidence, and the thought of falling into deep water will no longer be one of fear.

Remember: *it is panic that drowns most people.*

When the worst happens—perhaps an undermined river bank collapses, or a shingle bottom slides away beneath your feet—and you suddenly find yourself plunging fully clothed, rod in hand, into the deeps—*don't* open your mouth and shout. Pay no attention to those stories of drowning men coming up three times. If you ship enough water first time down you won't come up at all. So—*keep your mouth shut.*

Provided you don't wave your arms about above your head you will soon bob up again. A living body is very buoyant. (Even if you can't swim, there is sufficient air trapped in your various garments to keep you afloat for several minutes, if you only give yourself half a chance.)

Float on your back. Keep your head lying well back in the water and let your legs come to the surface. Once in this position you can start shouting for help.

If in a river *don't* try to swim against the current. Let yourself drift downstream, feet first; then it will be your boots that will strike a rock, and not your head. Paddle away with your hands and gradually edge in towards the bank.

This sequence is reproduced from *Falkus and Buller's Freshwater Fishing*, for which it was taken. The part of the hapless angler was played (most gallantly) by Frank Plum. Fred Buller took the pictures.

A fisherman wading in a strong current on steep shingle . . .
takes a step too many.
The shingle slides away underfoot; the current sweeps him forward . . .
and down he goes, into deep water.
This type of accident can happen in any river, whatever the nature of the bottom. Within seconds of being safe and sound you may find yourself floundering out of your depth. It is the unexpectedness of such accidents that carries the greatest threat to safety—the shock of a sudden plunge into cold water; the fear that your waders may drag you down. *They will do nothing of the sort.*

136

Don't turn round and try to swim back against the current. *Turn on to your back* and let the current take you with it. If you cannot swim and hold your rod too, let it go. With line out, there should be a good chance of recovering it later.

Float on your back, head upstream. Kick with your legs, paddle with your hands, and *keep your head back.*

The classic "safe" position. Head well back. Legs up. Arms outstretched. Once in this position you can start shouting for help.

Keep on your back. Float downstream feet first with the current and gradually edge in towards the bank by paddling with outstretched hands.

But *don't* try to pull yourself up a steep bank out of deep water. The weight of sodden clothes and waders full of water will quickly exhaust you. Resist the temptation to cling on in a hopeless situation.

Keep on down the pool. Head back, legs up. Don't drop your legs to feel for the bottom: a vertical body will sink at once.

138

When you reach the shallows, *don't* try to stand up and walk out. Tired, suffering from shock and exposure, you may stumble and injure yourself. Roll over on to hands and knees . . .

and crawl out.

Wading Risk in Strange Water

Angler at A wades out to B in order to cover fish lying under the right bank. Wading along a shallow underwater ridge he fishes down to point C. There he comes to deeper water and finds he can wade no further downstream. He is unable to retrace his steps upstream owing to the strength of the current. Not realizing he is on the end of a spit he attempts to wade in towards the left bank along the line CD. Almost at once he steps into deep water and is swept off his feet by the current, downstream towards E. (See photographic sequence.)

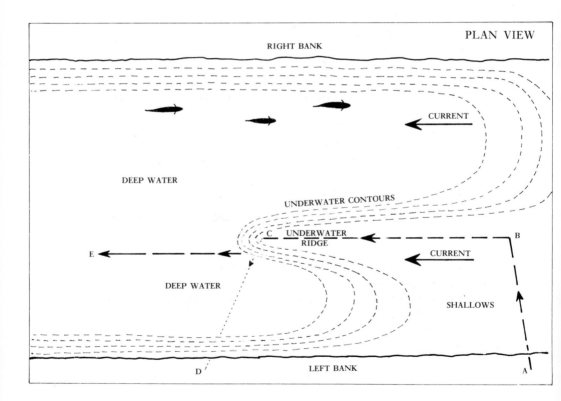

This seems to be as good a place as any to have something about storing and cooking the fish we spend so much time and trouble trying to catch. First of all, four Cragg Cottage breakfasts.

1. Clean and dry a small sea trout (1–$1\frac{1}{2}$ lb.).
   Wrap the fish in a slice of bacon.
   Place fish on a rack inside a roasting tin.
   Cook in a hot oven for about twenty minutes.
   Serve hot with extra slices of bacon, slices of fried bread and slices of cold tomato.

2. Clean and fillet a sea trout ($1\frac{3}{4}$–$2\frac{1}{2}$ lb.).
   Coat with oatmeal.
   Fry in bacon fat. Turn when golden brown.
   Serve hot with slices of bacon, fried bread and cold tomato.

3. Clean several herling.
   Melt some butter in a pan.
   Add a tablespoonful of olive oil.
   Add some cucumber rings.
   Fry for approximately one minute.
   Add the fish.
   Fry slowly until almost cooked, then crisp the skins by increasing heat.
   Lift out and place on a hot dish.
   Clean pan and add fresh butter.
   When butter bubbles add fresh cucumber rings and cook for about one minute.
   Pour the lot over the fish and serve.

   Note. Also delicious with blanched almonds instead of cucumber, but cooked in the same way.

4. Clean several herling or a sea trout (up to $2\frac{1}{2}$ lb.).
   Salt the fish inside and out.
   Sprinkle the tray of an ABU fish smoker rather sparingly with sawdust (supplied by the makers).
   Place the fish on the grid and close the lid completely.
   Place the smoking chamber on its stand on a stone floor out of a draught.
   Slide a tin holding approximately 5 fluid oz. of methylated spirits

underneath the smoker. (The tin supplied by the makers is suitable for herling-sized fish, but not for a larger fish if it is to be smoked in one session. At Cragg we use a 2 oz. tobacco tin.)

Light the meths and leave it. When the tin is dry the fish is done.

Bone the fish and serve cold with slices of hot bacon, rings of cold peppered tomato and homemade brown bread. (Out of this world!)

Fresh or smoked, a $1\frac{1}{2}$–3 lb. early summer sea trout straight from the sea is surely the most delicious of all fishes. For smoking I can recommend the ABU smoker. Served with a green salad (French dressing) smoked sea trout makes a splendid "starters" for dinner. It is a meal in itself when eaten with salad, fresh garden peas and new potatoes.

The equipment:
    Smoking chamber with tight-shutting lid, containing a grid.
    Stand for chamber.
    Tin for methylated spirits.
    Methylated spirits.
    Bag of sawdust (supplied by makers).

Having cleaned a sea trout (of up to $2\frac{1}{2}$ lb.), cut off its head and tail and rubbed plenty of salt into it, sprinkle the floor of the smoking chamber sparsely with sawdust.

Place the grid on top of the sawdust and the sea trout on top of the grid.

Slide the lid on.

142

Make sure the lid is tightly shut.

Fill the tin with methylated spirits. Place underneath stand, and light. Align chamber on top of stand.

You can now go away and forget about it. When the meths is burnt out (in about 15–20 minutes) the fish is smoked. Leave it where it is to cool off.

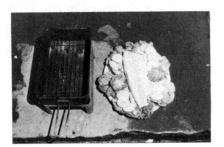

Bone the fish and serve as desired.

Note: It is advisable to use the smoker on a stone or cement floor. A draught-free corner of the garage is ideal.

143

And now two more main meals.

Cragg Cottage Hot Baked Sea Trout (in sauce)
1 sea trout (3½–5 lb.).
1 or 2 tins condensed mushroom soup (according to size of fish).
3 fresh mushrooms.
1 bunch chives, or . . .
2 small shallots.
½ bottle dry white wine.
2 sprigs parsley.
Pinch of thyme.
1 tin asparagus tips.
3 slices streaky bacon.
2 oz. butter.
Salt, black pepper.
2 butter papers.

Place the fish in a deep roasting tin or any other suitable utensil.
Dilute the mushroom soup with wine to a creamy consistency.
Chop chives (or shallots) and parsley. Add to mixture, together with the thyme and a pinch of pepper and salt.
Chop the mushrooms and put inside fish, adding a little butter.
Pour the soup/wine mixture over the fish. This should come about half way up the side of the fish. If necessary add more wine.
Place bacon over the top of the fish and dot with remaining butter.
Cover with butter papers and bake in a moderate oven (15 min. per lb.).
15 minutes before the end of cooking time add the drained tin of asparagus to the mixture around the fish.
Serve hot with rice and garden peas, using the liquid the fish was cooked in as a sauce.

Cragg Cottage Cold Baked Sea Trout (in tin foil)
1 sea trout (upwards of 3 lb.).
1 oz. butter.
Sprig of parsley.
Tablespoonful of olive oil.
Salt and black pepper.

Clean the fish and sprinkle inside with salt and black pepper.
Chop sprig of parsley and mix with butter. Dot in small dabs along the inside of the fish.

144

Rub the olive oil over the outside of the fish. Leave for half-an-hour.
Wrap the fish loosely in tin foil, making sure that the parcel is water-proof so that the natural juices are retained.
Place on a rack inside a large baking dish. Cover bottom of the dish with warm water.
Bake in a moderate oven (15 min. per lb., i.e. 1 hour for a 4 lb. fish).
Allow fish to cool before opening the tin foil.
Split open the fish and remove backbone. Spoon the juices (retained in the tin foil) over the fish.
Serve cold with salad, fresh garden peas, asparagus and new potatoes.

Deep-Frozen Sea Trout
Contrary to what I have often been told, sea trout will deep-freeze very well *provided they are in top condition*. At Cragg we freeze only the fish that are caught early in the season straight from the sea, preferably with sea lice on them.

A fish to be frozen is wetted, placed in a polythene bag and taped up. Its weight, and place and date of capture are written on a label attached to the parcel and the fish is put in the quick-freeze compartment.

We eat frozen sea trout throughout the winter and find them excellent. The last of the previous summer's catch is consumed in time to provide freezing space for the new fishing season.

For me, a sea trout at Christmas is something of a ritual. To admire the fish once more; to read the details on the label and look them up in my fishing diary, adds another dimension to angling. A winter wind whines outside the kitchen door as I go back in memory to a dusk-shadowed pool and the enchantment of a summer night long past . . . The gnats are dancing. There is the scent of bog-myrtle; the sound of water from the weir. Owls are hooting in the darkening woods. I feel the slow draw of the fish as it takes the fly; the nerve-tingling excitement as we fight it out in the darkness . . .

It is this necessary quietness and loneliness of peal fishing at dark which some town-bred people seem to find so eerie. The yowl of a vixen traversing the oak wood a hundred yards behind you, the sudden overhead cr-a-a-ak of a heron, the nostril-blowing of a sleepy steer, or even the hooting of an owl, seems to give some of these people the jitters. Their scalps wrinkle at any unexplained noise, and I am sure that some of them imagine that the river bed on the wading side is dotted with bottom-less pits into which they will step at any moment after dark, to be held down by the warlocks of the water, never to be heard of again . . .

L. R. N. Gray, *Torridge Fishery* (1957)

V
Night Fly Fishing Strategy

PART ONE: THE APPROACH

So far we have studied the fish and chosen some of our lures and tackle. Next to be considered is a plan of attack.

Provided he has sufficient experience of night fishing, by far the greater part of a river sea trout fisherman's bag during the season will be caught in the darkness and most of these fish will be taken on the fly. Both bait and spinner can, of course, be used at night—depending on the type of water to be fished—but only occasionally is either so effective as a well presented fly.

Ledgering at night suffers from the disadvantage of having a distinctly passive approach. Once the angler has decided on his pitch and cast in his bait, it is left to the fish to provide victory or defeat. Except for an occasional sly movement of the bait, there is not much an angler can do to overcome the effects of changing conditions.

The fly fisherman, on the other hand, can and indeed must seize the initiative; and to do so he has at his command a tactical variation of considerable range.

For the benefit of the novice I might mention *en passant* that there is absolutely nothing so disenchanting as bait fishing when the eels are biting (especially the bootlace size, with which my river seems to be riddled), and eels fling themselves at a worm on ninety-nine nights out of a hundred.

There is, however, an amusing and quite skilful method of fishing a moving worm at night with fly rod and line. When fish are exceptionally dour, or as a change from other methods, this ploy is occasionally worth a try—if you happen to have some worms handy. We will deal with it in Chapter X.

Spinning offers more opportunity of attack than ledgering, but as we shall see, many of our fish at night are caught close to the bottom—and in the darkness it is almost impossible to fish a minnow deeply and slowly enough to entice fish without getting it snagged at every cast. In addition to this, for reasons already discussed, a minnow by its very construction is not so effective as a fly which, if correctly dressed, provides a more attractive lure. As described in Chapter XIII, I have done well enough on a Mepps spinner late at night in salt water over a sandy bottom, but then the fish were on the feed and very active. It is different in the river when fish are "lying low". Either way, my preference is for the fly.

Nothing I have written is intended to imply that night fly fishing is easy. If such an impression has been given I hasten to correct it. Anyone who experiences a sense of satisfaction from mastering what is difficult will soon discover that fishing after dusk presents unique opportunities for enjoyment!

But, of course, night fishing is not to everyone's taste; not every fisherman is temperamentally suited to the sport. Like wildfowling, it has a strong, rather weird mystique, an appreciation of which demands an affinity with solitude in wild and remote places. Anyone who does not derive a deep delight from long hours in the darkness by some lonely river, with only the wind and water as his companions, should abandon thoughts of serious night fishing.

To a small but devoted band of anglers, however, sea trout night fly fishing represents the very cream of sport. And it is interesting to reflect that their dedication can be rewarded by material as well as spiritual satisfaction—for there are few fishing nights during the season when sea trout cannot be caught.

Not everyone will agree with this. It is a view which, I am well aware, is at variance with much that has been said on the subject. Some writers are of the opinion that night fishing is a chancy sport, worthwhile only in certain favourable conditions, rarely profitable after midnight, and that many blank nights may be expected. Such an opinion is not formed without reason. But it results, I venture to suggest, from a faulty approach to the sport; a basic error in thinking, and insufficient observation of the fish themselves. It was partly because for years I had seen so many fishermen fail—simply through missing opportunities they seemed unaware of—that this book was first written.

My fishing diary provides evidence of what can be done if there is a good run of fish, and sufficient time and energy is devoted to catching them. During one not untypical season my friends and I fished on 87 nights. Fish were landed on 84 of them. (One night was totally blank.

On two nights fish were hooked but lost.) These figures are given merely to illustrate what is possible.

Not every night, of course, offers the same chances. There are bad nights, good nights, even exceptional nights when sea trout seem to fight to get at the fly so freely do they take. It is on record that a hundred sea trout were taken in one night by a single rod; and on my own water, there was a well-remembered occasion when the fish showed such eagerness that as an experiment I removed every piece of dressing from the hook, leaving only the silver painted shank—and still they took it. Little skill is required to catch a large bag in such circumstances; and whether the lucky fisherman derives much pleasure from such a hollow victory depends on his philosophy, for it is in itself no criterion of his craft.

He is a disappointed man who looks for such success every time he goes to the river. Nights such as those I have just described are extremely rare, especially today when runs of fish are only a shadow of

Some sort of water gauge is essential on every fishery. If there isn't already a gauge on the water you fish, then make one, as I made this. It has helped me to catch a lot of fish. To be able to check the height of water and the rate at which it is rising or falling, at any hour of the day or night—simply by looking at a painted post—enables anyone who knows his river to accept many a chance of catching fish that he would otherwise miss.

149

what they were before U.D.N. But even when fish are plentiful, there is always the problem of change in weather conditions—to which sea trout are very sensitive.

It is seldom, the weather in these islands being what it is, that some very plausible reason cannot be found to explain night fishing failure. Excuses are legion. The water is too warm or too cold; the river too high or too low; the night too clear; the air too chill; the wind is invariably from the wrong direction, or there is no wind at all; the glass is rising or falling too quickly; the fish are too stale, or too fresh—or there aren't any! The unsuccessful fisherman protests bitterly against bright moonlight and starlight, beats his head at the sound of thunder; whereas lightning, tempest, rain and mist reduce him to a state of impotent despair.

Provided there are fish in the river only one excuse is valid: that the river is in spate and the water coloured. No other conditions preclude the catching of fish at night, and although it would be foolish to pretend that some weather conditions are not decidedly more unpropitious than others, the would-be successful sea trout fisherman should never allow them to deter him from fishing. They will reduce his chances, certainly; but fish can still be taken—provided he understands how these conditions are affecting the fish, and presents his lure accordingly.

This is the "art" of fishing. The measure of a fisherman's skill, the true meaning of *success*, is not the number of fish he catches when sea trout are coming eagerly to the fly, but what he can achieve on the numerous occasions when they are not.

The fowler who waits for his birds to settle before shooting them will make neither a skilful nor successful shot. So with sea trout fishing. Don't wait for the perfect night that so seldom comes. Ignore the wise-acre who hangs up his rod and speaks of thunder; let others tap the glass and funk the ground mist; don't worry if the air is dry or the grass is wet or the wind is north, south, east or west, if you want to fish—then fish. And, which is more, go on fishing—however poor the conditions—because you will neither gain experience nor catch many fish if you don't.

If free to do so, fish all night. Don't give up simply because the sea trout have "gone down", or your bag is still empty at one o'clock in the morning. You won't fill it lying in bed. If you present the right lure in the right way you will get an offer at some time during the night. Perhaps only the one, and you may have to fish hard to get it, but that one may be the fish of the season—perhaps of a lifetime. I have known it happen.

150

During periods of really heavy rain, fishing is usually poor. But *it can be very good when the rain stops*. Sea trout often take well just after a thunderstorm has passed by, or during the intervals between heavy showers. The picture shows a simple, inexpensive but practical fishing shelter. It is set with its back to the prevailing wind, and fenced against farm animals. A rain shelter of this type is of great value to the sea trout night fly fisherman: it helps him to catch fish. Here he can sit out the heaviest storm in comparative comfort, and take advantage of weather conditions which, otherwise, might drive him home.

The man who said: "If you want to drink champagne you must think champagne", could have applied his maxim equally to fishing. Fishermen who want to catch fish must think fish—and nothing else. People who spend their time on the water talking, listening to the owls or thinking about their income tax will never catch much. Always provided it is behaving properly, there is no moment of any cast when the fly may not move a fish. How often some chagrined angler relates how, after hours without an offer, his rod was almost pulled from his hand— just when he wasn't expecting it!

Never lose confidence. Never surrender to a feeling of hopelessness or inferiority. Everyone makes mistakes at night. Don't let them ruffle you. Nothing must be allowed to undermine your confidence, for nothing can be done on the river without it. There is great truth in the saying that the best fly to use is the one you believe in. Unless you have faith in your fly you won't fish it properly. Why? Simply because you will not fish with sufficient concentration. Concentration is vital to successful fishing.

For this reason, fish in silence.

Unless you are fortunate in a companion who appreciates the value of silence, you will catch most when you fish alone.

I am aware that some anglers are quite incapable of fishing alone after dusk. Not being countrymen, they are apprehensive of being by themselves among the strange noises of the night, faced eventually with the ordeal of fumbling their way home through the dark, owl-haunted woods. Obviously, anyone who feels uneasy when fishing alone at night must have companionship. Nevertheless, if he wants to catch sea trout he will choose companions who know when and when not to chatter. Nothing interferes more with concentration than the sound of the human voice.

Apart from some auditory assistance—the whirring of a piece of grass caught on the fly during casting; a fish that makes its presence known by splashing at the head of a pool, and so on—night fishing is carried out almost entirely by the sense of touch. The feel of the line in the air tells the distance cast; the feel of the fly in the water informs how it is fishing in a fast "run"; the drag of a sunk line gauges the depth at which the fly is working in a deep, slow pool; only by feel is the touch of a drifting leaf distinguishable from the gentle nudge of a big fish—a fish that may be caught if detected and cast for again. It is concentration that enables the angler to acquire this delicacy of touch. But that is not all.

As the result—or what I assume to be the result—of intense concentration over many years of night fishing, I have become conscious of a rather strange faculty: that often I know beforehand when I am going to catch a fish. Very likely you may scoff at this and say that such a thing is impossible. I assure you it is not.

During recent years this odd prescience has become more and more pronounced, especially after long quiet periods of fishing when nothing has been moving. It manifests itself by a sudden "tingling" of the senses; a vague feeling that I am about to hook a fish; that now is the time; that such and such is the place, or that a certain fly should be used. I act accordingly . . . and bingo—there he is!

The only explanation I can offer is that it may be due to a subconscious assessment of some change in conditions the conscious senses have not become fully aware of. A change so slight as to be almost imperceptible, but which is sufficient to bring a fish into a "taking" mood.

After all, when salmon fishing, we gladly welcome a gleam of sunshine on a cold spring day, a breath of wind that provides a ripple in June. When fishing for sea trout at night, we watch for a cloud to hide the moon; the softening of a hard, bright, starlit sky, or a sudden rise in temperature. But there are changes less noticeable, though no less important, and in the darkness the sea trout fisherman's senses should be attuned to draw an inference from such changes. When experienced, he will find himself acting on this "information", although hardly aware of *why* he is doing so.

This is a rational explanation; but whether it is in fact the reason for this strange pre-knowledge, I really don't know. One is reluctant to write of extra-sensory perception in connection with the sport of fishing, and yet I am drawn to the conclusion that something of the sort exists.

An instance of this "feeling"—and I have experienced many similar— occurred once when I was fishing a trout lake. Conditions were very poor and nothing was being caught. While wading, I suddenly became conscious of "knowing" that there was a big fish lying just beyond a weed bed at no great distance from me. Although there was no visible sign of the fish, I had a feeling of certainty not only that the fish was there but that it was a "taking" fish. I was about to cast across it when a friend arrived on the bank. Particularly anxious he should catch a fish—it was the last day of his leave—I pointed out the place where I thought the fish was lying and suggested he should try for it. He joined me in the water, put his fly out exactly as directed . . . and immediately hooked a splendid brown trout of just over three pounds!

Coincidence? The possibility cannot of course be rejected. But in my own mind I know otherwise. It has happened to me too often, for too many years.

If, as I believe, such experience is the result of intense concentration, it represents an asset that any angler might develop with advantage. But such a degree of concentration is not easily attained. It is probably impossible unless you are fishing alone, or with very experienced companions. It cannot be "switched on" suddenly, at will. So, start to "receive" before you actually start fishing: as you make your way to the river, or set up your tackle. Allow your mind to become as one with the sound of the water and the wind in the trees. When you can observe and record without consciously seeing and hearing, this "instinct" has begun to emerge.

Don't be too sceptical. One day it may help you to fill your bag—as I am sure it helps those successful solitary fisherman, found on every river, who catch fish when all others fail.

*   *   *

This intuitive faculty is, I believe, an atavistic survival; a part of man's hunting instinct. Although it has been long submerged I feel certain that with help it can be brought to the surface. And I suggest that one way of doing this is to develop one's ability to see, read and understand the "stories" of the countryside—a skill that must have been second nature to early man, but is now almost entirely forgotten. To do this we must learn to use our eyes and brains in a new way—or, rather, in a very old way: the way of our ancestral hunters.

Almost everywhere out-of-doors there are opportunities of doing some nature detective work. On plants, bushes, rocks or the bark of trees there are tell-tale signs. In wet grass, sand, mud, snow or soft earth are footprints, scrapes, scratches, scuffles, and even where the ground is too hard to register an imprint there may be feathers, droppings, scraps of fur and other clues from which we can deduce what creatures have been there before us; what they have been up to, and why.

Although they are not often seen by day, otter and fox, like the badger, tread the river bank at night, and so does the roe deer and the water vole and the stoat and the hedgehog and a host of others. They are our companions, with whom we share our "pitch", and they merit our attention. Many of them are nocturnal, but all of them leave tracks and signs from which, in daylight, they can be identified. If we care to use our eyes we can find these tracks they leave, and begin to "read" stories of their night's activities which, in interest, are as compelling as anything the waterside has to offer.

Along a muddy lane on our way to the water we may see badger or rat or pheasant tracks. In the woods, fresh scars on tree trunks where the bark has been peeled by red deer; in a woodland glade, branches that have been nibbled back into a distinct "browse line" by feeding roe deer;

The author and his wife ford the rain starved summer river at a place where roe deer come down to drink. No signs are visible on the shingle, but slot marks in bankside mud lead to the spot. And here, roe can frequently be seen at dusk.

155

a fraying-stock—perhaps a juniper bush with ravaged stem and earth pawed bare at its base—where a buck has been "staking-out" his territorial boundary. Bitten leaders in a new plantation show evidence of hares and rabbits. In sand or mud beside the water are prints of heron, wild duck, roe-deer, fox or otter. Pellets disgorged by such species as owl, buzzard and rook divulge what these birds have been eating. Some signs are extremely simple: mole-hills, worm-casts, rabbit burrows, a woodpecker's hole. Others are equally unmistakable though far less numerous: a thrush's anvil, a sparrow-hawk's plucking-block, a red stag's wallow. So, too, is the badger's sett, with its mounds of earth-works—sometimes the result of generation after generation of badger families—run-ways through the undergrowth and nearby lavatories. From their droppings we can identify, among others, red deer, roe deer, pheasant, grouse, blackcock, fox (whose dropping may be packed with beetles) and badger. On the edge of the dunes are rabbit feeding-scrapes, and the sloughed skin of an adder. Rabbit mating-rings are scuffled in the sand—which also holds criss-crossing tracks of skylark, hedgehog, stoat and mouse. Near the sea pool are the probing holes of oystercatcher, curlew, redshank and other waders. An empty gamebird's egg devoid of membrane, among typical dragging footprints, shows where a carrion crow has been at work. A rifled rabbit-stop requires more thought, although footprints in the freshly turned earth or sand and the nature of the kill prove whether it has been dug out by a badger, or raided while open by a fox.

Nature detective work such as this contains a curious paradox. Far from absorbing an angler's time and attention to the detriment of his fishing, its indulgence will in the end help him to catch more fish. By reading a few of these simple stories before we reach the water we have had to use our eyes and our brains. We have become hunters before we start to hunt.

All angling techniques, from fly to float fishing, are subject to infinite variation. Each tackle and method has to be modified to suit the water that is to be fished in the conditions of wind, weather and light prevailing at the time. It is the ability to make a rapid assessment of these factors and to "read" the situation correctly that singles out the expert angler.

Good angling books are of great value. They can teach a novice the various methods of angling; they can show him how to tie reliable knots and how to assemble his tackle; they can advise him on a choice of lure or bait and how to present it. But they cannot teach him how to "read" water. Without "water sense", no matter how advanced his technical skill, an angler will never rise above an average level of competence.

By giving an angler the chance to flex these wasted hunting instincts, which—like wizened muscles—have been inhibited by centuries of urban life, nature detective work sharpens his powers of observation and deduction. This increased awareness of what is going on around him puts him in harmony with his outdoor environment and leads him towards a deeper understanding of animal behaviour. It will not help him to cast his lure farther or more accurately, but it will help him to decide what to cast and why. If he trains himself to notice what is happening on and around the water he may begin to notice and, which is more, to understand what is happening *in* the water.

As I have implied in earlier chapters: if their powers of observation had been a little sharper, a lot of sea trout fishermen in the past might have caught a lot more fish.

*   *   *

The man who sets forth with a rod knowing nothing of the environment in which he goes to hunt is only half an angler. He sees without comprehending. The waterside has a language he does not understand. The multitude of stories it offers him he cannot read. He is out of sympathy with his surroundings. In consequence he is, all too often, the man who when darkness falls fears to fish alone.

"Men fear death as children fear to go in the dark." But not only children fear the dark. Many a fisherman has suffered feelings of nameless dread as the dusk closed round him on some lonely river, lake or stretch of coastline. Even on my own water, a friendly little beck, I have known men who would not fish alone at night. "What—go up there alone through those spooky woods? Not me!"

Although few care to admit it, many fishermen do not fancy fishing by themselves after the light has gone, and many a chance of catching sea trout has been missed because some companion failed to arrive on the water at an appointed time. Finding himself alone beside a darkening river, the nervous angler heads for home.

His apprehension is understandable. How different it all seems when daylight disappears—and the darkness becomes full of strange sounds. Things *do* go bump in the night! There are squeaks and grunts and screeches and gurgles and rustles and plops. Stones rattle, shingle slides, bushes move and swish, eyes gleam, ripples spread across the water from unseen swimmers; a fox screams from the fellside; a deer barks;

Marram grass, sand dunes, river and beach. A low tide scene familiar to many a sea trout fisherman. In locations such as this, as well as in the mud and sand of the river bank, "stories" of our waterside companions abound.

owls hoot from shadowy woods. The creatures of the night are stirring: badger, otter, hedgehog, stoat, weasel, rat, feral mink, nightjar; all of them at some time or another will share the waterside with us. But to the novice who comes unprepared into this elemental and seemingly hostile jungle of the dark, these animals are strangers; the sounds they make he does not understand—and what man does not understand, he fears.

For this reason the owl was long prominent in stories of the supernatural. It is a bird of more than usual interest. For a vertebrate its hunting ability is unique. Probably, no animal has contributed more towards man's feeling of uneasiness at night. Mainly the tawny owl, whose long, wavering call sounds so eerie in the darkness.

Tawny owls are particularly vocal late in the summer when the adults defend their territories against their young. The young owls that fail to establish territories of their own probably die quite soon—of starvation.

Then the barn owl, that glides ghost-like over the water meadows at dusk with its terrifying screech. The sight of a white shape that floated screaming into the night must have started many a ghost story. As Gilbert White noted: "White owls often scream horribly as they fly along. I have known a whole village up in arms on such an occasion, imagining the churchyard to be full of goblins and spectres."

To our forbears, darkness was a symbol of death. It was natural that the mysterious owls, being pre-eminently creatures of the night, should become associated with death and disaster.

The Romans hated them. As the sight of an eagle before a battle signified victory, so an owl presaged defeat. Ovid called it: "Cowardly owl, an omen dreadful to mortals." To Pliny, it was "The bird of death, and utterly abominable." Virgil's owl ". . . prolonged his mournful and prophetic note", and when Herod Agrippa entered the theatre at Cæsaraea, it was an owl perching on a rope above his head that warned him of his coming end.

Our own literature, too, abounds with references. Chaucer wrote of: "The owl that eke of death the bode bringeth." And Shakespeare: "Out on ye owls, nothing but songs of death." It was his ". . . fatal bellman that gives the stern'st goodnight." And as some anonymous poet observed:

> Thy note that forth so freely rolls,
> With shrill command the house controls.
> And sings a dirge for dying souls.
> Te Whit! Te Whoo!

159

The purposeful "trod" of a hedgehog that during the night came into this camp on the sand dunes (top of picture) and raided the larder! An interesting sidelight on hedgehog hunting behaviour, discovered by elementary nature detective work. We can see where this animal has set off again on its long journey back across the estuary sand at low tide. On its way it must have crossed what was at high tide the homeward route of many a salmon and sea trout.

The belief that owls are birds of ill-omen exists even today. I remember an aged Devonshire angler shaking his head in dismay one sunny afternoon when a barn owl crossed our path as we made our way to the river. "We'll do no good today!" he prophesied. And later, on our way home having caught nothing, the old sage wagged his head knowingly. "It was that bliddy owl, m'dear. I told 'e t'would put a blight on us!" Loving him, I contented myself with thinking of the low water and blinding sunlight (to me, more rational reasons for our failure) and said nothing— not that anything I could have said would have changed his opinion.

Undoubtedly such superstition has its origins in the uncanny ability of some species of owls to hunt not only at night but in utter darkness. The owl has remarkable night vision; but no creature, however good its sight, can *see* in utter darkness.

A recent theory was that an owl's eyes responded to infra-red radiation from its prey. But this has now been disproved. Experiments have shown that in the daytime, on starry nights and in moonlight, owls hunt by sight. But on very dark, cloudy nights they locate and pin-point their prey by *sound*. This is made possible by their noiseless flight and asymmetrical ears—owls being the only vertebrates to have such ears.

Of the ghostly silence of an owl's flight, that fine naturalist and fisherman, St. John, observed: "If we take the trouble to examine the manner of feeding and the structure of the commonest birds—which we pass over without observation in consequence of their want of rarity— we see that the Providence that has made them has also adapted each in the most perfect manner for acquiring with facility the food on which it is designed to live. The owl, that preys mostly on the quick-eared mouse, has its wings edged with a kind of downy fringe, which makes its flight silent and inaudible in the still evening air. Were its wings formed of the same kind of plumage as those of most other birds, it is so slow a flier that the mouse, warned by the rustling of its approach, would escape long before it could pounce upon it."

(What St. John did not, perhaps, appreciate was that the silence of the owl's wings works two ways: it certainly prevents the mouse from hearing the flight of the owl, but it also enables the owl to hear the rustle of the mouse.)

When we think of their exceptional eyesight and sense of hearing, their soundless flight and eerie, terrifying calls, it is not surprising that owls occupy so large a place in country legend. Nor is it surprising, even in these so-called enlightened days, that for so many people the lonely darkness still holds vague feelings of unease.

But the angler who interests himself in the animals of the waterside and can identify the signs and sounds of his unseen companions, need no longer fear "things that go bump in the night". When he regards the river bank with understanding, it will present a world of fresh interest and fascination, and he will await the coming of dusk with new-found eagerness. Already, he will be a better angler—for he has become a better hunter.

Alone in the summer twilight, with the bats flickering above the tree-tops and a barn owl hunting silently along the hedge, he may remember those evocative lines of Meredith's:

> Lovely are the curves of the White Owl sweeping
> Wavy in the dusk lit by one large star.

And watch his fellow hunter with delight as the owl swoops low over the shadowy fields, with Venus brilliant in the west.

*   *   *

There is another, quite different, aspect of the angler's approach which will repay careful analysis: an understanding of his motives; a consideration of *why* he wants to go fishing.

There is a strange form of self-deception practised by many anglers. It is a "belief" that they fish not from a basic desire to catch fish, but for the pure joy of fishing. It is a kind of Orwellian double-think; an armour to protect their confidence. Alas, it is an armour full of chinks—for it consists of humbug.

Some writers, lost in dreams, eulogize the angler's sense of spiritual values; they speak in romantic terms of a deep inner contentment springing from an awareness of natural things. This may be true of the Dedicated Dry-Fly man—intent on deceiving a trout with an imitation of the natural insect. To him, the fish itself is of secondary importance. It may also be true of the solitary Coarse Fisherman who, content with the enchantment of his surroundings, spends long, drowsy, flower-scented hours in contemplation of his float. Such a man has my admiration. The end product of his sport represents neither a financial investment, nor a competition prize—nor yet a tasty meal. He neither sells his catch nor eats it. He lands it, admires it . . . and sets it free.

Some salmon and trout fishermen are inclined to look with scorn on their coarse fishing contemporary. And yet (with the exception of those who go to the waterside in droves accompanied by the bookies) as a sportsman he is their superior. Apart from the D.D–F. man already mentioned, was there ever a "game" fisherman yet who, by the end of a fishless week, gave a damn about the birds and the flowers, or the view, or anything else? His sense of deep inner contentment springs from one thing only— a fish on the bank. If such a person as a happy unsuccessful game fisherman exists, I can only say that I have never met him.

Years ago, to augment my income as a writer, my wife and I housed Game Fishermen as paying guests. For season after season I was able to observe the species—in close-up, so to speak.

It was all very interesting. I live in one of the most beautiful valleys in England. When a G.F. came to stay, looked at the view, took a deep breath and announced that in the midst of such beauty he really wouldn't mind if he caught nothing—my heart sank. I knew him immediately for a liar, or an extrovert so lacking in qualities of self-analysis as to be a fool. Either way, if the river was dead low, or hopping up and down, I prepared for a tricky week.

Sure enough, as day followed fishless day, the familiar symptoms emerged. The view no longer enthralled, and over all an air of dis-enchantment hung. By the fourth or fifth day, neither bodily nor spiritual comfort could assuage the nagging sense of frustration—until, suddenly . . . fish! In a flash, all was changed. Dejection and despair vanished like summer clouds. Never was the view so magnificent. Never sang the birds so sweetly. Never was the world so gay.

Anyone who has endured the horrors of a fishing hotel during any week of poor fishing conditions will know exactly what I mean. Like bad driving, fishing failure draws up the very dregs of human nature— except that on fishermen the mask of Satan shapes more slowly. On the road, the metamorphosis happens instantly; on the river it is gradual and insidious.

It is all very understandable. The ego of the unsuccessful angler is sensitive and raw; vanity is outraged; pride is wounded, and the cut goes deep. Let another rod succeed in the face of his failure and it is acid in the wound.

Well, it is a matter of temperament and there is something of it in all of us, however well it may be concealed behind a façade of good sports-manship. It is necessary for every would-be-successful fisherman to face this from the outset, *before* he goes fishing. The reason for much fishing failure is not the state of the weather or the water, or the reactions

163

of the fish; it is the fisherman's lack of self-understanding.

Fishermen react to failure in different ways, according to their natures. Some give up. Some resort to darker methods. Most flog gamely on— but the seeds of failure quickly sprout and, as they blossom, confidence withers. Once confidence has gone the fisherman's success is doomed, for confidence and success are inseparable.

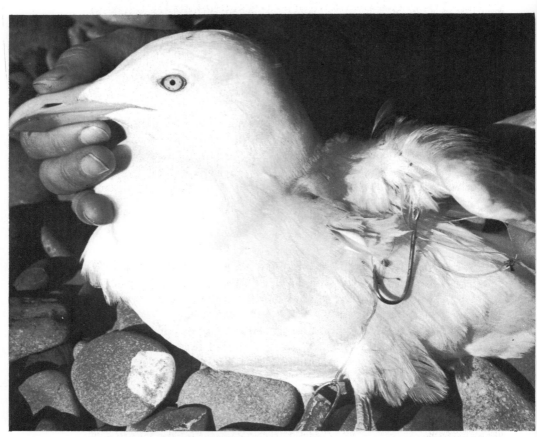

Each angler should remember that the waterside is not used by him alone; he shares it with a host of wild creatures. Lengths of nylon left lying about can get wrapped round legs, bodies and wings, causing mutilation or death. All too many anglers are guilty of this thoughtless behaviour. An awareness and understanding of the animals that keep us company lends another dimension to our sport. The waterside would be immeasurably poorer without the flash of the kingfisher, the song of the willow warbler or the heron's harsh croak. A blank day is soon forgotten, but a badger seen at dusk (pausing, perhaps, to sniff the air and peer inquisitively at us) is long remembered.

Never leave an unwanted leader, or yards of tangled monofilament line lying about at the waterside.

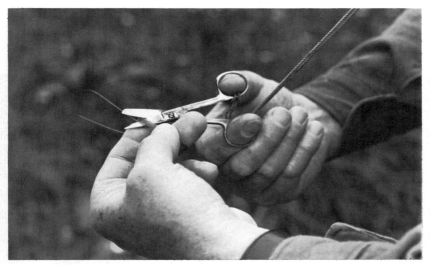

When you wish to dispose of a length of nylon, wind it round two fingers in a small tight coil, then cut the coil with your scissors.

This reduces it to a bundle of tiny pieces that cannot get wrapped round anything.

Concealment. No matter what species you are fishing for, never stand against the sky-line either in daylight or darkness. The second position is better than the first—but why not adopt the third?

Note. A place where one wades easily when the river is low can be a good "lie" for sea trout and salmon in spate water. Position 3 contains such a "lie"—not a yard from the angler's legs. From it, a $10\frac{1}{2}$ lb. sea trout was hooked at dusk when the river was up a foot and running clear. (See also, high-water "lies", p. 303.)

After *concentration* and *confidence* must come *stealth*—the stealth of the hunter. However skilfully your fly is fished it is pointless if the fish have fled. Speaking to a fellow fisherman may not affect the fish, but a heavy footfall most certainly will. So, be stealthy. Move quietly both in and out of the water. Sea trout are very sensitive to vibration. When fishing from a high bank, crouch; go on hands and knees, crawl. Don't show yourself against the skyline, no matter how dark the night.

For wading, felt soles are quieter than nails; they also have a better grip on slimy rock. By the way, don't believe the myth that wading should be avoided at all cost. The reverse is very often the case. Naturally, it depends where you are fishing; but on most rivers, *provided you wade with great care*, you will have far more chance of success standing thigh or waist deep in the water than clumping about on the bank against the skyline. When "backing-up" a sea trout pool in body waders at night, I have many times hooked fish in places close to where I was standing only a few minutes earlier.

When wading is helpful, don't hesitate. Get right in there, and the deeper the better. The less of you there is sticking up above the water the more your movements will escape a trout's field of vision and the closer he can be approached—as you can prove easily enough in daylight. Wade like a heron, that most stealthy of birds. To do so requires much practice. Let nothing stop you practising.

But wade at night only where you know the river well.

And after *stealth? Persistence.* Don't give up. Keep on fishing.

Many novices become easily disheartened. They expect to hook a fish at every cast. This expectation, while unquestionably the right approach to fishing, is not a short term policy and demands a continuity of effort. Alas, so often when the fish eventually "come on", their erstwhile would-be captors with short-lived confidence are halfway home—or sitting disconsolately on the bank with a bottle.

The best time for catching sea trout is the hour after dusk. But not always. It is possible to fish without an offer from dusk until, say, two o'clock in the morning in late July and still take the bag of the season. Not often, perhaps; but it happens. So, why not give yourself the chance? After all, if like many sea trout night fishermen you are able to fish only at week-ends or during your holidays, why not regulate the domestic arrangements accordingly? The short dramatic nights of June and early July are short enough—a mere three to four hours from dusk to daylight—it seems silly not to take advantage of every fishing moment.

Imagine that you are fishing with me and staying at my cottage. This is the sort of programme everything is geared to.

During conditions of low water when night fly fishing is in force, as it usually is, you will be out from dusk until dawn. After which, we shall sit and drink coffee and whisky, admire each other's catch, discuss the night's events and watch the sunrise. Then, bed.

Breakfast at one o'clock. Then a leisurely reconnaissance of the river—to observe where fish are lying, and height of water; to recover flies lost during the previous night's adventures—and so on.

After this, drinks, and talk, and fly-tying, and a lie-down, before lunch–tea–dinner combined—which, during June, July and August, takes place between 7.30 and 8.30 p.m. Plenty of time afterwards to set-up tackle and prepare for the next night's fishing.

Obviously, as the days shorten and the nights get longer, the times of fishing and eating change. The short dramatic nights are past. Fishing no longer starts at 11.30 p.m., as it did in June. As we move through July into August and August into September we start earlier and finish later—but by mid-September we are not fishing the whole night through. Dinner (which up to now has been getting earlier) suddenly shoots back to about 10.30 p.m. and forms a welcome interlude during the long darkness which, by then, starts around 7.30 p.m.

All this relates to night fishing arrangements. But suddenly—rain, and the river starts to rise. No matter what the date, whether in June, July, August or September, the whole rhythm of life undergoes an immediate change. Fishing switches at once from night to day. Early to bed. Up at first light. Meal times adjusted accordingly.

This, very roughly, is how we operate during the fishing season. It is merely an idea of the sort of plan I suggest you should work out if you want to fish seriously for sea trout and to give yourself the best chances of success, whether over a week-end or over a week.

When conditions are suitable, the temptation to fish for sea trout by night and salmon by day is almost irresistible. Many a time I have returned to the river to fish for salmon all day after fishing for sea trout all night. Conscious of life's brevity I have always gone to the limit. But as we get older the sheer physical effort becomes increasingly more difficult. The time comes when some sort of discipline is necessary. My advice to ageing anglers like myself is to make up your mind which species you are going to fish for during the next twenty-four hours—and stick to it.

Now—after this digression on to *fly presentation*.

A fly may be presented to a sea trout in a number of different ways, but a fish will take it only when its behaviour is consistent with the

An 18 lb. summer salmon taken before breakfast on a size 12 double, after an all-night sea trout session. Gillie, Kathleen Falkus.

Angler wading in steady current at the head of a pool. A common enough position at night, especially when fishing a sunk line. *But*, when a fish is hooked the angler should get out of the water as quickly as possible.

To be playing a fish at close range from this position is all wrong. The fish cannot have failed to see the angler and, in consequence, taken fright. A frightened fish takes considerably longer to land. The angler should have played the fish while standing well back on the shingle bank *out of sight*. Only when he was sure the fish was beaten and ready to land should he have moved forward. Then, he should have *knelt* at the water's edge with landing net extended at arm's length and lying on the bottom in front of him — ready to be raised to encompass the fish as it is drawn in. (See also, *Netting a fish*, p. 124.)

prevailing conditions. As these conditions change, so the behaviour of the fish will alter, and so too must the fisherman vary the action of his fly. From which it is clear that the more sensitive he becomes to such changes the greater his chances of catching fish, for the more accurately will he choose his fly and the way in which to fish it.

Choice of lure is one thing, method of fishing it entirely another. All fishermen are familiar with the old country saws such as: "When the wind is from the north the fish won't venture forth." And: "With the wind in the east the fish bite the least." And so on.

Not inspired verse, perhaps; but sound enough in spirit. And for obvious reasons. Usually, north or east winds are cold winds, and whenever the air temperature is much lower than the water temperature conditions are seldom good for fishing. So that, on those evenings when a chill ground mist blankets the river; when the sky clears after a hot day and the air temperature goes diving down below the water temperature, fish no longer show much inclination to rise to the fly. There is little surface movement of any kind. Fish which may otherwise drop back to the shallower water at the tail of a pool tend to lie deep and unmoving. There is no wallowing in the shallows, no rolling about, no splashing underneath the bushes; the surface of the pool flows even and unbroken with none of those exciting ripples that follow the slosh of a big sea trout.

Obviously, on nights such as these—and they occur frequently—fish are difficult to catch. Seemingly intent only on their breathing, with little inclination to indulge in any unnecessary exercise, they lie in the deeper water and regard with indifference a fly that passes high overhead. No lure, whatever its reputation, is likely to succeed in moving a fish unless its presentation is in sympathy with these adverse conditions. It is clear, for example, that as the fish show considerable reluctance to come to the top, a fly fished near the surface is unlikely to meet with much success.

There are two fundamentally different ways of fishing a fly: on or near the surface; and very close to the bottom. Both methods involve a number of important variations—the principle in each case being quite different—nevertheless, they may all be placed under two headings: *Floating Line*, and *Sunk Line*.

The object of a floating line is to fish a fly high in the water. The object of a sunk line is to fish it deep. I make no apology for these rather obvious statements, since I have known a number of fishermen who laboured under the impression that a sunk fly could be fished properly (i.e. deep) with a buoyant line.

I must assure you at once that it can not!

When we wish to fish sunk fly for sea trout at night, the fly cannot work correctly unless the *line* is completely sunk.

Let the newcomer to sea trout fishing burn that on his memory with letters of fire, for the failure to appreciate this simple truth is the reason why so many fishermen fail to achieve success on a cold night.

You may wonder why, if the fish is experiencing no pangs of hunger, it should take a fly at all on these cold evenings. The answer is that (with the exception of the Surface Lure, which will tempt an occasional fish to come to the top) it won't—unless the fly is fished *very deep and very slow.*

There are two possible reasons for this. One concerns the fish's physical reactions to a sudden drop in temperature, which will be considered in Chapter VII. The other is that a sea trout, when feeding at sea in similar conditions, would not expect his food—which our lure represents—to be swimming close to the surface.

A sea trout while in the sea feeds mainly on small fry, and the staple diet of fry is plankton. Anyone who has watched a plankton feeder, such as a basking-shark, knows that on a warm day, the shark is likely to be swimming close to the surface, with dorsal and tail fins showing. His title is, of course, a misnomer, for he is not "basking" and never does bask. He is cruising steadily along, feeding; his huge mouth wide open to sieve up the plankton on which his life depends and which in warm weather exists close to the surface. But when the temperature drops, not a shark will be seen; the plankton drifts have gone deeper and, in consequence, the sharks have followed them down.

This is rather how we might expect sea trout to behave if, indeed, it is through habit that they take our lure. On a summer's day, or on a warm night, they should accept a fly that is fished close to the surface— since it represents their old sea-time prey which would in turn be feeding close to the surface. On a cold spring day (in rivers that hold sea trout in this season), or when a summer night turns cold and the temperature is considerably lower than the day temperature, the fish—if they take at all—should do so when the fly is deep down and close to the bottom.

I confess at once that this theory is rather shaky. But whether it is right or wrong is of no real importance. It is the empirical that concerns us here. In practice this *is* how sea trout tend to behave.

On an average night, therefore, in order to give yourself the maximum opportunity of catching fish, you should be prepared at dusk to fish a fly fairly fast and close to the surface. Later, when the air temperature falls, you should fish it slowly, close to the bottom (indeed, since the fish will be feeling sluggish and lacking in any desire to rush about it must be put right in front of their noses).

This means that since both floating line and sunk line tactics may have to be used on the same night, the minimum tackle requirements for a night's fishing will be a suitable fly rod and two lines: floating line and sinking line.

A better arrangement is to use two rods: one fitted with a low density line (floater; floater with sink-tip, or slow-sinker—depending on the strength of current), the other with a high density line. And unless you go to the river so equipped you will be denying yourself considerable chances of success. On many nights, the fisherman who through lack of equipment or experience cannot fish a sunk fly properly will catch very few fish.

First, however, we will consider the floating line—since on many nights this is what we shall start with.

In the Night usually the best Trouts bite, and will rise ordinarily in the still deeps; but not so well in the Streams. And although the best and largest Trouts bite in the Night (being afraid to stir, or range about in the Daytime) yet I account this way of Angling both unwholesom, unpleasant and very ungentiel, and to be used by none but Idle pouching Fellows.

James Chetham, *The Angler's Vade-Mecum* (1681)

Ah well . . .

VI
Night Fly Fishing Strategy
PART TWO: FLOATING LINE

In the first edition of this book, having been brought up on silk lines and grease, I did not write kindly of the "... new type of unsinkable fly line." It was, I suggested, unsuitable for sea trout fishing. "The length of line to be fished wet varies from pool to pool and from night to night, and it is essential to use a line whose buoyancy can be altered as required."

Well, all that was true, and the principles of "greased-line" fishing remain as valid today as they were then. But fly lines, like fly rods, have come a long way in the last decade. We no longer need to change the floatability of a line to suit a change of conditions—we simply change the line.

Our intention in this chapter is to fish the fly at a depth of between four inches and a foot. Given the same length of leader, this means that less line should be allowed to sink in slow or sluggish water than in medium or fast water. It is usually advisable, however, for the join of line and leader to remain underwater, otherwise the line knot, or loop, may cause excessive surface disturbance.

The type of line chosen to fish a fly near to the surface depends primarily on the strength of current, as shown in the diagram. To prevent the fly from being carried too far down, a buoyant or semi-buoyant line is used; but only knowledge of the water in question will determine whether it should be a floater; floater with sink-tip, or a slow-sinker.

The speed at which a fly travels through the water is of paramount importance. To generalize: it is true to say that a fly should be fished high and fast; deep and slow; and some reasons for this were considered in the last chapter. But "fast" is meaningless in the absence of other data. What must be taken into account is the size of fly and strength of water in which it is being used.

If ever you are in doubt as to whether (in rapid water) your fly is

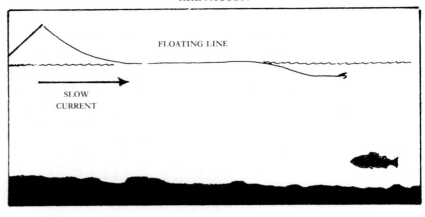

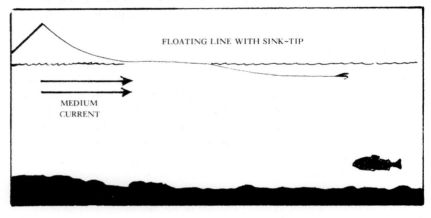

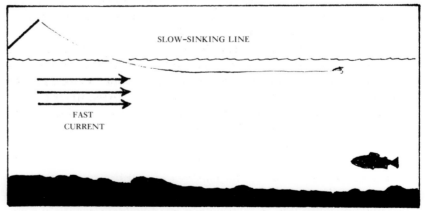

In each case, irrespective of difference in current strength, the fly is fishing at the same depth. The principle also applies directly to summer salmon fly-fishing with modern lines.

fishing too fast—and I anticipate that in nine cases out of ten it will be—calculate roughly the speed of the current, then take a good long look at your fly—and think. A sea trout seizes a fly in mistake for some sort of living creature. If, as I suggest, our general purpose "fly", or lure, represents a small fish, its speed all the time it is fishing should not exceed the maximum speed at which a small fish of that size can actually swim. If a larger fly is used, its speed may be slightly increased; a smaller fly fished more slowly. The speed of a fly depends on its size.

Of course, when fishing nymph or something like an imitation moth or shrimp, we must also consider the shape and purpose of the fly; but a short, fat creature seldom attains the speed of one that is long and slender, and in this chapter I am assuming the use of a Medicine, or some similar lure, which resembles a little fish.

Minnows and other small fishes swim at maximum speeds of between 2 and 4 m.p.h. Supposing the speed of the current in which we are fishing is 5 m.p.h., and the maximum speed of the little fish that our lure represents, 3 m.p.h., it is obvious that the lure can never fish naturally against such a current. Furthermore, it cannot even hang motionless against the current, because a small fish swimming flat out in that position would be drifting tail first downstream at a steady 2 m.p.h.

This is all so elementary that I would be ashamed to mention it were it not for those fishermen who, year after year, pull tiny flies through the water at speeds which, applied to creatures of that size, can only be described as fantastic. The fish must regard such phenomena with the same startled surprise that we would experience if we saw the postman zoom up the lane at 90 m.p.h. on his push bike.*

The only time a fly may actually be pulled through the water in the conditions just described is when it simulates a little creature swimming at maximum speed *downstream*—in which case it would attain a ground speed of 8 m.p.h.—and the reason why a rapidly-moving fly or spinner *fished upstream* sometimes succeeds when downstream fishing fails is, I suggest, largely because of this. The fish, for once, is offered a lure that is travelling at a natural speed.

Fishermen casting across a fast current are sometimes mystified when the only fish to take does so the moment the lure touches the water. Whenever this happens it is regarded as something of a fishing miracle. The sad truth is that only at the moment of touchdown is the fly or bait fishing at a speed reasonable enough for the fish to accept!

The experienced "greased-line" salmon fisherman fishing down from

*Or, rather, as we would have done years ago before the introduction of those little red postal vans!

the fast water at a pool neck, through the middle slacks to the streamy tail, may change his size of fly perhaps three or four times in the course of fishing out that pool. And although the sea trout fisherman has greater latitude, in that his standard size of fly is larger, there are times when he should be conscious of the need to do the same.

The problems involved in fishing fast water are shown in the diagram—which is by no means accurate, but gives a rough indication of the path a fly should follow if it is to fish naturally.

A fisherman at A casts to B and allows his fly to swing round to C along the arc BC, marked X. This is a theoretical path, however, because as soon as the fly begins to swing round, a belly will start to form in the line; so that the actual path of the fly will be the "S"-shaped curve, marked Y. This belly in the line will cause the fly to whip round even faster than it would have fished in the theoretical path which, itself, is too fast for the water speed and the size of the little fish, which the fly represents.

If we assume the speed of the little fish to be 3 m.p.h., its actual path—if it wishes to cross the river from B to the side AC with the minimum of downstream drift—will be something like that shown by the dotted line BD, marked Z.

Swimming at maximum speed with its head into the current and edging over towards the side AC, it will at first be swept backwards a considerable distance. Then, gradually, as it crosses over into less powerful water, it will lose less ground until, in the 3 m.p.h. portion of the current, it will be at its furthest point downstream and able for the first time to hold its own against the stream.

So that, if our fly is to "hang" motionless against the stream, with its water speed 3 m.p.h. and ground speed nil, this is the first position in which it can be made to do so—if it is to appear natural. After this point has been passed, the little fish will start to creep slowly upstream, its ground speed gradually increasing until, having achieved the slack water by the bank at D, it will be swimming at a ground speed of 3 m.p.h.

This, then, is approximately how a lure should behave in similar conditions if it is to be acceptable to the fish. We may not, of course, be fishing in water so fast, but the speed I have assumed for the lure is rather high. In practice, it is probably less than this.

How can we best fish a piece of fast water? It is clear that to stand at A, cast at forty-five degrees across the stream and let the fly swing round is not going to be very effective. Obviously, the speed of the fly must

PLAN VIEW

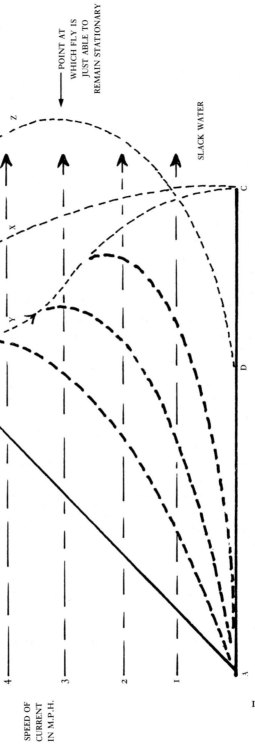

FLY UNABLE TO "HANG" AGAINST CURRENT

POINT AT WHICH FLY IS JUST ABLE TO REMAIN STATIONARY

SLACK WATER

Z

X

Y

B

C

D

A

6

5

4

3

2

1

SPEED OF CURRENT IN M.P.H.

MAXIMUM SPEED OF SMALL FISH REPRESENTED BY FLY = 3 M.P.H.

179

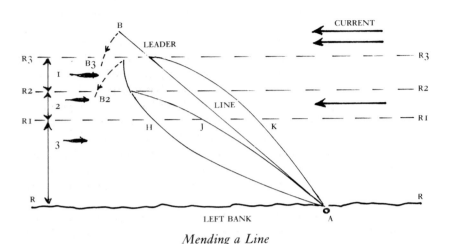

Mending a Line

Note. The diagram is far from accurate. Its object is merely to illustrate the principles involved for the benefit of the novice. The increases in effective casting range: R1–R2, R2–R3, have purposely been exaggerated.

a. An angler at A casts his fly to B. On its swing round it will cover three fish, Numbers 1, 2 and 3. As soon as the line touches down, however, the strong current will cause a pronounced belly and the line will quickly adopt the curve H. In consequence, the fly will whip round across the first two fish too quickly to be acceptable. Not until it reaches slacker water will it be fishing correctly. R–R1 is, therefore, the approximate *effective* casting range, and only fish Number 3 is likely to be attracted by the fly.
b. The angler at A casts to B. The line again bellies with the current into the curve H. This time, however, the angler switches the line-belly over into the curve J. This has the effect of slowing down the fly—which swings round towards B2 at a speed acceptable to fish Number 2. Due to this "mend" in the line, the effective casting range has been increased to R2. The fly now has *two* chances of attracting fish.
c. The angler at A casts to B. Now, however, as soon as the line touches down he switches it over upstream and at the same time shoots two or three yards of slack. This enables the line to adopt the curve K. The fly is now able to swing round to B3 in a manner acceptable to fish Number 1. Effective casting range has been increased to the line R3, and all three fish can be covered correctly.

Note. A mend consists of switching the line over from rod top to the join of line and leader (or close to it), *not* to the fly itself. If too much power is used the fly is jerked violently backwards, often out of the water. When this happens the mend defeats its object, since the result is to scare fish rather than attract them.

be slowed down, and for downstream fishing there are four ways in which this can be done.

1. We can "mend" the line. This consists of lifting it off the water the moment it has been cast and switching it over with an upstream loop. As the line is switched over, extra line is shot to create an upstream belly.

This method of controlling a fly can be of great value, but seldom at night. In the darkness it is very difficult to mend a line without jerking the fly—which is precisely what we are trying to avoid. Furthermore, to switch a line over without causing surface disturbance is impossible. On broken or rippled water this will do little harm, but much of our night fly fishing takes place on flat, fast glides at pool tails. Sea trout will tolerate much more disturbance at night than they will by day, but not the splashing of a mended line on such a smooth surface. The ability to mend a line expertly is a very useful trick for every fly fisherman to have up his sleeve—and that is where it should stay for much of the time.

2. As soon as the line touches down, an extra yard or two is shot. This has the effect of slowing down the fly, but it requires careful calculation. Unless the correct amount of line is shot at exactly the right moment, the fly will lose its balance and drift until, suddenly, the current tightens the line and causes the fly to whip round. This is roughly the effect we try to create when fishing Surface Lure; but then it is our intention to let the lure drift lifelessly for a few yards before creating the *drag* which, I feel sure, is what attracts the fish rather than the lure itself.

3. A more practicable method. Take a pace or two downstream as soon as the line has been cast and, at the same time, allow the rod to swing round with the fly, extending it at arm's length if necessary. This will enable the fly to fish out the important first half of its elliptical path. Once it has crossed into easier water, the fisherman can begin very slowly to work it in towards the rod.

4. Go upstream and throw as long a line as possible. Probably, this is the most satisfactory solution. No amount of juggling with rod and line is likely to be effective unless the angle BAC is reduced.

There is a quaint notion that, because in the darkness fish are less able to see the fisherman, a long line is never needed. It is an example of those little fallacies that creep into fishing and seem so often to be accepted without thought (many of which are examined in this book). As every fisherman must surely know, his first precaution when casting to a fish is to keep out of sight. But the reason for casting a long line at night is not, primarily, the need for concealment; it is to ensure the correct working speed of the fly. Often, it is possible to reach the same piece of water with a much shorter line. But merely to cover fish and have the fly whizz over them is of no practical value whatsoever.

> *Note.* Another method of slowing down fly speed in fast water is to cast the fly upstream. In my experience, however, there are very few occasions when upstream fly is so effective for sea trout as downstream fishing.

Needless to say, if only to avoid unnecessary trouble, everything should be done to minimize casting distance—by wading, for instance, and wading deep—but when circumstances demand a long line, a long line must be cast if there is to be any chance of an offer.

It has already been suggested in this chapter that correct fly presentation depends largely on speed. This fly speed depends on the speed of the current which, in turn, depends on the amount of water in the river. A spate river rises and falls very quickly, and the speed of the current suffers an equally dramatic change. The sea trout fisherman (like the salmon fisherman) must be ever aware of this change and its effect on the way he should present his fly.

A certain pool with which I am well acquainted provides an example of fishing a known "lie": the position of a (usually) big sea trout that lies by itself on or beside a rock in four or five feet of water a few yards from the fisherman's bank. The current sets close in beside this bank, and shortly after a spate when the river is clear but running high and fast the method of attack is to cast a long quick-sinking line from a position beside the water's edge well upstream of the fish. (See diagram No. 1 opposite.)

In this strong current, the line is put down close to the angler's bank so that the fly has only a small angle to subtend on its swing round. This is a tricky cast, especially in anything of a wind, for it requires absolute accuracy in direction as well as distance. A slight error puts the fly either into the angler's bank or too far out into the current. If too far out, belly will quickly form in the line and the fly swing across the fish at too great a speed. If the fly is slapped down too hard on top of the fish it is almost certain to be ignored. But if, when first presented, the fly is moving correctly, the chances are that the fish will take it. This is doubly to the angler's advantage. Such "lies" are seldom vacant for long: as soon as one fish goes, another moves in.

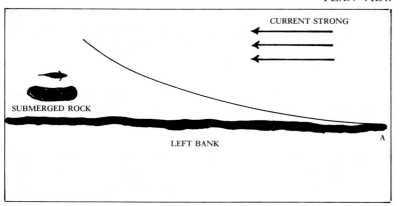

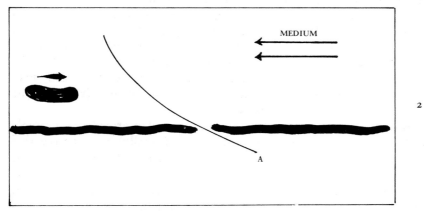

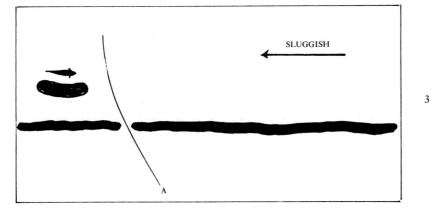

A few nights later, when the river has fallen and the current decreased, a medium length cast is made more squarely to the fish with a sink-tip line, and partly overland (diagram No. 2). To avoid any possibility of movement being seen against the skyline, it is advisable to keep well back from the water's edge and to fish on hands and knees. In order that the fly shall retain its balance in the now rather sluggish stream, a small belly is allowed to form in the line. This is an example of *using* belly to work the fly which, if the cast is made correctly, should be swung across the fish at just the right speed. But, as before, complete accuracy is required, for the fly must fall only a short distance out and at the right angle.

When the river has dropped to summer low and there is practically no current at all, a floating line is fished mostly overland (so that the angler can keep back from the skyline) from further downstream still; the fly put just beyond the fish and worked across by hand (diagram No. 3). Care must be taken not to get *too* square to the fish, or to put the fly too far out, for only leader and fly should pass across the fish's field of vision. Another fascinating exercise in judgment of angle and distance.

If the exact position of the "lie" were not known, and the cast not carefully planned, seldom if ever would this fish be caught.

The example illustrates a very important point: *fish do not always lie under the opposite bank*! I have watched fishermen march into a pool at dusk, stand practically on top of the only "lie" and cast towards empty shallows. Truly, it can be said that sea trout fishing failure is not always the fault of the fish!

Sometimes, however, fish *do* lie only under the opposite bank and these often acquire the reputation of being "difficult". In many cases this is simply because the line is cast too squarely to the fish. An example of this is a pool of mine where sea trout lie in a strong current very close to the left bank from which it is impossible to cast. Although it is an excellent "taking" pool, it defeats anyone who underestimates the speed of the current where the fish are lying—or, indeed, does not realize the fish are lying there. By the time his fly is fishing properly it is in empty water. These fish may be caught by casting upstream, but by far the best method is to go well above them, wade in as far as possible and cast downstream with a long line (see diagram opposite).

Success in many sea trout and salmon pools depends upon such simple tricks. The successful fisherman is held in awe by the unsuccessful; but examination of the water invariably shows that this apparent wizardry consists of nothing more than correct presentation.

184

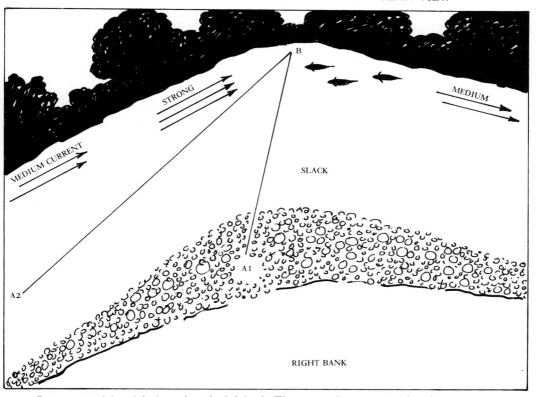

Sea trout are lying tight in against the left bank. They are easily covered with a short cast from A1. This is ineffectual, however, owing to the strength of the current. The angler should wade in to position A2 and cast a comparatively long line to B.

It is worth nothing that correct presentation consists not only of controlling a fly's depth and speed, but the angle at which its longitudinal axis appears to a fish—especially when a fisherman is wading deep and the fish is lying straight downstream. A fly that finishes up downstream of the rod "at the dangle" is sometimes attractive to a fish—seeming to stimulate some "taking" instinct, rather in the way that a nymph-like lure jigged up and down in front of a fish will sometimes induce a take. But a fly taken in this position usually secures a poor hold. This can be avoided if the fly is *led* across the fish's lie by moving the rod round in advance.

185

Fly-Leading

This is another little trick that can help a fisherman to present his fly correctly. The diagram and photographs show a fly being led across a pool tail in a medium current.

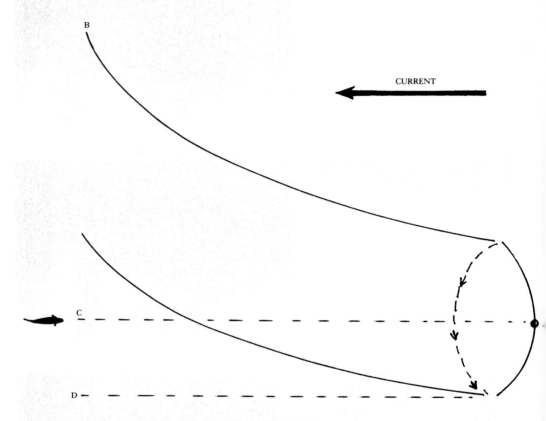

Plan view of pictures opposite, showing relative positions of rod and line while the fly is being led across the river. Angler at A casts to B. Fish lies at C, straight downstream of the angler. This is where the fly will finish up "at the dangle" unless it is led across to D by rod movement (see position 3).

Note. Fly-leading is by no means confined to sea trout fishing. It is a little ploy that the salmon fisherman can note with advantage. A salmon, too, is often poorly hooked when it takes a fly at the dangle.

Leading a fly across a pool tail in a medium current.

Here, the angler is using the full length of his arm and rod to help slow down the fly's speed during the early part of its swing.

Here, the rod has been raised to the position recommended on p. 211 and is moving round in advance of the fly.

Here, the fly is still on the right-hand-side of the angler. It will not finish up straight downstream at the dangle, however, since the rod has been brought round at right angles on the inshore side, and the fly will be led across the downstream position. Now, if a fish takes straight downstream of the angler, there is a good chance of it being well-hooked. These pictures show the advantage of using a long rod. Note also the position of the wading staff. Owing to its heavily-leaded butt it remains ready to hand during every moment of the cast, in spite of the angler's movements. (See also, p. 118.)

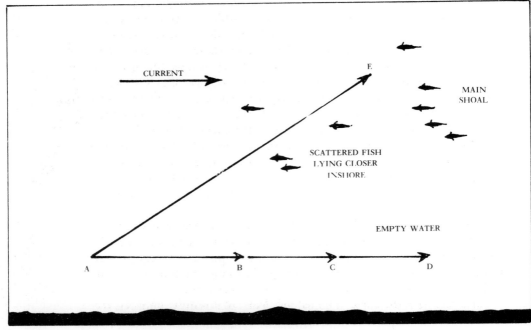

To false cast over water that may be holding fish is a mistake made by many trout and salmon fly fishermen. In the diagram, an angler wading at A wishes to cast to E to cover a shoal of sea trout. It is greatly to his advantage to avoid scaring any scattered fish that may be lying between him and the shoal. A frightened fish may transmit danger signals. Since the water close to his own bank is shallow and empty of fish, he can use it for lengthening line. He starts by laying a couple of rod's lengths of line on the water at B; strips off line and casts to C, and repeats the procedure by casting to D. Now, with sufficient line out, he casts to E, resists any temptation to false cast, and leaves his line where it falls. When his fly has swung into empty water he can retrieve and cast again.

> *Note.* This method of lengthening line at night cuts out a lot of rather dangerous swishing to and fro. It helps to avoid wind knots and is kinder to leaders and flies—especially when there is anything of a wind blowing.

It is easy to be beaten by the various conditions that combine to hamper us at night. If these are to be overcome, technique and tackle must be good enough to provide the best possible chance of hooking a fish at any particular moment. However beautifully we may cast afterwards, it is pointless if a clumsy cast has already slashed the surface and put down the only taking fish in the vicinity. It is pointless, too, if we are trying to reach that taking fish with a line that will not carry into wind.

As we have seen, minimum tackle requirements are: one rod and two reels. Whether two rods are used is a matter of convenience; but if they are (and I recommend it) I see no point in using a less powerful rod for floating line than for sunk line. The Surface Lure will be fished on the former as well as fly, and only a strong rod will push a Surface Lure out against the wind. An equally powerful rod will be needed for fishing Sunk Lure on a high density line. So—why not a "matched pair" of ten-and-a-half footers?

Successful night fly fishing calls for a high standard of casting that can be performed with mechanical rhythm. In this it is analogous to the golfer's swing—and as with the scratch golfer, practice makes perfect. But *don't* practice while you are fishing. Swishing the line backwards and forwards over the fish will not help you to catch them.

False casting is the curse of fly fishing. Most of it is quite unnecessary. The trouble is it becomes a habit, practised by anglers who, intent on distance, seem to forget they are trying to catch a fish. Sea trout are frightened when lines flash to and fro overhead or slash the surface— even at night. If you must false cast, do it over empty water, then switch direction, make your cast to the fish—*and leave it*. The ability to cast a long line is very useful, but distance alone is not enough.

No matter how far a fly may be cast, it is wasted effort if it is not cast accurately. Merely to punch a fly somewhere out into the darkness, let it swing round on its unknown course and then pull it in again, is not going to catch many fish. We must know exactly where the fly has to go, make sure it goes there, and sense its position and action during every moment of the cast. This requires great concentration. But once sufficient accuracy is attained, night fishing becomes considerably more exciting. Like the fish described on p. 198, sea trout that have been marked down in daylight and whose positions are known, can be fished for.

Accuracy comes with practice. The knowledge of where sea trout lie comes partly with experience and partly from careful daylight reconnaissance—and I *mean* careful. Fish spotting does *not* consist of tramping along the edge of a river bank with a pair of polaroid glasses. Use the glasses by all means, but never, never show yourself to the fish. (This advice must sound drearily repetitive to many of my readers; and yet—each year I see it all happening: the lack of stealth; the seeming inability to understand that fish can see and hear and be frightened.) Never mind how silly you may think you look, crawl up to the waterside on your stomach, taking advantage of long grass or bushes; and move slowly. Few fish are easily seen. The grey shapes, lying like shadows against the shingle, blend with their surroundings, and to detect them needs practice. So, take your time—and don't stand up!

Even if you are unable to see the fish themselves, you can spend some very profitable minutes trying to identify possible "lies"; watching the set of the current, with its swirls and eddies; noting snags that may foul the line, and places suitable for landing fish. Good landing spots can make a lot of difference to the number of fish you take home. The time to find them is *before* you hook a fish, not after—especially when you will be fishing in darkness.

A hooked sea trout will either be beached or netted. If you decide to beach it you will need a gently shelving bank of sand or shingle. If you net your fish, you will find it much better to do so in deep than in shallow water. A "lay-by" just off the current, holding a foot or more of slack water, is ideal. Look for it in daylight.

Except for the fish that are running, sea trout do not move about very much at night. Fish responding to the hatch of fly that occurs on some rivers will soon reoccupy their "lies". Spate-river fish show little sign of this activity and are content to stay where they are. If the night turns cold, sea trout will move up a pool into deeper water; if the evening is warm, some fish will drop right back to the sill of a pool tail; just before daybreak there is sometimes a strange movement into the shallows near the head of a pool (see p. 196), but these represent only a comparatively small proportion of a pool's population. In most rivers on most evenings, fish will be found in much the same positions that they occupied during the day. (In lakes, during calm, warm weather, sea trout tend to move out of the deeper water into shallows where they are seldom found in daylight—but we will deal with these in Chapter XIII.)

There is plenty of sea trout activity when the first effect of a spate is felt, and when a sea-pool fills with the tide; but in these conditions night fishing chances are usually poor. When the river is at normal height and you go down at dusk to fish over a shoal of sea trout located during the afternoon reconnaissance, you may confidently expect them to be lying where you saw them—unless in the meantime there has been a considerable change in temperature—and you have every chance of success. Every chance, that is, if you don't frighten the fish. While dusk turns to darkness, you must fish with extra care.

Start by fishing down to the head of the shoal, but go no further downstream. Let the leading ranks of fish see your fly, but try to prevent the line from passing over them. This can be done accurately provided the position of the shoal has been lined up with some prominent feature on the opposite bank—a bush or tree which is easily seen in the darkness. The moment a fish is hooked, walk him upstream so that he can be played and landed well clear of the others. It is likely that the shoal will gradually drop back. As they do so, move down with them. Fish after fish can sometimes be taken in this manner if you cast skilfully enough and move, either on the bank or in the water, as quietly as a ghost.

Everything considered in this chapter applies equally to fishing the Surface Lure, with this exception: that as the usual size of this lure is larger than most of the flies in use, it can be fished a little faster. Nevertheless, care must be taken not to drag it against a stream which is obviously too strong for a creature of that size to stem.

We can form some idea of how to fish it when we watch small creatures that are swimming across a river: small voles, frogs, toads, all of which must get taken from time to time by both non-migratory and migratory trout. I have more than once caught brown trout that contained mice; and there was the sea trout that took the little toad, shown on p. 77, and immediately afterwards took a Surface Lure.

It is most important that the join of line and leader does not itself cause a wake. When using silk line I would leave the last few yards ungreased—so that it dipped under slightly and avoided surface disturbance anywhere near the lure. Similarly, in a fairly strong current, a modern sink-tip line can be used. Provided the leader is attached to the lure a little way back from the nose (see illustration on p. 72), and the lure is not fished too slowly, this slight dipping of the line should not be sufficient to drag the lure under.

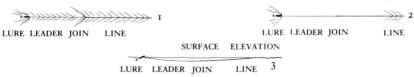

PLAN

LURE LEADER JOIN   LINE   1   LURE LEADER JOIN   LINE   2

SURFACE   ELEVATION

LURE   LEADER JOIN   LINE   3

1. Surface Lure on floating line. Disturbance caused by leader and leader/line join.
2. Surface Lure on sink-tip line. Leader and leader/line join dip beneath the surface film. No disturbance.
3. Elevation view of 2.

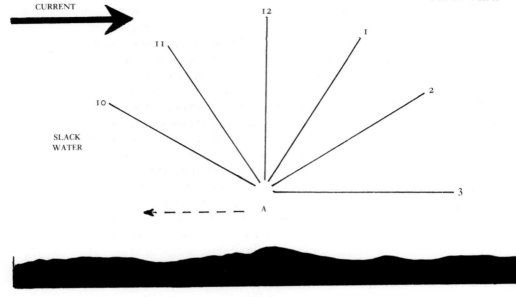

CURRENT

12

11

I

10

2

SLACK
WATER

3

A

RIGHT BANK

While the fish within casting range remain undisturbed the angler (at A) does not change his position, hooked fish are brought to the net and despatched where he stands. He should start at the pool tail and gradually work his way *upstream*.

ELEVATION

SURFACE

DROPPER or
"BOB" FLY

LEADER

TAIL FLY

"Medicine" on the tail. Hackled "Bumble" type fly (dipped in Permaflote) on the dropper. Leader made up with a Water Knot or Double-Grinner. A long rod is essential for this form of fishing.

Note. One can, of course, fish Round-the-Clock using only a Surface Lure.

"*Fishing-Round-the-Clock*"

There is an exciting method of fishing both on and underneath the surface after dark, in sluggish or slack water, known as "Fishing-Round-the-Clock". Make up a leader with one dropper. Tie a Medicine—or some other fish-like fly—on the tail, and a "mothy" hackled type of fly on the dropper.

Wade very carefully to a position from which fish can be covered with a short line, and stand perfectly still. Body waders, needless to say, are a great advantage.

Start fishing by casting upstream at an angle of, say, 10 o'clock (see diagram). As soon as the leader touches down, draw the flies towards you by raising the rod and stripping line with the non-casting hand as shown on p. 83. Work the flies so that the tail fly fishes just below the surface and the dropper drags along on top, leaving a tiny wake. (Dipped in Permaflote, p. 126, the dropper fly will stay afloat all night if need be.)

Don't let the flies slow down or stop, but recover in the same smooth movement and cast again, this time to, say, 11 o'clock—and so on, "round-the-clock". If a fish rises and refuses, don't cast over it again too soon. Make several casts in other directions first.

In my opinion, Fishing-Round-the-Clock provides the only sensible opportunity to use a dropper at night. Droppers can be a curse in the darkness and will, in the long run, cause the loss of more fish than they will catch. With the short line used for round-the-clock fishing, however, a dropper can be very effective—particularly if it is fished, as described, along the surface.

This method of fishing can give very good sport. The best time for it is in the late dusk of a warm, windless night. With a light, long rod and fine tackle it is a splendid way of catching herling and small sea trout during late July and August, when the river is low and the shoals are lying widespread over the "flats", or near the tail of a big pool—provided the current is not too strong. As only a short line is needed, round-the-clock fishing gives excellent practice to the angler who has had no experience of casting a fly in the darkness. (If he is a complete novice, however, he will be wise to dispense with the dropper.)

There are times when fish will continue to rise long into the night although, as may be imagined, owing to the weather conditions which prevail during an average summer, such occasions are limited.

Fishing gives us so many memories, apart from catching fish. . . . I was fishing a small, black pool in the dark. I could reach the whole of it from one spot on the grass which extended down to it from the bank about twenty yards behind. I had caught two fish of two lbs. or so and laid them on the grass, well back from the river. Another fish came my way and when I had put it where I thought the others were, the darkness put doubt in my mind as to whether they were really there or a little farther along the bank. I killed a fourth fish, but could only find my third one. I thought of cats and rats, but the culprit I caught with one of the fish was a hedgehog. The other fish had vanished completely and I do not know what happened to them. The hedgehog kept his fish and I took two home.

Charles C. McLaren, *The Art of Sea Trout Fishing* (1963)

VII
Night Fly Fishing Strategy

PART THREE: SUNK LINE

A fishing night may be split up into three periods: from dusk until approximately midnight; from midnight until, say, one o'clock in the morning, and from then until daylight. The first period we will call—to use a sporting metaphor—the "first-half"; the second period: "half-time"; and the third period, the "second-half".

It will be found that roughly sixty per cent of the fish caught during a season's fishing will be taken in the first-half; about ten per cent during half-time, and about thirty per cent during the second-half. But it is worth noting that the second-half will provide many of the big fish that are caught.

There is also a short period at daybreak—I call it "extra-time"—that will occasionally produce fish. It is a comparatively brief period and varies in merit with different water. On my own water, for some reason, it is most irregular. On the other hand, some rivers provide a regular period of dawn activity that extends well into daylight.

Of course, these figures must not be taken too literally. Like all generalizations, they are intended only as an indication of what may be expected. On some nights fish may be caught only during the first hour; on others, not until perhaps two o'clock in the morning. Sometimes, the fish are "on" all through the night and an exceptional bag is taken; but such nights are rare.

Apropos of "extra-time", two points are worth mentioning.

1. When fishing Surface Lure (both in the sea and in the river) I have noticed a very strange thing: at dawn, sea trout will sometimes take the lure in almost broad daylight; whereas in a similar intensity of light at dusk they will simply splash at the lure, or ignore it altogether. I can think of no reason for this.

2. During the thirty or forty minutes of broadening daylight I have often made good catches of sea trout right up in the shallows at the head of a pool. This has been in water where, later in the day, they are seldom if ever seen.

A rather dramatic example of this occurred not long ago. A friend, having fished without success from dusk until just before dawn, returned tired and despondent to the cottage kitchen where (having a deadline to meet) I was busy writing.

Convinced that sea trout could be caught, I gave him tea and whisky and insisted that he went back to the river—assuring him that if he fished at the head of a certain pool and stayed there until broad daylight he would get an offer.

I don't think he believed me. Not for a moment. But (cheered perhaps by the whisky) he complied, fished where I suggested, and returned an hour or so later with the two biggest sea trout of his life.

The incident is mentioned merely to stress the point that there are many anglers who, stopping too soon and missing the magic moment, never realize the chances they have missed. I urge my reader not to make this mistake; but to persist; to experiment, and try to find these "taking" places where fish sometimes lie for a short time at daybreak.

A taking place at daybreak. The head of a pool. Under the sycamore branches on the far bank is an age-old lie for a big sea trout.

With the exception of those clear, cold evenings when the temperature drops sharply with the setting sun, floating line tactics are likely to be in operation during the first-half. That sea trout usually take best of all during this period there can be no argument—and there are few fishermen who will not agree that, after a glorious burst of activity lasting for anything from half an hour to, say, an hour and a half, the sea trout stop "taking" and go down. At least, that is the pattern of their behaviour on most fishing evenings and the possible reasons for it have already been discussed. They are, I have suggested, the sea trout's feeding habits formed during his life at sea; or a change in conditions—or both.

This sudden cesssation of sea trout activity is the start of what I call "half-time", and it varies considerably. There is never any doubt when it happens, however; the fish themselves "blow the whistle" and the river suddenly seems strangely lifeless. The fisherman can relax, because during this period he may as well fish for sea trout in his bath.

It is at this point that so many people lose heart. They flog on unsuccessfully for a while and then, thinking the fish are "off" for the night and unlikely to show any further interest in a lure, take their tackle to pieces and go home.

They may be right. But on nineteen evenings out of twenty they will be wrong.

Indubitably, the fish are "down", and the chances are they will stay down—quite literally—but that does not mean they cannot be caught. Indeed, on most nights the fly-fisherman will enjoy occasional opportunities of catching sea trout from half-time all the way through until dawn—and after—provided he recognizes those opportunities and presents his lure correctly.

I have said earlier that the second-half will produce many of the bigger fish, and generally speaking this is so. Over the season, more big sea trout will be caught after than before midnight; the *average* weight will be heavier. The reason for this is simply that tactics during the second-half consist mainly of Sunk Lure and Surface Lure fishing, and these methods sometimes tempt a big fish that a smaller lure on floating or semi-floating line has failed to move. A sea trout that declines a fly fished near the surface will sometimes accept a lure which is dragged *across* the surface or bounced off his nose!

That the period when sunk line is used should also be most propitious for the Surface Lure may seem contradictory; but it should be remembered that darkness is all-important for Surface Lure fishing, and on most

197

nights—at least, early in the season—it is never really dark until after midnight.

What I have written is not intended to imply that *all* big fish are caught late at night. I mean only that you have a better chance of catching a whopper after than before midnight. You may not, of course, ever catch one at all. But if anything I write gives you the incentive to fish on into the night (or early morning) after other fishermen have gone home, I shall at least have helped you to take the first step towards landing one.

Many anglers fish for a lifetime without catching a sea trout larger than five or six pounds; the reason being that they never devote themselves to the capture of a really big fish. The hooking of a large sea trout is regarded as a matter of chance, and a very unlikely chance. For many years I thought the same; but experience taught me otherwise. These big fish *can* be caught—if you fish for them.

Obviously, luck will still play its part, as it does in all fishing. But at least we shall give ourselves a better chance of success if we take the trouble to find out where a big fish is (or is likely to be) lying.

This glimpse of the obvious merits no acknowledgement of regret. Many night-fishermen go to the river without knowing for sure that the water they intend to fish is holding sea trout, either big or small, let alone where they are lying.

Rivers vary greatly in the opportunities they present for observing sea trout. In some, fish are almost impossible to see, except in conditions of dead low water. But many rivers run clear very quickly after a spate, and in these the noting of sea trout shoals and large individual fish is not difficult.

The best chance of hooking a big fish is when he is newly arrived in a pool, fresh from the sea. The longer a sea trout lies in the river the harder he is to catch. So, when you spot a big fellow, don't wait for a couple of days, get after him the same night.

But first, a careful daylight reconnaissance is necessary. Study his "lie" until you have a clear picture of it in your mind. Mark his position by means of easily recognizable features on the bank. Calculate the length of line needed to cover him. Note the depth of water where he is and the proximity of any snags. Decide the spot from which you will fish for him, and don't underestimate the speed of the current. Remember, whatever lure you offer must swim at the right speed and depth; on this will depend the length of line you will have to cast. Plan your fishing night mainly round that one big fish and think of little else—unless by

198

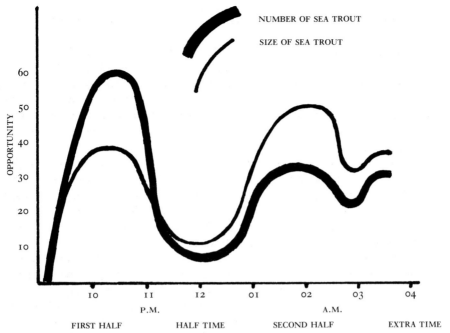

NUMBER OF SEA TROUT

SIZE OF SEA TROUT

OPPORTUNITY

60
50
40
30
20
10

10   11   12   01   02   03   04

P.M.   A.M.

FIRST HALF   HALF TIME   SECOND HALF   EXTRA TIME

Time/opportunity curves for a typical August night. River at average height. Weather conditions favourable.

$11\frac{1}{2}$ lb. female "harvest" sea trout.

At its best, the sea trout is superior in flavour to the salmon. But seldom in its larger sizes. Although tremendously exciting to catch, these big late-season sea trout are disappointing on the table. Smoked, grilled or fried, a fresh-run $\frac{3}{4}$ lb. herling is delicious during most of the season. But to my taste, a June/July sea-lice covered two pounder is the best eating of all.

some happy chance you have a second monster marked in another pool!

When you go to the river at dusk, don't start fishing too soon. Starting too early is the most common of all sea trout fishing errors. Wait until it is dark. If the evening is warm, fish first of all with a floating or sink-tip line and then, later on when the temperature drops, change to a sunk line.

Try him first with something like a Medicine. When it is dark enough, and not before, try the Surface Lure. After this, try the big Sunk Lure; then the Secret Weapon.

Naturally, these methods don't follow each other in quick succession, but at intervals throughout the night. Each time you try for him, fish down to where he is lying and no further. If he refuses to co-operate, leave that piece of water and go elsewhere. He may, of course, have gone under some roots, or dropped down to the tail of the pool, or just be having a cruise round. Never mind, leave him. You will be trying him again many times, later. Unless he has run, the chances are that sooner or later during the night he will return to his original position. It is a "lie" you know intimately, and that is the place to get on terms with him.

If your monster has been in the river only a day or two there is a good chance of hooking him. If he has been out of the sea for a week or two or longer, his capture will require some luck and a great deal of persistence. He can still be caught, however, so keep at him, with reasonable intervals between each attempt (during which, of course, you can go and fish elsewhere), until daybreak. And before you finally leave it, fish that pool right out.

By the way, if you ever hear a big fish slosh late at night—between, say, one-thirty and three in the morning—put on a big Sunk Lure, wait for a few minutes, and then try for him. If the current is not too strong, use a floating or sink-tip line, for in these circumstances the lure should be fished fairly close to the surface. If this is refused, try him with a Surface Lure. The chances are he will take the first lure he sees, especially if he happens to be lying up at the head of the pool in streamy water.

I have caught a number of large fish in this way, after hearing them lunge on the surface in the early hours of the morning. But they must be given plenty of time. I have learned from experience that it is a mistake to cast for them too soon after they have moved. Wait for about five minutes. Years ago, I used to make myself wait while I smoked a cigarette. Now, having given up smoking, I bridge what seems to be eternity by talking to my dogs.

Many attempts to catch these big fellows will end in failure, but memory of failure quickly fades. The moments of success are unforgettable. Like most of fishing's more exciting incidents, these golden moments usually occur when least expected; so, no matter how hopeless your efforts may seem never relax your concentration. Whatever the outcome, nothing can parallel the excitement and anticipation of a fisherman who goes down to the river at dusk determined to catch a large sea trout in a known "lie". All else pales beside it. It is the quintessence of fishing.

Unfortunately, such tactics are almost impossible on many rivers today. The man on association or ticket water is lucky to find a place to fish that doesn't already contain a queue of waiting rods. A pool to himself to fish as he likes is a rare luxury. Nevertheless, sooner or later his chance will come. I hope that what I have written will help him to recognize and take advantage of it when it does.

In addition to catching big sea trout in the early hours, there is this interesting business of the salmon—an example of which was quoted in the Introduction. Since catching that fish I have taken quite a few salmon with Sunk Lure late at night, and so have some of my friends. And they have done so on at least ten different rivers.

Why aren't more salmon caught late on dark nights? Is it because so few people fish for them? I have an idea that, except at dusk and dawn, the orthodox sea trout fisherman fails to catch them because his flies are too small. (They are often too small to catch the very big sea trout, too!)

Perhaps I am wrong. There may be numerous instances of salmon taking small flies at night. But I haven't heard of many. I am not, of course, referring to mid-summer twilight fishing in low water on Scottish rivers; but *dark* nights, from mid-July onwards, when there has sometimes been a blanket of ground mist.

I sometimes wonder what might be done at night with Sunk Lure on a major salmon river by anyone who had the time and opportunity to experiment.* Any reader who *has* may be interested to know the

*In a recent letter relating to night fishing for sea trout in the River Tay, Mr Leslie Stout tells me:

"In five seasons—late May to October—I took a total of 11 salmon on the big Sunk Lure, the best being an autumn fish of 16 lb. I was purposely avoiding the known salmon lies for the benefit of estate guests the next day. I'm positive that if I had set out specifically to fish for salmon, the total would have been very much higher."

conditions which have, so far, attended every instance of my catching salmon at night.

1. The taking time has been after midnight, between approximately one o'clock and three-thirty a.m.

2. The night has been dark. If there was a moon, then thick cloud has covered it—although one well-remembered salmon did take in light diffused by high cirrus.

3. On several occasions there has been thick ground mist, with accompanying drop in temperature. Admittedly, this condition has not "attended every instance" but often enough to merit comment.

4. The river has been low and clear.

5. The salmon has been lying in from three to six feet of water, usually near the head of a pool.

6. The Lure ($2\frac{1}{2}$–$3\frac{1}{2}$ inches long) has been moving fairly quickly, so far as I could judge about six inches to a foot from the surface.

7. The fish has moved shortly before it took.

> *Note.* That this taking fish *was* the fish that moved is, of course, only an assumption. But although there is no absolute proof, I am certain that in each case they were one and the same fish. Nevertheless, perhaps it would be more accurate to say: On no occasion have I caught a salmon in these circumstances when a fish had not moved shortly beforehand, in the same position as, or very close to, the fish that took.

*　　　*　　　*

As we have already discussed, during the "first-half" the fly is fished high and fast—always with the proviso that its speed should be reasonable for whatever creature it is supposed to resemble. Later in the night, however, the fly should be fished deep and as slowly as possible. Provided it keeps its balance and, therefore its attraction, it cannot be fished *too* slowly. The reason for this is not, primarily, size or shape of fly, but the behaviour of the fish.

Consider the sea trout: he is lying close to the bottom, his habitual sea-time feeding hour has passed, there is no longer any instinctive reaction to a fly fished near the surface and actual food is of little interest for he is not hungry. He has no intention of running and is quite content to remain where he is.

Being cold-blooded, the rate at which a fish's metabolism can function is largely determined by the ambient temperature. That water is always coldest at the bottom of a pool is well known to anybody who dives in, and at the bottom the sea trout find conditions restful and soporific.

There can be little doubt that the rate at which they can generate energy for physical activity depends strongly on temperature—for the same reason that the rate at which chemical reactions proceed usually increases very rapidly with a rise in temperature. We can be fairly certain, therefore, that in warm water the fish can take in and burn oxygen more quickly than in cold water with a similar oxygen content.

Assuming the water to be saturated, i.e. to have dissolved all the oxygen from the atmosphere it can hold at the particular water temperature, and taking a temperature in the region of 55 degrees Fahrenheit as representative, then we can say that the amount of dissolved oxygen decreases by slightly more than one per cent for each degree F. rise in water temperature. For each degree F. fall in temperature there would of course be the same increase in the amount of oxygen that could be dissolved. An increase in atmospheric pressure will cause more oxygen to dissolve, whereas a decrease will cause oxygen to be given off. These changes would be directly proportional to the pressure change, i.e. a one per cent change of atmospheric pressure would lead to a change of one per cent in the amount of dissolved oxygen. But this applies only to *equilibrium* conditions. Unless the external conditions change *slowly*, there will not be equilibrium and the figures cannot be applied directly.

When the night turns suddenly cold, the surface layer of water will begin to cool and will therefore increase in density. This will tend to cause the surface water to sink—almost certainly before it has had time to take up from the air the greater amount of oxygen that it could hold on account of its lowered temperature.

In the conditions we are considering, however, it is unlikely that the behaviour of the fish is determined *solely* by variation of oxygen content of the water. Fish appear to be extremely sensitive to temperature change, regardless of any concomitant change in the oxygen content; indeed, their metabolic rate changes very appreciably with changes in temperature. So that, although the drop in temperature may be small, we can expect our sea trout to be lying close to the bottom in the deeper water, feeling rather sluggish, with no incentive to indulge in unnecessary exercise, and concerned only with their breathing.

Whether I am right for the wrong reasons does not matter. What does matter is that, in the conditions we are considering, the sea trout have most certainly gone down. They have lost their first fine frenzy, and are no longer prepared to dash after our fly. Now we must *tempt* them to take. And clearly, if we are to succeed we must offer the fly in such a way that the sea trout can take it with the minimum of effort.

For this to be accomplished satisfactorily, it follows that the fly must be sunk to the bottom and manoeuvred so that it swings round in front of the fish *as slowly as possible*. And unless the fly is fished in this manner, very few sea trout will be caught on a cold night.

The fisherman who thinks that sunk fly fishing consists merely of sinking his fly is deluding himself. The assumption that, because it has to fish deep, a heavy or weighted fly should be used is a fallacy. It is the *line* that must sink. It is the line that maintains the position of the fly close to the bottom, and the fly will fish correctly only when its longitudinal axis forms a direct continuation of that line. Obviously, a line that is buoyant or semi-buoyant will prevent the fly from swimming as it should.

The Sunk Lure, with which much of our sunk line fishing is (or should be) carried out, is intended to represent the impression of a diminutive fish; and however small they may be, fish do not swim on a steady course at a constant depth with their heads pointing towards the surface. A line otherwise than completely sunk will tend to lift the nose of the fly as soon as it is moved. It will also bring the fly up into the surface layers, where the sea trout are no longer inclined to follow it.

The use of a heavy fly is of value only in strong water. When the current is slack, it is very difficult to fish a heavy fly as slowly as we wish without it getting caught on the bottom—and it is in the slower, deeper water that most sunk fly fishing at night is carried out. True, the fly must fish deep; but it must also fish slowly without getting snagged up and *without losing its trim*. For this reason a fly dressed on a light iron is much more effective than a heavy fly. In this context, the disadvantage of the tube fly becomes apparent. Although the tube itself is very light, there is a treble set right at the very end which makes the tube tail-heavy when fished in the type of water we are considering. For other than use in fast water, to weight the nose of the tube destroys our purpose. At whatever depth it may be fishing, a fly that is swimming well has always the chance of attracting a fish; an unbalanced fly, even if initially attractive, is seldom taken. As I have seen so often when watching the passage of a tail-heavy spinner across a pool, the fish show interest in the lure and may even follow it—but at the last moment turn away.

All the time it is in the water the fly should move smoothly and steadily, with nothing erratic about its behaviour. Some anglers have a habit of waggling the rod up and down as they fish, presumably under the impression that they are giving the fly some assistance. So they may be, if fishing a nymph for brown trout. But we are doing nothing of the

Fast run-in at the head of a pool. Edge of the current clearly defined. No fish will accept a fly which falters as it swings into the slack water seen in foreground.

sort and I am convinced that this rod movement is a very bad habit. Our fly represents a little fish, and far from creating additional "life", these bursts of acceleration must appear most unnatural to a sea trout.* Irrespective of whether floating or sunk line is in use, the rod should be kept still. Where there is insufficient current to work the fly, all necessary movement can be given by drawing the line steadily through the rod rings with the non-casting hand. The exception to this is Round-the-Clock fishing; but even then, the rod is raised with one steady, even movement.

*A reservoir brown trout angler often deliberately creates this movement to make his lure more attractive to fish that are "sticklebacking". The stickleback tends to move about in a series of jerks.

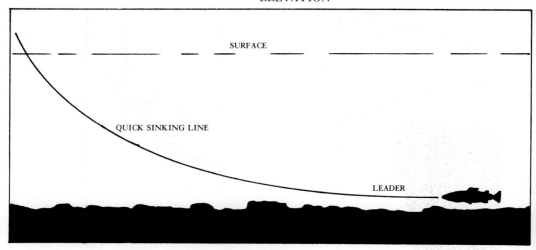

For late night ("second-half") fishing: Sunk Lure on quick-sinking line. The same line can be used for fishing fly-maggot.

Yes—all that is valid. But as my old friend Maurice Wiggin once wrote: "It is true of fly-fishing, more perhaps than of any other branch of angling, that no sooner have you made a flat statement than you have to qualify it." And like many other statements in this book, the previous paragraph is no exception. There *is* a time when we can profitably waggle the rod up and down using a high density line—that is, when fishing a weighted jigger-type lure to sea trout that are lying in deepish water close to our own bank, preferably under the rod-top. (See diagram.)

This is a form of what is known today as "sink-and-draw": a method that started life hundreds of years ago as: "trolling". (The terms "trolling" and "sink-and-draw" mean the same thing. The method of dragging a lure along behind a boat is not "trolling", it is "trailing". But all this will be discussed in Chapter XIII.)

The use of this weighted lure excites my friends F.J.T. and brother Ken, who occasionally report dramatic results while jigging in the darkness. But on most water the opportunities of fishing it are limited, and we will return to the more usual and convenient approach to sea trout: casting across the river.

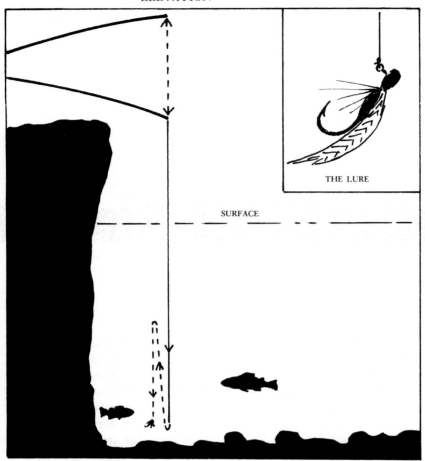

THE LURE

SURFACE

Fishing a "jigger" lure.

Generally speaking, when floating line is fished—either with fly or Surface Lure—the rod should be held at an angle of about thirty degrees to the water. Owing to the way in which a sea trout often (although by no means always) takes a fly fished on or close to the surface, the slight belly of line thus formed between rod tip and water will assist the fish to hook himself as he turns away. But with sunk line, the rod point is held close to the water in order to give the line every opportunity to sink. Also, the angler is in more direct contact with his fly. This is very

207

important, for during late night fishing sea trout frequently do *not* turn away with the fly; in consequence, the angler should tighten instantly— a point we shall return to shortly.

The less line hanging between rod and water the less a gusty wind will affect the movement of the fly. This is a point to remember when fishing sunk line: action of wind on the line may considerably increase the fly's speed, and there are times when it is necessary to hold the rod tip beneath the surface.

The rod point should also be kept low when we are fishing a floating line in a strong wind. In this case, a small loop of line is held ready to let go in the event of a fish taking. This is similar in effect to the loop of slack held in readiness when we are salmon fishing. But unlike fly-fishing for salmon—when line should always be given to a fish the moment he takes—this is by no means the common practice during sea trout fishing and is employed only in certain circumstances, about which more later.

Far too much time and effort is wasted at night by flogging empty water, or fishing down a pool cast and cast again. The result of this chuck-and-chance-it fishing is, all too often, a weary and disconsolate fisherman whose flagging concentration finally deserts him at the moment he most greatly needs it.

Wherever you fish at night—especially with sunk line, which is a much slower business than fishing floating line—cast only where you know or where you *think* a fish is lying. Plan exactly how and where the fly is to fish and concentrate on making it behave in the way you intend. Direct each cast at some particular sea trout and work the fly as carefully as possible over the position in which this fish is assumed to be. The assumption will by no means always prove to be correct; nevertheless, fishing to a definite plan will lend valuable support to confidence and concentration, and in the long run many more sea trout will be caught by fishing in this manner than in a more haphazard fashion.

When sunk line is fished in deep, sluggish water, there will be a considerable amount of underwater sag from rod-tip to fly, and allowance must be made for this. The distance cast when attempting to cover a known "lie" with sunk fly should be sufficient to allow the fly to reach the fish *when the line has sunk*. Clearly, if only the surface distance to the fish is cast, the effective, or bottom, distance will decrease as the line sinks, and the fly when sunk and in an operational position will finish up short of the fish. Further allowance must be made for sideways belly formed in the line by the current.

ELEVATION

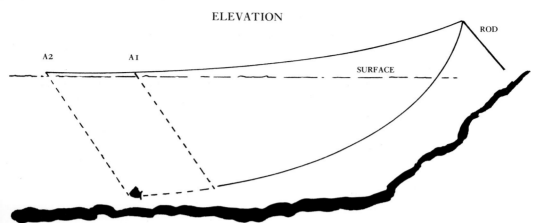

Even in slack water a sunk fly cannot be put in front of a fish merely by casting the distance between fish and bank (A1, see diagram). To allow for line sag, extra distance must be cast (A1–A2).

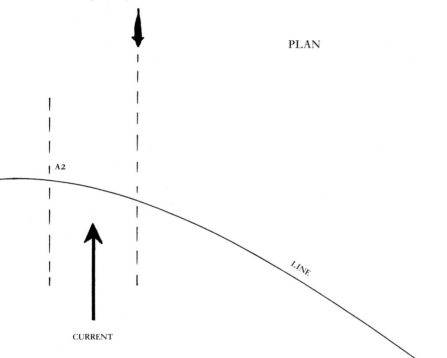

PLAN

In a current, a further distance must be cast to allow for belly in the line (A2–A3).

To judge casting range from the pitch of the fly on the surface can be misleading. Many novices forget that the fly will finish up far short of the fish when the line has sunk, and bellied.

Factors to be considered when making allowance for this downward sag and sideways belly are: strength of current; depth of water, and the time taken for the line to sink—all of which can be determined only by daylight reconnaissance, which is essential if night fishing is to be successful, particularly on strange water.

Everything relating to sunk line fishing applies equally to fly/maggot. Fly/maggot consists of fishing a sunk fly with one or more maggots impaled on the hook (the method is described in detail on p. 256). It can be a deadly method of catching sea trout and will sometimes succeed when other forms of lure are refused. The secret—as you may guess— is to fish it as slowly as possible. Maggot can be used with any type of fly, but is most effective on a very small fly. This is because it is much easier to hook a sea trout when maggot is fished on a small hook than on a large hook. (But see also, notes on fishing the Secret Weapon, p. 60.)

This question of hooking sea trout is a vexed one. It all devolves on the apparently simple question: should a fisherman strike—or tighten— when a sea trout takes the fly?

In the case of salmon the question can be answered quite simply. To tighten on a salmon too quickly is a certain invitation to failure. But then, the "take" of a salmon is usually quite different from the "take" of a sea trout. On the subject of hooking sea trout many conflicting opinions have been given. Some writers advocate fishing a loose line, others suggest that quickness of strike is essential—so that the inexperienced angler reading first one and then another may be forgiven if he finds himself in a state of some confusion. What he wants is a direct answer to his question: "Should I, or should I not strike a sea trout when it takes my fly? This writer says I should; that writer says I shouldn't. Which is correct?"

The answer is—both.

There are times when we *should* strike a sea trout (or, at least, *attempt* to do so), and times when we *shouldn't*; and the choice depends on a number of factors which, as this is a question of some importance, we will consider in detail.

When a sea trout takes a fly properly—that is, with determination— he turns away with it in his mouth. Nine times out of ten this fish, when landed, will be found to have the hook firmly in the angle of the jaw; in the "scissors" as it is called. A sea trout is most likely to take a fly in this manner during periods of settled weather; in other words, when fishing conditions are good. In these circumstances, no strike is necessary.

When a sea trout takes a fly in a half-hearted manner—by nipping it or treating it to little tugs and tweaks—the fish does *not* turn away with it. This fish will be poorly hooked and, usually, the fly will be found in the front of the mouth. Sea trout behave like this when weather conditions are unsettled; during the approach of rain or thunder and lightning; when the air temperature drops sharply so that the air is considerably colder than the water; and occasionally (probably for the same reason) in bright moonlight. When fishing in these conditions we should be prepared to strike.

Generally speaking, the times *not* to strike are:

1. When fishing sink-tip line in fast or medium water.
2. When fishing sink-tip or floating line across slack water in conditions of settled weather.
3. When fish are taking the Surface Lure with determination.
4. When a fly is "hung" on a long line straight downstream of the angler.
5. When fly/maggot is fished on a small single hook.

The times when we *should* strike a sea trout are:

1. When fishing sunk line late at night.
2. When fishing floating or sink-tip line in slack water and fish are merely pulling and tweaking—which usually happens when the glass is falling.
3. When fishing the Surface Lure and fish are taking very gently (see Chapter III).
4. When fly/maggot is fished on a large single hook.
5. When fly/maggot is fished on the Secret Weapon.

By "striking" I do *not* mean a big jerk, but just a turn of the wrist; a tightening of the line.

As I have witnessed many times in daylight, sea trout "take" in a variety of ways. Fundamentally, our decision to strike or not to strike hinges on whether the sea trout when he takes the fly, turns away with it. When he does so, no strike is needed. Quite the reverse in fact. To tighten on such a fish too quickly is a certain way of hooking him badly, and it is for this reason that the rod is sometimes held at an angle of about thirty degrees. The resulting belly of line which hangs between rod tip and water forms a cushion between reel and fly, so that a fish can turn away with the fly without it being pulled out of his mouth. When fishing strong water, however, it is advisable to keep a foot or two of slack line in readiness to let go the moment a fish seizes the fly. It is not trapped against the rod by fingers of the casting hand, but held between forefinger and thumb of the non-casting hand with just sufficient force to prevent the current from pulling it out.

When a fish does *not* turn away with the fly, the strike should be made as quickly as possible. This happens most frequently with sunk line. The fish takes the fly into his mouth and then blows it out again. At least, this is what I *think* he does—and since I have seen it happen in daylight, I assume that something similar is happening at night. But whether I am right or wrong does not affect the angler's immediate action—which is to tighten, the instant he feels the fly stop.

A fish will sometimes take a fly with the very front of the mouth, give it a decided shake and let it go. This, I think, is what happens at night when we feel that strange double "knock". Something of the sort probably accounts for the sudden vicious pull, which never develops. This pull is so strong at times that a white line of spray is visible on the surface, an instant before the hook flies back overhead (almost invariably into the bushes, to add injury to insult!).

I have never learned how to hook the fish that takes like this. Which is hardly surprising since, if what I suspect is true, the fly is never properly inside the fish's mouth.

There is, however, an amusing variation on the theme of hooking sea trout on the sunk line: the time when we should not only strike, but *anticipate* the strike. Indeed, the line should be tightened *before* we feel the fish actually touch the fly. This sounds wildly improbable and demands careful explanation.

In unsettled weather, especially when they have been in a pool for some time, sea trout often refuse a fly that is fished near the surface and merely play with it when it is sunk. They seem to nudge it, or mouth it and let it go. With the approach of rain they give the fly little tweaks, probably by pulling at the wing dressing. As mentioned before, when thunder is imminent and lightning is flashing behind the distant hills, they take the fly with the front of the mouth and give it a nip (rather in the way that a salmon sometimes nips a prawn), and in every case they do no more than give the fly a half-hearted pull. They do *not* suck it in and turn away with it as they do on the occasions when they take properly. All the angler feels is a series of infuriating little tugs.

These fish are seldom hooked because only very rarely are we quick enough with the strike. The fish don't give us time; they don't hold the fly long enough to give our reactions a chance—especially when there is belly in the line. But a fish behaving in this manner will often go on tweaking the fly time after time, and this fish can be hooked. The way to do it is to anticipate the "take" and tighten *just before the fish is felt.*

Let us assume you are fishing a sunk fly which is swinging round in a sluggish current, and that fish are behaving in the manner just described. Wait for a moment or two after feeling a fish tweak the fly and then cast again over exactly the same place without, of course, altering length of line or moving your feet. This can be accomplished by lining up the direction of the cast with some bush or tree on the opposite bank. Start to count from the moment of casting until you feel the fish touch the fly again. It is common for a fish to give the fly a pull cast after cast, although it may not do so *every* time.

PLAN VIEW

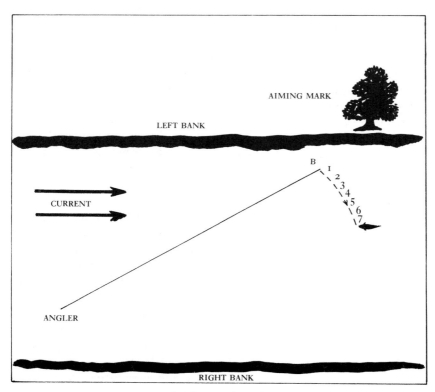

Anticipating the strike
Fish tweaks at count of seven. Cast as before. Count to six—and tighten.

Suppose for purposes of illustration that the fish tugged when you had counted seven. Repeat the procedure and again start to count. On reaching six—tighten. It is surprising how often a fish is hooked. The time taken in reacting to your own decision to strike bridges the gap between then and the moment the fish takes hold of the fly. Naturally, it doesn't work every time—far from it—there are too many variables: timing or direction may be faulty, the fish may have moved his position, you may have moved yours, and so on. But it can be done—perhaps more often than you may think.

Like all fishing tricks it requires practice, split-second timing, precision casting and, above all else, intense concentration. But it is utterly absorbing and gives great satisfaction when it works, for it results in fish being caught in most unfavourable conditions. Bear this in mind, however; most of the fish hooked in this manner will have the fly right in the front of the mouth. Often, therefore, they will be poorly hooked. Don't let it worry you. After all, few of them would be landed if you didn't know the trick.

There are two other ways of dealing with tweaking sea trout. The first is to fish a small nymph-like fly, or (better) a size 12 double. This is a difficult lure for a sea trout to tweak without getting hooked, and the double hook secures a firm hold in the gristle on the edge of the fish's mouth. Nevertheless, it *can* be tweaked with impunity, and when this happens you will be wise to change immediately to the Secret Weapon. This lure was specially designed to deal with the "tweakers"!

But not even the Secret Weapon with its tail treble can *guarantee* a firm hold on a half-hearted sea trout. Which brings me to the problem of the lightly-hooked fish.

Whether on sunk or floating line, a lightly-hooked fish usually comes straight to the surface and splashes about on his side. These antics are almost invariably a signal that fish and fisherman are shortly to part company. Except that the fish may be trying to shake out the hook, sensing in some way that it has a poor hold, I can think of no good reason for this strange behaviour and have never heard an explanation of it. Nevertheless, this fish comes to the top and splashes, and when he does so the fisherman's heart sinks.

Having tried every means of coping with this unhappy situation, I am of the opinion that only one course of action is worthwhile: that is, try to get the fish ashore as quickly as possible. The moment this shivering business starts, put pressure on the fish and walk steadily backwards (if you are able to) and bring him straight in to the bank. If fishing from gently shelving shingle you may land him. The moment he touches the stones he will jump—usually up on to the shore. You will need to move quickly, though, to prevent him from hopping back again, for he will certainly have come off the hook when he jumped.

When wading, there is little you can do except try to bring him straight in to the net. This can be done only if you are fishing a short line, and have the net ready in time.

These tactics often fail to land the fish—but you were going to lose him anyway.

Other methods you may care to try are:

1. Moving to one side or the other of the fish—preferably downstream —and trying to give the hook a better hold by pulling it from a different angle.

2. Dropping the rod point; if necessary, pushing it underwater. (The idea behind this is to try to stop the fish from flapping about, and so help to prolong what hold the hook has.)

3. Stripping off line and giving the fish a lot of slack.

4. Playing the fish very gently.

Frankly, I haven't much faith in any of them. It is true that when wading I automatically push my rod point underwater if a hooked fish starts to thresh about; but I would far rather be ashore and walking backwards. That is the best method I know—and even that doesn't work very often.

On that sad note we will bring this chapter to a close.

Never allow some well-meaning friend to assemble your tackle for you. Never, never, never. Always do it yourself. Then if a rod-ring has been missed, or there is a turn of line round the rod and the line won't shoot properly (most irritating at night, when you can't see what is happening); if the reel falls off when a fish is running; if a knot slips in the best fish of the season—you have only yourself to blame.

Falkus and Buller's Freshwater Fishing (1975)

VIII
Night Fly Fishing Tactics

PART ONE: THE "FIRST-HALF"

You have, we will assume, arrived at the river. At your disposal are several pools and an unbroken "run" or glide. Ample for a night's fishing. This water, together with the "lies" it contains, is not imaginary but an actual stretch of fishing I know intimately, and the suggested methods of fishing it are those which in the beaten way of experience have proved successful. (The pool and "run" described in this chapter are shown in the diagram on p. 219.)

> *Note.* All the examples given in this book are factual and taken from rivers, lakes and stretches of coastline in various parts of Britain. Nevertheless, I must emphasize that they are intended only as a "guide". It is not my purpose to tell you what to do on your own water, but to suggest certain lines of approach that may help you to experiment and to think things out for yourself. I write what I know to be true of the waters I have fished. It seems to me not unlikely that it may also be true of many waters I have not fished.

It is the second night following a spate—which is the best of all. A fine, warm, rather cloudy mid-July evening with a slowly rising glass; a light westerly wind; the river running crystal clear, moderately fast and showing ten inches on the gauge. Altogether, ideal conditions for catching sea trout.

For the sake of convenience, two rods have been set up: one with a floating line with sinking tip; the other with a quick-sinking line. The fly selected to start with is a size 4 Medicine (described in Chapter II) tied with a Grinner Knot (see p. 117) to a 10 or 11 lb b.s. monofilament nylon leader. For most night fishing 6–7 ft. of leader is sufficient. In the half-light or on moonlit nights, a longer leader 9–12 ft. can be used with advantage.

There is nothing, *nothing* in the whole sport of fishing so enchanting as a sea trout spate river in the drowsy dusk of a warm summer evening. And the evening in question is no exception. The smooth pool tail is dimpled with the rings of rising parr and small trout. In deeper water beside the long, undulating roots of a leaning alder, a big fish rolls lazily on the surface, setting a spread of ripples racing to lap the distant shingle. Downstream, where the river shines in the slowly fading light, a myriad gnats dance in a shimmering cloud. An early bat flickers above the trees. Westwards, over the fells, an evening star shows palely. But the grey and blue stones of the river bottom are still clearly visible and you must resist every temptation to start fishing.

I must emphasize again that to steal a march when fishing in clear water for sea trout is fatal to success. There is no greater mistake. Once it is dark, sea trout may accept a faulty cast; but no disturbance of any kind will be tolerated until the shadows have lengthened sufficiently. For the sake of a few minutes the best of an excellent evening's fishing may be ruined. To begin too soon is a common fault and not only among novices. I have known supposedly experienced fishermen go into a pool a good half-hour or more before time—and then express bewilderment when, in seemingly favourable conditions, the sea trout showed no enthusiasm to co-operate. Those fishermen who, once rod and line are assembled, find it impossible to contain their impatience, should start by fishing a stretch of fast, broken water; they will do less harm there.

But of course there is no need to sit and twiddle your thumbs. Go first to some empty water, perhaps the outflow from a pool, and test your fly. Make sure it doesn't tend to swim upside-down, or on its side, and that its body doesn't stick out at an angle from the leader. If it does, cut it off and re-tie it.

Next, mark the water level—with a stone, or by pushing a stick into the bank. It is important to watch for any sign of a rising river. Although no rain may fall in your locality, a storm farther up the valley can start a sudden spate which, in the darkness, may take you by surprise.

If you still use silk lines, strip off a quantity of the ungreased (or sinking) line and the last few yards of the greased line, and leave them together with leaders and flies to soak in some shallow pool among the stones. Wetting all tackle in advance ensures the correct working of line and fly from the moment fishing starts. Neglect this precaution and the initial five or ten minutes are squandered in trying to induce sufficient line to sink to a fishable depth; the fly, meanwhile, skidding ineffectually on the surface. This amount of time on a good fishing evening is far too valuable to be wasted in such a manner. The night's best fishing chances

218

are likely to come within an hour of dusk and once it is time to start not a moment should be lost.

Nothing must be done now that will in any way disturb fish. All necessary reconnaissance was carried out earlier when the water was sunlit. Then, with the aid of polaroid glasses, positions of each shoal and large individual fish were carefully noted. The pool contains a main shoal of fifty to a hundred sea trout which are lying about two-thirds of the way down (Position 10). They are stationed close to the left bank, and the head of this shoal—which holds the larger fish—is level with a clump of broom which leans out from a small overhanging ledge. It was from behind this clump, lying full length in the long grass, that you scanned the pool earlier in the evening. There is a scattering of fish some distance above the shoal (Positions 9 and 8), and further upstream still, in streamy water at the pool neck, a very fine sea trout of perhaps eight or nine pounds (Position 7). There is another scattering of fish below the main shoal (in Positions 11 and 12).

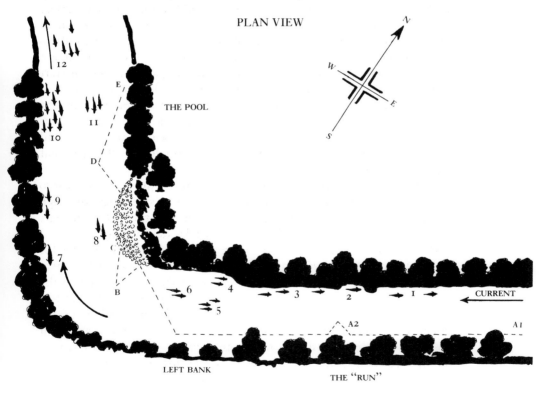

PLAN VIEW

Provided you keep well away from the water's edge, the time of waiting can be usefully spent in noting places convenient for landing fish (although, of course, this should have been done earlier). Before starting to cast, whether in daylight or darkness, it is essential to know exactly where fish are to be landed. Wherever possible, choose a piece of quiet water well upstream of the main shoal and preferably with cover of some sort behind the rod.

Never attempt night fishing without first smearing hands, face, neck and wrists with insect repellent. As the shadows lengthen, particularly on a warm, moist evening, midges become increasingly active. This activity promises well for sea trout fishing chances, for usually when the midges are biting so are the fish. But if you approach the river without some form of anti-midge lotion, the attention of these little creatures will quickly remove all pleasure from fishing.

The sun has dipped behind the distant fells whose eastern flanks are now a dark purple in the afterglow. A gleam of light springs from cottage windows far across the valley. A moth flutters over the pool and falls spinning on the surface—which is already ringed by the splash of a jumping fish. A white owl glides silently across the water meadows; the faint night wind flutters the leaves; the fascination of a darkening river deepens, and where the current chuckles against mossy stones beneath overhanging branches, all is shadowy and mysterious.

It is time to start. Not on the quiet, sheltered and unruffled pool tail—which should be left undisturbed for at least another forty minutes—but on the faster, more rippled water of the "run" above.

Although you wish to begin with floating line tactics, it will be better—owing to the speed of the current—to fish the fast water at the head of the "run" with the sinking line, and change to the floater further down where the current has less force. Accordingly, the latter is left at a convenient place about halfway up the "run", close to Position A2.

> *Note.* A rod is not easily seen once the light has gone, especially among bushes and trees. To avoid wasting precious minutes searching for it later on, mark the spot with something that will show up in the darkness: handkerchief or fish cloth.

This done, you go into the river at Position A1.

The fish in this stretch of water lie close to the bushes on the right bank (in the numbered positions) all the way down to the flat tail at the bottom where they tend to spread out evenly towards the left bank.

In case there is any confusion over which bank of a river is which, the right bank is on an observer's right hand when he is facing downstream.

The "run". River at dead summer low with very little current. Angler casting to fish in position 3. Position 2 (described on p. 225) is in the dark "hole" that can be seen behind the angler's right shoulder.

Note. The foliage on both banks has been carefully undercut to form a sort of tunnel. The shadow and shade remain unaffected, but now (with the exception of the bushes above Position 2, which have purposely been left uncut for fear of disturbing that particular "lie") no branches hang low across the river. Every inch of the water can be covered with a fly. This is of great importance since (as shown in the diagram) fish tend to lie close to the opposite bank. Once the night fly-fisherman has determined the angle at which to cast and the exact length of line needed, he can fish with confidence, however dark the night, and put his fly within inches of the other bank.

It is necessary to wade the whole length of the "run" owing to a heavily bushed left bank, and as there are no convenient places for beaching a fish, every sea trout hooked must be brought to the net. But before going further, it is worthwhile to consider what happens when a sea trout takes the fly.

As a general rule, when a sea trout rises to a fly he positions himself to intercept and seize it when it is approaching his "lie" broadside or partly broadside on, swimming upwards and forward to do so. And having risen and taken the fly in his mouth, he turns away with it and dives back towards his original "lie". This turn is nearly always made away from the fisherman and towards the opposite bank; the probable reason being that the fish wishes to regain his "lie" as quickly as possible; also, that when he turns in the direction from which the fly has come he is automatically heading back towards deeper and safer water. This means that for a fisherman casting from the left bank, the fish is most likely to be hooked in the right side of the mouth. And *vice versa*. (Of course, there are exceptions to this, one of which occurs sometimes when a sluggish pool is fished from the deep side.)

A fish that comes well to the fly will take with great rapidity and power. If the line is too taut this sudden snatch will result in a poorly

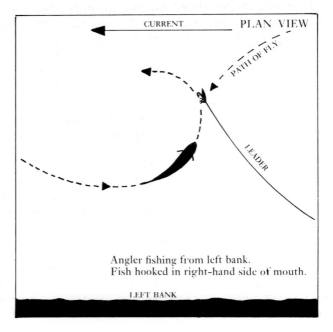

Angler fishing from left bank.
Fish hooked in right-hand side of mouth.

LEFT BANK

hooked fish. Sufficient slack line must be provided, so that the sea trout is able to turn away with the fly without it being dragged straight out of his mouth. It is for this reason that the rod is held at an angle of about thirty degrees or so (as illustrated on p. 187). Indeed, in fast water— such as the head of the "run" just described—a couple of feet of slack line is lightly held, ready to let go the instant a fish takes.

When wading, it is a golden rule to get out of the water as quickly as possible after hooking a fish. But many sea trout "runs" flow between high or heavily wooded banks which make immediate retreat from the water impossible. In conditions such as these a fish must be played and landed pretty well on the spot. The fisherman, thigh or waist deep in water, is unable to move very quickly either upstream or downstream and can do little more than take action to prevent his rod top fouling overhead branches while bringing a fish to hand. The technique of playing a fish hooked in a fast "run" is, therefore, rather different from that employed in a pool where the fisherman has at his disposal many yards of open bank or shingle along which to manoeuvre.

A sea trout, having turned away with the fly and felt pressure from behind—i.e. upstream—as he does so, is likely to go tearing off on a long downstream rush. This behaviour is in itself no cause for alarm. Provided the fisherman has played his part correctly, the fly should be firmly in the corner of the fish's mouth—and the reel contains (or *should* contain) plenty of backing. Unless the fish is heading for some obvious and formidable snag, no attempt should be made to interrupt this first powerful run. There is not only the fish's strength to contend with, but the weight of the current as well. Any sudden check at this point will almost certainly result in a broken leader.

It is worth mention that the more pressure put on a fish as he runs, the more leverage is likely to be exerted by the shank of the hook against his jaw, either to break the hook or tear it free. A point in favour of the short-shanked treble used with a tube fly.

Note. It is, of course, this downstream run that pulls the upper hook of the Sunk Lure so firmly in the outside of a fish's jaw and provides a firm double hold (sometimes the only hold) in an early season fish (see p. 66). For this reason, early fish hooked on Sunk Lure should be encouraged to run downstream. This can be done by giving them a bit of "stick" as soon as they are hooked. Nowadays I always do this when fishing the big S.L. and wait for the fish to complete his downstream run before starting to walk him upstream. Although these tactics probably result in some disturbed fish among a shoal, they certainly help to maintain contact with a good fish already hooked!

An early season fish is sure to have a soft mouth, and the hook will quickly form a slit in the flesh (as illustrated on p. 37). But the moment of danger, when he is most likely to rid himself of the hook, is yet to come. Unless he is a very big fish and determined to return to sea, he will eventually stop his downstream rush, turn and begin to swim quietly back again. All that is necessary is to keep in light contact. Provided he is not bullied, he will usually swim steadily up past the fisherman who should do nothing until the fish is upstream of the rod at an angle of about forty-five degrees. At this point he can be given a little "stick", to prevent further progress upstream.

Now is the moment of truth. If the fish turns towards the rod and jumps—and it is a common reaction—there is a danger that the hook will shake free.

So, as the fish leaves the water the rod point is neither dropped nor kept still, but instantly raised so that pressure is applied while the fish is in the air. Unless an exceptionally large fish is hooked, or very light tackle is in use, there is little risk of breakage; for the fish is airborne and the leader merely pulling against a weight well below its breaking strain. Besides helping to maintain the hookhold, this putting the pressure on a sea trout when he jumps seems to remove a lot of his bounce; his subsequent movements are made with considerably less *élan*, and usually it is not long before he is ready for the net.

With the exception of the lightly-hooked fish discussed in the previous chapter, any attempt to net a fish too soon is a serious mistake. Unless he is exhausted, sudden fright caused by the dark bulge of a net will send him off on a final determined fling which, if it catches the fisherman unawares, may break the leader or tear the hook free, besides unnecessarily prolonging the fight. Always wait until a fish has turned on his side. On all but the darkest night, the flash of silver flank is plainly seen.

In anything of a current it is a bad policy to allow a beaten fish to finish downstream of the rod. Unless he is a small fish it is no easy matter to drag him back to the net. A tiring fish should always be manoeuvred upstream—which is why he is allowed, indeed encouraged to pass the rod on his return journey. Once he is upstream he usually stays there—because of the pull of the line from downstream.

The net is sunk well below the surface and the fish brought backwards with the current. As he passes over the net it is raised with one steady, unhurried movement.

Once your fish is safely in the net, carry out the following drill. First put the net handle between your legs and pull some line off the reel. This is to avoid jerking the fly, which is still in the fish's mouth or, if it came away when line slackened as the fish was landed, is entangled in the net. Then, put the rod in the crook of one arm (or, if body waders are being worn stuff the rod butt down inside them), reach for the "Priest" and knock the fish on the head while he is still in the net. Having done so, take him by the gills and slip him into your fish bag—and re-sling your net.

With a little thought and practice all this can be done quite safely and easily while you are standing in the river, and will prevent a lot of splashing in and out of the water. But remember this: all movements at night—from wading to changing a fly—should be deliberate and unhurried. Never try to do anything too quickly. Haste in the darkness is the biggest time loser of all. *Always take your time.*

So much, then, for coping with a fish once he is hooked. Now to return to your position in the river at the top of the "run". A small but important point is that you are fishing from east to west; i.e. towards the last of the light. It is dark below the line of bushes and trees on the opposite bank, but the western sky above still glimmers brightly. Vision in this half-light will be greatly assisted if you pull your cap brim low down over your eyes so that it comes below the line of the tree tops. This blots out the glare from the bright sky and enables you to see very much more clearly into the shadows. For a time, the pitch of your fly may be just discernible.

Fish that are lying in the upper part of the "run" (Position 1 in the diagram), are in fast water. If the fly is to cover them at a reasonable speed, as long a line as possible must be cast at an acute angle downstream. There are no trees behind the rod to start with, so that a normal overhead cast can be used.

As each cast is made, a pace is taken forward down-river and the rod brought round with the fly. There is always the possibility of a fish lying further over towards the left bank, or following the fly across, so keep the fly moving smoothly and steadily as it swings into the slacker water and bring it upstream towards the rod by drawing in a full arm's length of line with the left (or non-casting) hand. This slack is shot when you cast again.

The "run" is fished in this manner down to Position A2.

Opposite to you now is the known "lie" of a good fish. He is in a small bay on the far side of the current which runs underneath overhanging bushes that jut out just above (see diagram). These bushes make downstream fishing impossible. The wall of trees on the left bank makes a "broadside on" approach very difficult. This is an instance when the fly should be fished upstream. The method is to wade well out just below the fish—both to keep the rod movement behind his line of vision and to shorten the casting distance as much as possible—and put a line across and at a slight angle upstream, so that the fly lands a yard or two above and beyond the fish.

Since a floating line is easier to handle upstream than a sinking line, the other rod—which has been left in readiness at this spot—is now pressed into service.

Strip line off the reel and let it drift down with the current until you estimate you have sufficient line out to make the cast. You can, of course, calculate the length of line stripped off by retrieving it in arm's lengths from downstream and letting it go again. For instance, if the length of rod is 10 ft. 6 in. and 6 ft. of leader is being used, 4 arm's lengths of line will give approximately 13 yd. from the fisherman to the fly: four yards, plus twice the length of the rod, seven yards, plus the length of the leader, two yards. Total: thirteen.

Another method of measuring the length of line out in the darkness is to have markers tied on to the line at certain intervals. But such markers are easily moved and so are unreliable.

Provided you know the water well and have reckoned the distances between various points—and indolence is the only excuse for not having done so—complete accuracy, so far as distance is concerned, is possible even on the darkest night. And when fish are lying close to an opposite bank which is lined with bushes, accuracy is of no small importance.

Should you find yourself fishing strange water without having had an opportunity to inspect it in daylight, one method of determining distance is to tie on a fly with no point. Cast across the river, gradually lengthening line, until the fly clatters on the leaves opposite, or lands on the bank; then measure the amount of line you have out. This will give the width of the river, and you can then replace your fly and, allowing for wind and differing angles of attack, fish that water with confidence.

When casting for the first time in the half-light it is a good plan to try a practice cast well away from the "lie" you wish to cover. Plop the fly hard down into the water. If its pitch is visible in the shadows the length of line is easily judged.

In Position A2, you are trying for a good sea trout with a very tricky cast and it is worth taking pains. Merely to disturb the fish, or hang

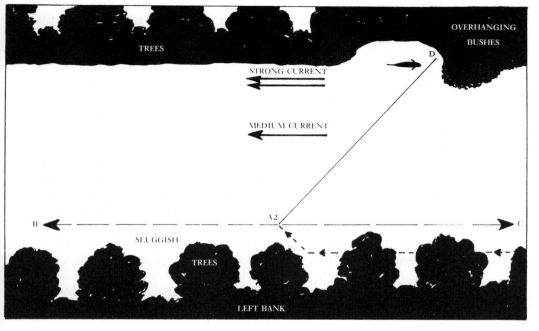

Fishing Position A2

1. Let line out to drift downstream to B. Measure in arm's lengths as already described.
2. Cast to C. Plop the fly hard down. Surface disturbance here will do no harm.
3. Bring the fly back along the path A2/B. Then cast straight to D.
It all looks simple enough on paper (or in daylight). It is not so easy after dusk. The fly must be presented correctly first time. If the river is low, a second chance is unlikely. Disturbed by a bad cast the fish may have moved. It is the ability to recognize and take chances such as this that enables the expert angler to catch fish when others fail.

leader and fly in the bushes for want of a little thought and care is plain stupid.

When confident of covering the fish, cast boldly across and slightly above him. Then, raise the rod and bring the fly towards you so that it resembles a little fish swimming diagonally downstream a few inches below the surface. The fly can be fished quite fast because, as we saw in an earlier chapter, this is how a small fish might reasonably behave when swimming such a course. It will therefore seem quite natural to the sea trout, whereas a fly fished at that speed against the current would appear most unnatural.

If the fish takes this fast-moving fly he will do so with a rush; but the belly of line hanging from the raised rod tip to the water should provide sufficient slack for him to turn away with the fly and hook himself.

It may be that on feeling pressure from a downstream direction, he will make his first run *upstream*. If he does, be ready for him to turn because, immediately, he will come whizzing down past you with full assistance from the current. Unless you are prepared for it, a great bag of slack line will form; and if this happens there is likely to be a short, sharp display of acrobatics in the shadows under the bushes somewhere downstream—before he shakes out the hook and departs.

Should you succeed in landing him he will undoubtedly repay the trouble you have taken. These difficult "lies" often hold big fish, and he could well be the heaviest caught during the night.

As you fish on down the "run" over the fish lying in Position 3, a form of switch cast is made, to keep the line clear of tree branches behind the rod. The fly is thrown straight back upstream parallel to the bank, the rod being held well out at arm's length over the water at an angle of forty-five degrees, or less. The more downstream the angle of cast the easier it is to position the fly with the forward stroke, so fish as long a line as possible. The current is slackening all the way down to the tail of the flat below, so you continue to fish with the floating line, the other rod being left on the bank to be recovered later.

But as the current slackens, the fly not only slows down during its swing round, *it doesn't swing round so far*. Indeed, by the time you are ready to cast for the sea trout in Position 4, the fly no longer finishes up straight below you, but stops in slack water some little distance out towards the opposite bank (Position C, in the diagram).

From such a position it is easy to get caught up on the back-cast if the fly is thrown behind in the usual way. One answer is to roll cast the fly to the fish at Position 4, but this is not really very satisfactory. It is

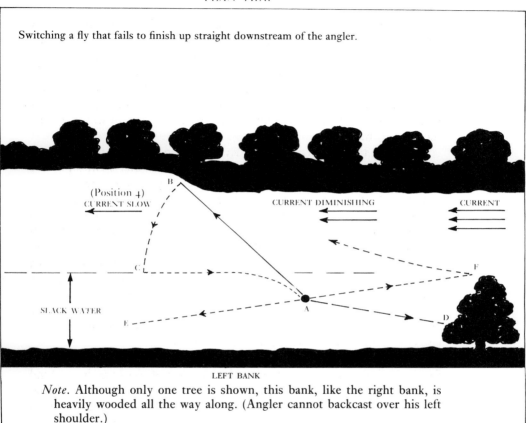

Switching a fly that fails to finish up straight downstream of the angler.

Note. Although only one tree is shown, this bank, like the right bank, is
heavily wooded all the way along. (Angler cannot backcast over his left
shoulder.)

Angler at A casts to B where fish are lying. The fly swings round on a slow current,
but can travel no further than C—where it comes to slack water. Now, if normal back-
cast is made in direction of D the fly will be caught in tree branches. Instead, angler
roll casts to E, lifts the line straight back behind him towards F, and then, before the
fly touches down, switches it to B.

Note. Accurate roll casting is very difficult at night. To attempt to roll the
line direct to B from C is likely to result in a splashing line, which may
disturb fish. No harm will be done by splashing the line down at E, since
there are no fish lying anywhere near.

very difficult to roll cast accurately at night. The fish at 4 are in quiet water and a heavily splashed line is likely to put them down. As shown in the diagram, however, a roll cast can put to good service—although not directly towards the fish.

But although by roll casting to E and switching to B we can present the fly properly, Position 4 is still a very tricky "lie". A gust of wind will blow the leader into the bushes just ahead of the fish. As with Position 2, the loss of leader and fly must be balanced against the chance of hooking a good sea trout.

The fish in positions 5 and 6 are easily covered. The current here is gentle, but on the floating line the fly will swing across the "lies" at about the right height and speed. It is necessary merely to cast well across the river, allow the fly to swing round for a short distance towards your own bank and then work it in through the slack water—either by stripping the line, or using the "Finger-Ring" Figure-of-Eight method of coiling the line in the hand, as shown on p. 86.

Each cast is fished out completely, the fly being brought in much closer to the rod than hitherto. In this slacker water, fish often follow a fly for some distance before taking it. Sometimes, they will swim close behind it and snap at it just as it leaves the water. It is important, there- fore, that the fly should not lose its action when coming from the current into the slack, nor move jerkily. For this reason the rod is held quite still.

Having fished out the "flat" at the tail of the "run", back quickly up again, casting every two or three yards as you walk steadily backwards, until you reach the other rod (left at Position A2). This is always worth doing. It is surprising how often sea trout are caught when water that has just been fished down is taken in reverse. The reason may be that the fly did not cover that particular fish properly on the way down, or (possibly) that some sea trout, like salmon, have a delayed reaction to a fly, or (probably) that the sudden appearance of the fly is more stimulating —resulting in what is more or less an "induced" take. Whatever the reason, however, backing-up a pool is a very productive method of fishing—both for sea trout and salmon (see also, p. 240).

Having retrieved the other rod, ford the river below the tail of the "run", crossing diagonally. Moving water is easier to ford on a down- stream diagonal; besides which, the shallowest route across a river is seldom the shortest line between the two banks.

You are now on the shingle above the pool. It is dark enough to fish this water, and the place to start operations is at the head (Position B).

Angler in position B.

In position C.

On the way to D. Now the net can be propped up on the bank beside the landing-place to which each hooked fish will be "walked".

231

Position 7 marks the "lie" of the big sea trout seen during the afternoon reconnaissance. The water at that point is fast, so wade well out (to Position B) in order to narrow the downstream casting angle as much as possible. There has been no adverse change of weather conditions; the evening is still warm; the sea trout show no signs of having gone down, so continue fishing the sink-tip floating line.

Start well above the big chap and work carefully downstream, making sure the fly is fishing correctly before putting out the important cast that is likely to cover him. If he takes, all well and good. If not, leave him. He has either seen the fly and declined it, or he has gone for a cruise. As we shall see when fishing the sunk line, there are times when it is advisable to cast over a fish again and again, but this is not one of them. Better to leave him alone for the time being. You will be trying for him again, later; the "lie" will be fished a number of times before daybreak.

There is one point I want to make clear. This big fish is not left alone because we are chary of "over-fishing the 'lie'". *Provided it is fished properly, a sea trout "lie" (or a salmon "lie" for that matter) cannot be over-fished.* This view is contrary to much that has been said on the subject. Nevertheless, experience has taught me that provided a fish has not been frightened by poor casting, shadow, the sight of the fisherman or an unsuitable lure, he is quite capable of accepting a bait or fly which has been cast consistently for perhaps half-an-hour, or longer, and which he has already seen umpteen times. (For examples, see Surface Lure, p. 78; and worm, p. 328.) Our attack on the fish in Position 7 is broken off simply because to concentrate on one particular "lie" so early in the night is to waste time. Big sea trout tend to take more readily later on.

Below the big fellow there are sea trout lying on both sides of the river: in Positions 8 and 9. It is a mistake to cast for those under the far bank first. By doing so, you will merely disturb the sea trout close to the right bank before they have had a fly put over them. So, concentrate first of all on the fish in Position 8. These are lying in quite shallow water, close to the shingle and on the edge of a fairly strong current. To *avoid* hooking a fish from Position 9, cast to a point well to the right side of the centre of the river. As the fly swings round its comparatively short arc and comes into the slacker water, keep it moving at a steady speed and bring it across the fish on a slightly upstream path.

Immediately a fish is hooked, pressure should be applied in an attempt to restrain him from rushing across the river. If he starts splashing about

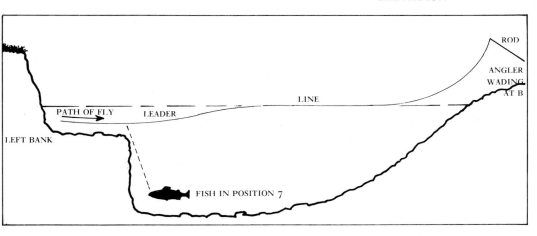

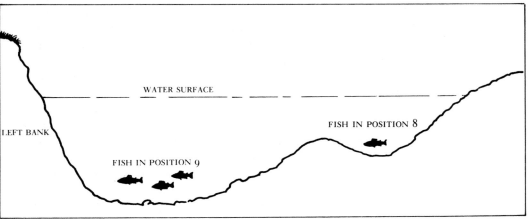

Elevation showing the changing underwater contours of the pool. See plan view on p. 219. Fish in positions 7, 8, 9. (Since we are looking downstream the fish should be shown facing us, head–on—but I can't draw them that way.) The fish in Position 7 is close beside a steep ledge. "Lies" of this nature are common. The lure should be put well across the river into the shallow water beyond, and out of sight of, the fish. Its *sudden appearance* as it swings across the ledge into view often induces a fish to take. This is a little ploy that can be used to good effect in many similar situations—when fish are lying on the angler's side of a submerged rock, etc.

among the fish lying under the opposite bank the chances of catching one of them will be greatly reduced—at least, for a time. Needless to say, it is pointless to run any risk of being broken, but the necessary "stick" can be given by dropping the rod point over on to the river side and applying pressure *away* from the bank. When this is done the sea trout often solves the problem himself—by rushing ashore!

What (I think) happens is that the fish takes the fly at speed after it has passed him on its inshore course and then, feeling pressure from the direction of apparent safety, accelerates in alarm and shoots aground. On touching the stones he makes a prodigious leap . . . and sails up on to the shingle.

Such behaviour is disconcerting to the fisherman who doesn't expect it. Indeed, the situation is very comical. There he is, standing out in the water, playing a fish that is flopping about high and dry on the bank. Unless he quickly realizes what has happened and gets ashore in time, the fish shakes out the hook and jumps back again.

This happened to me so often years ago on the pool under discussion that Kathleen, my wife, would crouch on the shingle close to the water with the landing net. The instant a sea trout took, I would give a warning shout. As often as not the fish dashed straight for the shore and jumped— sometimes, quite literally, into the net. That one could induce a sea trout to behave in such an obliging manner never ceased to delight me.

Today in that particular place the trick no longer works, for with the changing years the fish have changed their "lies". All the same, it illustrates an important point. In many pools, close-lying fish such as those in Position 8, are seldom caught—for the very good reason that they are seldom fished for. Unless the angler is aware that fish sometimes lie very close to his own bank he is apt to march straight to the water's edge, wade in, and start casting as far as he can towards the other side of the river. No further chance of catching those close-lying fish is possible. Not surprisingly they have fled at his incautious approach and, in doing so, have in all probability spread alarm among sea trout lying farther out. As a result, the angler stands on one "lie" and casts over another which holds only disturbed fish.

As I have witnessed often enough, the mistake is common. It explains the comparative failure, in otherwise favourable conditions, not only of the fisherman responsible but any other who is unfortunate in fishing down behind him.

Having dealt with the inshore "lie", we can take action against those fish in Position 9. It is quite straightforward fishing but a long line should be cast at as much of a downstream angle as possible, for these fish are lying in a fairly strong current and the speed of the fly must be controlled.

By now the sky is quite dark. The light in the west has faded to a dull glow which dimly outlines the distant hills. The night breeze is a whisper and over the river and meadows has fallen the hush of late evening. There is the ever present soft sound of the water; an occasional screeching of young owls from the branches of a dead oak in the spinney behind the pool; the splash of a fish rolling in the shallows. Where in daylight the river runs clear over the pale stones all is black and mysterious. It is the witching time—time to start on the best piece of water: the pool tail.

So far, it is mainly rippled water that has been fished. Here, in the lower part of the pool, the river is a steady glide with only the faint night air to ruffle its glassy surface. To a quickened imagination, the dark water gurgling beneath the alder roots surely holds some leviathan sea trout that will hurl itself at the fly in a sluther of foam—and the heart leaps suddenly as a fish lunges across the pool and sends the ripples scudding.

You are naturally anxious to start. But first, a tackle inspection.

1. Strip line off the reel and re-wind (see p. 266).
2. Examine the leader for wind knots. Wind or no wind, they appear at night as though by magic.
3. Test the fly and make sure of its point.

The fish in Position 10 represent the large shoal already mentioned. Those in Position 11, some scattered fish that are lying well to the right of the pool on the edge of the current; and those in Position 12, fish that have dropped back to the extreme tip of the pool tail where the water quickens and flows out into a shallow, stony "run" beyond.

The sea trout in the main shoal present no problems. It is possible to wade to a convenient position (D in the diagram) from which the fish can be covered with a cast of medium length. They are lying in a steady current of easy pace that will work the fly nicely, provided the angle of cast is sufficiently downstream to avoid too much belly forming in the line.

The head of the shoal, as marked earlier in the day, is in line with the overhanging clump of broom. From your position low in the water this is still visible against the skyline. Start by fishing a few practice casts down to your marks. They may not be visible much longer in the darkening twilight, so measure (in arm's lengths) the amount of line in action and count your steps from the shingle bank: this will ensure that after hooking and landing a fish you will re-start no farther downstream.

Earlier, when wading the "run", it was not possible to get ashore; each fish had to be played and landed where he was hooked. Here, however, you are able to beat a quick retreat. So, immediately a fish is hooked he is removed from the proximity of the others in the shoal and landed in the quiet water beside the shingle bank.

With the exception of Sunk Lure fishing—when a fish is encouraged to make an initial run downstream (see p. 223)—it is advisable to start "walking" a fish as soon as possible whenever you are in a position to do so. It takes the heart out of him, reduces his resistance and shortens the fight. But any delay is fatal. A moment's hesitation and he is likely to go shooting off on a long acrobatic rush across the pool. To interfere with such a run is to invite disaster. An attempt must be made to control him the moment he is hooked. This does *not* consist of putting a finger on the reel and hauling. You are not indulging in a trial of strength but the art of gentle persuasion. And although, naturally, not every fish will respond to such treatment, it is surprising how many will do so—provided you act at once.

The moment a fish takes the fly, turn away from him and begin to walk upstream, the rod held absolutely steady with the butt set firmly against your body, the point at an angle of about forty-five degrees to the water and at right angles to the river. It is now that an extension to the rod butt (mentioned in an earlier chapter) becomes so important, for it is almost impossible to "walk" a fish successfully unless the rod is anchored fast against the body. Should the handle of the reel catch in loose clothing, the danger incurred by a fish making a sudden rush is obvious. In darkness it is not always easy to avoid this, especially when the reel is fastened to the very end of the butt. Such a position for the reel is the logical one—in theory. In practice it is quite different. In my opinion, to fish with a rod that has no extension below the reel is to accept an unnecessary handicap. Certainly at night.

Lest there should be any misunderstanding I must make it absolutely clear that when "walking" a fish you do *not* tow him up the pool. Nor do you try to pull him along. Don't haul, or jerk, or allow the rod to vibrate, or hold the line fast against the rod. At the first gentle pressure the fish either comes forward or he doesn't. If the move is made soon enough he usually does, but there is no question of trying to force him.

236

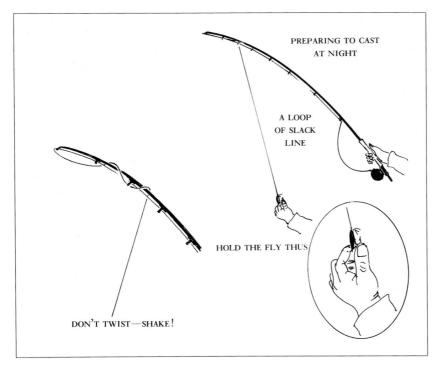

PREPARING TO CAST
AT NIGHT

A LOOP
OF SLACK
LINE

HOLD THE FLY THUS

DON'T TWIST—SHAKE!

It is very easy to get into trouble at night when starting to cast. Some sort of preparatory drill will save much loss of time and temper—and so lead to more successful fishing. I recommend the following:

1. While the fly is still hooked in the butt ring, draw off a loop of slack line between reel and the first rod ring.

2. Detach fly (for safety's sake holding it as shown in close-up) and pull on the line.

3. If the line runs smoothly through the rings, straightening the loop, all is well; carry on with the cast. If it does *not*, the line is obviously snagged and to start casting will lead to worse trouble.

A common cause is shown in simplified form in the third drawing. The line has looped round the rod and caught on a ring.

At this point, unable in the darkness to see what has happened, the novice makes the mistake of twisting the rod round and round. Unless he is lucky, the line merely becomes more securely snagged.

Correct procedure is to tension the line lightly—and *shake* the rod. Nine times out of ten the line will free itself. The moment it does so the loop will straighten and you can start to lengthen line.

Note. If on the back cast you feel the fly hit the rod, something has undoubtedly gone wrong. *Stop casting at once.* If you have some yards of line stripped in, don't move your feet. First, reel in the slack line. Then inspect the leader. It will probably be wrapped round the rod. If it is clear, there will almost certainly be a "wind" knot in it.

A bag of twenty-one sea trout and two herling (average weight $2\frac{1}{4}$ lb.) taken during the "First-Half" between ten-thirty and midnight.

If you give him too much stick the chances are he will jump and then dash madly away. When he comes forward you will not feel his weight, for he swims steadily upstream urged on by the belly of line that quickly forms between him and the rod. Only the drag of the line through the water is felt.

Often, you may think the fish has escaped and, in sudden despair, tighten too savagely. This has disastrous results; he will certainly go tearing off, dragging your line among the other fish in the shoal—the one thing you are trying to prevent. So long as a steady but unhurried progress is maintained upstream, the fish will follow quietly. In fact, he will gain ground. By the time a previously selected landing place is reached he is usually somewhere out in the middle of the river and conveniently opposite the rod.

You are now some distance from the main sea trout shoal and in the best place for playing the fish. Indeed, if he has been "walked" far, most of the playing will have been done. There is no point in continuing further upstream, so stay where you are and keep well back from the water's edge. If there is a background of bank or foliage behind the rod, so much the better.

After a "walking" session a fish is not usually inclined to run far, and it is not difficult to prevent him from rejoining the shoal. If he jumps, pull him sideways while he is in the air—a trick that he seems to find very disheartening. It is easy to tell when a fish is going to jump by the peculiar "shivering" feeling transmitted along the line just beforehand. Of course, if he is a large fish be careful of the leader—drop the rod point and provide some slack line. Generally speaking, however, the larger the fish the less likely he is to leap clear of the water.

The flash of his flank will signal defeat. Sink the net (as described on p. 124) and when you are sure he is beaten, shorten line and draw him firmly in with one steady movement.

Having knocked him on the head, re-wound the line, examined the leader for knots or damage and, if necessary, re-tied the fly, wade carefully back to the same place as before and start again.

Fishing fly in this manner on a suitable night is the most deadly of all methods of killing sea trout. Fish after fish can be taken from a shoal, even on a calm, still night with the river at summer low, provided great care is taken—both when wading and casting—not to disturb the water. Each fish should be "walked" upstream and played well clear of the others, and landed without the aid of a flashlamp. Most important of all: the exact position of the shoal must be known.

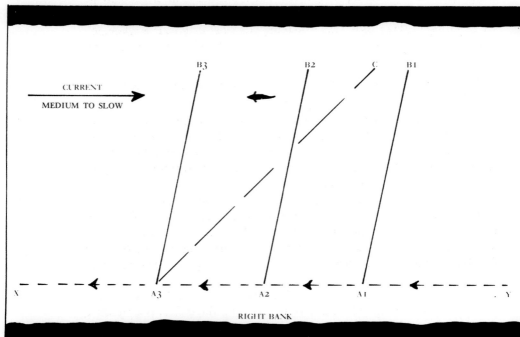

The object of backing-up a pool is to present the fish with a lure that behaves differently from the way it did when the pool was fished down.

When fishing down in the usual way, an angler casts approximately on the line A3–C (depending on the strength of current), and continues down the pool.

When backing-up he casts from A1 to B1, walking backwards towards A2 as the lure fishes round; then casts again, this time to B2; and so on, along the line Y–X, keeping on the move the whole time. An important aspect of this method is that a fish (such as the one lying above B2) is approached *from behind*. The lure suddenly appears—instead of approaching gradually, cast by cast, as it did when the pool was fished down.

This sudden appearance of a lure often induces a fish to take.

When there is moonlight or bright starlight, only the fly should be allowed to pass over the fish. On these occasions a longer leader can be used with advantage: say, nine or ten feet, or even longer. If a "Needle" knot is used (see p. 109), there will be no danger of the line/leader join catching in the rod rings.

> *Note.* In a gusty wind a long leader can be a curse. But, since the water is likely to be rippled there is less need of it.

If the sea trout in the main shoal become disturbed, that piece of water should be rested and fishing resumed higher up. Later, attention can be given to the fish that are lying farther down. Those in Position 11 are easily covered; but those in Position 12 require further wading (to Position E) and are best left alone for the time being.

It is never tactically sound to fish a pool right out early in the night. Less disturbance will be caused when hooking and landing a fish from the sill of a pool tail once the night is really dark. As indicated in the diagram, a fish hooked at 12 will almost certainly drag the line through fish lying immediately above, unless it can be kept downstream and landed at E.

When you do start fishing from E a Steeple cast will be needed (see p. 91), for there is a heavily-bushed bank behind the rod. It is a valuable cast for all night fishing when there are obstructions behind you, and also when you are fishing with a wind at your back. To cast with a straight arm is no bad habit; it helps to keep the fly out of danger and virtually lengthens the rod by two feet or so.

E is a good position from which to try "Round-the-Clock" fishing. After which, the pool can be "backed-up" to the shingle.

By now, however, the fish no longer respond. Midnight has struck, and the last light has gone. The earlier cloud bank has rolled away leaving a sky full of flashing stars. With the accompanying sharp drop in temperature, the night has turned chilly. The river seems suddenly empty; no fish are moving and the surface of the pool is still and unrippled.

It is time to rest and consider the next move, for the whistle has blown and it is half-time.

Viator: May a man take a stool and sit down on the ground by you?

Piscator: Yea, so that you sit not over near the water.

Viator: Nay, I trow, I will sit far enough off for slipping in.

Piscator: I do not mean therefor, but I would not have you sit so that the fish may see either your shadow, your face, or any part of you.

Viator: And why? Are they so quick of sight?

Piscator: Look, what they lack in hearing, it is supplied into them in seeing chiefly . . .

Viator: Well, now I am set, may I then talk and not hinder your fishing?

Piscator: Spare not, but not too loud.

Viator: Do the fish then hear?

Piscator: No, you may talk, whoop, or hallo and never stir them, but I would not gladly by your loud talking that either some bungler, idle person, or jester might resort unto us . . .

The *Arte of Angling* (1577). Author unknown.

IX
Night Fly Fishing Tactics

PART TWO: "HALF-TIME"

In practice, of course, not every fishing night lends itself to such neat dissection as that used to illustrate these chapters. In warm weather, a floating line, or a sink-tip line, may be fished unchanged throughout the night. On cold evenings, it may be better to start, and continue, with a sunk line. But although much depends on the conditions of weather and water, such nights are exceptions rather than the rule, and the divisions of first-half, half-time and second-half create the sort of pattern to which the majority of fishing nights conform.

At the start of half-time, when the first fine flurry of action is over, sea trout seem suddenly hard to catch, and at this stage many fishermen decide to pack up and go home. This, as I have already suggested, is a great mistake. Provided time is at your disposal, the second half can offer splendid opportunities of catching fish—meanwhile, this is the chance to rest and make any necessary change of tackle. For instance, the sink-tip line can be exchanged for a floater fitted with Surface Lure; a Sunk Lure substituted for the Medicine on the sinking line.

Rushing about at night is always foolish, and during the period of half-time utterly pointless. If fish are not taking on what you know to be a good stretch of undisturbed water, it is unlikely they will be doing so elsewhere. Rather than pant from pool to pool, it is better to select a piece of water that you know holds fish and stay there.

> *Note.* There is, however, one important exception to this. It occurs during the very early part of the season (on the rivers I usually fish this is in the middle of June) when the river holds only a scattering of sea trout. During these short nights, when I have to "search" for a fish, I take one rod, travel light, and cover as much potential holding water as possible.
>
> But as soon as the main run starts and there are shoals of fish in the pools, one good holding pool and a "run", or two pools with a "run" between them, is more than sufficient for a night's fishing.

I am assuming, naturally, that your movements are unrestricted. It is unfortunate to acquire the reputation of being a "water-hog". Should you have a private stretch at your disposal you may, of course, please yourself how, when or where you fish. But if you are on "ticket" water, it is most ill-mannered and unsporting to "sit tight" on the best piece of fishing (should you have arrived there first) and prevent others from having a cast. There is much ill-feeling engendered on some waters by such selfishness and it extends, I regret to say, throughout the whole range of angling. Only quite recently, claims to fishing places on both the famous Royalty Fishery and on Chew Reservoir were settled by punch-ups.

Shades of Sheringham! To this has it come!

It is unlikely that anything I write will influence such louts, and there is little point in preaching to the converted, so I will content myself by suggesting that when you find yourself on a good beat which others wish to share—as they most certainly will on promising nights—it is wise to confer with them, preferably before fishing starts, and make some amicable arrangements. When dealing with beginners, try to be tolerant. It is, I know, depressing to watch the ineffectual efforts of a novice in a good holding pool; but such moments are, surely, a test of character. We were all inexperienced, once. Perhaps a kindly word of advice may react to mutual benefit.

On the other hand, to consider the opinions of a fisherman more experienced or with a better knowledge of the water than yourself, is not only polite but profitable.

Although half-time may be a period of rest for the fisherman it is not necessarily so for the fish. Now that darkness has fallen, a run may be under way; a general movement of fish upstream from pool to pool. Sea trout show little interest in a lure while engaged in this, so that even on the best fishing nights such activity contributes towards the slackness of half-time.

When running from salt water during a spate, some fish will go straight through to their intended pools and stay there until shortly before spawning. Some will run only short distances, remain where they are for several weeks, ignore a succession of spates, and then run many miles. Occasionally, when the river dwindles during a long, dry spell, fish from some of the lower pools drop back to the estuary; and they will sometimes do this early in the season if the nights turn very cold. Some fish, however, make their way gradually up-river from pool to pool in conditions of dead low water, taking weeks to reach their final resting places—and these are the fish we see and hear at night. These late evening runs are most common during the early part of the season. But fish will not move if the air temperature drops too sharply at dusk, nor when the barometer is falling. Sea trout seem very sensitive to any forthcoming change of weather. When rain is imminent, they will lie where they are and wait for it.

There is no mistaking this night movement once it starts. Much splashing is heard above and below the pools as fish force their way up through the stickles, and a fisherman motionless in shallow water will often see the surface "V"s caused by running fish as they swim up past him, at times almost brushing his legs. It is as well for the fisherman to rest during this period, for seldom will these running fish take a fly.

Although sea trout may move up at any time during the night (and I think that some do so just before dawn), the main run begins as soon as the sky has darkened sufficiently. It extends throughout the length of the "operational" part of the river and lasts for perhaps an hour or so, after which only an occasional fish is heard splashing through the shallows.

Having run a certain distance and arrived in a fresh holding pool, some fish (I think) prowl round it for a time—often lying for a while in shallow water at the tail. They will now take a fly very readily.

As evidence of this, I remember an afternoon early one season when my wife and I, while making a reconnaissance of one of our pools, spotted a biggish sea trout that could be easily identified by a scar on its back. I caught this fish the same night in very shallow water in the tail of the pool above. It weighed just over 6 lb. The river was low. In order to find its way into the pool where I caught it, the fish had to splash its way through only an inch or two of water. In doing so, a sea trout of this size would have made a lot of noise. But while fishing down the pool (about an hour or so after dark) I had heard nothing. Clearly, the fish must have run up earlier, just at dusk and either been lying in the tail ever since or dropped back from deeper water.

Even while resting, never relax your concentration. As I have re-marked in an earlier chapter, if you wish to succeed at night it is essential to remain *en rapport* with your surroundings. And the darker the night, the more your ears take over from your eyes. For instance, always be on the alert for otters.

Often, otters will station themselves where running fish are most easily intercepted, and any undue splashing from a fish coming into a pool should be investigated. A sea trout flopping through the shallows is an easy prey. But it is not my intention to denigrate these fascinating animals. Many was the hour I used to spend lying in the dew-wet grass at dawn watching them at play. (Not today, alas. There are few otters in my part of England now.)

I have noticed that fish seem to possess the strange faculty of knowing when otters are on the hunt, and therefore dangerous. I have watched a pair of otters gambolling quite close to a shoal of sea trout, rolling over on the bank and sliding down after each other into the water—the sea trout, meanwhile, holding their positions apparently undisturbed. At

". . . a biggish sea trout that could be easily identified by a scar on its back. . . . It weighed just over 6 lb."

other times I have seen fish show signs of great agitation some minutes *before* the arrival of an otter.

It is not difficult to sense an otter's presence at night. An ominous stillness seems suddenly to spread over the water, and the fly swings across the pool untouched. I remember an evening some years ago: I had fished without an offer down a magnificent stretch which was in perfect condition and full of fish. Sitting on a rock at the tail of this "run", my mind dark with doubt, I became suddenly aware of movement on the shingle at my feet. Sure enough—there he was! I remained absolutely motionless while, for a long moment, he stared at me in the half-light, a quizzical look on his little round face. Then away he slid into the shadows, as silently as he had come.

That otters kill a number of salmon and sea trout is beyond dispute. But I do not grudge them their fish. Their main diet is thought to consist of eels, so in all probability they do more good than harm. Judging by the fish that I have found, whose death could with certainty be ascribed to otters, I don't think an inordinate number are killed. Game fish are beset by enemies from the moment the eggs are laid and otters, surely, must be low on the list. They cannot be compared to such predators as cormorants, goosanders, mergansers, herons, feral mink, and eels. I resent an otter's company only when we wish to share the same water. To fish a sea trout pool after an otter has given it the works is to cast in vain. But the otter's darker points do not, in my view, provide a strong enough case for his destruction.

Should an otter put in an appearance on water you are fishing, make your presence known at once. He will quickly leave you in possession.

* * *

But the accommodating behaviour of the otter and other wildlife predators is by no means common to all pests. Sea trout are easily disturbed, and many good fishing chances are missed through no fault of the angler. Bathing parties; canoeists; happy holiday-makers; stick-retrieving dogs; River Authority workers who (with impeccable timing) come with dredgers, bull-dozers, rock-tippers and slashers to canalize the river or trim up the bank just as the main run of fish is due; "creeping" anglers, who stare with feigned surprise when told they are fishing private water; stampeding cattle; children with shrimping nets; hikers in hordes; stone-throwing hippies . . . I have suffered them all! Unless his boundaries are mined, anyone trying to protect a fishery in modern England has a busy time of it.

Consider the appalling treatment to which so many rivers are subjected. Apart from those grim ogres, Pollution and Extraction, what has the angler to contend with? Has he a fair chance at those fish which, surviving capture in estuary nets, have reached their resting pools? Has he, at least, a reasonable chance of fishing undisturbed water?

Frankly, no.

When low-water conditions prevail, ease of transport makes poaching so simple in many rivers that poaching gangs threaten not only the existence of the fish, but sometimes even the fisherman. As quoted in the first edition of this book, a man fishing on an expensive beat of a famous Cumbrian salmon and sea trout river, was given his marching orders by a dozen or so poachers who arrived to net his pool. Hopelessly outnumbered, threatened with cudgel and stones, what alternative had he but to vacate the water? That incident occurred in 1960. Today the situation is no better.

It is unfortunate that such a large proportion of the British public regard the poacher with the sentimental affection usually reserved for dogs and bears. He is pictured as a romantic individualist victimized by the minions of some wealthy riparian owner. Much of this rubbish is the fault of certain ignorant writers whose opinions are expressed in radical slush founded on the man-trap and spring-gun iniquities of a bygone age.

There is nothing the public likes half so much as the story of Little Man being hounded by Big Man—and finally doing him down. A great quantity of classic romantic literature is based on this simple plot, and the story of the poacher is no exception. Hearts that suffer no greater exertion than the daily pound along Leadenhall Street beat faster at the mention of his name. The very word "poacher" evokes pictures of a shining moonlit night, with the wind in the trees, and a rushing river; our salmon-snatching hero out-witting brutal bailiffs by means of river lore and homely guile . . . eventually flogging his meagre catch to feed his starving children.

What nonsense it all is.

Poachers, using poison, can ruin half a river and cause thousands of pounds worth of damage in a single night. And they do. Rivers are raped with click-hook, leister and net; and poisoned with everything from household detergent to cyanide. Skin-diving suits with flippers and masks are used to recover fish killed and stunned by explosives.

At his worst, the poacher is an organized gangster who works as a full-time professional fish thief; an armed thug who, with knuckleduster, cosh or knife, does not hesitate to injure anyone who attempts to interfere with him. At his best, he is a local loafer who works alone and sells his "clicked" salmon and sea trout at the pub for booze. Unfortunately there is no control over the sale of game fish. Salmon and sea trout command a very high price. An illegal catch is far too easily disposed of.

Of course, as an astute reader will have realized, the elementary nature detective work discussed in Chapter V is of considerable help to anyone trying to protect a fishery. Poachers cannot work without leaving signs of their activities and these are easily "read" by anybody who can use his eyes and knows what to look for.

Sand, gravel, mud and even stones show human footprints: lichen trodden off a rock shows up as clearly as a print in snow. It is extremely difficult for the human body to move through undergrowth without leaving a trail. Broken twigs and branches; trampled bracken; a "trod" through dew wet grass to a fish "hod" beneath trailing alder roots.

Equally glaring are patches of algae rubbed off stones on the bottom of a deep pool—where a diver wearing flippers and mask has groped. Clean stones lying among slime-covered rocks show where a salmon has been pelted, to move it into a snatchable position. Disturbed gravel or shingle with scattered fish scales shows the place where a net has been dragged ashore. Fresh tyre marks in the lane end.... All these are obvious to the man who knows his river. Often, the signs of a poacher's reconnaissance can be spotted and the river saved from harm.

I recommend every keen angler to acquire some practice at detective work. There are times when the ability to read tracks and signs may help to explain his failure to catch fish. Sport is not likely to be brisk if the pool has been netted the night before!

So much for the poachers. But what of the anglers? Are they blameless? Do some of them not contribute towards the general ruination of sea trout and salmon fishing? Indeed they do. This is an age of plenty, and more and more rods are flocking to already congested rivers. The behaviour of many of these so-called sportsmen is disgraceful.

It is an unhappy feature of much modern game fishing that an increasing number of fishermen regard their sport as something of a business speculation, relying on money accruing from the sale of their catch to offset fishing charges and accommodation—even to the extent of feeling disgruntled if they fail to show a profit. In a sport whose basic pleasure springs from the aesthetic rather than the material, this is a matter of regret. To these angling "fishmongers" a game fish represents little more than its current market value. Small wonder that the edges of "sportsmanship" have become blunted.

The pall of commercialism that has spread across game fishing has enveloped the creed stating that the end is all, success everything, and the Way to Success of no account. In other words: get the fish on the bank and who the hell cares how? It is a reflection of our present cynical, materialist society, that to speak of ethics is to invite a snigger. Be that as it may, a code of behaviour is urgently needed if both fish and honest fishermen are to be given a chance of survival.

There is an increasing number of anglers who, when the water is low, readily succumb to temptation and start foul-hooking. The fish caught by these snatch-and-run characters are negligible compared with the hauls of their professional brethren, but the damage to the fishing is considerable. Have you ever tried to catch sea trout or salmon after they have recently been stroke-hauled? Perhaps more often than you may suspect—and the reason for your failure to catch fish may have puzzled you at the time!

This "foul-hooking fever" becomes a form of compulsion that attacks some anglers and develops very quickly. Success acts on them like a drug. Soon, they abandon all pretence of fair fishing and concentrate exclusively on their snatch tackles. In a very short time they are in the semi-pro class.

To prevent all this there is, perhaps, one bailiff who may have to cover several rivers many miles apart. He has no enviable job. He suffers damage to his transport and property and runs the risk of severe physical injury. To smarten his wounds, the offenders when caught all too frequently escape with ridiculously small penalties. The next poaching expedition pays their fines—with interest!

Many anglers live in blissful ignorance of the crooks that form this fishing underworld. It is time their eyes were opened. If the visiting "ticket" angler arrives at the wrong time his chances are not bright. Sometimes it is a wonder he catches anything at all. Often he doesn't. And it is hardly surprising.

*   *   *

A method of fishing we have not yet considered in detail is fly/maggot. This entails mainly the use of sunk line and forms part of our repertoire during the second-half—so, a note in advance will not be out of place.

But first, a word or two concerning bait. It is often questioned whether the use of maggots—or any other form of bait—in the killing of sea trout is "sporting".

Over the years I have discovered that most people who condemn bait-fishing have no idea what they are talking about, since they have never tried it and therefore have no practical experience of the skills involved. Nevertheless, an analysis of angling "sportsmanship" is overdue, and we may as well deal with certain aspects of it now.

When conditions are suitable, fly/maggot can be a killing combination. This in itself does not make it unsporting. The killing of fish is a matter of individual conscience, which every fisherman must rationalize to his own satisfaction. A dead fish remains a dead fish, and it is absurd to suppose it is any more unsporting to kill that fish on a fly that has a maggot attached than on a fly alone—whether wet or dry—or on a worm, or a dock grub, or a shrimp, or a sand-eel, or a spinner, or any other legitimate lure. *Clearly, all legal methods of angling are equally sporting. The merit of any particular method at any particular moment depends entirely on the behaviour of the angler concerned.*

What makes any form of fishing—fly fishing included—unsporting, is the manner in which it is fished. It is not the method that is either sporting or unsporting, it is the man.

Ledgering for sea trout and salmon on some association waters is to be deplored simply because it becomes a selfish method in the hands of so many fishermen: fishermen who squat in one place for hours on end and deny the use of that water to anyone whose lure is not connected to a lump of lead.

And as many of us have discovered when waiting to fish a pool, there are plenty of fly fishermen who behave just as badly.

I have no objection to fishing bait. On the contrary, as later chapters indicate, there are several bait-fishing methods that demand great concentration and skill. My criticism of ledgering in certain circumstances applies to *any* form of fishing—whether with bait, spinner or fly—that is selfish, or unsuitable for the conditions in which it is being fished.

There is an unfortunate type of angler who boasts of fishing very fine "to give the fish a chance". He is a fool. There is nothing in the least sporting in giving a fish the chance to escape with a hook in its gullet. A fish will decline tackle that is too coarse and strong. It will break and tow away tackle that is too fine. The *sporting* angler, knowing he must use something in between, chooses the strongest tackle that will enable him to hook *and land* the species he is fishing for in the conditions existing at the time.

This seems an appropriate place to enlarge on the American system of assessing the merit of a catch (mentioned on p. 99). Briefly, this system encourages an angler to fish for big fish with light tackle: the heavier the fish, the lighter the line, the greater the merit. Thus, to catch a large fish on, say, 20 lb. line is adjudged a more praiseworthy feat than to catch a fish of the same size and species on a line of 40 lb. And so on, up and down the scale according to the species. From trout to billfish.

It is an indication of how sick some notions of modern sportsmanship have become when such an insensitive approach to the killing of wildlife for pleasure should be tolerated—let alone encouraged—by a supposedly civilized society. The American "sportsman" is not noted for his enlightened outlook. But British anglers need not feel smug on this account. It may seem incredible, it is nevertheless true, that an attempt is being made to introduce this iniquitous system into Britain. The stupidity of such an idea is cause for alarm on the part of all responsible anglers. It can only bring angling into disrepute. A growing number of people in Britain are opposed to field sports; to the killing of wildlife for pleasure, fish included. That they have not yet thought out a convincing argument against angling is no reason to suppose that they are not doing their best to conjure one up. To provide them with a case so obvious as the American System is an act of the greatest folly.

Any reader who thinks me guilty of exaggeration may care to absorb the following extract from a news item published in *The Daily Telegraph* for 20th April, 1974:

"*Angling may teach children violence, says sociologist.*

"Teaching children how to fish might be conditioning them to become violent towards each other [a] lecturer in sociology . . . claimed yesterday. He is urging that a national survey be made of the effect of fishing on young minds.

"[He] believes that by learning to fish children are being taught to inflict cruel injuries. And this, he claims, could make them insensitive to violently harming people . . .

"[He] made his objections after the renewal of a licence for an angling club. Now he is asking the Liberal party to begin a survey.

"Yesterday he said: 'I am very concerned that once children become insensitive to harming fish they could feel the same towards human beings. I know that fishing is a sport enjoyed by millions, but I am very worried that people can get pleasure from something which involves hurting harmless creatures.

"'The moral and mental consequences on children of this gruesome sport need to be studied.' he added." !

* * *

The author (in 1957) with a 13½ lb. sea trout. Curiously, this fish ran itself aground almost immediately after being hooked and was landed in under a minute.

In 1973. Sea trout, $11\frac{1}{2}$ lb. This fish made the most determined fight to avoid capture, taking the better part of half an hour to land. It is the same fish as shown on p. 25. Note the scar on the flank. Almost every fish has some sort of distinguishing mark by which it can be recognized (see also, p. 246).

254

The use of bait is often denigrated because, it is claimed, it is too deadly. From this, tedious arguments have been adduced by so-called "purists" to illustrate the superior "sportsmanship" of fly fishing. These arguments are ridiculous because they are founded on a false premise. The right fly, properly fished, is often the most killing lure of all. If anyone objects to the use of a lure because it is too deadly, then obviously the first he should abandon is the fly!

Anglers go fishing to enjoy themselves, and each has his own favourite method or methods. Provided he uses tackle of suitable strength and does not interfere with anyone else's sport, he is no less a sportsman when fishing bait than he is when fishing fly. I prefer the use of the fly rod to, say, the ledger rod—because it gives me more pleasure, not because I consider it more sporting.

So-called "fly" fishing for salmon and sea trout cannot be compared to brown trout fly-fishing. To start with a generalization: the salmon or sea trout "fly", whatever its construction, is not really a fly at all. It is a lure. It is very seldom intended to simulate a natural insect, and its use is nothing for anyone to get toffee-nosed about.

The difference between fishing for migratory fish and for what are known as "coarse" fish—with which, in this context, I classify the brown trout—is that the latter *feed* and the former *do not*. This, to me, is the fundamental distinction between "game" fishing and "coarse" fishing. Admittedly, there are occasions when sea trout and, more rarely, salmon, seem to search for food; but (apart from the young "first-year" fish mentioned earlier in the book) these are the exceptions. For all intents and purposes, when fishing for sea trout and salmon we are trying to entice fish that are not hungry; fish which, carrying their rations on their backs so to speak, have no need of food. Whereas, at some time or another, at fairly regular intervals, all other freshwater species must eat.

A migratory fish, I contend, accepts bait for the same reason that it accepts anything else—because it is enticed. But the notion that bait is necessarily more deadly than any other form of lure—simply because it is bait—is a fallacy.

If this is so, the novice may reasonably ask, why is bait so popular? The answer is simple. With certain exceptions, to be discussed in a later chapter, bait-casting owing to the invention of the fixed-spool reel has become much easier than fishing a fly. To attain a reasonable standard of fly casting is not difficult—but *to fish the fly correctly* is entirely another matter. And it is, in my opinion, largely because of this that, on some rivers, bait proves much more successful than fly: the water conditions prevailing make correct fly presentation extremely difficult.

How deadly is the maggot? Like the worm, skilfully presented it will kill fish by day in low water when fly is almost useless. By night the success of fly/maggot is subject to great fluctuation. As the result of much experiment on almost every fishable night the seasons through for many years, I would say that the fisherman who relies for his success on festooning his fly with maggots is doomed to many disappointments. The usefulness of this method, like any other, depends on conditions, and often these are unsuitable. Nevertheless there are nights—usually chilly and when the water is very low later on in the season—when fly by itself is refused but fly/maggot accepted. And even when, curiously enough, the maggot alone is refused, although fished in a similar manner. And the only explanation I can offer is that the use of maggot in these conditions of low water and temperature permits the fly to fish at a slow speed while still retaining an appearance of being alive. Any loss of balance due to the fly's loss of speed being off-set by its tail of wriggling maggots. The chief success of the fly/maggot combination lies more with stale rather than fresh fish, and it is not impossible that the reasons for this are those suggested in an earlier chapter.

These are academic points, however; what concerns us at the moment is that on certain nights little interest is shown in any form of lure other than fly with maggot on the end, and it is sensible to be prepared for these occasions.

Fly/maggot is fished deep and slow. If the water is high and there is much current the addition of maggot to the fly is unlikely to be of any great advantage. Maggots require careful casting. They will stand a surprising amount of ill treatment, but they won't live long if jerked about in the air. Try to cultivate a soft, easy casting motion, making as few false casts as possible. It is impossible to fish fly/maggot properly with a sticky line: a smooth, well polished line which shoots freely through the rod rings is essential. The modern *Wet Cel* line, which seems to do all the work itself, is ideal.

The drill is to impale two or three maggots on the fly by hooking them through the tail—i.e. the blunt end. Let the fly sink, so that it drifts round very slowly in front of the fish a few inches from the bottom. The all-important angle at which you cast will depend on the position of the fish and the strength of current. When the water is very low, the current slack and the bottom clean, allow the fly to sink completely and lie on the bottom for a time. This gives the fish a chance to recover from any disturbance caused by casting in such low, still water. Then, after a suitable pause, begin slowly to work the fly in: *not* by raising the rod, which will draw the fly towards the surface, but by gently stripping line with the non-casting hand; keeping the rod point as low as possible— under water, if necessary. Provided the cast has been made correctly, fish are likely to take as the fly begins to move; and the first yard or so of recovery is the most important. This is noticeably so late on a cold night when fish are not disposed to move either quickly or far.

(The ledger angler who lets his bait lie for a short time and then gives it movement by inching it in across the bottom of a pool, will more than double the bag of the man who puts his rod in a forked stick and keeps his bait stationary.)

Correct presentation at night in conditions of dead low water requires skilful casting and an exact knowledge of where fish are lying. It is very helpful to have a clear picture of the river bottom in mind, so that the action of the fly is "seen" not only in relation to the fish but to the various rocks and snags. This exercise of the imagination, which plays a major part in successful night fishing, is made possible by concentration and careful daylight reconnaissance on rivers that are clear enough to permit it.

Readers who have made it as far as this will not be surprised to learn that the reaction of sea trout to fly/maggot varies considerably:

1. They will gulp fly and maggots straight down.

2. They will simply arrest the progress of the fly by nipping the maggots. (I have seen them at it in daylight.) It is done with extreme gentleness and without any pull whatever. The line just stops—so that to an unsuspecting angler it feels as though his hook has lodged behind a stone. Instinctively, he slackens line. Then, realizing his mistake, he gives it a jerk. Too late, the fish has long since let go. This behaviour is similar in effect to the uncanny way in which a sea trout will "stop" a Surface Lure (as described in Chapter III).

3. They will treat the maggots to a tiny tweak—releasing them at once, without even squashing them. The frustrated angler can feel it happening during cast after cast. It was to put an end to this that the Secret Weapon was designed (see Chapter II).

Fishing fly/maggot is delicate and exacting work. Try to sense every movement of the fly and the touch of a fish by "reading" the line with the wetted tips of forefinger and thumb of the non-casting hand.

Secret Weapon baited and ready for use. Maggots impaled at the blunt end on top hook only.

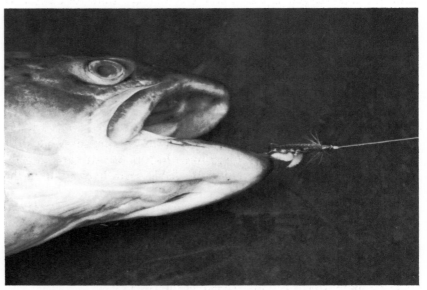

Sea trout hooked by treble right in the front of the mouth. When fish are "taking short" they are frequently hooked like this. Only a tweak would have been felt if this fish had taken maggot fished on a one-hook fly.

258

When fishing maggot on a large fly (Medicine) or on the Secret Weapon, tighten immediately a fish is felt. With the small, single-hooked Maggot-Fly, do nothing. Give the fish time to gulp. Tighten only when he moves away and you feel the strain come on the line. This fish will have the hook in his throat and a fish so hooked is never lost, unless you are clumsy enough to let him break you—in which case you should hang your head in shame.

Apart from the disturbance caused and the loss of a good "taking" fish, to leave a fish swimming with a hook stuck in him is surely unfortunate. Briefly, it is thought that injury to the gills, or to the skin along the medial—or lateral—line will cause pain, and that elsewhere on the fish it will not; and that it is unlikely a fish suffers pain from being hooked. This is probably true; but what we *think* is, I submit, of small importance. From our point of view as sportsmen the issue is clear: until we can establish beyond doubt that a fish with a hook lodged in eye, tongue or throat, and with a leader trailing behind, suffers no discomfort, we should assume that he does and make every effort to avoid being broken.

Further to this: a fish should be knocked on the head as soon as he is landed. Excess oxygen *may* stun him, but we don't know for certain, so don't let him flop about on the ground—despatch him at once.

Don't, unless it is unavoidable, handle any small fish you wish to return alive. If possible, take hold of the hook by the shank and lightly shake the fish off into the water. If it is necessary to take hold of the fish, first cool your hand by wetting it. The active squirming of parr when grasped preparatory to their unhooking and release is probably due to the searing touch of a dry hand along the sensory nerves of the lateral line. It is fallacious to suppose that every little fish which, on his return, swims quickly away, is necessarily saved. One danger of handling fish is the disturbance of protective slime which all fish are covered with. Removal of this slime may promote the fish's death by permitting the growth of fungus and disease.

The unfortunate killing of parr and small trout that have swallowed the hook provides a strong argument against the use of maggots on a small fly. These little fish are strangely active on certain evenings, and when such a night of activity is encountered the use of fly/maggot should be discontinued, or the small fly exchanged for a large one. Parr are more likely to be lip-hooked on the large fly.

Note. I am unable to offer any opinion regarding the sensations experienced by a maggot when impaled on a hook. That I sometimes use maggots myself exposes my own moral fallibility.

Some bait fishermen colour their maggots red, green, orange and so on, in the belief that this makes them more attractive. It may—although my own experience has produced nothing to support this. To my way of thinking, the virgin maggot in its natural podgy paleness is the best. Dye them all the colours of the rainbow, however, if it gives you confidence; for confidence is of far greater importance than colour, whether of maggot or fly.

For convenience when fishing, carry the night's ration in a small tin which has a hinged lid. A throat pastille tin is ideal.

Maggots are sometimes difficult to obtain just when they are most needed, so—if you are lucky not to live in a built-up area—you may as well breed your own. A simple but effective maggot-pit can be made at the bottom of the garden. I don't pretend any expert knowledge on this subject, but here for your consideration is a procedure which, from practical experience, I can recommend.

Dig a hole about two feet square and eighteen inches deep. Put some suitable food in it—fish heads are good—and cover with a grid that is strong enough to withstand the depredations of scavenging cats and dogs. Shortly, a supply of maggots will materialize. When the maggots are nice and fat, lift the fish heads up with a pair of fire tongs and shake them over a bowl. Store the maggots in a wooden box full of bran or sawdust, so that when you come to use them they will be clean. Replenish the pit with fish heads when necessary. This method should provide a steady supply throughout the summer. Needless to say, it will not commend itself to everyone!

The life of a maggot can be extended by temperature control. For several weeks, maggots can be prevented from turning into chrysalids if kept at a low temperature—a few degrees (F.) above freezing point. An ordinary domestic refrigerator is ideal for this purpose.

If maggots are allowed to get too dry they shrink in size and their skins become tough. This toughness of the skin makes them more likely to burst when impaled on a hook. To prevent this, add three tablespoonfuls of water to each pint of the sawdust mixture the maggots are kept in.

A highly skilled fisherman of my acquaintance has a theory that sea trout prefer smelly maggots to clean maggots. This will not be appreciated at home when the tin comes open in your pocket. But if you fancy the idea, don't bother about the bran. Leave your maggots to do nicely thank you in their little bed of rotten fish until shortly before use.

On those (I hope very rare) occasions when the Medicine and other patterns of fly, Surface Lure, Sunk Lure, fly/maggot and all else has failed, try as a last resort a thin, inch-long sliver of sea trout belly on the bend of the hook. Fish it on a Medicine; deep, but rather faster than Sunk Lure or fly/maggot. Again, this method of "fly-fishing" will not be received with acclaim by all members of the fraternity. Illogical though they may be, they are entitled to their opinions. I can assure others that there are times when this gimmick can be surprisingly effective.

And now let us look on the other side of the angling "balance sheet": misfortune.

It is frustrating when, having fished with care and concentration through the lonely hours, often persisting in the face of unpromising conditions, we miss the chance of hooking a fish—or lose one we have hooked—through some elementary mistake. These failures are sometimes due to the fish; sometimes to a faulty fishing technique, and some of the problems involved have already been considered. It may be helpful, however, during this period of half-time rest, briefly to summarize the reasons for failure before fishing out the second-half, which we shall be doing in the next chapter.

First of all, there is the sea trout that is never hooked and whose presence is rarely suspected: the fish that moves to a fly but refuses it. The reason for this refusal is either because the fly is swimming incorrectly, or fishing at the wrong speed or depth, or simply because it is a poor fly.

Then there is the fish that pulls a fly without being hooked. This nibbling at a fly seems to be governed by air and water temperatures and by impending weather conditions. A fish behaving in this manner may sometimes be hooked by employing one of the following stratagems:

(a) Anticipating the strike, as described in Chapter VII.
(b) Fishing maggot on the Secret Weapon.
(c) Fishing a small, nymph-like fly tied on a size 12 or 14 double.

Thirdly, there is the fish that is lost either because it breaks a part of the angler's tackle, or because it comes off the hook while being played. The latter, which is always irritating, may be due to the fish's soft mouth; faulty striking; bad handling, or pure chance.

Every fisherman is destined to lose a percentage of the fish he hooks, and the wise man faces this loss philosophically in advance: he knows it will happen sooner or later and that it is senseless to let it result in more than a momentary irritation. I must admit at once, however, that on occasions the most rational among us are sorely tried.

Since the dawn of angling wild-eyed men have babbled of fish hooked and lost, their plaintive voices echo down the years and the anguish is understandable—at least, by those of us within the brotherhood. To hook a fish (after hours of fruitless flogging) only to feel the line go slack is one of life's sadder moments. The wretched angler, gazing at straightened hook or broken leader, is left with a feeling of regret that he hooked anything at all.

Of course, breakage is by no means the only cause of loss. All too often a fish just comes off: the hook simply loses its hold. This sometimes happens time after time in sequences so strange as to verge on the uncanny. In this respect some people seem to be more unfortunate than others. I suppose it all evens out in the end, but I have certainly known anglers who for no accountable reason seemed to have more than their share of misfortune. Most of us have experienced one of those inexplicable "runs"—when fish after fish is lost—and I am no exception. To those of my readers who account themselves unlucky the following anecdote may give some heart.

It was a night I recall with great clarity. Indeed, much of it is burned indelibly on the mind. My wife, Kathleen, was with me for part of the time—fortunately (in one sense), as you will understand, since what happened is almost unbelievable.

I started fishing at dusk. The river was alive with sea trout, all eager, it seemed, to seize the fly. With my second or third cast I hooked Number One.

It went splash, splash, splash down the pool—and came off.

I cursed, and cast again. Almost immediately I was into Number Two. I played it to the net, where it rolled over and departed.

Numbers Three, Four, Five, Six, Seven and Eight followed in fairly quick succession. About these fish I remember no details—except that they all came off.

But Number Nine is fixed. Kathleen had been counting, and I remember this fish well enough. It distinguished itself by running aground. While it was flopping about on the shingle the hook came free, I tried to grab the fish, but it slithered out of my hand, bounced back into the river and swam away.

At that point I nearly packed up.

Had I obeyed the impulse this episode would have taken its place beside a day of misery in Banffshire just after the war when, in a snow-storm, I pricked eleven salmon. But I reckoned those fish had had nine lives and that, surely, was enough.

Doggedly I wiped the sweat away, lengthened line and cast again into the shadows. At once there was a savage pull. My rod bent, and bent. . . . Then, bang, splash—and away went Number Ten.

I played Number Eleven very carefully. It seemed well hooked. I felt that if this one came off I would start to gibber.

It came off.

So did Number Twelve.

Number Thirteen was a heavy fish. It didn't even do me the honour of showing itself. It just swam steadily up the pool while I held my breath and the reel sang. Then the line went limp.

I am not normally a superstitious man. But by now everything had become unreal. My senses were beginning to tremble. I felt slightly unhinged. An old story came to mind—of trawlermen who (in addition to rabbits) forbade the mention of women while the net was down for fear of a curse upon their catch.

Kathleen's figure was ghostlike in the dusk. The sweat prickled on my neck. Here I was, actually fishing. . . . Then, suddenly, I was into Number Fourteen.

It followed the others.

I staggered up the bank.

"Look", I said to Kathleen. "Leave me alone. There's a dear. Go home and go to bed."

She went home.

I sat on the bank for about an hour and smoked cigarettes, and looked at the stars and the light of the cottage window winking from the distant fell. Then, not for the first time, I changed my fly, tested the hook and started again.

The sea trout proved just as eager. But now, incredibly, every fish I hooked stayed on.

I went home with sixteen.

Altogether, I think you will agree, a most remarkable night. Thirty offers. Thirty fish hooked. The first fourteen all lost. The following sixteen all landed. Riddle me that if you can.

For anyone interested in figures, my fishing diary informs me that these events took place some twenty years ago on the night of 6th August;

that the sixteen fish weighed just under 50 lb.; the smallest $1\frac{3}{4}$ lb., the largest $5\frac{1}{4}$ lb.

There is a moral in all this. It shows that persistence is sometimes rewarded; that it pays to fish on for sea trout well after midnight; that in angling almost anything can happen; that no matter what you do and no matter what armament you use, single-hooks, doubles, trebles (and I had tried them all during that mind-shaking "first-half") some fish stay with you and some don't.

One cynic to whom I told the story suggested the obvious moral: that only a fool takes his wife fishing. But I think we might forget this one.

*   *   *

Frequently, more frequently than some of us care to admit, our misfortune stems not from chance but our own ham-handedness or lack of attention to detail. Here, for your consideration, are twenty ways of losing a fish. They are compiled from my own experience, and for each of them the angler is responsible.

1. *Unsound tackle*

To be broken is a disaster common to all fishing wherever a line is thrown. There can be few fishermen who have not, often enough, suffered this indignity, and seldom does it result from anything other than sheer carelessness. Tackle failure is usually the cause.

The question is sometimes asked: "What is the secret of successful fishing?"

There is no *secret* of successful fishing. What "secret" there is has been told often enough. It is, of course: *attention to detail*. In no aspect of angling is this so important as choice and care of tackle.

Unsound tackle is clearly the fisherman's fault. Every item should be overhauled and tested before fishing starts. Leaders get damaged by rocks or a fish's teeth and should be inspected at regular intervals. So should rod-rings and their whippings; reel fastenings; reel handles; landing nets and, indeed, every other piece of equipment that is used to hook and land a fish. Most important of all, it should be remembered that to buy cheap fishing tackle and to hoard nylon is nearly always false economy.

2. *Hook failure*

A lot of fish are lost because a hook straightens out. Most modern hooks are suspect, trebles in particular. Every hook should be tested before use.

264

A broken hook is due either to poor casting or to poor quality metal. In both cases the angler is at fault; in the former for clumsiness; in the latter for not testing the hook.

Nothing is more disheartening and frustrating than to feel the line go slack immediately after the strong, decided pull of a heavy fish, only to discover that we have been fishing with a barbless hook! It can happen easily enough, especially in the windy darkness among rocks or shingle. One faulty cast may rob the hook of point and barb, so that a fish seizes it with impunity. Only correct casting and frequent inspection of the hook will prevent loss of fish through this all-too-common cause.

3. *Failure to re-tie hook or fly*
Impatience is usually to blame for this. A hook should always be re-tied after a big fish has been landed (or the leader pulled free from tree branches or bushes). If you are in any doubt whatever, don't hesitate to fit a new leader.

4. *Failure to re-wind line*
Always strip the line off the reel and re-wind it tightly and evenly after a fish has been played. If, while the fish was played, one coil of line has bitten down among loose coils, the reel will jam when the next fish runs. I have known some very big fish lost because of this.

5. *Fishing too fine*
This is both pointless and unsporting. To be broken by a fish is a disgrace.

On a bright, windless day, in conditions of low water, only the very finest tackle has any chance of moving a sea trout. The fly-fisherman is wise to leave such water until dusk when, besides enjoying more opportunities of sport, he can fish with tackle of reasonable strength.

6. *Wind knots*
An overhand knot in a nylon leader can reduce its strength by as much as 40 or 50 per cent. Wind or no wind this miserable little knot (often the result of faulty casting) appears in a leader as though by magic. When fishing in the darkness it is a simple matter to test for these rogue knots (or kinks or roughness) by running the fingers down the leader. Unless a knot is newly formed and has not been pulled tight, don't bother to undo it. Scrap the leader, or that particular section of it, and put on another. It is the height of foolishness to risk the loss of a good fish for the sake of a few pennyworth of nylon.

7. *Reel jamming*

This is due either to bad maintenance or lack of attention while you are fishing. To put the butt of the rod down into dry earth or sand may result in the reel becoming clogged. An extension to the rod butt helps to avoid this, even so it is a good habit (especially in the darkness) to place the butt of the rod on top of your foot.

When a fish is being played it is easy for the reel handle to catch against loose clothing. If this occurs while a fish is running, disaster is almost certain. A rod butt extension helps to avoid this. But above all, be alive to the possibility of it happening.

As already mentioned, another reason for a reel jamming is when tight coils of line bite down on loose coils underneath. *A line should always be stripped off and re-wound before fishing starts, and after a big fish has been played.*

8. *Leader knot jamming*

If, when a fish is being landed, the line is wound in too far, so that the join of leader and line jams in a rod ring, a sudden rush may enable the fish to break free. The use of a Needle Knot avoids this. If a Figure-of-Eight knot is used, make sure that the leader is not too long for the rod. For most night fishing, 7 or 8 feet is ample. Another method of joining line and leader is to whip a loop in the end of the line and join loop to loop. In addition to being a more convenient join, the loop will slip through the rod rings more easily than a Figure-of-Eight knot. (For instructions on tying these knots and loops see Chapter IV.)

9. *Striking too hard*

Bad fishing. The most likely moment for a break is just as the fish is hooked. Striking consists of *tightening* on a fish—not giving him a great jerk, like a sea angler hooking cod.

10. *Holding a fish too hard*

Apart from faulty striking this is the quickest and most certain way of getting broken. It is a fault common among novices, who when they hook a fish cannot bear to let him get further away from them. The only time a fish should be "held" is when line or backing is almost exhausted, or when the fish is running towards an obvious snag: perhaps the middle arch of a bridge. But the fault often lies with the fisherman for allowing the fish to get into a position from which such a disastrous run is likely. In many cases, prior action such as "walking" the fish will prevent it. No fish should ever take us by surprise. All eventualities should be considered *before* we start fishing. The successful landing of sea trout, or salmon, or pike, or any fish that swims, depends on careful thought before a line is put in the water.

11. *Trying to land a fish too soon*

Very common fault. The fisherman has shortened line and, with net extended, hauls the fish towards him. The fish responds and obligingly comes almost within reach. Then, frightened by the sight of net or fisherman, he turns and dashes off in alarm. The reel fails to react quickly enough, or a handle gets hooked up, or the line knot jams in a rod ring— and the leader snaps. *Wait until the fish has turned on its side*

Even so, a fish is not *scooped* out but *lifted* out. When a fish is almost ready to land, sink the net to the bottom so that it cannot be seen. Then, when the fish is on his side, *and not before*, draw him firmly in and raise the net to encircle him.

267

12. *Touching a nylon leader with a cigarette end*
This somewhat bizarre accident is hardly likely to happen to a non-smoker. I am ashamed to say it occurred once when I was bending down to land an exceptionally large salmon . . . !

13. *Leader nipped in joint of landing net*
A miserable business which happens from time to time in the darkness, when a folding net is snapped into position. Having uneasy doubts about all folding gadgetry—whether undercarriages, nets or chairs—I prefer a solid outfit as described in Chapter IV.

14. *Hole in landing net*
Very irritating, but sheer carelessness. Having, as the angler thinks, been safely netted, the fish suddenly sets off with renewed vigour—leaving the angler to play him through the hole. This is very comical to watch, but not amusing to the participant. It usually results in the loss of the fish; sometimes a broken rod tip.

15. *Fish knocked off the hook*
This might be called the "willing helper syndrome". Invariably, the bystander, anxious to help in landing a fish, goes into action too soon. Except in emergency, it is advisable for an angler to land his own fish. Then if it gets knocked off the hook by the landing net he has only himself to blame.

16. *Line/backing splice draws*
No fly fisherman should ever allow anyone else to splice his fly line and backing for him. If the splice draws he loses not only the fish (usually a big one) but the line as well. If he does the job himself, and tests it thoroughly, it will not draw. (Where possible, use a Needle Knot.)

17. *Snags*
A frequent cause of disaster. Some rivers have clean banks and are comparatively free from obstructions, others contain snags of every description: jagged reefs, weed beds, tree roots, stumps, coils of wire, sunken logs and rows of ancient posts that once acted as bank supports. These posts form desperate obstacles when a fish is being played, for in many cases the bank, owing to erosion, has receded and left them submerged and well out into the stream. But the loss of many fish can be avoided by careful examination of the river beforehand. If the position

of a snag is known, prompt action may prevent a fish from reaching it.

The time to get on terms with a fish is the moment he is hooked. To wait until he has run halfway down a pool or gone to ground in a weed bed, before they do something constructive, is the fault of many anglers on hooking a fish. A surprising number of people seem to be ignorant of how a fish should be "walked", or even that a fish *can* be "walked". (For details of this, see p. 236.)

Posts that once acted as bank supports, exposed by erosion. Here the river is at dead summer low, the posts can be seen and their position noted. In spate water they are invisible, and have cost unwary anglers many a fish.

From observation of disturbed fish, some idea can be formed of how they will react when hooked. For the benefit of the beginner, I should mention that a hooked fish rushing towards a snag doesn't do so with the intention of draping the line round it. The fish runs underneath or behind the snag in order to gain protection from danger—just as he will at any time during the day when frightened, whether hooked or not. The subsequent cutting of the line or leader is incidental.

It is significant that hooked fish frequently fail to take advantage of some very obvious means of freeing themselves from the line; they will swim within inches of a sunken post or stump but make no effort to use it. And it would be remarkable if they acted otherwise, for the snags in question are not those to which the fish automatically run to seek shelter. On the other hand, to a fish lying beside a weed bed the weed represents his natural and readily available place of concealment, and the moment he is hooked he will probably head straight in that direction. If this is suspected, steps can be taken to prevent it, and one way of doing so— as I have already suggested—is to start "walking" the fish immediately he takes the fly.

All this, however, refers mostly to fishing in daylight. A fish is far more likely to snag the line during daytime than at night. Once the light has gone, a frightened fish is less inclined to run for cover, and places into which hooked fish are certain to rush in daylight are often ignored in the darkness. An example of this is a pool, well-known to me, in which sea trout when hooked by day invariably make for a section of undercut bank shored up by stakes. Once a fish gets underneath among the maze of posts he is as good as lost. But only rarely does a fish run underneath at night.

This is not to imply that the danger of being snagged at night can be ignored. Far from it. There are plenty of obstructions in most rivers that a fish can take the line round—by accident, if not design. The frequency with which it happens depends on the number of these snags and on our knowledge of the water.

But there are snags other than those underwater. Overhead branches that catch the rod top while a fish is being played have been the cause of many a disaster. It can happen very easily when a bushy run is being fished at night.

Another snag, oddly enough, can be the angler's own landing net— which at times defeats its purpose. This happens when a fish is being landed on a multi-hook tackle: fly leader with one or more droppers; Stewart or Pennell worm tackles; spinning flight; quill minnow with flying trebles, etc. As the fish is drawn towards the net one of the upper hooks attaches itself to a mesh, and the fish—now held tantalizingly just outside the net's rim—can be brought no further. At this point he usually stages a sudden recovery, wrenches the hook out and departs.

". . . a section of undercut bank shored up by stakes." Solid on top, with a platform of stones, but hollow underneath—a place of concealment for many sea trout and salmon.

271

Snags are a perpetual threat in every river. They can appear after any spell of heavy rain. The tree stump in the middle of the picture (brought down by a midsummer spate) cost Tom Rawling his heaviest-ever sea trout—probably one of the biggest ever hooked in my stretch of fishing. In Tom's words: "I knew the snag was there . . . I just felt that if the fish ran downstream it would stop before it got there. Or hoped it would . . . I still tremble a bit when I think about it. I walked the fish up into the pool above. [A hundred yards upstream from where it was hooked.] The line strummed and cut through the water like a U-boat superstructure. And then, when I gave the fish some stick it just ran and ran and ran . . . and in my innocence I thought: 'I have plenty of backing, it will stop by the bridge and come back.' The Sunk Lure came back, quite intact—after the fish had got off!"

18. *Fish jumps back again*

Not infrequently, a fish, having been hooked and landed successfully, succeeds in jumping back again—leaving the unfortunate fisherman with thoughts of suicide. This is a desperate business which, however unlikely it sounds, happens to most of us sooner or later. (I regret to say it has happened to me more than once.) Except when wading under a high bank where it is difficult to get ashore—in which case a fish should be knocked on the head while still in the net—never handle a fish until well away from the water. When beaching a fish, have the net close behind his tail and always get between him and the water before attempting to pick him up. Failure to observe these rules has cost me several fish.

19. *Waterside thieves*

A fish is not necessarily safe even when landed and killed. Rats, cats, mink, otters, badgers, pigs and humans have all been known to snitch dead fish from a river bank. Never leave your catch lying out on the grass; always hang it up out of reach, or put it away in a bag.

This simple precept was not fully appreciated by my old friend "Briggy" Wilson, until the day he lost a 4 lb. sea trout and half a 7 lb. salmon in a droll encounter with a herd of hungry swine. Wading, and unable to save his sea trout, he got ashore just in time to seize the tail end of his rapidly disappearing salmon. The engagement was brief but dramatic; the combatants parting with honours even.

20. *Threats domestic*

Finally: even when a fish has reached the house it is not entirely free from danger. Many years ago, an Irish friend of mine—a magnificent fisherman—caught a record trout. Everyone to whom he proudly showed the monster agreed it should be sent at once to Limerick to be stuffed. Alas, a sense of urgency dwindled as the celebration of its capture grew, and on his eventual home-coming he "absent-mindedly" left his great fish on the kitchen floor.

He awakened the following afternoon with a feeling of having forgotten something. Then memory hit him like a thunderflash and moaning, he dashed downstairs. Too late—the cat had. . . . But you have already guessed the terrible ending.

A moon that wades through a sea of clouds need
not disturb the angler very much, but one which
converts night into day is not loved by the keen
fisher who desires some sport with sea trout. In
these circumstances he must exercise the greatest
care, study his every movement, approach the
water quietly and always keep himself concealed
from the trout, use the finest tackle, and throw the
lightest of lines; in short, he must stalk his fish,
and in the end his reward, if any, will not be great.
It will, however, be highly creditable. A single
capture is a triumph; more than that constitutes a
glorious night's sport.

R. C. Bridgett, *Sea Trout Fishing* (1929)

X
Night Fly Fishing Tactics

PART THREE: THE "SECOND-HALF"

On those evenings when a run of fish takes place at dusk, the second-half may be approached with sanguine expectation. Indeed, it may well get off to a dramatic start. After a quick cruise round, some of the sea trout that have recently entered a pool may lie for a time in the extreme tip of the tail, often in little more than a foot or two of water, before joining the shoals of fish already in residence. When in this position they will take the fly savagely; so that, if fish have been seen or heard moving up, it is well worth trying the pool tails first.

Of course, not all sea trout hooked in the shallows of a pool tail are fresh run. Some may be stale fish that have dropped back from deeper water. But if, earlier in the evening, sea trout have been splashing up into a pool, there is a good chance that some will be lying far back. If the pool is not too far from tidal water, the clean appearance of these fish (when caught) together with the presence of sea lice, will give evidence of their freshness. It is almost certain that no run will take place if the evening is cold or the barometer falling: conditions that invariably provide difficult fishing. If sea trout are to be caught in these circumstances, it will be mainly with Sunk Lure; occasionally, Surface Lure.

So far, the evening in question has been warm and floating line tactics have been used. With fresh run fish in the pools and the water in good condition success should have been comparatively easy. Now, however, the night has turned colder and in consequence the fish are less likely to respond so readily. To tempt them, the fly must be put in front of their noses. This means that with the exception of Surface Lure and the chance of a floating line at dawn, it will be sunk line fishing from now on.

The second rod (with sinking line) is set up ready—indeed, it has already been in action—and the rod with floating line is made operational simply by exchanging the fly for a Surface Lure.

It is by no means always necessary to wait until the second-half before trying surface fishing. As described in Chapter III, the success of this method depends on the sky and there are times when it can be used earlier, during the first-half. Should there be a dark, cloudy sunset, a good plan is to change to Surface Lure—and at least give it a try— immediately after fishing a pool down with fly; that is, as soon as dusk has deepened into night. But without the assistance of heavy cloud, nights early in the season are seldom dark enough until after midnight— although the lure will sometimes take fish on water shadowed by high banks or overhanging trees.

On a warm night in late June or early July watch for any sign of cloud forming and be prepared to start fishing Surface Lure as soon as the sky darkens. At this time of year, the light may be suitable for, perhaps, only half-an-hour or so during the night. If the chance is missed there will be no other. That missed chance may deprive you of a big fish.

On moonlit nights the order in which your water should be fished is very important. This order will depend on the time of moonrise and your position in relation to the moon. Sea trout fishing can be quite good in moonlight, but not with the moon at your back or shining straight down a pool.

Bright moonlight, from whatever direction, is less propitious than a clouded sky. This is due not so much to the amount of light but to the air temperature. A clear sky usually means a colder night. But if the night remains warm, sea trout will take well no matter how bright and clear the sky—*provided the moon is in front of the rod*, preferably hidden or partially hidden by trees, and at right angles to or behind the fish. It is fly or Sunk Lure that should be used in these conditions, for although sea trout sometimes splash at the Surface Lure in moonlight, they seldom take it.

Of all adverse conditions, a moon behind the rod gives least chance of catching sea trout; so make sure that any water fishable only from an easterly or south-easterly direction is fished first—*before* moonrise. Water that can be fished from a westerly or northerly bank can be left undisturbed until some time after the moon has risen.

A very simple and straightforward example of this is shown in the drawing on the next page.

It represents a beat with three holding pools: A, B, and C.

In fish-holding capacity their order of merit is: C, B, A.

They may be fished from the right bank only.

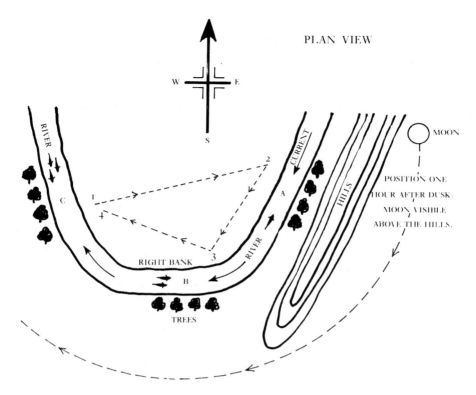

The moon is due to appear above the eastern hills about an hour after dusk. In what order should you fish these pools?

For a long time after the moon appears, C (your best pool) will be out of action. To start with, the moon will be behind the rod; later, it will be shining straight down the pool. So—fish this water first, *before moonrise.*

After the moon has risen, fish pool A. This you *must* do. A is in shadow from trees and the moon is in front of you, whereas the moon is shining straight down B, your next best pool.

When the moon has moved round to the south, pool B is in shadow and, again, the moon is in front of the rod. You can now fish your second-best piece of water without fear of disturbing it.

Later, when the moon has reached the south-west, you can return to pool C—which by now will be in shadow.

Therefore, to give yourself the best chance of catching sea trout, the order of fishing should be:

1. Pool C. (Best pool).   2. Pool A. (Third-best pool).
3. Pool B. (Second-best pool).   4. Pool C. (Best pool).

When the moon is shining downstream from behind the angler's shoulder, flickering shadows of angler and rod can stretch the length of a pool. Fish will be frightened long before they have a chance of seeing the fly.

278

On our imaginary evening, however, we will assume there is no moon and that the night has not yet been sufficiently dark for Surface Lure to be used. So that, in the absence of cloud, you will start fishing the second-half with sunk line.

Successful sunk line fishing is deliberate and unhurried. The technique is—deep and slow. Any undue haste; any attempt to cover the water quickly is to make failure certain. The senses of a naturally impatient fisherman will need the stimulus of confidence: a knowledge of where fish are lying: faith in his fly; belief in his technique. It is the antithesis of floating-line fishing. No putting the fly here-and-there, seeking fish, as you do when fishing a short line Round-the-Clock in a pool tail, or when searching under the bushes in the dark, dancing ripples of a "run". Cast the fly only where you know, or have reason to think fish are lying. Each cast is a long, slow, separate adventure, fished patiently out with absolute concentration: the rod unmoving, the line a slender, probing antenna; the fly slowly gliding over the stones in front of those sleek, silver fish that hang hardly moving in the deeps.

Give the line every encouragement to sink. Minimize any effect of wind by keeping the rod point low, almost touching the surface. If the line will not sink sufficiently, or the wind is strong, hold the rod point beneath the surface; push it down as deep as you like.

Fish with tense anticipation; the line held in sensitive fingers, both wrists flexed ready to tighten at a touch. Once the fly has sunk sufficiently it is the first yard or two of the cast that is most likely to move a fish: during the initial draw of the fly, or the early moments of its unhurried swing.

The "take" is extremely gentle. A fish will simply close his mouth on the fly as it floats past—and almost immediately, with as little fuss, let it go again. A moment's delay in the strike and your chance has gone. The odd fish may be missed through striking too soon; but, in these conditions, not many. Never strike from the reel, or with the line trapped against the rod. Hold the line with thumb and forefinger of the non-casting hand (as illustrated on p. 83). Raise the rod point and tighten line simultaneously. This applies to all sunk line fishing, except when using maggot on a *small* fly. Then, take no action at all: the fish will do all that is necessary to hook himself, so let him get on with it. Not so with Sunk Lure.

Sometimes, without even so much as a tweak, the fly will suddenly stop. A moment later you *may* feel the rod bend as a sea trout turns away with the fly, and realize that the hook has found a fish and not a

279

rock. More probably you will feel nothing of the sort. Few fish turn away with the fly in these conditions. To hook those that don't you must tighten the instant the fly stops.

Nothing, ABSOLUTELY NOTHING should be allowed to interfere with your concentration. Complete concentration is important whatever you may be fishing; with sunk line it is a vital necessity. The sudden hooting of an owl is distracting enough—conversation is out of the question. If you accept no other pieces of advice offered in this book, at least take heed of this: never, *never* fish with anyone other than a mute. To be encumbered with some talkative ass throughout the long watches of the night when you are trying to fish the sunk fly is an invitation to lunacy. You will invoke the aid of demons in the disposal of such an incubus long before the dawn.

> *Note.* After the first edition of this book a certain reviewer—who evidently knows as much about sea trout fishing as I know about horse racing— took it upon himself to treat the previous paragraph with derision. His approach to night fishing, seemingly, is a jolly prattle with his friends over a midnight barbecue. If yours is the same, so be it. But don't write me angry letters when you take home an empty bag.

*   *   *

A sunk line can be a brute to handle in the darkness and it is essential to use a rod capable of lifting it. Great care must be taken during the recovery. A sudden snatch is certain to result in the line springing from the water like an angry snake, striking the rod and falling in coils around your neck. If you have a long line out, first bring it to the surface by raising the rod and drawing in line with the other hand. Then, lower the rod point, taking in more slack as you do so. Having accomplished that, start again—this time carrying the recovery straight through into the back-cast. The slack line accumulated will, of course, be shot as the forward cast is completed. Use the full stretch of your arm during the back-stroke. This lengthens the rod and keeps the line as high in the air as possible. Holding the rod well up in this manner is often useful when a fish is being played; it helps to keep the line free from snags and prevents it from being drowned.

Most stretches of fishing contain a few "lies" which, although they may be fished easily from the bank with a comparatively short line, are impossible to cover correctly except by means of deep wading, and a very long line. There is a "lie" of this nature (Position 13), in the second pool at your disposal—a pool you may fish only from the left bank.

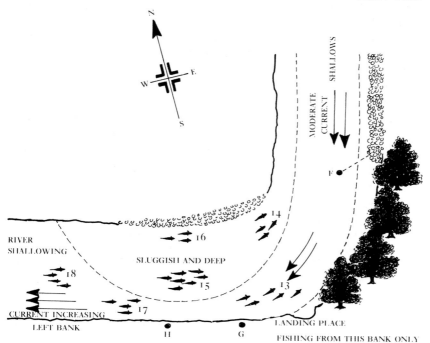

On the whole, it is not an easy piece of water. The current sets hard into the left bank at a point downstream of the four trees and then flows through the pool keeping very close to this bank until, on approaching the tail, it spreads out as the river begins to shallow.

The fish in Position 13 are easily covered from just below the trees, but the fly cannot be presented correctly from there, for the current will carry it straight in towards the bank. Clearly, the cast must be made from a place further upstream; and for the fly to work as required, this point can only be at F, the last wadeable position downstream of the shingle bank. Only when fished from here will the line be able to sink sufficiently, and the angle of cast be such that the fly can "hang" in front of, or (better) work slowly across the fish.

As a general rule of "wet" fly fishing, the shortest line to a fish is seldom the best. It is the angle of presentation that contributes most towards a fly's natural behaviour, for this angle controls its speed. The novice who keeps this in mind and stops to think before he casts will soon become a successful fly fisherman, irrespective of his casting ability. When his fly arrives in front of fish it will be moving in a manner likely to attract them. Although it may cover fewer fish, it will hook more than that of the man who casts more powerfully but with less thought. The line to be cast from F is a very long line indeed; but neither the novice nor anyone else has any need to waggle his rod about—he has merely to wade into position, strip off line and allow the fly to drift down with the current.

In most rivers there are "lies" similar to that in Position 13, which are difficult or impossible to cover correctly from the bank. The ability to wade deep is a great asset to every fly fisherman. (For notes on wading safety and technique, see pp. 132–140.)

Although scattered fish may be found anywhere in a pool, sea trout seldom spread themselves out evenly, or lie all together in one big shoal. In most pools of any size there is a main shoal, a number of subsidiary shoals, and the occasional big fish that usually lies by himself. For example, in the second pool under consideration, Number 15 represents the main shoal, and Numbers 13, 14, 16, 17 and 18 the subsidiaries. The order in which they are fished is of some importance.

The pool. Angler in Position H.

282

The fish in Position 18 present no difficulties. But to cast for them means fishing a long line from H, which is practically on top of the fish in Position 17. These fish are also easy to cover, but to do so successfully entails fishing a long line from G—which is, in turn, close to the fish in Position 13. And so, positions 13, 15 and 17 should be covered before attempts are made to cast further afield.

The fish in Position 13 have already been discussed. Those at 15 can be dealt with easily enough from G, but the rod should be held well out over the water to keep the line clear of the narrow stream of current which, at that point, is setting close to the left bank; also, the fly must be worked by hand.

The fish at 16 are not easily caught, while those at 14 are very difficult indeed. The latter can be reached from F, but belly in the line caused by the current will quickly drag the fly through the slack water before it has had time to sink, and unless there is sufficient ripple, a mend will defeat its own object. The best chance of hooking one of these fish is to cast a long line, upstream and just beyond them, from G. A tricky cast, for the fly must fall just inside the edge of the current—which is marked on the diagram by the dotted line—and brought very slowly across them on a slightly downstream path.

In the conditions prevailing, and using a sunk line, the pool is fished

The landing place. A fish has been manœuvred upstream and is being brought back with the current over the net. Note fishing shelter in background and compare with flood picture on p. 300.

283

SEA TROUT FISHING

as follows: 13 from F; 14, 15, 17, 16 from G; 18 from H; in that order.

Unless I have failed lamentably in my explanation of the principles of sunk fly fishing, the reason why a *long* line is cast for the sea trout in Positions 17 and 18 (which, as can be seen in the diagram, could be covered easily with a very short line), is surely obvious.

Landing a fish on the shingle bank behind Position F is a simple matter. It is not so easy to land fish when casting from G or H. The bank there is steep and, when the river is low, the long reach down to the surface makes a net awkward to use. More important, however, a fish played out in that part of the pool is likely to disturb many of the others. As suggested in Chapter VIII, it is advisable whenever possible to "walk" a fish away from a shoal and land it upstream. Here, over-hanging branches prevent access to the shingle bank; but just down-stream of the trees is a tiny bay where it is possible to get to the water's edge. In addition, there is a patch of slack water in front of this landing place into which a fish may be drawn and netted without difficulty. So, each hooked fish is taken upstream to the head of the pool and dealt with in this manner. True, playing fish from this position will disturb those at 13; but they have already been thoroughly covered when fishing was started from F.

If the glass is falling and a change of weather likely, sea trout may well start to play with the fly, "nipping" it with the front of the mouth and giving it little tugs and tweaks. The fish in Position 18 are in an ideal place for you to try trick striking—or anticipating the "take"—as described in Chapter VII. They are lying in a moderate, even current, and on a long line the sunk fly swings across them at a gentle pace. When a tweak is felt, concentrate on that fish and neither lengthen line nor move your position. Continue to cast so that the fly fishes the same piece of water at the same depth and speed.

If you fail to hook the fish, withdraw the line—not by winding up the reel, but by stripping in by hand—and (if you are using a fly and not a Sunk Lure) put a couple of maggots on the hook. If these are nipped, change at once to Secret Weapon and concentrate for a time on fly/maggot fishing (see pp. 60 and 256 for details of this technique).

*   *   *

At this point my reader may complain that many of the fishery examples in this book are taken from small rivers rather than big rivers. Quite true, they are. And the reason is that big rivers present fewer problems

284

than small rivers. The latter have a greater variation of swirl and eddy; more sudden changes of height and current; more "intimate" holding places, which are vastly more difficult to cover effectively at night than those in the broad sweep of a big river. The sea trout night fly fisherman who can catch fish consistently in fast, bushy, overhung, rocky little rivers, can catch them anywhere.

Many major salmon rivers have good runs of sea trout. For the angler who is not exhausted after a day's salmon fishing, there is every chance of sport with sea trout at night. Clad in body waders and armed with a suitable wading staff (see p. 118), he will encounter few problems when fishing these wider waters. In the long, broad tails of the big rivers, it is not so much *where* you fish, but *what* and *how*.

I have fished many of the big salmon rivers in Britain that hold sea trout. All the night fishing methods described in these chapters have served me well—and Sunk Lure, in the small hours, has often provided the bonus of a salmon. Indeed, for most of my night fishing in the strong, steady draw of a big pool tail, it is mainly in the Sunk Lure that I pin my faith. It seldom lets me down.

The repertoire of: Medicine; Sunk Lure; Surface Lure; Secret Weapon, and Small Double—plus any experimental flies and lures you care to try (and some lobworms) should provide sport on most fishable nights of the season.

No two rivers are the same and no two pools on any river. Each presents its own problems; each is a separate study in itself, but the basic principles of the methods used in fishing them do not alter. Technique is modified to suit a particular river, or any pool on that river, with this in mind: each visit will require a different fishing approach from the last. Apart from the effects of wind and weather prevailing at the time, there will be a change in water level, with a corresponding alteration in strength of current and, therefore, the positions in which fish are lying.

However well a fisherman knows his river, the planning of a successful night's fishing demands a daylight survey of the water. Spate rivers suffer frequent change (a point to remember when wading at night) and not only are the banks of shingle constantly shifting, the "lies" in the pools are shifting, too. Where only a few weeks ago the bottom was plain gravel, rocks have emerged; or a waterlogged tree trunk, swept down by a recent flood, become embedded.

Even those lake-fed rivers that suffer no dramatic change, offer fresh problems each succeeding night as the water level drops during a spell

285

of dry weather. Where the current was too strong to hold fish the week before, there are now fish lying; where there was sufficient stream to work the fly the water has slackened and the fly must now be worked by hand. Here, the current has altered its course; there, a back-eddy has formed, and so on. Much of this is impossible to ascertain in the darkness, and it is on such knowledge that success depends.

PLAN VIEW

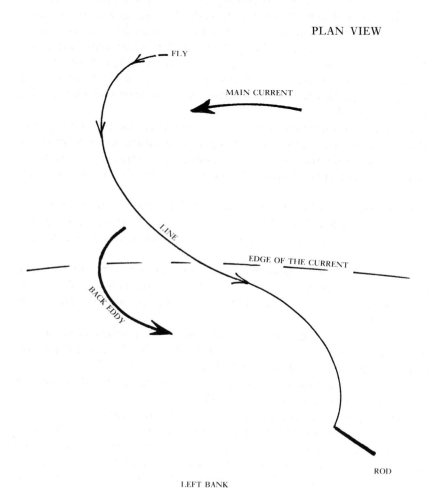

Effect of strong back-eddy on line and fly.

286

Of all problems faced by the sunk-fly fisherman, back-eddies pose some of the most difficult. The third pool to be fished on our imaginary night is an example of this (see diagram, p. 288). At a certain height of water a vicious back-eddy forms just off the shingle bank where the river curves to the left. Although most fish are to be found towards the tail of the pool, some tend to lie about halfway down near to the opposite bank in fast, fairly deep water. These fish are almost impossible to catch when a sunk line is cast across and downstream in the usual way. The fly simply doesn't have time to sink. As soon as the line touches down it is quickly snatched by current and back-eddy into the shape of a distorted "S". The fly fishes poorly. The line is awkward to retrieve. It is a situation common to many pools in many widely differing rivers.

Although such water is never easy to fish (particularly at night), one way of coping with a back-eddy is shown in the diagram and photographs of the third pool.

The fish in question are lying in the main current near to the opposite bank (at G). To attract them the fly must fish deep and move across their "lies" at a reasonable speed. This cannot be accomplished unless we negate the drag of the back-eddy and prevent the line from becoming "S" curved.

When starting to fish the pool, we cast in a conventional manner between points A and B for fish in the pool neck. At B we wind up and walk downstream to point C. From there we cast a long line upstream to E.

As soon as the cast is made we start to walk steadily upstream, holding the rod well up and keeping as much line as possible clear of the water. Our speed upstream should roughly equal the speed of the fly downstream.

At D, if all has gone well, the line should be roughly straight, the pronounced "S" curve having been avoided. The fly, meanwhile, has reached F and had a chance to sink. The current will do all that is necessary to work it across the river, and on stopping at D and tightening line, we may find we have hooked a fish.

Many anglers miss golden opportunities because they never seem to realize that an occasional fish (and a big one at that) sometimes lies close to their own bank, even though most fish in the pool are under the opposite bank. This point has been stressed earlier, but I make no apology for repeating it. The situation occurs frequently, on every type

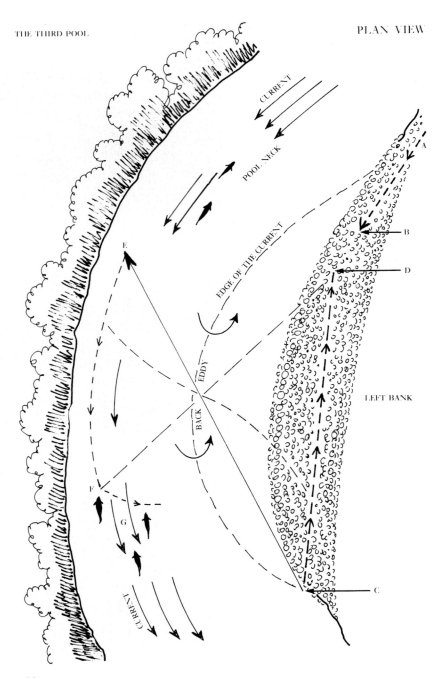

CURRENT

POOL NECK

EDGE OF THE CURRENT

A

B

D

LEFT BANK

C

E

EDDY

BACK

F

G

CURRENT

Angler at head of pool, fishing between A and B.

Angler, Position C, has cast upstream to E.

Angler has walked upstream to D. The lure has reached F, and sunk. The line has straightened out.

of water, and failure to take advantage of it often makes the difference between success and failure, whether by night or day.

An example is shown (Position D) in the diagram of the fourth pool at our disposal. This pool is worth a glance, since it also illustrates the method of upstream-night-worm-fishing (mentioned on p. 147), which we will deal with first.

Most of the fish in this pool lie close to the left bank from which, owing to dense undergrowth, night fly fishing is virtually impossible. To catch the fish at the head of the pool (Position A) and those in the tail (Position C) is quite straightforward. Ways and means of coping with similar "lies" have already been discussed. But the fish in Position B are a very different proposition. As shown by the dotted underwater contour lines, these fish are lying in water of considerable depth, close to the far bank and in a fairly strong current. Late at night, when sea trout are reluctant to rise to the fly, and when sunk line fishing is in operation, the fish in Position B are very difficult to catch.

True, they can sometimes be taken on a Surface Lure, fished by wading the shallows above the shingle bank, but when they seem disinterested in anything on or near the surface and are lying with their chins firmly down among the rocks, it is not easy to get a sunk fly anywhere near them—in that current, in that depth of water.

This is an ideal opportunity to try a worm, fished upstream on fly rod, fly leader and sinking line.

Preparations are simple. The fly is exchanged for a bare hook on which one or two lobworms are threaded. The bait is cast upstream, at an angle of about forty-five degrees, well above the fish, and allowed to drift down with the current, sinking as it goes.

If the bait stops, do nothing. Wait. You will soon know if it is a rock by the dead drag of the current. A fish usually takes very gently and then swims upstream. Tighten only when you feel him move away.

It is an exciting method, requiring no small degree of sensitivity. To fish it effectively at night is a considerable test of skill.

The behaviour of migratory fishes makes them quite difficult enough to catch, whatever method is used. They do not need to be hedged by convention. Nor does one need to justify the use of bait. Any "purist" who thinks that casting a worm at night is an easy or "unsporting" way of catching sea trout should go and try it at once. It needs practice. I remember a hilarious night on the "fourth" pool with that fine angler, Fred J. Taylor. He wrote about it later in the magazine *Angling* . . .

". . . I *knew* the water was low and clear and I *knew* that I needed my

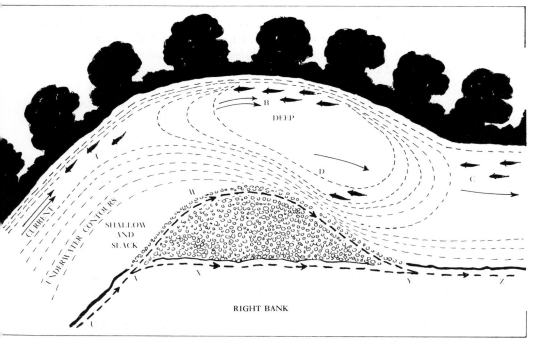

There is a time to wade and a time to fish from the river bank, but (although there are many, usually very obvious exceptions) as a general rule: when wading, wade deep; when fishing from the bank keep well back from the water's edge.

worm tackle with me but I was talked into leaving it behind by Hugh, who was in a very light-hearted mood.

"'Bring your worms by all means my dear chap,' he said, 'but let us use the fly first and later we can fish the worms on the fly rods.'

"... Did you ever try to cast a lobworm on a fly outfit? Sunk line? Fifteen to twenty yards? In utter blackness? ...

"Every few casts, because I could not make the necessary distance without throwing off the worm, I'd get a little tweak and then a steady pull on the line. Each time I thought it was a fish, and each time I reeled in an eight inch eel. New hooks to be tied. Lines to be untangled. Bad language and utter chaos. And Falkus laughed, and like little Audrey, laughed and laughed again.

"'I'm not laughing *at* you, my dear chap,' he gurgled. 'I'm laughing *with* you. You *must* believe me. I'm laughing *with* you.'

"After that I gave up. Then I drank the rest of the Scotch and I laughed too. We both laughed *with* each other!"

Fred, of course, is a worm fisherman of uncommon skill who, to heighten his humour, wrote with undue modesty. Nevertheless, even he was impressed by his first experience of upstream night worm-fishing on the fly rod!

A word of warning. Whatever success you may have when trying out this method, don't be misled. It is no angling "philosopher's stone". Very often it fails. I mention it because I have found it to be a skilful and highly diverting technique that will occasionally provide a fish I might not otherwise have caught.

*　　　*　　　*

Now for the fish in Position D. These lie in quiet water only a few yards out from the angler's bank, which is steeply shelving. Over the years this spot has yielded some good fish to anglers who approached it with stealth. But only a few have done so. The common practice has been to fish along the bank from U to V then carry on down the pool keeping close to the water's edge, following the path W.

Wrong.

The clatter of shingle and sight of the angler looming up against the skyline destroy any chance of hooking fish at D. They are no longer there!

If, instead, the angler turns right at V and follows the line X, walking on the grass and *keeping off the shingle*, casting his line overland, any "taking" fish that happens to be lying at D is easily caught.

Of course, one reason why Position D is seldom fished properly is that fish are never seen there in daylight. It is a "lie" that seems to be used only in darkness.

But this is really no excuse. The sea trout angler should know that where a shingle bank slopes steeply away there is always a chance of finding a fish at night, and the axioms: "Always fish the nearer water first"; "Keep quiet"; "Stay out of sight", seem such obvious points.

And yet. And yet . . . !

*　　　*　　　*

Having fished out the other three pools at our disposal on our imaginary night, we will return to the first pool, below the "run", and try again for the main shoal in Position 10 (shown in Chapter VIII)—not forgetting the big sea trout lying in the pool neck.

Watch carefully for any change in conditions. Clouds are starting to form and the pool begins to darken as the stars disappear. Now there is a splendid chance to try the Surface Lure, which is set up ready on the second rod.

The use of two rods is a great convenience, for if fish refuse the lure you should return at once to sunk line. With one rod, this would mean another change of reels.

The Surface Lure, cumbersome to cast, whirrs through the air like a shuttlecock. Standing deep in the river you put it out into the shadows under the bushes opposite, shoot a yard or two of extra line and keep the rod point well up.

The lure floats down under the bushes, then checks and begins to swing round on the current. Suddenly, a fish splashes at it. . . . Then another, closer to your own bank.

You recover and cast again. Another fish rises. . . . Then several more. The pool, which a short time ago seemed empty, is now alive with fish. But although they rise with splash after splash there is no pull on the line. Not one of them actually touches the lure.

To anyone who has not fished Surface Lure before, this reaction must be astonishing. (Indeed, although I first experienced it many years ago I still have the same feeling of surprise; of wonder. . . . The same thrill.)

Perhaps it is still not quite dark enough. Stop casting, stand where you are, and wait. Already, more cloud is building up. Suddenly, this heavier cloud bank blots out the streak of light that has glimmered all night in the northern sky and the surface of the pool blackens. This is the moment you have been hoping for.

As dawn begins to show and the wake of the lure becomes visible, change back to fly. Fish out the pool tails completely—and, before it is too light, don't forget to have one last try for the big sea trout at the head of the pool!

Now, shadows under the opposite bank dissolve. The mystery and enchantment of a darkened river begin to fade and once again you see the water running clear over the pale stones. Wind in your line, for it is time to stop.

The hilltops are tipped with gold. Through the trees there is a glimpse of distant hayfields. Under the pink clouds, larks are singing; a ribbon of mist lifts from the water-meadows, and high against the fellside the cottage windows glitter with early light.

Sit awhile at leisure to breathe the morning freshness and catch the beauty of the sunrise.

And let your garments Russet be or gray,
Of colour darke, and hardest to discry:
That with the Raine or weather will away,
And least offend the fearfull Fishes eye:
       John Dennys, *The Secrets of Angling* (1613)

XI
Daylight Fishing

PART ONE: HIGH WATER

A large portion of this book is devoted to night fishing because on the majority of sea trout streams it is in the darkness that we are most likely to be successful, sport by day (certainly with fly or spinner) being confined usually to those times when the water is high. Rivers vary considerably in their opportunities for catching sea trout other than by night. Lake-fed rivers, although some may rise rapidly, have a comparatively slow rate of fall. Rivers that do not flow from large lakes may lift and fall as much as six or eight feet in twenty-four hours, and generally speaking it is in these spate rivers that sea trout fishing is at its best—certainly there, I think, that the fish are most exciting. It is mainly of such rivers that I write.

The wild beauty of a spate stream seems in harmony with the nature of the fish it holds. From some tiny spring, high in the hills, it hurries seawards over grey, weedless stones; among great boulders and banks of shingle; through shallow, rock-strewn rapids flecked with white water that foam down between long, deep, gin-clear, tree-girt pools. Such a river, with its quick rise and fall is ever challenging. Except on stretches of fast, broken water, fly-fishing offers little chance of success in daylight when the river is low. Conversely, fishing after dark in high, coloured water, is largely a waste of time.

As a general rule, the best daylight spinning and fly-fishing can be expected when a river is falling and clearing after a moderate rise following a dry spell of no longer than a week or ten days. The stage of a spate when sport may be approached with most confidence depends on the time of high tide and the quantity of matter suspended in the water. Should the rise follow too long a period of drought, the water may come down black with peat drainings; tar and oil washed from road surfaces; and a mass of dirt, drifting leaves and sticks—to say nothing of branch

295

loppings, tin cans, drowned sheep and cattle, an occasional tree trunk and a profusion of plastic bottles and bags. Any pleasure in casting is quickly dispelled by the constant hooking of leaves and other pieces of rubbish, and chances of catching fish will be slender until this filth has been swept out to sea. But provided the time of high tide coincides with cleaner river conditions (certainly on those rivers whose estuaries run to shallows at low water) there should be every likelihood of sport during the later stages of the spate; for then, with the water dark but not dirty, fish will probably be running. At any rate, this is the time that the fish—whether fresh-run or resident—are most likely to take.

Your arrival on flood water must be timed not to the right day, but to the right hour or even half-hour, for at a certain stage of the spate most rivers produce a "magic moment" when fish suddenly come "on" and take furiously. This applies not merely to one "lie" or even one pool, but to a whole stretch of river. Hours of blank fishing may precede and follow such a period of activity—which, even when you have an intimate knowledge of the river, is by no means easy to predict.

The truth of this was pressed home rather painfully many years ago. It was about two o'clock on a hot, sunny August afternoon; the ground steaming after heavy rain; the "streamers" out on the fellside; the river in high spate. I was sitting at my desk by an open window, writing. Later that afternoon, when the water had dropped a bit, there would be splendid opportunities of catching fish. But not just yet. I had it all worked out. (Why not? I knew that river. I knew its every whim. After all, I'd been fishing it long enough.) There wasn't a hope of any "magic moment" before about four o'clock. Five, more like it. Say, between four-thirty and six.

My father-in-law, carrying a fly rod, came down the lane from his farm above the cottage. He stopped by the window.

"Are you coming fishing?"

"No," I said. "It's too soon. I'll be down later."

He wagged his head and walked on.

"Silly old bugger," I thought. "He'll tire himself out. He'll want to pack up just when it all starts."

I went on writing.

At four-thirty, exactly as planned, I took my rod from the pegs in the shed and went down to the pool. I found the old man playing a sixteen-pound salmon. He'd had it on for half-an-hour in heavy water and was exhausted. He'd hooked it with his fourth cast. His first three casts, all from the same place, had accounted for a twelve-pound salmon; a nine-pound salmon, and a five-pound sea trout. They were stretched out on the grass behind a gorse bush.

He landed his third salmon—and went home to his tea.

I fished until dark—without an offer.

*　　　*　　　*

If you are fishing on a river's lower reaches, a close familiarity with the local tide tables is of great assistance, since a run of fresh fish during the cleaner stages of a spate—at least, in those rivers whose estuaries dry out—depends on the time of high tide. Sea trout will come up an estuary and enter a river with the tide, if the river water is in reasonable condition.

Supposing the time of high tide is, say, 10 a.m., and that the spate begins to fall at about this time, or a little before; the chances of some good fishing may be expected during the late morning and early afternoon—between, say, 11 a.m. and 3 p.m., depending on the fisherman's distance from the sea. Certainly, he would be ill advised to go home to lunch. Undoubtedly, his best plan would be to choose some likely piece of water which experience has shown to contain several good high-water "lies", and stay there. Rushing from place to place is unlikely to increase his chances of success and, however hot the sun, any temptation to spend a lunch hour loafing on the bank should be resisted. The "magic moment" does not provide the only opportunity of catching fish, but it is a splendid time while it lasts and often of short duration. It is a pity to miss it for the sake of a corned-beef sandwich.

Provided that the time of high tide coincides, the early hours of a hot summer's day are most propitious; necessary conditions being: high tide at dawn, with the river falling after a moderate spate caused by overnight rain. But you must be up before first light and on the water by sunrise. By breakfast time the water is likely to have cleared and dropped, the "magic moment" long since gone, and fly fishing over for the day. There will be little hope of further sport until that evening when, with luck, night fishing may be in operation again—although the following night will undoubtedly be better.

As the water drops, certain of the bait fishing methods described in Chapter XII can, of course, be tried. But when fish go off the "take" during the latter stages of a spate they are likely to remain dour for some time. They seem to need about twenty-four hours to settle down, and until the second day, or night, are difficult to catch whatever bait or lure they are offered.

297

When several small spates follow each other in swift succession, so that the river keeps rising and falling from day to day, fishing is almost certain to be poor. Unlike salmon, sea trout are intolerant of unstable conditions—judged by their reactions to a lure. It is the settled sea trout that takes a lure most readily, whereas it is the unsettled salmon that so often becomes a "taking" fish. As the experienced salmon fisherman knows, there are several tricks that in "hopeless" conditions of dead low water will sometimes induce salmon to take a fly: making a lot of splash, by throwing large flat stones into the pool; swimming a dog across, or getting a companion to go in; fishing a very big lure down and then backing up with a tiny fly, and so on. All these tend to agitate the fish, but not necessarily to frighten them. There is a very important distinction. An agitated salmon may take; a frightened salmon will not. A salmon may leave its "lie" for a number of reasons; for example, he may have been prodded out of it. But *provided he has not seen the angler or the shadow of a moving rod, he remains a catchable fish.* Indeed, if he has been persuaded to go for a swim in the conditions just described, he is likely to be much more catchable.

But this is a digression. Apart from an occasional big fish, whose reactions are not unlike those of a salmon, sea trout do not behave in the same way. And so, when conditions of weather and water are unsettling to fish, and especially when spate quickly follows spate, don't expect sea trout to respond with much enthusiasm.

Like most rules, however, this one is not entirely without exception. Spates occurring in quick succession result in a clearance of the impurities which drain off the land into the river; so that, by the second or third rise of water the river, although fairly high, is running free from colour. This does not provide good daylight fishing, for the sea trout are unsettled and most of them are not occupying their normal "lies"; but, when the water is high and clear there is a good chance of taking a *big* sea trout after dark on a Sunk Lure. Several of my friends have caught some very big fish in similar conditions.

Few of the places that hold sea trout in low water are worth fishing— or indeed possible to fish when the river is high. Unless you are fortunate in having an expert adviser, either gillie or knowledgeable local angler, only your own experience together with an understanding of the sea trout's habits can tell you where to expect fish.

It is invariably flood water that brings the village worm expert on the scene. Much information can be gained from watching him at work. He will saunter along the river bank, stopping here and there to push his big rod through some gap in the bushes and drop a bunch of worms into a piece of quiet water beside the torrent. These are places which, from long experience, he knows will at some time or other during the spate provide a temporary "lie" for resting fish. But don't feel too disappointed or hurt if such characters reward your thirst for knowledge with some degree of taciturnity. Some local fishermen are co-operative, many are not. That they may resent the intrusion of strangers on "their" water nowadays is understandable. Stretch after stretch of sea trout water has been bought or rented for prices that a few years ago would have seemed fantastic. Until quite recently on many of our northern streams the farmer/owner of "a bit of fishing"—often not interested in the sport himself—has not considered it to be of much value. Nowadays the farmer's bit of fishing may be worth as much as the farm itself.

Naturally, anyone who pays such money reserves the water for his own use, and who can blame him? Who can blame the farmer for taking advantage of his good fortune? It may be regrettable, it is certainly ineluctable, that the elementary economics of supply and demand should play their part equally in fishing. Never has the demand been so great, and most of those places where a local man enjoyed a "dip in" for the asking have long since been let or sold. Now the local angler is dependent almost entirely on association water—if there happens to be any in the vicinity. It is hardly surprising if he looks with suspicion on well-dressed strangers who approach him for information.

*   *   *

The bewilderment of an angler who, having hitherto seen a spate river only at its normal summer level, comes to fish it after a night of heavy rain, is easily understood. In its bank-high, swollen state, full of unexpected swirl and eddy, the river is unrecognizable. Quiet, clear pools have become black, boiling cauldrons; the steady glides, roaring torrents. Where only the day before the angler picked his way dry-footed among the stones, there is now eight feet of racing water. The sill of the weir has become a great, smooth wave that bends suddenly downwards and breaks with a bubbling roar thirty yards beyond. He may well spend most of his time searching hopelessly for a place to fish.

Everything depends on local conditions, and the best I can do for the inexperienced angler is to suggest some places, common to most rivers, where fish are likely to be found at some time or other during a spate. But first, it may assist him to know what the fish themselves are up to.

A pool shrunken by summer drought. Looking upstream.

The same pool in flood water.

Further upstream. Fish are resting on the edge of the current—among the broom!

Looking downstream. The pool is the same as that shown on p. 282, and photographed from roughly the same angle. A dramatic difference!

When the spate arrives—and if the angler was out on the river the previous night, sea trout behaviour might have enabled him to predict it—three "classes" of fish are available. These are:

1. Fresh fish coming up from the sea.
2. Fish already in the river, but which during the spate will run higher up.
3. "Resident" fish that have no intention of running, spate or no spate, and just stay where they are.

The "resident" fish may not run higher until later in the season, or they may never run at all—simply because, being destined to spawn in some stream close to their present positions, they have already reached their "intended" pools. Such fish are not easily caught; as soon as conditions become uncomfortable they will go underneath the bank, or among the rocks, and stay there until the water has dropped sufficiently to allow them to re-occupy their customary places.

Sea trout fresh from the sea take more readily than stale fish, so it is mostly fresh fish that are caught during the spate. Thus, the time of high tide is important on some rivers. But, an inconvenient tide needn't deter the fisherman from going to the river. The absence of a fresh run doesn't prevent him from catching fish, it merely reduces his chances. There is always the possibility of sport with those fish already in the river —although they offer more limited opportunities.

It should be mentioned here that the degree of spate depends not on local rainfall but the amount that has fallen in the hills higher up the valley. A cloud-burst fifteen or twenty miles away may bring the river down in flood although not a drop of rain has fallen locally. Such an occurrence is not at all uncommon. Spates of this nature can happen with great suddenness and it is advisable to treat them with respect. An unthinking tourist who left his motorcar close to the river one thundery afternoon, returned to find his parking place a maelstrom. Two of the car wheels were subsequently recovered many miles downstream by a local farmer—who fitted them to his trailer.

After a time, running fish will swing in to the side and rest. These resting places change as the level of the water drops. Each will hold fish only while the river is at a height which makes that "lie" acceptable. After the river has fallen past a critical level, that particular "lie" will not hold fish until some future spate. The successful high-water fisherman must therefore know not only where these resting-places are, but at what stage of a spate fish are likely to use them.

Two views of a great highwater sea trout and salmon "lie": the "Fence-end". Here, the river is seen at summer low, but when the foreground is covered by coloured flood-water, an angler standing thigh–deep beside the fence post has fish a rod's length from him. Where grass and shingle meet, they rest for a time on the edge of the current—moving on upstream as the water level falls.

Having from instinct, experience or local advice, selected a good place, the fisherman should stay there. Sooner or later it is bound to hold fish. But as the water level falls, the time will come when that "lie" will hold fish no longer, and he must change his ground.

Often, a stranger's chances of sport will depend on his "fisherman's instinct", that weird quality which springs from some sixth sense and develops with experience. Some anglers have an unerring eye for a fish. A glance at the water and they will unhesitatingly pick out the best fishing spots. To others, this proclivity is for ever denied. Most people, however, can learn to "read" a river—if they will only take the trouble to use their eyes, and their brains. As a start, the following examples may be helpful:

Easily identified resting-places are the little bays that form where cattle go down to drink. Similar bays are found at entrances to fords where, in low water, farm vehicles cross the shallows.

Avoid fast water and the turbulence of whirlpool and eddies. It is

Here again the river is seen at summer low. When floodwater approaches the top of the bank, fish lie between the two heaps of rocks in a sort of backwater. In a position such as this they are usually caught on worm or spinner, more seldom on fly. When resting in these "lay-bys" fresh fish that have been running straight from the sea are often ready takers. But in this case note the snags—both upstream and downstream—old stakes that once provided bank support.

such water that the fish themselves most carefully avoid. Search for stretches of quiet water, just off the main stream, which are free from turbulence caused by tree-roots or rocks. These places are usually close beside the bank, often beneath overhanging bushes and trees. Because of this they are often very difficult to fish.

Some fisheries are wretchedly maintained, and many chances are lost because trailing branches make high-water "lies" unfishable. This is a pity, because although these "lies" are not often fished they can be very profitable when conditions are right. On my own stretch of fishing, such places are carefully tended: branches, bushes and brambles being cut back each season, and the bottom kept free of snags. Often enough, a little work on a river bank makes all the difference between failure and success—and why so many fishery owners and Associations don't look after their water better than they do defeats me. Time spent on river upkeep pays handsome dividends.

The end of a little roadway leading to a ford. River at summer low. The patch of gravel where the dogs are sitting forms a favourite "lie" for sea trout and salmon when the river is in high spate and coloured. In these conditions the road end is a quiet lay-by just off the main current; a resting place for fish that have run up the rapids below. Here they will lie for a while in no more than two to three feet of water.

305

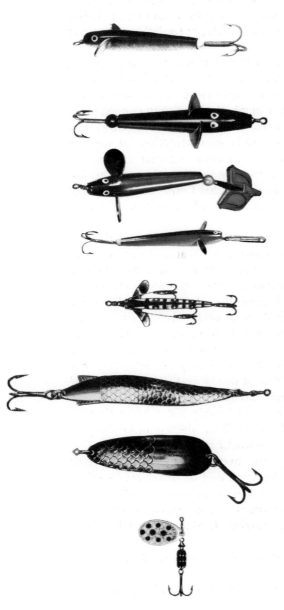

Devon Minnow. The Devon appeared during the latter part of the 19th century. In spite of changing fashions it is still one of the most popular spinners. Made in almost every colour or colour combination; from about ½ inch to 4 inches in length. Sea trout sizes: 1–1¾ inches.

Wooden Devon. Very light. Spins on an even keel at low speeds owing to position of the vanes. Good colour combinations are blue and silver; brown and gold. Sea trout sizes: 1¼–2¼ inches.

Hook-Hoods prevent trebles getting tangled up in the tackle box.

The Devon *Mount* is separate from the body shell. A paper-clip keeps them together when not in use.

Quill Minnow. A very good lure. Due to its lightness it is better than the metal Devon in shallow water. I prefer them without the two flying trebles. Sea trout sizes: 1¼–2½ inches.

Toby Spoon. A very popular lure with many salmon and sea trout anglers. It has superseded the natural minnow (noticeably so on Loch Lomond). I have used it for many years when spinning for salmon, sea trout and bass. In my experience, it is a wonderful attractor, but a poor hooker. Sea trout size: 2¼ inches.

Bergen Spoon. It has a half-scaled silver finish on the outside, gold inside. I have found it to be a very successful lure. Sea trout size: 1⅝ inches.

Mepps Spoon. This little spoon, which is made in several sizes, has a well deserved popularity. The low friction bearing attachment allows the blade to flutter when fished at very low speeds. A splendid lure for upstream fishing when a stream is clearing after a spate. Its weakness is the treble hook, which is inclined to straighten. Sea trout sizes: 0. 1. 2.

Water most suitable for fly fishing is the slack, just off the main stream, alongside an undercut bank or the edge of a shingle ridge. But some of these highwater spots are impossible to cover with fly and can be fished only by dropping a worm between the branches, or by flicking a spinner out through a gap in the bushes.

To be on the river armed only with a fly rod does not preclude the use of a small spoon. Handle it as you would a fly. Cast out, allow it to work not too quickly round a piece of water fairly close to the surface, and then draw it steadily towards you through the slack water underneath the bank. It is a good looking lure when the water is very peaty. The flash of silver as it slowly twinkles round is most attractive—at any rate it is to the angler, and so fills him with confidence. Significant, however, is the number of fish that follow a minnow or spoon but, at the last moment, turn away. It is not without reason that I reiterate the value of the fly. Work it how you will, fish after fish will sometimes follow a metal lure right up to your feet.

The reason why the spinner has acquired a reputation for being the only practical lure for spate fishing is probably because, being so much larger than most orthodox sea trout flies in general use, its action in heavy spate water, owing to its size/speed ratio, appears more natural to the fish. Whatever water we are fishing, the relative speed of the lure is of great importance. Often, a big fly is a superior lure, even in dark, heavy water, provided there is room to fish it properly. Frequently, of course, there isn't room, and those places which for all intents and purposes are impossible to fish with fly can usually be covered with a spinner because of the ease with which it can be cast from an awkward position. For this, the fixed-spool reel and spinning rod are needed.

Most fixed-spool reels will carry considerably more monofilament nylon line than is needed in actual fishing. The addition of backing to, say, a hundred yards of casting line is a useful economy.

For maximum casting efficiency, the line level on the majority of fixed-spool reels should be fractionally less than $\frac{1}{8}$ in. below the lip of the spool. In cases where the spool's rim has an extra-wide radius curve the line level should be fractionally more than $\frac{1}{8}$ in. below the lip.

Over-filling the spool will cause tangles. Under-filling will reduce casting range.

To ensure correct filling, carry out the following procedure:

1. Wind one hundred yards of new line on to the empty spool.
2. Join line to backing.

3. Wind backing on top of line until the correct level is reached, then cut off.

4. Reverse line and backing. This can be done either by running it off the spool across a field (or round and round the garden) or by winding on to another reel and thence on to a second reel. (Old centre-pin reels are useful for this job.) The end of the backing is now uppermost.

5. Tie end of backing to spool and wind on. The line will now finish up on top of the backing and the level will be exactly right.

The last few yards of a nylon line suffer considerable wear and tear during the course of a day's fishing. As a result its strength may be considerably reduced. Several yards should be cut off before the angler tackles-up.

Continued removal of line lowers the line level on the spool. With a fixed-spool reel the line must be "set up" to proper level again—either by increasing the amount of backing, or by fitting a new line.

On the subject of spinning rods, here is a fascinating little item of information relating to the butt or "gathering" ring. It was ferreted by my friend Fred Buller.

For many years anglers and rod-makers alike have been convinced that a large butt ring was a vital feature on any rod used with a fixed-spool reel. This has been based on the belief that coils of line coming off the spool in spiral fashion need to be "gathered" by a large ring in order to "pour" smoothly through the smaller-diameter intermediate rings—just as liquid has to be gathered in a funnel before it can be poured into the narrow neck of a bottle.

It all seemed very plausible. I had thought so myself. Experience, however, teaches otherwise. Tournament casters (and who should know better?) are now convinced that *two smaller-diameter butt rings* placed within one inch of each other are more effective.

As percipient readers will have gathered from the tone of this book so far, I am no great lover of the spinning rod, preferring the fly rod whenever possible. This has no "sporting" connotation. It is simply a matter of personal pleasure. Casting a fly gives me more satisfaction than casting anything else.

It is a strange quirk of human nature that a sense of satisfaction derives from doing what one finds difficult. And how true this is of angling. If fish could be hooked at every cast how many fishermen (other than the "fishmongers") would bother after a day of it?

This situation was in fact the subject of a neat little story concerning a fanatical dry-fly fisherman who, if memory serves me, woke up on the bank of a chalk stream to find himself faced with a rising fish. He cast to it. It took at once and was duly landed, $2\frac{1}{2}$lb. exactly. No sooner was this fish landed than another of the same size rose in the same place. This, too, was landed. And another. And another ... The lie was never empty. No cast failed to hook the fish. The story ends with the angler's dreadful realization that he is doomed to precisely similar sport day after day into eternity; that he is indeed in hell.

And to those of us who cherish the sport of catching wild fish in wild places, hell it would be.

Spinners and mounts have always presented something of a carrying and storage problem. If they are kept in tins or plastic boxes (as mine are!) they get jumbled up and the mounts get tangled—wasting time at the waterside. There is also the danger of rusting when a wet spinner is returned to the box. The American box, with its series of hinged trays honeycombed with individual compartments, solves the first problem but not the second. The picture shows the Buller Box. Vertical packing ensures drainage and ventilation, thus eliminating the problem of rust.

It would seem unnecessary to stress that all tackle should be kept in good order. And yet the main reason why so many large fish are lost is because hooks or mounts are seldom replaced until lost on the bottom—or in a fish! There are wire mounts and nylon mounts. Both are suspect and should be tested each time they are used. So, of course, should the hooks. Remember: The loss of a fish due to breakage of any kind is almost always your own fault.

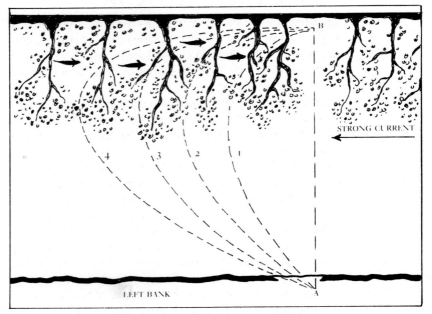

Note. It is likely that overhanging branches may trail in the water when the river is high. Having cast from A to B, the angler should drop the rod point, holding it beneath the surface if necessary while the cast is fished out.

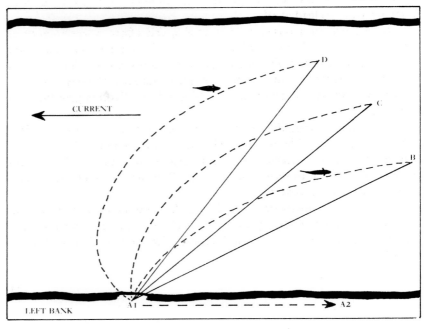

I am not suggesting that spinning is hellish—even though some of the early "spring" salmon fishing (laughable term) comes fairly close to it. As the diagram on p. 315 illustrates, successful spinning demands much skill (even in wildfowling weather!). So too does one's approach to fish on a small tree-girt river in summer.

There is an aesthetic satisfaction in placing a spinner within inches of an overhanging branch, paying out line and letting the lure twinkle down to sea trout and salmon lurking under the leaves. This demands great skill, and so provides great satisfaction.

An example of this is illustrated in the diagram. Remove the trees and there is no trouble; the fish lying under the opposite back can be covered easily enough; the angler has only to avoid over-casting. But *with* the trees; *with* those overhanging branches (and I can think of many a stretch just like it), covering those fish is a very different proposition.

There is just one place to cast—from A to B, through the narrow gap between the branches that hang low across the river. As each successive cast is fished (1, 2, 3, 4, etc.) the lure is allowed to drift further downstream, sinking as it goes, the angler (with the bale-arm of his fixed-spool lifted) paying out line, a little bit more each time. To start with, a fairly heavy anti-kink lead will be needed. After a cast or two, during which the spinner has crept further and further downstream, this anti-kink lead must be exchanged for a lighter one. If he is to fish right down under the opposite branches without getting snagged on the bottom, he will probably have to change his lead three or four times and may finish up with no lead at all.

Catching fish in a position such as this can afford a great sense of achievement. It calls for casting accuracy of a high order, and good judgement in releasing line for the downstream drift—which depends on correct assessment of current strength; amount of weight on the leader and the time it takes to sink. There is no "coffee grinding" in spinning of this sort.

The second diagram illustrates a simple example of upstream spinning, a method made possible by the admirable Mepps spinner. The best time is when the water is clearing, is in fact perhaps too clear for the fly, and the fish are tending to return to their "lies" in the centre of the stream, or on the edge of shingle ridges.

From A1, cast upstream to B. Bring the spinner back downstream (see dotted line) fractionally faster than the current, so that the little lure has its attractive "whirling" action without too high a ground-speed.

Ball-bearing swivel.

Diamond-eye swivel.

The swivel is an underrated but essential piece of tackle. For spinning, the ball-bearing swivel is the most efficient. Unfortunately, it is made only in one size. When a smaller swivel is needed, use a "diamond-eye". Made of rustless bright wire, it is strong and efficient.

Barrel swivels.

Anti-kink "Hillman" lead.

A swivel's primary function is to avoid line kink. The barrel swivel is not suitable for fast spinning, but in a small size makes a useful link between mainline and leader in a ledger rig.

Anti-kink vane.

Even a ball-bearing swivel cannot keep up with the revolutions caused by retrieving a spinner in heavy water. For deep-water spinning use a swivel with anti-kink lead. For shallow water use a celluloid anti-kink vane.

A simple spinning rig. The anti-kink lead is placed on the mainline end of the swivel.

312

Without changing position, make several more casts (C, D, etc.), before moving upstream to A2 and starting again.

This method of spinning upstream with a small Mepps (size 0, or 1) is very good for catching grilse in water I regard as being virtually hopeless for fly fishing. One point to remember, however: although you should tighten the moment the spinner is taken, *don't* tighten too savagely. If instead of a small sea trout it is a salmon that has taken, you will be left sighing with a straightened hook!

A Word of Warning

Always check the line on a spool before fitting it to your spinning reel. Some spools are shallow, some are deep. Make sure of the line's breaking strain and length. This advice seems obvious and unnecessary. It isn't. I know several people who have put on the wrong spool—and discovered their error while attempting to play a big fish. It happened to me once.

The river was up. "Go down and catch some herling for supper", said Kathleen. I was busy and thinking about other things. I found myself on the river bank with the wrong reel. It held about 20 yards of 3 lb. breaking strain. "Never mind", I thought, anxious to get back to what I'd been doing. "It's strong enough for herling. No bother." Of course, by the weird law that governs these things, I hooked a huge salmon. The current was very strong. I couldn't do anything with him. I would walk the great fish up the pool, watching the turns of line on the spool. Then he would set off downstream, and I would run after him. Then up we would go again . . . and down . . . This went on for an hour and a half. Up and down. Up and down. It all took place in front of a grinning audience of friends who by strange bush telegraph had gathered to watch the fun. Very irritating. At supper time Kathleen appeared, looking for her herling. The fish jumped. "Oooh!" said everyone. He was as fresh as ever. I felt utterly disenchanted. Just when it seemed likely we were going to be there all night the hook came away. I went quite numb. It was the only fish I can remember that I really didn't mind losing.

*   *   *

Before leaving the spinning rod and going on to other methods, there is one point worth considering. It concerns the strange "luck" of the novice who sometimes succeeds in hooking a fish when other anglers (who cast better but with little thought) have failed. It applies both to spring salmon fishing and to early season spinning for sea trout during April/May—or later in the season if the weather is cold.

The answer is very simple, as a glance at the diagram will show.

The fish are lying in a deep gully between C and D. To hook one of them in the conditions stated, *a lure must be sunk deep enough to swing round in front of their noses.* The underwater contours, however, make correct presentation very difficult. To fish a lure satisfactorily across these lies requires thought and skill. A semi-skilled angler, or one without knowledge of the river bottom, *thinks* his lure is deep enough (he has, after all, felt it touch bottom from time to time), and content with not getting snagged-up he fishes blithely away, cast after cast, his lure safe enough—but never in a place where a fish is likely to take it.

The novice can't cast as well as this. He throws his spinner to a point short of C (the limit of his range), gets his line caught up round the reel and pauses to free it. While he is fiddling with the line his spinner twinkles down towards the fish . . .

Having freed his line, the novice raises his rod and starts to wind in. As likely as not, his spinner is fast in the bottom. *But* there is also a chance that it may be fast in a fish. I have seen it happen many times.

The experienced angler knows all this and controls his lure accordingly. His fish are hooked by design, not accident.

Not long ago, a friend of mine was salmon-fishing in a pool similar to that shown in the diagram. For a time he kept touching the ledge at C.

"Better if you took some lead off," suggested the gillie.

My friend shook his head. "I need more lead, not less."

He increased the weight on his leader, cast a shorter distance than before and allowed the bait time to sink.

He took three twenty-pounders from the pool that morning.

This was Jimmy Skene, one of the wiliest salmon fishermen in Britain. The incident illustrates a basic truth about spring salmon fishing, but it applies equally to spinning for sea trout.

*   *   *

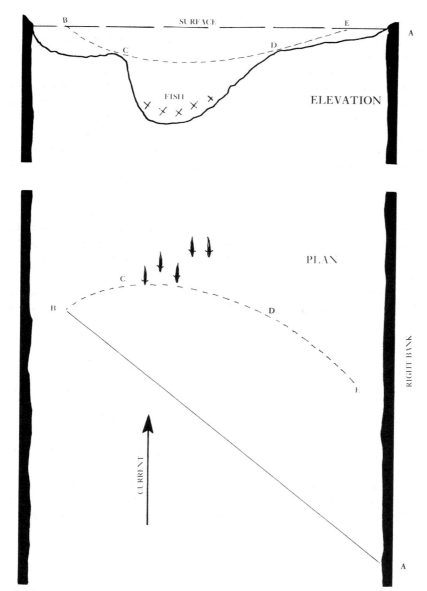

1. Angler at A casts to B.
2. Spinner starts to sink and to swing round towards C.
3. At C spinner touches bottom. Angler lifts rod. Starts to wind in line.
4. Spinner swings round towards D. This is the vital area, but the lure is nowhere near the fish.
5. At D spinner again touches bottom. This confirms the angler's belief that his lure has been fishing close to the bottom all the time. Again, he lifts the rod and recovers line more quickly.
6. Spinner is brought in towards angler's bank, at E.

And now, a glance at high-water worm fishing. First, something about the worms themselves.

There are twenty-seven recorded species of earthworms in Britain. We need concern ourselves with only five:

1. Lobworm (*Lumbricus terrestris*).
2. Big blue-headed lobworm (*Allolobophora longa*).
3. Small blue-headed lobworm (*Allolobophora caliginosa*).
4. Brandling (*Eisenia foetida*).
5. Redworm (*Lumbricus rubellus*).

Lobworms can be collected from the lawn or from any field of short grass, but seldom when the ground is dry and never when it is frozen. Warm, damp, dark nights are the best. On windy nights worms seem to be nervy and easily disturbed, and tend to expose less of themselves above ground. They are very sensitive to vibration and light (except red light) and both of these stimuli cause them to retire into their burrows— a feat they accomplish with astonishing speed. Theoretically, a red light should be used for hunting lobworms, since they are blind to this part of the spectrum, but my own use of it has met with mixed success. I find that although red light makes my approach less obvious to the worm it makes the worm more difficult to see. But of course this may be due to failing eyesight.

Stalking the lobworm in darkness is almost a sport in its own right. Choose a dark, damp night. Wear rubber shoes or wellingtons, and creep about with much stealth. Hold a small torch between the teeth as recommended for night fly-fishing (see p. 127). To have both hands free is a great advantage. Carry a worm-tin suspended from your belt on a string.

Frequently only a short length of worm is visible among the grass stems. This is by no means easy to see. When you think you have found a worm, *don't* prod him to make sure. He will disappear in a flash. Pin him down instantly with thumb and forefinger, or with both thumbs— one at either end. Next, locate the head of the worm. This is not so difficult as it sounds, since it is always the tail that is in the hole and there will be a movement in that direction. Hold the head firmly until the worm's peristaltic contortion thins the body sufficiently to allow you to withdraw him gently from the hole. Any attempt to pull a worm out too soon is disastrous, he will break in half. Naturally, if the whole worm is above ground and clear of the hole he is unable to make a speedy exit; you can simply pick him up.

Redworms favour old manure sites. Brandlings are found in fresh manure sites and compost heaps. Blue-headed lobs are found on the lawn; but, like the redworms, they haunt the soil underneath old cow pats.

Worms can be purchased from bait farms and occasionally from tackle dealers, but prudent and thrifty anglers will collect their own before the fishing season starts, and keep a supply alive throughout the summer. This not only ensures tougher worms but avoids the frantic flap that invariably occurs when thunderstorms bring a sudden spate. Many a time—either through improvidence or because some cad has rifled my bait-box—I have found myself out in the rain, digging furiously . . .

It is quite unnecessary. With good husbandry, worms can be kept alive and well for many months no matter how hot the weather. After a dry spell, worms are hard to get and the sensible angler (if he has friends like mine) will hoard his box of treasure, if not under the bed, at least well out of sight. Morals grow thin when worms are scarce and the river is foaming down and fish are running!

Lobworms should be kept cool during summer and insulated against frost during winter. The ideal temperature is 40–45°F. They will live far longer when stored in shredded newspaper than in moss.

Soak and squeeze enough torn-up newspaper to fill a biscuit tin. Add worms. Place a piece of damp sacking on top of the newspaper. On top of the sacking put a plastic container full of ice. Have two containers on the go; one in the deep freeze, one on top of the worms. Change them round daily.

Brandlings should be kept in bulb fibre, or peat, or compost from the worm bed—the top layer being used. The compost should not be too moist.

All the worms listed above will catch both salmon and sea trout. For preference, however, I would use a lobworm (*Lumbricus terrestris*) for sea trout in spate water, and for salmon at all times. For sea trout in medium water I would use blue-headed lobs. In low water, brandlings and redworms.

Spate worm-tackle is simple enough. A pierced-bullet rig (see p. 340) will serve the beginner very well to start with. All he needs carry is a small box containing some hooks, two or three leads of different sizes and some small barrel swivels and split-shot. My own tackle requirements go into a matchbox, carried in my waistcoat pocket. When wanting to try a worm during high water as a change from fly fishing, or to cover a "lie" impossible for fly, I merely cut off the fly, slip a pierced bullet on the leader, pinch on a stop-shot and tie a worm hook on the end.

This unsophisticated but highly effective rig is centuries old. The following description is by Colonel Robert Venables, in his book *The Experienc'd Angler* (1662).

> "Take a . . . small Pistol-bullet, make a hole through it, wider at each side than in the middle; yet so open in every place, as that the Line may easily pass through it without any stop; place a very small piece of Lead on your line, that may keep this Bullet from falling nearer the Hook than that piece of Lead . . . the Fish will, when they bite, run away with the bait as securely, as if there were no more weight upon your line, than the little piece of Lead, because the hole in the Bullet gives passage to the Line, as if it were not there."

Dried-up cow pat in a water meadow. Worms (*Allolobophora* in particular) will be found among the grass roots only a few inches below the surface. There is seldom any need to remain baitless at the waterside.

318

For variations on this theme, see the shot-link ledger *et al* p. 341. Apart from the substitution of differently shaped leads, and a tiny swivel in place of the stop-shot, this rig has never been bettered. Indeed it is still very much in use, and catches me a lot of fish each year.

Since for almost all spate worm fishing only a short line is needed, the 10 ft. 6 in. sea trout fly rod will serve admirably, indeed much better than a short spinning rod. Its length helps to keep the line clear of bushes and gives more control over a hooked fish. There are some bait rods on the market that will do the job still better (see p. 348), and if you go to the river to fish worm only, you will of course use one. I mention the use of the fly rod simply to encourage those anglers who, like myself, dislike carrying a lot of spare tackle about.

Lobworms from an Oxfordshire lawn living in damp newspaper. There is no difficulty in keeping worms in good condition for many months. These are very much alive-o after a prolonged heatwave (1973).

Note. Some anglers prefer freshly-dug worms, believing that fish find them more attractive. They may be right. But fresh worms are of little use for fishing upstream (see p.337) on account of their softness.

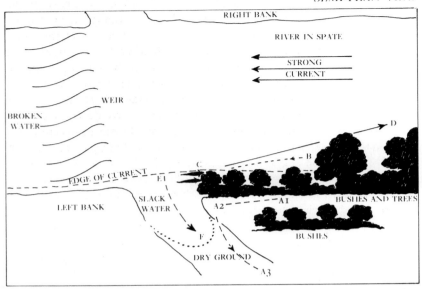

During high water fish often lie very close to the bank beneath overhanging bushes. The angler who can "read" his water starts with the advantage of knowing exactly where to put his worm. The problem is how to put it there. One example should suffice.

The diagram shows a high water "resting place" similar to that depicted on p. 305. A sunken pathway leading down to a farm ford has flooded and become a backwater E–F. Fish are lying under the bushes on the edge of the current at C. Having just run from the estuary they are likely to be "taking" fish, but simply to poke the rod over the bushes and drop a worm on top of them, or try to cast up to them from below, will almost certainly disturb them. Although the river is in roaring spate, the water where the fish are lying is gentle and fairly shallow, a splash close to the fish must be avoided. So, too, must the movement of the angler or his rod; fish can see remarkably well even in highly coloured water. A stealthy approach is just as important in these conditions as it is when the river is low. I have found the following drill to work very successfully when fishing the "lie" in question:

1. Stand at A1. Cast the bait to B, slightly upstream, according to the strength of current, to allow time for the lead to sink as it is swept quickly downstream.

2. Hold the rod at right angles to the river, through a gap in the bushes, and guide the worm towards the bank.

320

3. The lead will bump over the bottom to the edge of the current and the worm swing round in front of the fish. It is usually taken at once, before it has time to come to rest. If there is no "take", let the worm stay where it is for a minute or two. Then, holding the rod point close to (or under) the surface to keep the line clear of the bushes, draw the worm upstream an inch or two at a time, pausing for several seconds between each movement. In the event of a "take", hold the rod high overhead so that the line clears the bushes, and move down to position A2. This change of angle will encourage the fish to run upstream in the direction of D—which is where you want him, well away from the weir!

4. When the fish is getting exhausted and begins to drop back downstream, bring him in towards the bank. Then, when he is in the entrance to the bay, at E, put some pressure on him and walk steadily backwards towards A3, bringing the fish ashore at F.

The advantage of a long rod while all this is going on is too obvious to warrant further comment.

*　　　*　　　*

When the dark, peaty colour of the water lightens and takes on a resemblance to bitter beer, conditions are fine for fly fishing. In warm weather, as might be expected, fish are most likely to take close to the surface. The lower the temperature, the deeper the fly should be sunk. For much of this fishing, a floating or a sink-tip line will be used; but in a very strong current, or in cold weather, a high density line may be needed. So more than one reel should be taken to the river.

As the water falls, a smaller fly can be fished in the glides, or on a long line across the lower parts of a pool for, by this time, fish will be tending to occupy positions that more closely resemble their normal "lies". But sea trout seldom take well during the late stages of a spate, whatever lure or bait is used. As the colour goes out of the water, so the angler's chances diminish.

At this point, I suppose, we ought to have something about dry fly fishing. It will not be much, because I don't know much about it. I have caught very few river sea trout on a dry fly. (A floating fly dragged across the water after dark doesn't qualify. It will catch a lot of fish, but it is a small Surface Lure, not a "dry fly".)

There *are* rivers where sea trout dry fly fishing is a reasonable proposition, but the rivers I fish are not among them. Apart from the sea trout I have caught on the dry fly in stillwater (a very different proposition

321

that will be dealt with in Chapter XIII) the few sea trout I have caught on a dry fly proper were all in my own beck. What started me off was an incident one sunny August afternoon . . .

It was during the later stages of a spate. The fish didn't seem to be interested in anything. I was sitting idly on the bank looking at the river with nothing particular in mind, when a grasshopper came drifting past. I watched its progress, more out of interest in the set of the current than anything else. Then, a big neb appeared. There was a swirl . . . No grasshopper.

Well—back to the cottage. There, I rigged up a greased line with an artificial grasshopper left over from a trip to Corrib or Mask or somewhere. By dinner time that grasshopper had covered every stretch of holding water I had. Result, total failure.

But the sight of that disappearing insect had stirred my fancy. Surely if one fish would take from the surface there would be others? During the following weeks—and years—I put in a stint with the floating fly during the later stages of almost every spate. Not to *rising* fish; there weren't any. It was a case of fishing a dry fly rather than "dry-fly fishing" if you see what I mean. Anyway, eventually I had some sort of success— if you can call half-a-dozen fish in three or four years "success".

Funnily enough, the "taking" fly wasn't anything like a grasshopper, or any other insect. It was an ugly, gingery, hackled thing I had once tied (probably under the influence) for reasons now forgotten. Its very limited success occurred only when the river was "in between"; when the colour was going out of the water after a spate. Which is pretty well all I know about the subject.

It did of course occur to me that one reason for this comparative failure was my ineptitude. So naturally I got some experts in on the act. The most famous was my old friend, Eric Horsfall Turner, arguably the best dry-fly fisherman in Britain. I took him down to the river one morning and showed him a pool holding a shoal of about 250 sea trout ranging in size from a few ounces to five or six pounds.

"Now", I said. "Have a go."

The great man went into action—while I lay on my belly among the broom and watched the fish. As befitted a British Casting Champion, he fished with skill and stealth. It was a superb demonstration of fly casting. But it was unproductive.

He tried everything he had, including his renowned "Beetle", fishing both dry and wet. No good. Those fish showed not the slightest interest. They weren't frightened. There was no darting about. They stayed stolidly in their great shoal. But as time went by they gradually moved farther and farther away from whatever fly was floating over them. When Horsey paused for a rest and a pinch of snuff, they moved back again.

Nor did subsequent efforts prove any more successful.

Since then I have watched a lot of my friends have a go at it. Not one of them has ever hooked a fish. It makes me realize that what I achieved was, after all, comparative success!

It must be understood that Horsey and Co. fished in low water, while all my efforts were in (seemingly) more favourable conditions. Even so, it explains why the dry fly is no longer in my repertoire. I have long come to the conclusion that on the rivers I fish, the chances of success are too small to warrant the effort.

*   *   *

Whatever you are fishing, before starting to cast, try to form a clear idea of how and where a fish is to be landed. There should, of course, be plenty of backing on the reel, but if a big fish gets out into a heavy current and decides to go downstream he will be lost, together with line and backing, if you are not very careful. Whenever casting from a position whence you are unable to follow a fish that is making off fast downstream, check him before he runs out all your backing and fires his Parthian shot. Many an unfortunate fisherman has suffered the mortification of hearing that fatal "ping" as his backing snaps at the knot, and been left with an empty reel.

Don't, of course, jam the brakes full on. Do it gradually. If he won't stop, you will have to hold him—there is no alternative—in which case, if your backing is sound, you will probably lose only the fly. This is ignominious, but preferable to losing line and backing as well. To be broken by a fish is always most unsatisfactory—to my mind, disgraceful—so consider all handling problems *before* he forces you into that split-second decision when, in a hazy sweat, everything seems to go wrong.

Sometimes, after a fish has disappeared with a fly, the leader will have an ominous little curl at the end. This indicates that the knot has slipped! Should it ever happen to you, at least be sure that you alone are to blame. *Never* let your gillie, or anyone else, tie a fly on for you.

It has been said that a fish running downstream can be stopped by the fisherman stripping off line. This is a fallacy. A fast-moving sea trout or salmon can travel at 15–20 m.p.h., and the idea that line can be

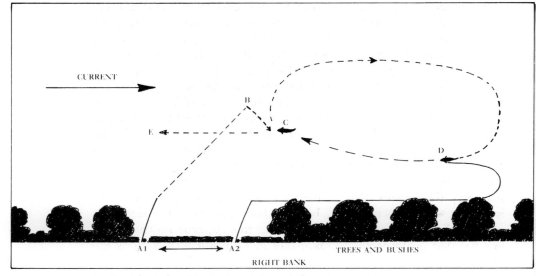

Angler casts to B and hooks fish at C.

Fish turns away and runs downstream, swinging round into the current at D.

Here, while the fish is fresh, a loop of line hanging below (as shown) will almost certainly induce him to move upstream towards his original "lie".

But don't be content to play a passive role.

The loop of line is merely a device for making a fish move when you are unable to move yourself. In the position shown you have the space A1–A2 in which to manoeuvre. Use it.

When the fish takes at C and runs downstream, follow it to A2. Then start immediately to walk it upstream (to A1). The chances are that the fish will continue upstream (towards E) and you will have him where you want him—upstream of the rod. If he makes another downstream run, repeat the manoeuvre. This time he is very unlikely to go as far as he did the first time. If he is a big fish and you know it will take some time to tire him, walk him back from A1 to A2 and then straight back up again.

324

stripped off quickly enough to affect a fish running so fast is chimerical. This method of bringing a fish upstream should, however, not be ignored. Properly applied it is very effective. It can be used when a fish has gone some distance downstream, but has stopped and is lying there. Then, if line is stripped off, a big belly will form below him; he will feel the pressure of this bag of line from behind and begin to swim upstream towards the rod (or, to be more accurate, towards his original "lie", see diagram). It can be used—indeed *is* used and *should* be used—every time a salmon takes a fly; particularly when you are wading. Then, if given plenty of line, the fish will start swimming upstream while you get out of the water; so that by the time you are up on the bank in a position to join battle he is somewhere opposite and just where you want him. It can be used when a fish is *beginning* to tire, and is below you, stemming the current. But the danger of losing a big fish downstream is greatest when he is *very* tired, because then he is unable to resist being carried off tail first by the current. When this happens no amount of line hanging below him will make him move upstream, for he is exhausted.

Whenever you are prevented from following a fish, one rule of angling entirely without exception is: never allow a big tired fish to get out into a heavy current. Unless your tackle is very strong, the moment the stream takes him past the rod he is lost. Once the fish is downstream you will never get him back.

Every eventuality of this nature should be considered before you start fishing. To cast for and hook a fish from a position in which you are not confident of landing him is most unsporting. There is an unfortunate type of fisherman who talks in boasting terms of being broken by a big fish. Such a person exposes himself not only as a bad fisherman, but an insensitive oaf.

Spate fishing often produces disappointing sport. But one advantage enjoyed in daylight and denied by darkness is the sight of a sea trout jumping. When fly is taken and line tightens in the sunshine, the stage is set for a magnificent and unforgettable scene. Almost at once, the surface breaks into a thousand sparkling drops and a writhing bar of lilac and silver bursts upwards, seeming to hang in the air for one, long, glorious moment, every dark spot on that shining flank instantly visible, before plunging down again and whizzing off in a rush that sets a fisherman's heart thumping to the music of his reel.

And the first and most important point in angling
is always to keep out of sight of the fish. Kneel
down, or hide behind a bush so that the fish cannot
see you. For if you do they will not bite. . . And
take care that you do not cast a shadow on the
water, for that will quickly frighten the fish—and
if a fish is frightened he will not bite for a long
time afterwards.
Dame Juliana Berners, *A Treatyse of Fysshynge
wyth an Angle* (1496)

XII
Daylight Fishing

PART TWO: LOW WATER

When the high sun blazes in a burnished sky and the shrunken river falls to low summer levels, there is little chance of daylight sport with sea trout on the fly. During these long, lazy, halcyon days, fish move into the deeper water. There they will rest: gray, unmoving shadows, each dark spot on their flanks standing out with vivid clarity, so transparent is the water, so still are the sea trout lying. Some fish are tucked away underneath the banks; others hang motionless under canopies of trailing alder roots, or in the leafy shade of overhanging branches. From many a crevice in the rocks the tip of a nose or tail protrudes; the fish's presence often unsuspected by a hidden watcher on the bank, until a few tell-tale silver bubbles wobble to the surface and break in the sunlight.

At such times, sea trout in the pools will not readily accept a fly until the sun has set and evening darkens the river. No matter how delicately the cast is made, fish will scatter at the first touch of a fly line on the surface. The shadow of fisherman or rod will send every fish darting for cover; so that in an instant the tranquil scene changes to one of swift movement, confusion and alarm. Fly fishing chances are negligible compared with chances after dark. The water will fish much better then if the sea trout are rested during the hours of daylight.

Nevertheless, no matter how low the river, *provided we have the right type of water at our disposal*, we need not despair of catching fish. Nor need hopes of using the fly rod be abandoned.

Depending on the nature of the water there are several methods of low water daylight fishing we can use. These will be discussed later in this chapter. But there is one outstanding method, which I have already mentioned and which in my opinion equals all others for sheer skill and enjoyment: fishing the upstream worm.

This method is one of the most difficult, and so rewarding, of all ways of angling, either by day or night. Quite apart from the concentration and excitement involved, it is the dexterity required that makes it so fascinating. It is worth remembering that the man who can fish the bait successfully, in addition to fly, is not only a good angler he is a complete angler; for apart from acquiring an all-round skill with a rod, he will have acquired a considerable knowledge of the habits of sea trout and salmon. In consequence, whatever rod he is using, he will catch a lot more fish.

The ability to fish moving worm in low water not only enables the angler to enjoy himself in what are often regarded as "hopeless" conditions, he will take large fish from water which the uninitiated would pass by without a second glance, let alone think of fishing.

I was fortunate enough to discover the existence of this delightful form of fishing many years ago. It happened one afternoon, quite by chance . . .

The river was dead low, the water crystal clear, the day windless, the sky like brass. I had fished greased line for hours without a touch; and then, in the heat of mid-afternoon, when even the stones seemed to be melting, I spotted a salmon.

He was lying on the edge of a fast current in about three feet of water, four or five yards out from a large rock. From a crevice in the rock a small bush was, mysteriously, growing. I crawled up behind the bush. The salmon was now only a few yards away, slightly upstream, and I could see every spot on his flank. I was using an old greenheart single-handed fly rod, but before taking up station behind the bush I had removed the fly from the leader and put on a bare hook. And on the hook—a worm, grubbed up from the bank.

With infinite care I cast the worm upstream and let it float gently down with the current. The fish regarded it without apparent interest. Again I cast, and again. The worm passed first on one side of the salmon, then on the other. Sometimes overhead. The fish took no notice whatsoever, except that when the worm seemed likely to hit him on the nose he moved very slightly to one side.

And all the time the sun was blazing down and my shirt was wet with sweat and sticking to my back. Not that I noticed it while fishing, I was altogether too fascinated. Cast followed cast. My tackle was fine; I was out of sight, casting a short line and fishing carefully. I decided that while the salmon stayed where he was I would do the same. It had become a most interesting little exercise: how long could I continue without disturbing the fish? I had no genuine hope of catching him.

And then, after about fifteen or twenty minutes of this, the salmon suddenly took the worm. There was nothing dramatic about it. He made no avid rush. It was simply that, as the worm floated past for the ump-teenth time, he moved an inch or two to one side and very gently took hold of it.

I held my breath and did nothing.

The salmon stayed right where he was, the worm dangling from his mouth almost as though it had drifted there by accident. It seemed to me that any action on my part would accomplish nothing useful—so I waited.

After what seemed a week, but was probably eight or ten seconds, the worm slowly disappeared. As it did so the salmon began to move lazily upstream. I raised the rod and . . . a few minutes later the fish was on the bank.

That incident, as I say, happened many years ago and it made me think. If salmon behaved like that with a worm, why not with a fly? So I tried "hanging" flies over fish on a long line from well upstream, and the results certainly justified my hopes; for the first time, probably, I was fishing my fly slowly enough. The most successful fly was a hairy thing tied with badger hair bristles from an old shaving brush—the most valuable piece of shaving tackle I have ever owned. Using it, I realized that a larger fly was needed in such fast water than I had been led to suppose. But even so it soon became obvious that in conditions of low clear water, fly tended to hook fewer fish than worm.

The reason for this I concluded was not the nature of the bait but the manner of its presentation. As will emerge from the following pages, fishing upstream worm causes far less disturbance than downstream fly.

The best water for the job is fast, rocky, clear, exciting "runs" where salmon and sea trout lie in conditions of low water and high temperature. They are also found in glides no more than a foot or two deep, among white, broken water where the river foams down between the rocks.

The most suitable tackle is a 10 foot, or 10 foot 6 inch single-handed rod, with a fly reel containing up to 200 yards of 16–20 lb. B.S. nylon. On the end of this nylon (which I shall call the "line") is tied a small

329

Perfect water for fishing the upstream worm.

swivel; and on the other end of the swivel, a 3 foot leader of much lighter nylon. On the end of the leader, a Stewart or Pennell Tackle. Line and leader are made fast to the swivel by means of the Grinner Knot shown on p. 117.

Heavy nylon is advisable on the reel because it is easier to shoot from coils in the hand than anything lighter than about 16 lb. B.S. The leader should of course be much lighter, but as heavy as the state of the water will permit. As a rough guide: for sea trout, use 6–10 lb. B.S. For salmon, 10–15 lb. For my part, when there is chance of hooking both species in the same stretch of water, I use 10 or 11 lb. B.S.

In my experience, comparatively few fishermen have mastered the technique of fishing the moving worm; most of those who try it use a fixed-spool reel. Now, the fixed-spool reel is a splendid invention. Together with monofilament nylon it has revolutionized certain angling methods. But it is not the tool for fishing upstream worm. As we shall see shortly, it is neither accurate nor sensitive enough.

When ledgering a worm it is a different matter. Then, the fixed-spool reel is ideal, as it is for casting float tackle. But except for the bait, there is no point of resemblance between ledgering and fishing upstream worm. Ledgering is practised in the pools, the upstream worm is fished in rapid, broken water and the worm is moving all the time it is fishing.

The object is to present a worm to the fish in such a way that it behaves as naturally as possible. To do this, it should drift with the current, without drag or hindrance, and precede the leader and line.

Throw a worm into a stretch of rapid, broken water and watch what happens to it. Off it goes with a rush; now quickly, now slowly; here it swings into a quieter patch of water and gently bumps along the bottom; there, quite close to the surface, it swirls rapidly down a steep glide; then turns over and over in some back-eddy, hangs behind a stone— perhaps lying quite still for a moment—before the current picks it up again and whisks it off further downstream.

This is how a worm should behave when presented to a fish.

The technique of fishing is quite different from that used for brown trout when the usual practice is to wade up river and cast almost directly upstream with a very long rod. For sea trout and salmon, we fish roughly at right angles to the river, casting slightly upstream and keeping out of the water as much as possible.

When fish are lying in fast, broken water and take just below, opposite, or just upstream of the rod, a Stewart Tackle is the best. In quieter water, where fish tend to take more leisurely as the worm bumps slowly

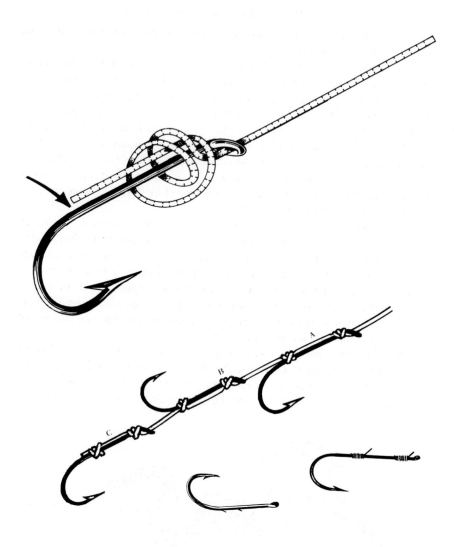

The sliced-shanked bait hook. If such are not available, whip a nylon bristle (or two bristles) to the hook shank to prevent the worm, or worms, from slipping down the shank and bunching-up on the bend of the hook. Bunched-up worms obscure the hook point and allow the hook to be pulled out of a fish's mouth.

Nothing new in this idea, anglers had thought of it hundreds of years ago: "... you may fasten some bristles under the silk, leaving the points above a straws breadth and half or almost half an inch standing out towards the line, which will keep him from slipping back."   Colonel Robert Venables, *The Experienc'd Angler* (1662).

332

round into the slack at the edge of the current downstream of the rod, a single hook is preferable.

Make your own tackles. They are simple to tie and will, I can safely say, be stronger and cheaper than any you can buy. Use the knot shown in the diagram. A small "snecked" hook is the best, size 8 or 10. And by a "snecked" hook I mean one that is twisted out at the bend. Tie on hook *a* first, leaving sufficient nylon to tie on *b* and *c*. Never go to the river without taking plenty of these tackles ready tied on 3 foot lengths of nylon and wound round cardboard frames (see p. 127). You are undoubtedly destined to lose a large number of tackles through getting snagged. This is inevitable, however skilled you may be, so it is well to carry plenty of replacements.

When preparing single-hook tackles, it is quite unnecessary to go to the trouble of whipping on eyeless hooks. Use a spade-end hook with the knot shown on p. 346. Or, if you prefer an eyed hook, use a single Stewart Tackle knot and then whip a quarter of an inch or so of the end to the shank of the hook. Give this whipping a couple of coats of quick-drying varnish and the worm will slide up over it with no difficulty. It is a good plan to whip in a bristle of nylon facing towards the eye of the hook to hold the worm in position.

When baiting a single hook, thread on two small lobworms and leave plenty of the ends hanging down. With Stewart or Pennell tackles, put on a single large lobworm upsidedown, so that the tail of the worm is uppermost on the leader, i.e. on the top hook of the two or three in tandem.

Stewart's original four-hook worm tackle. From the first edition of his book: *The Practical Angler* (1857).

W. C. Stewart first described his tackle in 1857. We may as well consider what he had to say about it.

"The advantages of this tackle are—that a trout can hardly take hold of the worm at all, without having one of the hooks in its mouth; that the worm lives much longer, and being free to wriggle itself into any shape, is more natural looking and consequently enticing; and lastly, that it is much more easily baited, particularly if the worms are fresh. Its disadvantages are, that it is more difficult to extricate from the trout's mouth; that it requires to be baited afresh every bite; and that the exposure of so many hooks is calculated to scare away some trout that would otherwise take the bait. But, upon the whole, the advantages, preponderate considerably over the disadvantages, particularly when trout are biting shy."

To which I have nothing to add.

Depending on the strength of current and depth of water, split shot or a twist of lead wire may be needed on the leader about 18 inches from the worm. Only practical experience of the water to be fished will determine the amount of lead required, but *it should be as little as possible.*

Let us assume that you are by the river. In front of you, flecked with white water, is a rapid, shallow, boulder-strewn "run" that stretches between pools which are, perhaps, two hundred yards apart. You have started at the bottom of this "run" and are gradually working your way upstream. At the moment, from where you are standing, there is the possibility of covering several promising "lies" that are roughly in the centre of the river.

Position yourself so that the top "lie" is just upstream. Strip line off the reel and hold it in two or three large loose coils in the left (or non-casting) hand. To facilitate the smooth shooting of line, a certain amount can be loose on the ground, or in the water, in front of you—although, if you are wading in much of a current it will *all* have to be held in the hand.

Swing the worm back behind you on a rod's length of line and with a smooth, easy flick, cast the bait upstream at an angle of about thirty degrees, shooting the line you have taken off the reel. The angle at which you cast will depend on the strength of current and depth of water. It should be sufficient to allow the worm to be fishing properly by the time it reaches the first "lie".

Immediately the worm starts fishing, maintain contact by drawing in line with the left hand, controlling it—if much has to be drawn in—with the forefinger of the right hand. As the worm passes you and continues downstream, allow this slack line to go out again, bit by bit (as shown in the diagram) so that the worm floats down quite naturally over the other "lies".

334

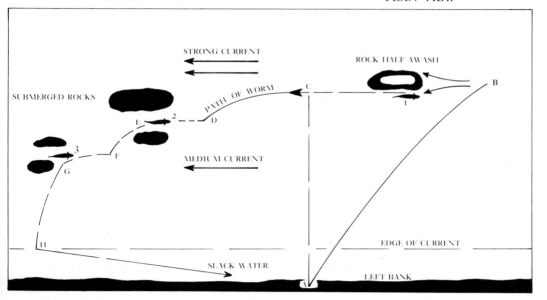

Key to diagram

1. To cover fish No. 1, angler at A casts to B, making allowance for set of the current (curved arrows) owing to water pressure on front of exposed rock.

2. Line is drawn in as worm drifts down towards C. At C, distance is shortest from casting point.

3. At C, line is tightened so that worm swings round to D, where line is released. Worm drifts past fish No. 2, to E.

4. At E, line is tightened so that worm swings round over submerged rock to F.

5. At F, line released again so that worm can drift over fish No. 3. At G, the length of line is once more the same as cast from A to B.

6. From G, worm swings round to H.

7. Worm recovered through slack water—and cast again to B.

8. Fish the "lies" in this way several times before moving to a new position.

335

When all the line is out, let the worm swing in towards the side, but as slowly as possible. If the current is strong, prevent the worm from coming to the top and skidding round on the surface by bringing the rod round downstream and holding it at arm's length.

All the time the worm is fishing know exactly whereabouts it is and try to sense what it is doing. Guide it over or round snags. If this is not possible, retrieve at once. Allow the line to pass between thumb and forefinger of the left hand. They alone are sufficiently sensitive to detect the difference between the touch of a rock and the nudge of a fish. A salmon may touch a worm several times before actually taking it. A sea trout, too, may play with a bait, but usually its "take" is more positive than that of a salmon.

It is when a fish is toying with a bait that the disadvantage of a fixed-spool reel becomes apparent; for, until the fish takes properly, the bait must cover the same spot cast after cast, and with the fly reel that exact length of line is already stripped off.

When, in a likely spot, the worm suddenly stops, *do nothing*. Keep the rod point well up and "feel" the line with the fingers of your left hand. Is the worm caught among the rocks, or in the mouth of a fish? To pull or jerk the line at this moment is disastrous. If the bait is snagged, you will merely fasten the hook more securely. If the bait is in a fish's mouth, you may drag it straight out. So *wait*!

If a sea trout has taken you, two or three distinct "knocks" may be felt. If it is a salmon, you will probably feel very little—merely a tremor, a slight "grating" sensation. In either case, do nothing until you feel the fish move. This will not be long in the case of sea trout. By comparison with salmon they move very quickly after taking. As soon as he moves, tighten. Downstream, if possible. At this point, a sea trout almost always, a salmon sometimes, jumps, and the sight of a large fish leaping from a piece of shallow water, which you might have thought held nothing but fingerling trout, is an exciting experience.

Sometimes the fish will forge ahead and run steadily upstream, sometimes he will go straight off downstream in one long tearing rush for the first piece of deep water below. Let him. He will be easier to play out and land when you have him there, and you have plenty of line. Make no attempt to check this rush. Follow the fish down, holding the rod high—if necessary at arm's length above your head—so as to keep as much line as possible out of the water and clear of obstructions.

And lastly, a few practical "don'ts".

336

1. Don't start fishing until you have examined the water very carefully. Mark down all likely places that may hold fish and decide how you are going to cover them. In particular, note all rocks and other obstructions that may snag you—not only while fishing but after a fish is hooked.

2. Don't expect fish to lie behind rocks. They very rarely do. Fish only lie behind rocks that have a smooth flow of water over them; then they will often lie on top. They are most likely to be found in front of, beside, or between rocks; or in steady glides.

3. Don't fish with freshly-dug worms. Use those that have been kept for several days, they are tougher. Fresh worms break very easily. It is most irritating when they fly off the hook each time you cast. Carry the day's supply in a tin that has a hinged lid. If the tin can be fastened to the front of your belt, so much the better. (For notes on care of worms, and worm species, see p. 316.)

4. Don't try to cast too long a line to start with. Fish the water close to your own bank first, before lengthening line to fish the centre and beyond.

5. Don't be in too much of a hurry. A fish may not take the worm the first time past. As always, it is presentation that really matters. Give every cast the same absolute care—not only to entice a fish into taking at that particular moment, but to avoid disturbing a fish that may take later.

6. Don't wade out to free a tackle that has become snagged. Break it and tie on another. This will lose you a lot of hooks; but to stumble about among the "lies" will lose you a lot of fish. The disturbance caused by wading in shallow runs lasts much longer than in a pool. In the pool a disturbed fish moves into deep water and soon returns. In shallows such as those described, there is no deep water nearby. A disturbed fish moves much further, and takes much longer to return.

7. Don't fish the fly down first. If you want to try both worm and fly, start with the worm. To present fly correctly in fast, shallow water of this nature makes wading—and therefore disturbance—inevitable. Besides, salmon (and large sea trout, too) often take a fly more readily after other lures have been fished over them; provided those lures have been carefully fished.

8. Above all, don't give up. It isn't easy. There are days when everything goes wrong; when every cast finds some hidden snag. As I know only too well, it is disheartening when tackle after tackle glues itself to the rocks. Nevertheless, persist. It is a difficult and exasperating method of fishing. It is tiring, for it demands intense concentration. But it is

337

also extremely fascinating and very, very exciting.

While learning, you will undoubtedly lose your temper and a vast amount of tackle. But of one thing I am certain—the thrill of your first leaping fish will be reward enough.

*   *   *

Not every river offers opportunities such as those I have described for fishing the upstream worm. This type of water is limited—there is less of it in England and Ireland, for instance, than in Scotland—and you may have to travel long distances in search of it. If you do, you will undoubtedly be rewarded. But even when transport facilities are available, it is not always possible to travel far from river to river except during holiday periods, and even then there may be difficulties in getting a "rod" on the water. One is usually restricted to a particular stretch of river during a fishing trip, and when weather conditions render one method of fishing hopeless, it is exciting to explore the possibility of other methods.

In addition to the upstream worm, there are several methods of fishing bait that will enable you to catch fish in low water provided:

1. They are legal.
2. The water is suitable.
3. They are properly fished.

These consist of: ledgering; long-trotting; float/ledgering; laying-on and stret-pegging. They entail the use of worm or maggot, either stationary or on the move, and fished with or without a float.

It may be that the very mention of a float makes some of my readers throw up their hands in horror. In case my comments in an earlier chapter have not been read, I should point out that it is never the method that is unsporting, it is always the man. Whatever the method, it is the way it is used that matters: its effect on the fish, and on other fishermen.

Apropos of this there is one very important point which must be emphasized. It applies both to bait and fly fishermen, and concerns the catching of first-year fish: the herling, whitling, finnock, etc. In certain conditions these little fish take very freely and not much skill is needed to make a big bag, either on bait or fly. Maggot in particular can be deadly, and one sometimes hears of very big bags being taken. This is regrettable. Many of these fish are non-spawners, and although no one knows their chances of survival when they return to sea, it is likely that they represent a large proportion of next season's run of 2–3 lb. sea trout. It is stupid to slaughter them in large numbers.

This is not to suggest that *none* should be killed. On the contrary, they can provide good sport on a fly at dusk, sometimes save a blank night—and are excellent eating. (My favourite breakfast is a fried herling and bacon.) I do suggest, however, that every angler should exercise firm self-discipline when these little fish are "taking" avidly. Supply your needs for the table—and call it a day.

With the proviso that their use does not interfere with other anglers' sport; that catches of small fish are restricted; that the angler takes every precaution to avoid getting broken (by using tackle of reasonable strength), the methods I have listed are as sporting as any other and, *if properly fished*, will do no harm to the fishery. I should stress, however, that although in my experience, worm or maggot when fished in moderation causes no injury to fly-fishing chances, *groundbaiting* in quantity with maggots may well do so. A stream of maggots drifting with the current through a shoal of fish often seems to cause agitation, especially among the smaller fish. "Feeding the swim" is, I believe, forbidden on most salmon and sea trout rivers. In my opinion, rightly so.

Equally, I see no reason why the use of bait should be banned altogether. It is true that maggot *can* cause the loss of smolts and parr. But I submit that if it is fished correctly, it constitutes no greater threat to these little fish than fly. (See lip-hooking, p. 356.) Nor will it affect chances with the fly that evening.

I have run a salmon and sea trout fishery for many years, and use every known angling method. Many times I have had excellent sport on the fly at dusk in water where, a few hours earlier, I had been fishing with bait.

Fly fishing is my chief delight—and indeed the method that catches me most fish—but I derive much satisfaction from fishing in other ways. In low water, a pool is always reserved for daylight fishing by my friends— who may use whatever methods they wish. Often enough this is in water where we are able to observe the reactions of the fish. This has not only given us great pleasure in fishing but has taught us a great deal about sea trout and salmon behaviour.

One of the joys of angling is to experiment, to try new methods. Bait fishing teaches the fly fisherman the use of entirely different tackle and gives him a fresh interest. In the same way, the bait angler's experience is considerably enriched by the use of fly tackle. I have seen both happen on my own water.

339

The simple float and ledger rigs and methods I have drawn and described in this chapter are merely basic examples of their kind. Tackles used in float and ledger fishing are subject to many cunning and subtle variations. The design and function of each tackle item (the float, for instance) is a study of its own, and there is not space for such a comprehensive survey. Nor is it necessary. For anyone interested, lake and river tackles and techniques are dealt with in considerable detail in *Falkus and Buller's Freshwater Fishing* (Macdonald and Jane's, 1975). Sufficient here to discuss in simple terms the possibilities of catching sea trout by day in conditions hopeless for fly fishing.

*　　　*　　　*

SOME LEDGER AND FLOAT RIGS

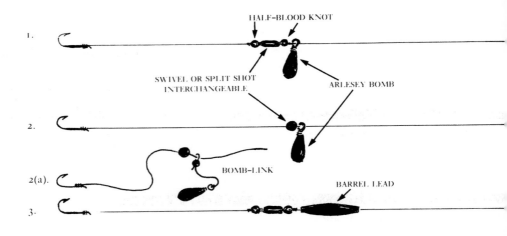

1.

HALF-BLOOD KNOT

SWIVEL OR SPLIT SHOT
INTERCHANGEABLE

ARLESEY BOMB

2.

2(a).

BOMB-LINK

BARREL LEAD

3.

PIERCED BULLET

4.

1–4: RUNNING LINES WITHOUT FLOAT

HOOKS: SPADE END OR EYED
LINES: NYLON MONOFILAMENT

346

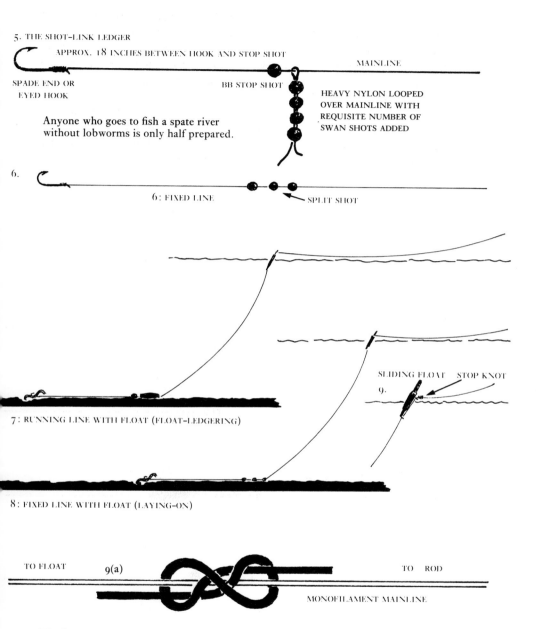

5. THE SHOT-LINK LEDGER

APPROX. 18 INCHES BETWEEN HOOK AND STOP SHOT

MAINLINE

SPADE END OR
EYED HOOK

BB STOP SHOT

HEAVY NYLON LOOPED
OVER MAINLINE WITH
REQUISITE NUMBER OF
SWAN SHOTS ADDED

Anyone who goes to fish a spate river
without lobworms is only half prepared.

6.

6: FIXED LINE

SPLIT SHOT

SLIDING FLOAT   STOP KNOT

9.

7: RUNNING LINE WITH FLOAT (FLOAT-LEDGERING)

8: FIXED LINE WITH FLOAT (LAYING-ON)

TO FLOAT   9(a)

TO   ROD

MONOFILAMENT MAINLINE

The knot as shown is tied very loosely for the sake of clarity.

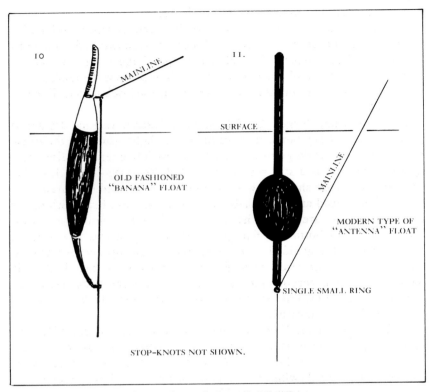

Two examples from the many different designs of sliding floats.

Note. These rigs are simple variations of the *fixed line* and the *running line* (with and without floats), two of the earliest recorded angling rigs. It is important to remember that the term "running-line" was used by early writers to describe a line that ran unimpeded through the lead—on the bottom, or (as they put it) "at ground". It did *not* mean a line running through the ring, or rings, of a rod; this is a recent error. The first angling book printed in English: *A Treatyse of Fysshynge wyth an Angle* (written, probably, between 1420 and 1430, printed in 1496), makes a clear distinction between a stationary line and a running line:

"Your lynes must be plumbid wyth lede. And ye shall pat the nexte plumbe unto the hoke shall be therefro a large fote and more. And euery plumbe of a quantyte to the gretnes of the lyne. There be thre manere of plumbis for a *grounde lyne rennynge*. And for the flote set upon the *grounde lyne lyenge* X plumbes Ioynynge all togider."

(My italics.)

Key to diagrams

1, 2, 2(a); variations on the Arlesey bomb theme.

1. A swivel makes a convenient join between mainline and leader when these are of different strengths. (The swivels shown in the diagrams are all out of proportion. They should be just large enough to form a stop that keeps the lead at an appropriate distance from the hook.)

2. A split shot can be used as a stop when the hook is tied direct to the mainline.

2(a). Bomb-link ledger. Useful for long-distance casting. Its shape prevents the Arlesey bomb from tumbling in flight—so often the cause of the terminal tackle getting tangled with mainline. In the diagram a split shot is used as a stop for the nylon link (the loop of which is also formed with a split shot). A swivel can of course be used if desired.

3, 4. Barrel lead and pierced-bullet ledger rigs have been with us for a long time. They are useful when a bait is to be rolled downstream with the current on a bottom of fine gravel. By fishing in this way a direct fish-scaring cast is avoided. If the lead gets caught up between stones, the line can still run freely through it if a fish takes the bait. If there is too much line drag through the lead, the fish may become suspicious and release the bait. Opening up the bore of the lead reduces line drag and increases the rig's sensitivity.

5. Shot-link ledger. Compared with the equivalent weight of lead in other rigs, this rig causes less disturbance when cast. If it becomes snagged, a hard pull will remove the weight from the leader. When other rigs become snagged (with the exception of the bomb-link, which works in a similar way) the terminal tackle is usually lost.

The addition or removal of one or more of the swan-shots on the link weight makes adjustment very easy. This is important when you need to adjust your lead to suit differing strengths of current in the same stretch of river. In ledgering, the calculation of weight can be critical and frequently makes the difference between success and failure. Experience soon teaches the number of shots required for varying currents, either for holding the bait still on the bottom or allowing it to bump along.

It is a good plan to prepare a stock of shot-loops holding, say, from two to ten shots. You can then start fishing with the loop you think has the right amount of lead for the current at the time. This saves a lot of fiddling about at the waterside.

Swan shots pulled off a loop can be slipped into your pocket, re-opened at home and used again.

343

6. A "fixed" line, weighted with split shot—usually the terminal tackle used when laying-on.

7. A float/ledger rig, using barrel lead and stop shot.

Note. The terms "laying-on" and "float/ledgering" often cause confusion, but the difference is simple enough. In both rigs the bait is not suspended from the float but fished on the bottom. *Laying-on has a fixed line. Float/ledgering has a running line.*

8. A typical laying-on rig, baited with worm. (See also, stret-pegging, p. 352.)

9. A sliding float, used when the depth of water exceeds the length of the rod in use. The Stop Knot is shown in 9(a).

10. Banana-shaped float. This was a most efficient design. It eliminated friction against the body of the float when line was being taken down to the Stop Knot by the weight.

11. Modern antenna-type float with single ring of very small diameter. Such a small ring needs only a very small Stop Knot. Most modern sliding floats are single-ringed. Friction is negligible.

Some of the best modern bait-fishing hooks have flatted or "spade" ends. Such hooks are by no means a modern invention, since almost identical models were in use thousands of years ago. The knots used by the ancients to fasten these hooks to their lines are not on record, but here are two present-day variations on the theme for use with mono-filament nylon. First of all, Method A.

Hold the hook, point up, in the left hand. Fold back eight or ten inches of nylon (fig. 1).

Grip the nylon against the shank of the hook (fig. 2). For ease of tying ensure that the line coming to the left hand is kept under tension.

With the right hand, wind the free end of the nylon round and round the shank, securing each turn by dropping the second finger of the left hand (fig. 3).

After completing six or seven turns, pass the end of the nylon through the loop (fig. 4).

While keeping a grip with the left hand, pull the mainline in the direction of the arrow until the knot pulls tight (fig. 5).

Slide the knot along the shank until it reaches the broad spade end. Give the mainline nylon a final tug with the right hand, while resisting this pull from the opposite end by holding the nylon stub between the teeth.

Trim the nylon stub.

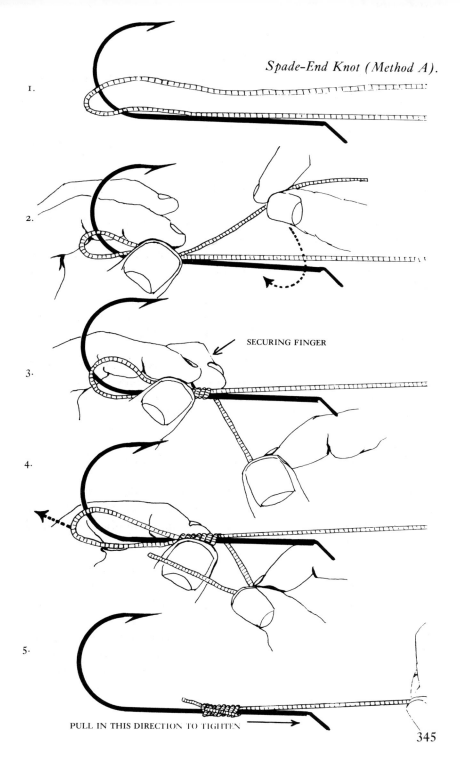

Spade-End Knot (Method A).

1.

2.

3. SECURING FINGER

4.

5.

PULL IN THIS DIRECTION TO TIGHTEN ⟶

345

Method B produces a neat, shank-hugging knot that is no more difficult to tie than the other; indeed, in poor light, it is easier.

Wind turns clockwise round the shank in the direction of arrow No. 1, *keeping each turn hard up against the left thumb.*

Make eight or ten turns, taking care not to wind them on too tightly.

When the last turn is made, pull the end of the nylon in the direction of arrow No. 2; gently at first, then firmly.

Slide the knot close up to the spade-end of the shank before snugging down. This is achieved by pulling on the line in one direction (arrow 3), while pulling on the end of the nylon in the opposite direction (arrow 2).

Spade-End Knot (Method B)

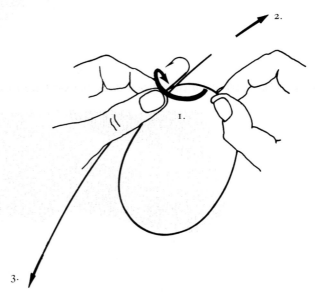

Although Method A seems to be popular, I much prefer this method.

The Spade-End Knot is equally effective for tying an eyed hook to a nylon monofilament mainline, the bulge forming the eye of the hook being treated as the spade-end. If hooks with upturned or downturned eyes are used, the mainline nylon is passed through the eye before the knot is tied. But in the case of a straight-eyed hook the eye is by-passed, and the hook treated as though it were a spade-end hook. (Otherwise it will stick out at an angle to the line.)

346

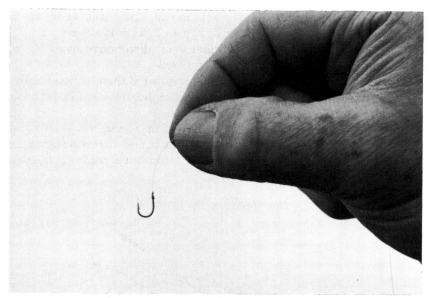

"Forged, Reversed, Flatted, Blued, Special" Hollow Point, Mustad–Limerick Hook.
Size: 10.

The Mustad, operational. A fine, exceedingly sharp point is an essential feature of a
hook used for maggot fishing. A blunt point bursts the maggot.

347

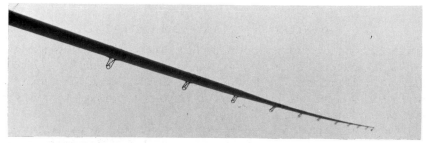

Bruce and Walker fibre-glass, compound taper, float-fishing rod.
Length: 12 ft. 6 in.

Stand-off rings hold the line clear of the rod and facilitate casting a float or a very light
lead. They should be made of stiff wire, hard chromed. The best standard end-rings
are made of tungsten-carbide.

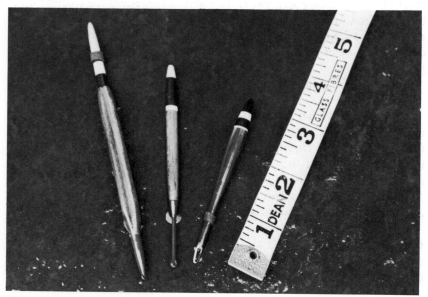

Recommended size and shape of floats.

A float acts as a bite indicator, a casting weight, and suspends a bait at a given depth
(or allows it to sweep the bottom). Although a float's shot-carrying capacity is related
to its volume, the same volume can be represented by almost endless combinations of
length and girth. Float patterns are legion, but for sea trout fishing these will do all that
is required.

348

When a boy I loved to sit and watch a float. And still love to. Ledgering a bait is sometimes more effective, but it is never so engaging. The float has a fascination shared by no other piece of tackle. Any angler who remains untouched by its magic is not only a deprived angler, he is at best little more than half an angler.

I caught my first fish at the age of four, over fifty years ago, and since that long-ago but never forgotten summer's day, float fishing has at some time or another caught me nearly every common species of British freshwater and saltwater fish. And the salmon and the sea trout are no exceptions.

I am not suggesting that the float should supersede other methods; simply that on occasions, when other methods fail, it offers the chance of some interesting and skilful fishing.

But perhaps more so with the float than any other method (whatever rig is chosen) final adjustment must always be made at the waterside. Success so often depends on some tiny but vital alteration to suit changing conditions of weather and water. The ability to sense these changes and to know how to deal with them separates the expert angler from the rest. The various float fishing rigs and methods have been studied in detail in a host of books. Here we need consider only a few elementary principles.

A float has five main functions:

1. It carries the bait to a fish-holding area, and avoids the disturbing splash caused by casting direct to fish. For this reason, if for no other, fish that would be frightened by fly-fishing can be taken on bait. One might think that the use of a float in low water would disturb fish. In fact, the reverse is true; *if properly used* a float *avoids* disturbance.

2. "Long-trotting" a bait downstream enables fish to be covered that are outside normal casting range.

3. It indicates a bite; also the direction the fish is moving in when the bait has been taken. This is important when worm is used. Both salmon and sea trout should be given plenty of time before the line is tightened. In the meantime it is useful to know where the fish has gone.

4. It keeps the mainline on the surface and so free of snags. The line is also prevented from "raking" through a shoal of fish when a bait is being retrieved or a fish is being played. This keeping of the mainline clear of the bottom is a great asset, and explains why float/ledgering, or laying-on, succeeds when plain ledgering fails.

5. It enables a bait to be manoeuvred over a wide area across and downstream (see stret-pegging, p. 352). Also, across and *upstream*. By crafty use of current and back-eddy, a bait can often be worked all round a pool, upstream, downstream and across. (See diagram.)

Key to diagram
Angler at A, casts to B_1, keeping the bale arm of his fixed-spool reel open.

The float starts to drift with the main current in the direction of C_1. The line on the surface between the rod and B_1 is dragged upstream by the back-eddy.

The line dragged backwards by the back-eddy will not impede the progress of the float (as might be thought), since the bale-arm is kept open; line will be taken off the spool and run out across the water in a big curve, as though it were running round a huge pulley wheel.

Every so often, the line is checked momentarily to hold back the float (see diagram on p. 354).

When the float reaches the area of C_1, down in the tail of the pool, the bale-arm is engaged. This causes the float to swing round towards D.

At this point, if the angler wishes to make another cast or to freshen his bait, he has only to swing his rod round inshore (upstream) and the float will be brought out of the back-eddy. It can then be retrieved, clear of any fish, through the slack water.

If he wishes, however, the angler can allow the float to fish right back upstream with the back-eddy towards G. In which case, he will lift his rod high and gradually wind in most of the slack line—picking it carefully off the surface.

When the float has come full circle it can be drawn in and cast again (to B_2 and B_3). Or, if the wind is offshore, it can be allowed to work back into the main stream, this time farther out, and go on another tour of the pool.

By skilful manipulation of rod and line the float (and bait) can be worked round and round a pool of this nature, covering every piece of holding water. Fish can be presented with a bait without a disturbing splash.

In fishing of this sort the fixed-spool reel comes into its own. And once more a long rod is shown to great advantage—as it is for every form of fishing. The 12 ft. 6 in. rod already recommended will serve well enough. I would certainly use nothing shorter. Line control is of paramount importance, and it is simply not possible with a short rod. This is a fascinating form of fishing, but it demands specialized tackle.

The diagram shows only a fraction of what can be done (with the right sort of rod, line and float) by using current, back-eddy and wind to work a bait to fish in a natural way and without disturbance.

> *Note.* For this type of fishing, maggot is not suitable since it needs a quick strike. Worm is by far the best bait. The great amount of slack line that may be out when the worm is taken will be a help rather than a hindrance, since the fish should be given plenty of time before contact is established. In the event of a take, do *not* snatch at the line with a jerk. This will only result in a lot of surface disturbance. Pause. Watch the float. See which way the fish is moving. When you think the bait has been properly taken, wind in carefully, bring the rod over downstream—and tighten.

PLAN VIEW

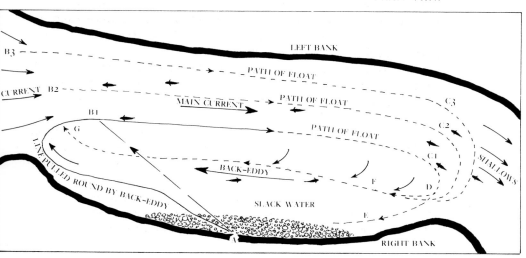

The depth at which the bait is set will depend on local conditions. When fishing a clean pool I prefer the bait to sweep the bottom. If the pool is rocky the bait will need to be set a foot or so clear of the bottom. (By the way, this is one of the most successful of all methods of fishing prawn for salmon.)

351

Stret-pegging is another method of fishing a bait at long range in running water without causing the disturbance of long-range casting. The bait not only covers a wide area, but reaches fish without breaking the surface nearby. The tackle is, in effect, a laying-on rig that is used to work a bait across a "taking" area to the stretch of water between current and slack where big fish often lie.

1. Set the float deeper than the water depth by about 18 inches.
2. Make a cast at right-angles across the river (A to B, see diagram). As soon as the cast has been made, hold the float back for a moment on a tight line. This enables the shotted leader and the worm to sweep the bottom on a short arc.
3. Release the line and allow the float to drift a yard or two downstream, then once again hold it back for a few seconds. During each pause (at C, D, E, F, G) the worm covers fresh ground. Gradually, in a rather crab-like fashion, the bait moves over towards your own bank, ending up on a much longer line than was originally cast, at H—where it can be allowed to lie for a time.
4. Bring the rod round so that it points downstream, then draw the bait quietly upstream through the slack water close to the bank. To retrieve the bait in this manner will cause no disturbance.

STRET-PEGGING

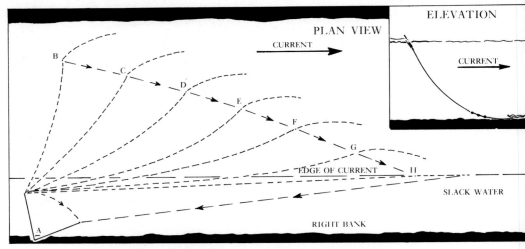

The first time down, the cast is made from A to B. Subsequent casts can be made at a more acute angle farther downstream, to cover water not fished hitherto.

Note. Stret-pegging is only possible where the bottom is clean—preferably sand or fine gravel. Fish may take at any point of the cast, but the "easy" water between current and slack is often good for both salmon and sea trout. Worm is the usual bait. But when conditions are suitable, shrimp fished in this way is deadly for salmon.

The head of a tidal pool in the heat of August. The river at dead summer low. In the absence of any freshwater current, Fred Buller is using the last of the ebbing seawater to work his float. For perhaps an hour or so there will be a chance of taking sea trout or salmon that have come up with the tide.

353

Later, when the tide had ebbed. Looking downstream towards the tail of the same pool. The light is bright; the water gin clear and unrippled. Anyone who condemns "bait" should try his hand at catching fish in conditions such as these. (A fly line falling across this mirror-like surface will put down every fish in the pool.) For anyone using maggot or worm, success is still possible. But it demands angling skill of the very highest order.

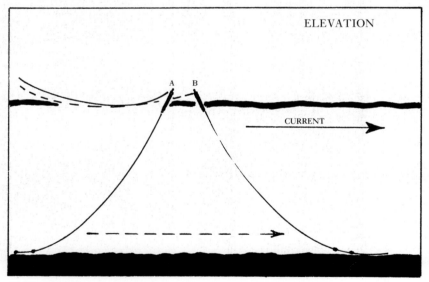

Holding back.
When a bait is trotted downstream, especially when it is sweeping the bottom, it tends to lag behind the float. This is indicated by the float's forward sloping attitude (A). The line should be tightened momentarily to allow the bait to be carried forward (B).

354

The result.
Fred Buller with three grilse caught (together with some sea trout) stret-pegging with worm in the "hopeless" conditions of low, clear water already shown. Note the distinguishing scar (insert) which enabled Buller to identify this fish as one he had previously spotted while making his reconnaissance.

355

Long-trotting is the best method of fishing maggot on float tackle. Wherever possible work from the bank under which the fish are lying. Try the bait set at various depths. Hold back at regular intervals as the float drifts downstream so that the bait always reaches the fish in advance. Keep in contact. The moment the float bobs—tighten. *When fishing maggot the object is to lip-hook every fish.* This is because maggot attracts and can be taken by very small fish. Lip-hooking ensures that immature fish can be returned to the water unharmed.

In the course of an hour or two you will undoubtedly make many tackle alterations to meet the changing demands of water, wind and fish: a different hook size; a variation in fishing depth (by increasing or decreasing the distance between float and hook); substituting a float carrying more shot to make the bait sink faster.

It is essential to *keep out of sight*. Stand or kneel twenty or thirty yards upstream of the fish and "trot" the bait down to them. Remember, the longer the range, the greater the strain imposed on your tackle when you strike—and quick striking is essential when maggot is fished in this way. Because of this, and because slightly heavier floats with more shotting are normally used in trotting, a strong, supple rod is best for this type of fishing.

When choosing from a number of floats, of different shape but roughly equal buoyancy, the most sensitive float is the best choice. A fish may become suspicious and drop a bait when it feels the resistance of a tubby float. Compromise is necessary, however, when a heavy shot load is needed, otherwise the float's length would be excessive. In low, clear water, a long float tends to "rub the backs" of the fish and frighten them. In fast, swirling water, a slim float is likely to be sucked under from time to time, whereas a more bulbous float will ride more smoothly and give fewer false bites.

There is a tendency for the novice to leave too much of his float showing. If a float dips half-an-inch when two or three inches were exposed above the surface, the "take" may go unnoticed. A float that dips the same distance when only half-an-inch was showing goes out of sight, and the bite is noticed immediately.

The underwater colour of a float is important if only for the confidence it inspires. Olive or yellow-brown is probably the best, since it represents the colour of natural flotsam. Fish are used to seeing all manner of twigs, bits of reed stem, grasses and the like pass over them. A float need be no more disturbing.

Brightly coloured floats are likely to flash during their passage through

356

the air, in the same way that a varnished rod, or a gun barrel, or a glass, can be seen to flash perhaps half-a-mile away. A matt finish is always best. Most animals can see as well as we can. Many of them have sight that is much more acute than ours, and what startles us is likely to frighten them. That sea trout have exceptionally good eyesight is well known to anyone who walks along the river bank!

There is no best colour for the visible part of a float. Choice depends on the prevailing light, but the following colour combination can be recommended. Starting at the tip, paint the part of the float that shows above water in three equal bands of orange, white and black. A float-cap of similar colour is then placed on the appropriate band.

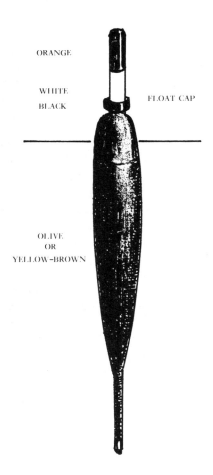

ORANGE

WHITE

BLACK   FLOAT CAP

OLIVE
OR
YELLOW-BROWN

No angler can avoid the occasional hooking of undersized fish. Such fish are protected by legislation; but size limits are pointless unless the angler takes care when removing the hook. All too often, undersized fish unhooked and returned to the water, die as a result of their rough handling.

The "V" prong disgorger in common use is both brutal and ineffective. A vastly better instrument is the cross-cut slotted disgorger. This is the most humane and efficient disgorger available today for use on small fish.

Hold the hooked fish, and tension the leader coming to its mouth. Let the leader drop in the cross-cut (A) before turning the disgorger through ninety degrees in the direction of the fish's mouth. The leader now runs right through the disgorger slots (B). Slide the disgorger down the line into the fish's mouth until the end of it takes in the shank of the hook and touches the bend. Now that the hook-shank is firmly held, a further push frees the barb. A half-twist and the hook can be withdrawn, as shown in the photograph.

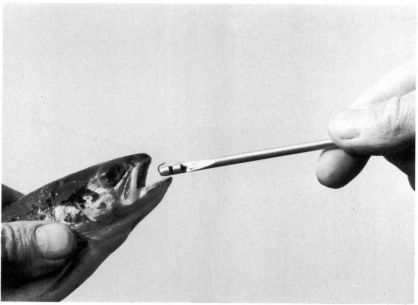

Cross-cut slotted disgorger removing hook from a small trout.

358

The "V" prong disgorger.

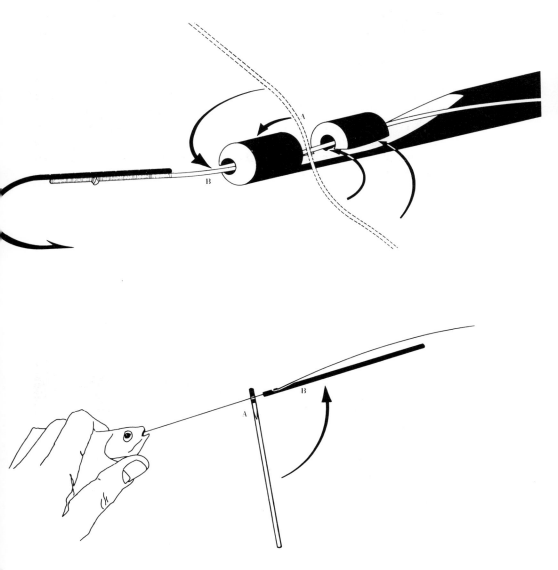

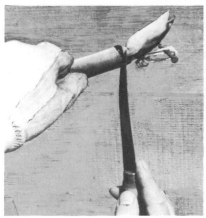

Sooner or later, bait fishing produces eels.
    To control a live eel hold as shown, between the fingers.
    Stun it by hitting it across the tail.
    Kill it by severing the neck vertebrae. (If you want to skin it, do *not* cut off the head.)
    Eels are delicious to eat.
    Some people simply cut them into chunks and fry them.
    Others prefer to skin them first.
    If you wish to do likewise:
1. Tie the head of the eel to a wooden upright.
2. Slice through the skin round the neck with a razor blade or very sharp knife.
3. Grip the skin with a pair of pliers and strip off.
4. Clean, salt, cut into chunks and fry.

And lastly, a word about attractants. Is there anything that will make a bait more attractive? Well—throughout the ages anglers, like mediaeval philosophers in search of their Stone, have sought potions for "alurring" fish. The history of angling abounds with "Irresistible Compounds". Here is an example:

> "Take Man's Fat and Cat's Fat, of each half an Ounce, Mummy finely powdred three Drams, Cummin-seed finely powdred one Dram, distill'd Oyl of Annise and Spike, of each six Drops, Civet two Grains, and Camphor four Grains, make an Ointment according to Art; and when you Angle anoint 8 inches of the Line next the Hook therewith, and keep it in a pewter box . . ."
>
> James Chetham, *The Angler's Vade-Mecum* (1681)

Does it work? I don't know. The difficulty of obtaining certain ingredients inhibits research. But frankly, while hesitating to knock something untried, I think Chetham made a lemon of this one. That fish should find the scent of Man (or Cat, for that matter) attractive seems unlikely. The reverse one would think would be the case.

Nevertheless, although so far as I know there has never been a "potion" that really worked, there is no reason to suppose that something of the sort is impossible. Fish have a fantastic sense of smell. Some substances undoubtedly attract or repel them more than others. I have a sneaky kind of feeling that there really is an "Irresistible Compound" lurking somewhere—if philosophy could find it out.

I hope it never does.

If a friendly millionaire were to offer me any white trout lake in Connemara I would choose Clogher. Always I pushed out from its shores with a feeling of anticipation and excitement. It has given a basket in half a gale and in complete calm. There was no telling where fish would rise best, or whether they were going to be large or small. Often disappointed, I never ceased to hope for the day which I felt was due to me, when morning and afternoon all over the lake, along shores and shallows, butt and islands, the big fish would be moving and I should bring *such* fishes back. It never came.

T. C. Kingsmill Moore, *A Man May Fish* (1979)

XIII
Lake Fishing
and Safety Afloat

The Approach

When we consider the widely differing lakes of north-west Britain and Ireland, each with its own particular character; each, for its mastery, requiring from the angler almost a lifetime's study of its moods, it is clear that nearly every statement about sea trout stillwater fishing needs to be qualified. To write a comprehensive summary of the fish and fishing in so many different locations would require considerably more space than this chapter can provide—and indeed more knowledge than I can offer.* My aim, therefore, is simply to express a few of the principles that are common to many fisheries and describe some of the tackle and methods I have found interesting and successful. (To avoid confusion between loch and lough, the term "lake" will be used throughout.)

A stranger to any water has a better chance of catching sea trout when going from river to river than from lake to lake. Nevertheless a lake can be thought of as a large pool in a river. Having run up the river that connects it to the sea, sea trout stay in the lake for a period of days, weeks or months before ascending the head waters to spawn—just as the river fish do, from their pools to the feeder streams.

But a river pool is so much more intimate than a lake. Fish are collected

---

* There are some good books that cover sea trout fishing in stillwater. I recommend the following: *Salmon and Sea Trout in Wild Places* and *Newly from the Sea* by the late Sidney Spencer, and *A Man May Fish* by the late T. C. Kingsmill Moore. Kingsmill Moore's book is in my top twenty list of best angling books. An enlarged second edition was published in 1979 and can be obtained from Colin Smythe Ltd, P.O. Box 6, Gerrard's Cross, Bucks.

in smaller and more clearly defined areas. Looking at a lake, a novice angler is easily dispirited by the vast sheet of water. For the most part, the fish are seldom seen; their "lies" are invisible. An angler new to the lake, however experienced he may be, relies mainly on his gillie or other anglers for a knowledge of the best "lies" and drifts and lures. There are, however, a few points which, when added to his water-sense, may help him to decide where, when and how to fish.

When sea trout first enter a lake it is likely that some will lie for a time near to the outflow, before making their way round the edges of the lake to the mouths of the feeder rivers in which they will ultimately spawn. But most of these newly-run fish travel at once through the lake to the area near feeder outflows. If the lake is one in a chain of lakes these fish will soon press on to waters higher up. If there are no further lakes the fish will start to spread out along the margins of the lake, in little bays and around islands—mainly in rocky shallows; sometimes in or near reed beds.

The area to which an angler should first direct his attention is the stretch of shallows off the mouth of a feeder river. Often, the bottom here is a ridge of sand that stretches down from shallows to deeps; a kind of "bar" formed by the fallout of sandy particles in the silt washed down the river and out into the lake by heavy floods. Invariably, such sand banks or ridges provide good fishing grounds. On the day following a spate, when there is every chance of fresh sea trout having entered the lake, this before all others is the place to fish.

Many of the bigger fish take up special "lies", occupying certain places in a lake at certain times. Some lies are tenanted early in the season, others not until much later on. They are occupied season after season and much of an angler's success depends on a knowledge of their where-abouts and when they are likely to be occupied. Small fish are sometimes inclined to cruise in shoals—certainly in some lakes, since they have been seen to do so. Gradually the fish spread out, some of them going into the deeps, with the result that the angler has fewer drifts over empty water.

Although sea trout in stillwater are often described as "active feeders" a little thought exposes this as a fallacy, and any angler who sets out expecting a rise of fish to coincide with a rise of fly is likely to be dis-appointed.

In earlier chapters we examined the sea trout's style of feeding in the sea. If the fish continued to feed as actively as this in the lake we might reasonably expect that the longer they remained in this new (and less fertile) environment the greater would be their efforts to find food, since if they retained their appetites after leaving their rich sea feeding-grounds the hungrier they would become. And it would be logical to suppose that the longer the fish had been lying in freshwater the greater the angler's chance of catching them. But this is far from being the case. On the contrary, in the lake as in the river, the most ready takers are the fresh-run fish. The longer the fish have been lying in freshwater the less interest they show in a food item, or an angler's lure. And, needless to say, the harder they are to catch.

Big sea trout are seldom found with food in their stomachs. Smaller fish, in the $1\frac{1}{4}$–2 lb. range, occasionally contain insects. I have caught sea trout of this size with fly larvae and beetles inside them—but strangely, never a stickleback, although small brown trout of only a few ounces caught in the same water were crammed with sticklebacks. (I have, however, heard of one Irish lake where small sea trout have been caught with the stickles "dripping out of their mouths".) Some of the herling remain avid feeders and, as might be expected, are ready takers. They are often crammed with food such as plankton and fly larvae—as indeed they may be in the river if sufficient food is available. But these are mainly immature fish uninhibited by any biological change. In the lake, as in the river, the majority of sea trout do little foraging. If a rise of fly occurs some of the smaller fish may interest themselves; but the appearance of food is by no means a guarantee of sea trout activity.

T. C. Kingsmill Moore makes the point so well in *A Man May Fish* that, with his kind permission, I quote him in full:

"Looking out over a calm lake, where the rises slowly spread and intersect like the Olympic rings, one is tempted to suppose that the white trout are making a meal of it, but four out of every five rises are made by small trout or parr. Even if the extra size or turbulence of the ring marks out a white trout, there is no guarantee that it is a feeding rise, for white trout like salmon will break surface for sport. White trout, moreover, seem very inept at taking a floating and motionless fly. Their sea feeding on sand eels and sprat has turned them into chasers rather than suckers-down, and from a becalmed boat I have often seen a white trout make two or three futile efforts to absorb a sedge or daddy and suffer the ignominy of having it snapped from under its nose by a small brownie.

"The feeding of white trout in fresh water is spasmodic and limited. This can be deduced from the rapid decline in their condition after

Mr Justice Kingsmill Moore, author of *A Man May Fish*. A great man. A great book.

they leave the sea, and is confirmed by examination of their stomachs. I ought to be able to present a table showing the stomach contents of several thousand fish, and I have wickedly neglected my opportunities for preparing such a monograph. From time to time I took out with me a magnifying glass, a white saucer, and a razor blade, and at lunch time eviscerated the fish, tipped anything found in their stomachs into the saucer of water, and examined it. In all I must have investigated about one hundred interiors. Rather over half had no food, except an odd water flea or Daphnia. About thirty per cent had the remnants of three or four insects, and about fifteen per cent had double that amount. No fish had as much as I would expect to find in a Slaney trout of six ounces after the morning rise. There were never any worms or traces of small fish. I found only small sedges, crane flies, assorted diptera, heather moths, and a very odd beetle. The herling— that is to say the sea trout grilse—seemed more disposed to feed than the adult fish.

"Admittedly the food supply in these moorland lakes is scanty, and a trout might be hard put to it to collect a dozen insects in a morning, but there are occasions when a moderate sprinkling of olives and small sedges are to be seen, and more often than not the white trout ignore them. White trout have their time of "taking", and if a rise of fly coincides with this time they will not overlook the natural, but a rise of natural will not necessarily bring them on the "take". The "take" seems to be the result of a sudden burst of activity quite unrelated to food."

Our approach to fishing for the stillwater sea trout is no different from our approach to the river sea trout: what we are trying to do is to stimulate his feeding habit; his response to the sight of something that is tempting—whether an insect or a tiny fish moving through the water; a dry-fly making little darts across the surface, or something big and hairy dabbled in the surface film. And the sooner we cast to a fish after he has appeared in the lake the more likely we are to catch him.

During spells of dry windless weather, stale fish can be very dour. They can, of course, still be caught, but like their counterparts in the river pools they need the stimulus of weather change to "bring them on".

Better, from the angler's point of view, is a rise of water to bring in a fresh run of fish. But even though fish may have run quite recently a lake may suddenly go "dead". There have been weeks when I fished

367

day after day without seeing a single sea trout move; catching the odd one or two at no particular times; being equally successful (or unsuccessful) by night as by day.

During difficult weather conditions it is wise to vary one's tactics. "Taking" fish are few and far between. A sea trout that declines a fly fished near the surface may take one fished deep on sunk line. One or two may be taken by trailing—either on "the metal" or on fly—or tempted by a dry-fly soaked in Permaflote and tickled across the surface. Modern nylon floss lines can be made to work in the lightest of winds: dapping no longer depends on the amount of breeze that the tackle of a decade or so ago demanded. And there is always the chance of a fish or two on fly after dark. Nevertheless, while conditions remain poor the fish, for the most part, are (as my favourite Irish boatman once described them) "sulky-boys".

For several days, perhaps, the wind remains light and variable with long patches of dead calm, gusting from the north towards evening. A cold wind that blackens the water in steely ridges. Nothing moves to fly fished near the surface. At dusk, although it is July, fingers are stiff with cold. The water seems lifeless. Pundits in hotel bars bemoan the lack of sport and blame the run of fish.

Suddenly the wind shifts to the south. It is a day of cloud and soft rain with breaks of sunshine. The sea trout are taking all across the lake. Boats come in with one or two salmon and a dozen or so sea trout apiece. Anglers who have arrived the night before bask in their good fortune, congratulating themselves and their companions on their skill. Those unfortunates that have flogged away the dog days and missed this golden occasion by a whisker, curse their luck. Unless he is fortunate in living beside the lake with the means to fish as and when he wishes, the stillwater fisherman must cultivate the comfort of a strong philosophy.

As an Irish gillie of long ago declared: "When fish are down any change is good, even if it's for the worse!" And it is true that on the lake as on the river a change, however slight, may bring a few fish on the "take". But all too frequently such bursts of activity are likely to be fleeting. With limited time at his disposal the visiting angler cannot afford to miss a trick. In addition to water-sense and a nose for weather, he needs the assistance of a sound technique.

*　　　　*　　　　*

Distinction between Brown Trout and Sea Trout
It would seem appropriate to include here an extract concerning the

distinction between these two fish which is of great interest to game fisherman and which occurs in a paper by T. B. Bagenal, the late F. J. H. Mackereth and J. Heron of The Freshwater Biological Association, Windermere.

"Usually sea trout can be easily distinguished from brown trout, though occasionally difficulties arise in separating them. These difficulties are most often encountered with large trout caught in lakes. The scales of brown trout that have been spawned in an in-flowing stream and later migrated to a lake show a great increase in growth similar to that shown on the scales of sea trout after they have migrated to the sea. Similarly some large trout have a colouration very similar to that of sea trout. Conversely fish are sometimes caught in the sea which if their place of capture was not known, would have been called brown trout. Over the last few decades large trout have occasionally been caught by the Freshwater Biological Association in gill nets set for pike in Windermere. The lengths, weights, sex and other details have been noted for each fish and a scale sample has been kept. At a later date it has become necessary in a few cases to confirm whether the specimen was a sea trout or a brown trout. It has been found that this can be done with certainty by an analysis of the strontium content of the scales. Sea water contains several hundred times more strontium than does freshwater, and it appears that unlike some other elements (e.g. halides) which are also commoner in the sea, the strontium difference is reflected in the scales of fish."

Note. Scales of brown trout contain less than 200 μgSr/g and those of sea trout more than 300 μgSr/g.

For the methods used and results obtained, see *J. Fish Biol.* (1973) 5, 555–557: *The distinction between brown trout and sea trout by the strontium content of their scales.*

Fly Fishing

The customary method of stillwater fly-fishing from a boat is to motor or row to the upwind end of a fishing area and then drift straight down-wind, keeping the boat's beam at right angles to the wind direction. The flies (usually two, sometimes three) are cast ahead of the drifting boat and worked back towards the angler. An oar is used only to keep the boat broadside to the wind, or to avoid rocks. But casting straight downwind is not very efficient. It covers less water, gives the fish—which

I think tend to head upwind—a less attractive view of the flies and increases the tendency to pull a fly out of a fish's mouth. In consequence, it is better to cast at an angle to the direction of the drift, so that the flies are drawn partly across the wind.

In my experience a method more profitable than the straight downwind drift is to fish on a zig-zag path *across* the wind. It must be emphasized, however, that the success of crosswind fishing depends on two factors:

    1. An experienced and sympathetic boatman. (By no means all gillies are in tune with this method and it is essential to have someone who is.)

    2. Sufficient wave to diminish the splash and movement of the oars.

Almost everything depends on the skill of the oarsman. In addition to knowing the best fishing areas he must be able to manoeuvre the boat at just the right speed with the minimum of splash. When a known "lie" is reached, or a fish has risen and refused, he must be able to check the boat and hold it in position without any downwind drift. This enables the angler to cover the fish several times, if necessary, without its being frightened by the sight of the boat. A fish that rises "short" will frequently take the fly if given another opportunity. But all too often, before such a fish can be covered properly a second time, a drifting boat is swept over it. Perhaps the sight of the boat's underwater shape reminds a sea trout of the seal—one of its main predators. For whatever the reason, sea trout are exceedingly boat shy.

In an earlier chapter I mentioned the need sometimes to throw a long line on the river at night. The reason was not concealment but to ensure the correct working speed of the fly. In stillwater a long line is even more important—and this time the reason *is* concealment. Unless there is a very strong ripple you must literally "throw out of sight"—by which I mean of course that you must be out of the fish's sight when he comes to the fly. I am aware that an occasional fish will take almost alongside the boat. But this is an exception. What concerns me is the fish that rises to the fly but refuses it because the boat is drifting too fast downwind. I am convinced that many chances are missed because of this.

While on the subject of concealment perhaps a word or two on outboards, stealth and over-fishing will not be out of place.

I don't know whether outboard motors upset the fish, but they certainly upset me. Horrible things! Silence is golden, and the droning outboard destroys it. Opinion about them seems to be divided. Some experienced

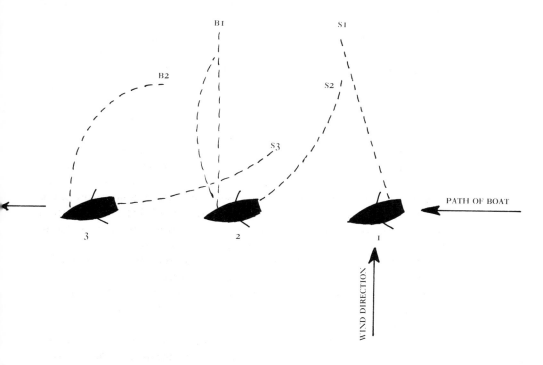

Crosswind Fishing.
Instead of drifting straight downwind the boat is rowed slowly and carefully on a path at right angles to the wind. To maintain this path the boat will head very slightly into wind, as shown.

Stern rod casts first each time—to S1 as shown in Picture 1. As the boat moves forward his flies will start to sink and then to swing round—S2 in Picture 2.

Bow rod now casts to B1 and mends his line towards the bows.

In Picture 3, stern rod's flies—S3—have almost completed their swing and he is ready to start working them in towards the boat. Bow rod's flies—B2—are curving round, owing to the mended line and forward movement of the boat, and working along the line of the waves parallel to the boat's path.

This system of casting ensures that neither rod interferes with the other.

anglers consider them a curse, others claim they do the fishing no harm. I cannot see how they can do it any *good*. I may be wrong. The vibration of a propeller may bring a fish on the "take". But I doubt it. (Outboards are forbidden on some lakes, so make sure of the rules before you use one.)

About the vibrations caused by noisy movement in a boat I am in no doubt at all. Keep quiet! Talk if you must, it will not affect the fish, but don't kick things about in the boat or rattle the oars or thump the floorboards.

Avoidance of the fish-disturbing shadows caused by casting with sun or moon behind the rod is just as important on the lake as on the river. The diagram shows parts of a lake. An angler has two beats (A and B) at his disposal for a day's fly fishing. B is the better beat for it is in the area immediately below the outflow of a feeder river, but in the morning anyone fishing it will have the light behind him. There is no doubt that on a sunny day he will drive many fish out into deeper water.

There are fewer fish in beat A (and also less ripple, for this water is in the lee of a hilly and heavily wooded island) but for much of the morning, because of the height of the trees, most of the water is in shadow. Obviously the best plan is to fish beat A before lunch; beat B in the afternoon.

A very elementary example; but I have watched many anglers make the elementary mistake of fishing across the best beat first, without a thought for wind and light.

Salmon or sea trout "lies" cannot be over-fished, *provided they are not disturbed*: i.e. the fish have not been scared out of them. But a boat drifting over shallow water does scare the fish out of it—for a time at any rate. Some of the best sea trout water is in sandy or rocky shallows only three or four feet deep. These areas are very easily disturbed. One drift across such water is enough for a morning. After that it should be rested to give the fish a chance to return and settle down, and should not be fished again until the next day—or perhaps, if there is a good enough ripple, on your way back in the late afternoon.

When fishing from the starboard side of a boat, bow rod should cast over his left shoulder, stern rod over his right. This reduces the danger of hooking the gillie, and the chances of the leaders becoming entangled. When two inexperienced rods have not previously fished together it is a good plan to announce: "Casting now" on each back-cast. A rhythm is soon established.

When crosswind fishing it is helpful to bow rod if stern rod casts first

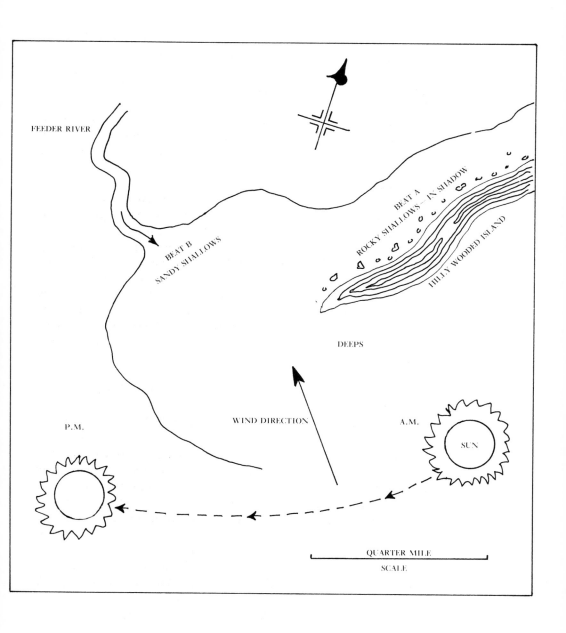

FEEDER RIVER

BEAT A
ROCKY SHALLOWS—IN SHADOW

BEAT B
SANDY SHALLOWS

HILLY WOODED ISLAND

DEEPS

WIND DIRECTION

P.M.

A.M.

SUN

QUARTER MILE
SCALE

373

A tumble of cloud on the mountains. A streamer in full spate after a night of rain—and a good wave for sea trout . . .

. . . or salmon. The stern rod has just taken a seven pounder that came to the dancing sea trout bob-fly . . .

374

. . . is duly netted . . .

. . . and admired. A beautiful fish, fresh from sea; rock hard and covered with sea lice.

Very calm conditions. The only hope of hooking fish is at long range. Line is stripped in; the coils held loosely in the left hand . . .

. . . Then finally the line is drawn back to the full extent of the left arm, while the rod is raised to bring the bob-fly dancing along the surface. The rod speed increases and continues into the back-cast. All slack line should be shot on the forward cast *without false-casting*.

A sea trout on dry-fly in calm water.

each time. This prevents the water from being "lined" close to bow rod's flies as the boat moves forward.

A good ploy for bow rod is to cast a long line at right angles to the boat's path, then to mend the line towards the bows. This helps to bring the flies back along the line of the waves well away from the boat, the tail fly fishing just under the surface, the bob fly skimming along the waves parallel to the boat.

Stern rod, too, can fish like this. But my own preference when in this position is to cast slightly forward of a line at right angles to the boat's path; allow the flies to sink while the boat moves forward; then, when the flies are roughly on the boat's quarter, start to bring them to the surface. This change of depth and direction seems to be very attractive. Sea trout often take just as the fly starts to swing.

Both rods will find that a variation of angle, depth and speed of fly recovery will add spice to their fishing. To fish out cast after cast in exactly the same way gets rather boring. Crosswind fishing has the great advantage of allowing considerable changes to be rung in fly presentation.

There are four methods of fly recovery. Assuming that the angler is casting with his right hand they are as follows:

1. When only a short line is cast it is sufficient to draw the line back with the left hand while raising the rod with the right.

2. A long line can be stripped in with the left hand and allowed to fall, or . . .

3. It can be drawn in with the Finger Ring method of Figure-of-Eight retrieve (see p. 86), or . . .

4. A few yards of line can be stripped in, held in coils in the left hand (see photographs), then the remaining line recovered by extending the left arm and raising the rod.

I use all of them during the course of a day's fishing. Each has its advantages and disadvantages. Loose line on the floorboards of the boat tends to get caught up in things. Too much Figure-of-Eight gives me cramp in the fingers. Coils of line sometimes catch in the butt ring on the forward cast. I suggest that you try them all and make your own choice.

Recovery of the flies is terminated by raising the rod and causing the nearest fly, the "bob" to dance on the surface and furrow along the line of the waves. The longer the rod, the lighter the line, the stronger the breeze, the further from the boat this can be made to happen and the more likely you are to hook a fish. The action of a bob fly is also attractive to salmon. This action is improved if the fly is dipped in Permaflote.

Don't hesitate to use a long leader. A Needle Knot (see p. 109) prevents the join of leader and line from getting caught in the rod rings when a fish is being brought to the net. But don't fish too fine. I would rather not hook a fish than lose one through getting "jagged" (an Irish boatman's highly descriptive term for getting broken). Apart from the disgrace that always attends such a disaster, I think it causes disturbance among other fish—especially in the shallows where many fish are hooked. Platil "Extra Strong" nylon of 9 lb. B.S. has the same gauge as standard nylon of 6 lb. B.S. I find this admirable for most lake fishing: fine enough for sea trout; strong enough for salmon.

A leader of 12–15 ft. is by no means too long. Certainly in calm conditions, or on a quiet moonlit night.

When fishing water that holds both salmon and sea trout make up your mind which species to attack. If you want to catch salmon you must fish for salmon. Similarly with sea trout. You may of course catch a salmon while fishing for sea trout and *vice versa*; but you will be more successful if you decide which species to fish for and concentrate on it. There are several reasons for this:

1. The "strike". When a sea trout takes the fly, *tighten*. When a salmon takes, *wait*—he will hook himself.

2. Size of fly. Generally speaking, larger flies should be fished for sea trout than for salmon.

3. Speed of recovery. A fly should be retrieved faster for a sea trout than for a salmon.

4. Fishing depth. As a very general rule, when fishing for sea trout concentrate on the bob fly. When after salmon concentrate on the tail fly. A salmon tends to take deeper than a sea trout, especially when a fly has been allowed to sink a foot or so and is being brought towards the surface. This is rather different from the reaction of summer salmon to the small fly in the river. In my experience the best taking depth for river "greased-line" fishing is about four inches. In stillwater, salmon frequently take the small fly at a depth of eight inches to a foot. I can think of no reason for this difference, but have noticed it many times; it makes the floating line with sink tip ideal for salmon in stillwater.

The novice is more likely to hook a salmon when fishing for sea trout than a sea trout when fishing for salmon. This is because he usually fishes too small a fly for sea trout and too large a fly for salmon. When

378

Reflections! Hopeless water for fishing wet-fly . . .

. . . But a fish or two may be tempted by a dry-fly, soaked in Permaflote, on a 12–14 ft. leader, cast well out and kept "on the twitch".

379

Sidney Spencer (left) fishing a nice sea trout wave on one of his beloved Irish loughs.

Fly fishing demands great concentration. Between drifts an angler should recharge his nervous energy. Such periods give him the chance to experiment; to trail different sizes and types of lures at varying speeds. Owing to the sudden changes in depth in some lakes this can be full of interest. Places where fish are hooked can be noted, and fished on another occasion with fly. Trailing over the shallows is not likely to improve fly-fishing chances, but in deeper water, from a boat under oars, it will do little or no harm.

380

fishing his small fly for sea trout he is unwittingly using the right size for a salmon. (Something very similar to this happens on the river on a hot summer's evening when the trout angler's tiny fly so often hooks a salmon. This is usually regarded with surprise—but not by the experienced salmon fisherman, who knows all about the salmon's preference for small flies.) Many chances of catching salmon are missed because the fly is too big; seldom because it is too small.

The lie of a fly in the water is very important. I am sure that many of the fish that "come short" do so because of the "wooden" way in which the fly is working. The fly's shape and colour interest the fish and bring him towards the surface, but the fly's unattractive behaviour seen at closer quarters inhibits the fish from taking it. So often one can see the fish in the side of a wave as he comes to the fly—only to turn away at the last moment.

One reason for a fly's lifeless action is the knot used to tie it to leader point or dropper. You have, I suggest, two knots to choose from: the Turle and the Grinner. Which you use will depend on the type of hook. For a straight or slightly-turned eye use a Grinner. For a pronounced turn use a Turle. (For diagrams of these knots see Chapter IV.)

"I never went to Cambridge, but I could beat most of them fellers!" A great oarsman of the west.

Stomach contents of a small sea trout: tiny fly larvae and a beetle. Food is seldom found in many of the larger fish.

Sea trout, 11¼ lb., caught by Mr R. B. Woodall on a Claret Pennell of his own tying. Loch Doilet, Argyll, 6th September, 1967. See colour Plate 2 opposite page 16 for a selection of traditional flies tied by him specially for this book.

At dusk in hot, calm weather, sea trout come from deeper water into the rocky shallows . . .

. . . and can sometimes be heard splashing among the reeds.

Lunch time. A tiny island in sea trout water of the far west. Country of wild and rugged beauty.

The chance of a fish at dusk? A wild light—but a nice ripple.

384

Regarding the flies themselves, there are dozens of patterns to choose from. Each fishery has its own list of popular fancies and the visiting angler is wise to give these local patterns a try first, but a combination of the following tail and bob flies will kill sea trout on most lakes. (See page 17 and colour plate 2.)

Tail flies		Bob flies
Kingsmill	Blae and Black	Claret Pennell
Snipe and Purple	Blae and Blue	Black Pennell
Mallard and Claret	Teal and Green	Donegal Blue
Grouse and Claret	Teal and Red	Black Zulu
Butcher	Teal and Silver	Blue Zulu
Bloody Butcher	Invicta	Claret Bumble
Peter Ross	Alexandra	
Black and Silver	Brown Turkey	
Dunkeld	Connemara Black	
Fiery Brown	Silver March Brown	
Cinnamon and Gold	Thunder and Lightning	
Pheasant and Yellow	Medicine ⎱ In rough	
Woodcock Teal and Yellow	Sunk Lure ⎰ weather	

Note: Detailed tying instructions for the Kingsmill and Claret Bumble are given in *A Man May Fish.*

When a fly is fished for sea trout in daylight there is little doubt that colour plays an important part. But the success of any particular colour seems to vary from lake to lake; sometimes, even, from day to day, and seldom if ever can the "colour of the day" be forecast. Occasionally, indeed, nature seems to go mad and turn logic on its head: for reasons unknown (certainly unknown to me) sea trout will show a predilection for one particular fly to the exclusion of all others.

So, be prepared.

Sea trout lakes are in wild, remote places. Village shops seldom have more than a limited range of flies, and anyway at the hint of a public holiday everything shuts down. When packing your tackle for a fishing trip always take some fly-tying stuff with you. *Always.* I once ignored this rule—with traumatic consequences.

Together with a friend—an angler of exceptional skill—I went to fish a very beautiful lake that was reputedly full of salmon and sea trout. On the first day, although the weather conditions seemed propitious and we fished with great care and concentration, neither of us hooked anything at all.

On the second day, while we were systematically working through our fly boxes trying all the patterns we had, my companion struck oil with a bright orange lure tied for reservoir trout fishing. It was dressed after the style of a Dunkeld. Quite why this fly should have been so successful I have no idea, but successful it most certainly was. No matter whether it was presented on the bob or on the tail the fish took it. Both sea trout and salmon. They would take nothing else.

One fly shared between two rods is somewhat restricting, but at least we enjoyed a measure of success and it was pleasing to see fish in the boat after so many hours of fruitless flogging. Then, suddenly—disaster. While extracting our precious fly from the gristle of a salmon's mouth I broke the hook shank.

We caught nothing else that day.

"Never mind", I said hopefully. "It'll all be different tomorrow."

But it wasn't. Like the first day, the third day was a blank. We tried fly after fly. The fish simply boiled at them. It was uncanny.

I thought longingly of my fly vice and box of hair and feathers. A few minutes' work and we would have been in business again. But my fly-tying stuff was hundreds of miles away. The local tackle shop had nothing like our streak of orange magic. Nor had the few other anglers on the lake (they weren't doing any good, either).

On our penultimate day we skirred the country round—and chanced on a fly-tyer who dressed half-a-dozen hooks according to our instructions. These flies hadn't the wizardry of our original, but they salvaged something from the wreck. On our last day we both caught fish on them. And, mark you, *only on them*.

Since then I have tried the same pattern in many other waters, but with no startling results. It has caught fish. But the success it had during that frustrating week has never been repeated.

On another occasion I had a similar experience with a homemade type of Fiery Brown. On the day in question in bright sunshine and the lightest of winds this particular fly accounted for a dozen good sea trout. A day or two later on a neighbouring lake it caught nothing.

Which brings me to another point.

Although the colours of a fly are undoubtedly important they may not work in quite the way that we sometimes think they do. The phenomenon of the fly that does consistently well in one fishery but catches comparatively few fish in another is an example of this. At the time, the failure of a favourite fly seems weird and, like myself, many anglers must have felt puzzled by it. Usually the blame is heaped upon the fish. They are being perverse, or unusually dour, or they are absent. And sometimes, of course, they are. But another explanation of it (at least in

386

part) occurred to me one sunny day not long ago.

I was sitting in a boat gazing absently at the water while the gillie rowed to the head of the first drift. For some reason he had that morning exchanged his usual grey-painted oars for a bright blue pair. As the oars dipped below the surface the coloured water of the lake changed the blades' bright blue to green.

I watched, fascinated. Then I suddenly realized that if an oar blade appeared to change colour when it went underwater a fly must change in a similar way. Although the exact degree of their colour vision is unknown, the salmonidae are certainly colour conscious. But a fish looking at my Medicine or Donegal Blue underwater from a range of several yards wasn't seeing what I saw when I selected that fly from my case. Because of the colouration of the water, which modified the fly's appearance, it is likely that what the fish saw on the morning in question was not a blue fly but a green fly.

It may be argued that this is of no importance; that what matters is not what the fish *sees* but what he *takes*; that if he takes what (underwater) appears to him to be a green fly it matters not if that fly (in the open air) appears to us to be blue. This is true—if we are fishing only on that water. But if not; if we fish a number of lakes—or rivers for that matter—the different colour tinge of the various waters may go some way towards explaining why a successful fly on one fishery fails to repeat its magic on another.

On some lakes the dap accounts for a number of very big fish. The customary tackle requirements are: a long, light rod, 12–16 ft.; a nylon floss blow-line; three feet of monofilament nylon leader and a big hairy lure soaked in Permaflote. (See colour plate 5.)

The lure is encouraged to waft out with the breeze ahead of the drifting boat and dance on the surface. From the angler's point of view that (apart from being careful not to strike too quickly) is about all there is to it. It is a simple method and, for the novice, has one great advantage over wet fly fishing: no casting is required. Although the beginner will miss a lot of fish through faulty striking, he can catch sea trout on the dap even if he has never held a rod before.

The "flies" mostly used for dapping (at least, those I have used myself) are large, bushy, hackled lures of the Black Pennell type; the Loch Ordie; forms of artificial Daddy—all in dark, nondescript colours. Although colour tones seem to play a big part in wet fly fishing they are unimportant in surface flies.

Dapping certainly has its moments. It can be nail-biting when a big fish comes up to the lure—for you can usually see it all happening. Dapping also offers chances of success in certain parts of a lake that are not normally fished with wet fly. In some fisheries, for reasons I have never discovered, it attracts sea trout from much greater depths than those usually fished with the conventional wet fly technique. But although there is much to be said in favour of dapping I get bored by the long periods of inaction.

For me, a more exciting method is to cast a large dry fly (pattern unimportant) well out from the boat and keep twitching it across the surface. This technique has a satisfying amount of action and, provided the angler is casting towards the light, is capable of catching fish no matter how calm and sunny the day. But again, don't be too quick on the strike.

Having recently read a delightful book on stillwater nymph fishing by Conrad Voss Bark,* it occurs to me that a technique based on his methods might work for sea trout, both in the lake and (under certain conditions) in the river, too. As I have never tried fishing the nymph quite as he describes it I cannot do more than suggest it as a possible field of research. It would not surprise me if an angler of enquiring mind, prepared to spend some time experimenting with this interesting method, found it rewarding.

Night fishing on most of the lakes I fish is inclined to be disappointing. I have hooked some big fish after dark on unconventional lures such as Surface Lure, Sunk Lure and Muddler Minnow (the reservoir trout lure), as well as the usual lake patterns, but never in numbers that fired my enthusiasm or led me to indulge in stillwater night fishing to the exclusion of daylight fishing.

Mind you, this is probably my own fault and due to a certain lack of persistence. It is the river that is always running through my mind. Darkness on stillwater has never meant as much to me; has never strung me to the same pitch of excitement. Fishing the lake at night is a very different business from fishing the river. The sounds and smells are not the same; the charm, the mystique of running water is missing. (I notice its absence by day too—which, I suppose, is one reason why I have chosen to live for much of my life beside a river rather than a lake. For me, stillwater fishing will always take second place.)

But all this is by the way. For the angler who is prepared to persist

*_Fishing for Lake Trout_ (1972), published by H. F. & G. Witherby Ltd.

388

and experiment there is sport to be had in stillwater at night. I have known occasions when fishing after dark has saved the day from being blank. It has also caught me bigger fish than I have caught during daylight. This has usually been in hot, settled weather, with the water low and glassy calm. At dusk in these conditions the sea trout tend to come into the shallows—from which they have been absent during the day. The lures and techniques I have used are much the same as those discussed earlier in the book: a floating line at dusk, changing to sunk line later in the night.

When Surface Lure is being fished the boat should be paddled slowly and very quietly at right angles to the breeze—which, of course, must not be strong or there will be too much ripple. Cast the lure at right angles to the boat's path and allow it to swing round, its wake being caused by the forward movement of the boat, then work it in for a few yards before casting again. You can catch fish by trailing the lure on a long line behind the boat. But I prefer to cast. When trailing at night, long distances may be covered towing a streamer of weed behind the lure.

*   *   *

Trailing

It is a pity that the terms "trolling" and "trailing" should have become confused. Many anglers speak of "trolling" when they mean "trailing" and of "sink-and-draw" when they really mean "trolling". The matter is summed up by John Bickerdyke in *The Book of the All Round Angler* (1888):

> "Dead-baits . . . are either arranged so that they spin when drawn through the water, or are placed on trolling-tackle, in which case they do not spin. Spinning baits are either cast out some distance, and drawn back through the water to the angler, or are trailed at the back of a boat. This trailing is often called trolling in Scotland and Ireland, a misnomer which has doubtless caused some little confusion in the minds of anglers. Trolling proper is the use of a dead-bait which does not spin, and is worked with a sink-and-draw motion in the water."

When the lake is at a good fishing height, especially when a spate has brought in a fresh run of fish, sea trout will be found mainly in the shallows near the mouths of feeder streams. But when the weather turns hot during periods of drought, the fish tend to move out into deeper water. In some

Trolling with the Gorge.
From *The Angler's Guide* (1833) 8th edition. T. F. Salter.

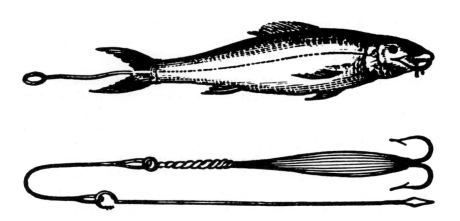

The Gorge Deadbait or Trolling Tackle (used for what is now commonly called "sink-and-draw") was described in *A Treatyse of Fysshynge wyth an Angle* (1496). It has survived practically unchanged until the present day.

lakes, notably those of northern Scotland, sea trout will rise to the fly (especially the dap) in deep water, but in many Irish lakes they will not. When chances of sport on the fly are poor, trailing is a profitable alternative—and not only for the fish it catches.

Deepwater trailing with the help of a depth indicator enables an angler to gain an accurate (and sometimes surprising) picture of what the bottom of the lake really looks like. This knowledge can be very valuable when next he fishes fly. A stretch of water thirty or forty feet deep may suddenly change to a small ridge of rocky shallows—ideal fish-holding ground. Marks can be taken and the place pin-pointed. Later, when conditions improve, this ridge can be fly-fished.

Most places of this nature are already common knowledge. But some are not. I have known even the most experienced boatman to be shaken by a line of soundings taken across a lake.

As a fishing method, trailing is often considered boring and lacking in finesse. H. T. Sheringham sets it all out in *Elements of Angling* (1908):

"There is what may by courtesy be termed spinning, the practice of trailing (it is often erroneously called 'trolling') for big lake trout in Ireland and Scotland. The angler simply sits in the stern of a boat and lets his spinning bait trail thirty yards or more behind while somebody else rows. The tackle and rod must be strong, as a big pike or a salmon is sometimes a possibility. No overwhelming display of skill is demanded of the angler, but the oarsman must know something about the geography of the lake and the nature of the bottom. Trailing may, however, be made something like an art if the angler does his own rowing, and is alone; in fact, there are few kinds of fishing which demand more promptitude and resource."

Sheringham was right. But there is more skill in successful trailing than he imagined. The fisherman who consistently takes good fish from the depths of what appears to be a featureless expanse of water is not, as many people seem to think, haphazardly dragging a bait about. His fish are caught by design, not chance. By using an echo sounder, and tackle that fishes at a specified depth, he gradually builds up a fascinating picture of the lake bottom together with the best "taking" places and depths. As a result he will, in the long term, catch more fish than the angler who moves aimlessly about, never quite sure of the depth of water he is fishing in—certainly not the depth at which his lure is fishing.

When my friend Fred Buller first made the acquaintance of that famous Loch Lomond angler, the late Harry Britton of Balloch, he was puzzled by the local method of trailing for sea trout and salmon. This method, although popular on the loch, was restricted mainly to fishing from power-driven boats travelling at a uniform speed—tactics that automatically cause a bait to fish at a uniform depth. The only variables, it seemed, were the type and size of bait, the choice of locality and, of course, weather.

This choice of fishing depth—or, rather, this self-imposed restriction of depth—seemed to F.B. to be unnecessarily inhibiting and in conflict with his own trailing experience. When deepwater trailing for charr in Windermere he had learned the importance of varying the depth at which a bait is fished. He had discovered that brown trout and charr that had deserted the upper levels would sometimes take a bait in very deep water. In addition, his experience of trailing different baits for different species on many other waters had made him aware of the need to fish baits at varying speeds in order to find the best "taking" speed for the day in question. This speed seems to vary from day to day. He writes as follows:

> "I ventured to suggest to Britton that anyone who fished in the customary Loch Lomond manner was not making the most of his opportunities. When his method of fishing produced a blank, only one inference could be drawn: that on the day in question no sea trout was interested in taking that particular bait trailed (say) 35 yards behind a boat at 2 m.p.h. at a uniform depth of $2\frac{1}{2}$ feet. (The figures are hypothetical, and used merely to illustrate the point.) Britton was so impressed with my argument in favour of fishing at different depths and at different speeds that he lost no time in trying out a modified experimental charr-trailing rig himself. It met with immediate success."

The following is an extract from a letter Harry Britton wrote to F.B. later that year:

> "So far the season and the weather have been atrocious—we have had little sunshine to warm up the water. The boats have been bringing back very few fish and things are very quiet for us all just now, but Fred before it went quiet I had the best ever start to a season—taking all my sea trout on your deep trolls . . . (they're absolutely terrific) so please keep our secret until I've had more time to experiment . . ."

Unfortunately, Britton was unable to carry out further experiments for he died shortly after writing this letter. But although all too brief, his experience of fishing Buller's deepwater rig in Loch Lomond points to a resource so far untapped in lakes holding runs of sea trout.

The Experimental Deepwater Trailing Rig

This rig is based on the Lake Windermere Plumbline Charr Tackle. The object of using it is to find out what bait or fly, if any, fish are taking and at what depth. That particular lure can then be fished with more appropriate tackle on a Downrigger (see pp. 397–401). One can of course fish the Downrigger without recourse to so complicated a rig as the E.D.T.R., but I give full details of it for the benefit of anyone who may be interested. I have, I may say, had enormous fun fishing the thing myself.

Like the traditional charr tackle, on which it is closely modelled, the E.D.T.R. has a heavy lead (approximately $1\frac{1}{2}$ lb.) cone-shaped in section and fashioned like a rudder to keep it from twisting when moving forward. This lead hangs straight down from the boat like a plumbline—hence the term "plumblining" for charr. (In fact, while it is fishing, the lead doesn't hang straight down but at a slight angle, see diagram. But we can ignore this.)

The lead is suspended at depth from a rod, or spreader, about 18 ft. long. The 20–26 yards of mainline that connects the tip of the rod to the lead is braided cotton, or cuttyhunk, between 60 and 80 lb. B.S. (The Windermere charr fishermen soak their lines in a mixture of lamp-black and boiled linseed oil. After a thorough soaking the line is hung out under cover for about three weeks to dry. This dressing helps to preserve cotton lines. It also stiffens the texture of the line and closes the braid, so that it becomes much easier to handle.)

Six droppers are attached to the mainline. The top dropper is tied 15 ft. down from the rod tip; the second, third, fourth and fifth at intervals of 12 ft. The sixth and last dropper is tied 8 ft. below the fifth dropper. The lead is attached 2 to 3 ft. below the sixth dropper.

The droppers, which are not tied directly to the line but to a brass wire charr-shackle, vary in length. The top dropper is 24 ft. with a 6 ft. leader: 30 ft. in all. Each lower dropper is 3 ft. shorter than the previous one. This has the effect of making the baits fish vertically in line rather than in echelon. For purpose of experiment, various types of spoons, spinners, lures and flies can be used. A dropper is about 30 lb. B.S. nylon. The leader, 8–10 lb. B.S., joined to the dropper by means of a swivel.

A "set" consisting of two "sides" of tackle is carried in a case with three drawers. Two drawers are for the made-up tackle; the other for various spares: leads, leaders, spinners etc. The drawers containing the complete rig are fitted with cork shoulders. These ensure that the hooks can be seated without snarling.

This highly specialized rig, devised by generations of charr fishermen, cannot be purchased. Even the Windermere charr baits are still hand-made. These are of two basic types: head spinners and tail spinners—tail spinners are preferred. All baits are made of thin sheet metal. The finish can be plain silver, or copper and silver—copper on one side and electroplated silver on the other—or brass and silver, or silver and gold-leaf. (Real gold was sometimes used in the making of charr baits—a thin strip that covered the side of a silver bait. Old-time fishermen believed that gold from an Australian sovereign had special charr-catching properties. This was beaten out to "the thickness of a butterfly wing".)

The lake is a mirror. A day for experimenting. Two charr rigs are being set up to explore the deeps (50-100 ft.) for charr, ferox and sea trout.

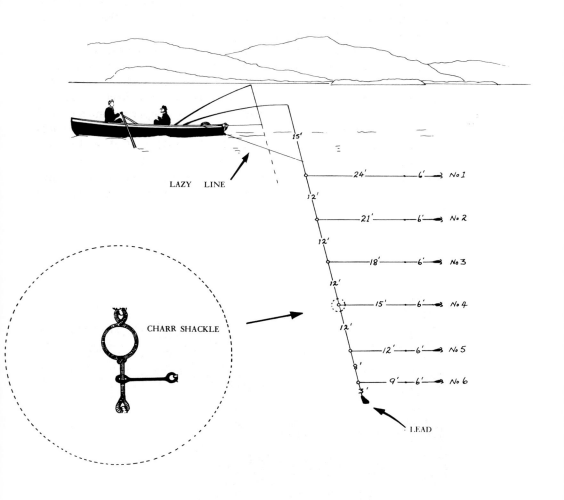

LAZY LINE

CHARR SHACKLE

15'

12'

12'

12'

12'

12'

24' — 6' — No 1

21' — 6' — No 2

18' — 6' — No 3

15' — 6' — No 4

12' — 6' — No 5

9' — 6' — No 6

LEAD

Deepwater Trailing Rig.
Based on the Lake Windermere Plumbline Charr Tackle. As an experiment, Loughs Mask and Currane were fished with the Deepwater Rig during a period of hot, dry weather when, according to reports, the fishing was "dead". In Mask, brown trout up to $5\frac{1}{2}$ lb. were caught 60 feet down. In Currane, sea trout up to $2\frac{1}{2}$ lb. were caught at depths of 25–35 feet.

Fishing procedure

The lead is dropped over the side of the boat and allowed to sink until the first shackle is reached. The big half-inch ring on the shackle is then placed over a nail that projects upwards from the gunwale.

The sixth bait is tossed overboard, the dropper held until the bait is seen to be spinning freely, then released.

As soon as the boat's forward speed tensions the dropper the shackle is lifted off the nail and the next section of mainline fed out until the next shackle is reached—and the process repeated.

When the top shackle is reached it is left on the nail until the line has been fastened to the rod tip.

A sea angler's bell is now clipped to the rod top. The butt of the rod is slotted into position and the top shackle released.

One end of a "lazy-line" (see diagram) has already been fastened to the mainline some 2 ft. or so above the top shackle; the other end to a brass screw-eye in the gunwale.

The best trailing speed is $1-1\frac{1}{2}$ m.p.h. (That is, for charr. For sea trout I would suggest $1\frac{1}{2}-3\frac{1}{2}$ m.p.h.)

A tinkle on the bell . . . and the mainline is brought to hand by means of the lazy-line fastened to the gunwale. *Note:* transducer hanging overside; depth gauge with its back to camera.

396

The welcome tinkle of the bell indicates a strike. The angler pulls in the lazy-line until the mainline comes to hand. Coiling mainline and droppers in the sternsheets, he pulls up until the appropriate shackle is reached. This is placed over the nail. He can now pull in the dropper and net the fish.

As the photographs show, F.B. and I have fished two rigs at a time, one on each side of the boat. For small fish such as charr this is safe enough. For larger fish I advise the use of only one.

All sorts of modifications can be made to this rig according to an angler's requirements. The overall fishing depth can be altered to suit deeper or shallower lakes; droppers can be added or removed; other materials can be used in its construction. But whatever its design, the successful handling of the E.D.T.R. requires skill—and a certain sense of humour. If anyone is disdainful of it, thinking it too simple and primitive a method, I urge him to try his hand at fishing it. Whatever his degree of success, he will find it highly diverting.

*   *   *

The Downrigger

On days of dead calm, when fly-fishing chances are slim, fishing an experimental trailing rig in deep water can be exciting and instructive. Since one is careful to avoid the shallows there is no interference with another angler's sport, nor any disturbance of the fly beats. From an angling viewpoint, however, one disadvantage of tackle based on the traditional Windermere charr rig is the heavy lead involved, combined with the fact that the rig is, in effect, a handline fished on spreaders.

All this is avoided in the Downrigger—an American method of deep-water trailing that permits a light rod to fish a bait (or fly) at whatever depth is required without the use of weight on the mainline. The principles of this splendid rig are shown in the diagram on the next page.

The rig is set up as follows:

1. A centre-pin reel of large diameter (A)—an old-time sea-fishing reel will serve admirably—holding about 40 yards of 60 lb. B.S. terylene line is fastened with the usual reel fittings to the back of the rodrest. the line is marked at intervals of 3 to 6 ft. with tags of wool (B). (Two-inch lengths of wool are passed through the braid of the line with a needle and tied, leaving an overhang of wool on each side.) A colour code is used so that the angler can tell precisely how much line is out at any time.

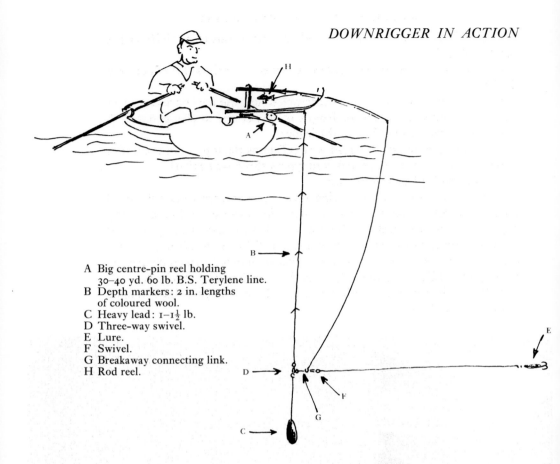

A Big centre-pin reel holding
    30–40 yd. 60 lb. B.S. Terylene line.
B Depth markers: 2 in. lengths
    of coloured wool.
C Heavy lead: 1–1½ lb.
D Three-way swivel.
E Lure.
F Swivel.
G Breakaway connecting link.
H Rod reel.

Rod tensioned downwards by clutch, or check, of reel and drag of line through the
water. When a fish takes the lure, breaking the connecting link (G), the rod will momentarily spring upwards.

Where water is deep enough to use it conveniently, the downrigger makes trailing depth
accurate to within a foot or two.

398

2. The line is fed through the rodrest and a lead of $1-1\frac{1}{2}$ lb. (C) is tied to the end.

3. Three feet or so above the lead a three-way swivel (D) is tied into the line.

4. Rod, reel and line are now assembled and the appropriate bait or lure (E) attached to whatever length of leader the angler chooses. A swivel (F) joins the mainline to the leader.

5. A link of cotton or thin lead wire (G) joins the top eye of the leader swivel to the centre eye of the downrigger's three-way swivel.

6. The rod is placed in the rest.

7. As soon as the boat is moving forward in an appropriate depth of water, as recorded on an echo sounder, the downrigger line is slowly payed out from the reel (A). The coloured wool tags passing the end of the rodrest indicate the length that is out. While line is being released from the downrigger reel the corresponding amount of line is automatically being pulled off the rod reel (H)—which is tensioned by its check.

8. When the required depth is reached, the downrigger line is looped round the reel handle.

The Downrigger set up. This rig provides excellent opportunities of sport on a light rod, trailing at depth without weight on the line.

Echo-sounder. An essential piece of deepwater trailing equipment.

The angler now knows the exact depth at which his bait is fishing. The echo sounder enables him to make any adjustment to the length of the downrigger line to accommodate variation in water depth. While a bait is being trailed the rod is curved downwards by the drag of the water on the rod line. As soon as a fish takes the bait and breaks the connecting link (G) the rod straightens, giving immediate bite indication. A fish hooks itself. The pull of the link immediately before it breaks is usually sufficient to drive the hook home. Exactly how strong the link should be can be found by experiment.

While the fish is being played, the lead-line is wound up to avoid any danger of entanglement.

Little imagination is needed to grasp the potential of this deepwater trailing rig. Any type of lure—whether spoon, spinner or fly—can be used on any type of rod and reel. It can be fished at any depth on terminal tackle that contains no lead whatever. Apart from the swivel joining leader to mainline there is no weight between rod and fish. If a fly is being trailed on fly rod and reel, even this swivel can be dispensed with. The link (G) can be fastened to the join of line and leader, or indeed anywhere along the line.

400

The use of a breakaway type of rig such as the Downrigger is by no means confined to freshwater. It holds great possibilities for the sea angler who wishes to trail at depth with weightless tackle on a light rod for species such as mackerel, pollack and bass. In addition to being very good sport, experimenting with a Downrigger when mackerel are plentiful soon teaches an angler how to adjust the rig for lake fishing, and to ascertain the best breaking strain of whatever material is used for the connecting link.

ELEVATION

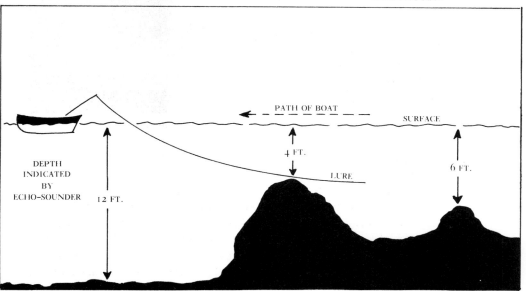

Echo-sounder used to determine approximate depth at which lure is fishing.

If while maintaining a steady speed the boat passes over a ridge, say, 6 ft. deep (as indicated by the echo sounder) and the bait follows the boat over without bumping, the bait's depth must be less than 6 ft. If, later, a ridge of 4 ft. is crossed and the bait bumps, you know the approximate fishing depth of that size of bait and anti-kink lead (if any) when trailed at that speed.

Whatever their size, shape or function, boats are potentially dangerous. Angling is a rapidly expanding sport and many anglers, whether they fish in freshwater or saltwater, are ignorant of boat handling. Each season has a depressing number of accidents almost all of which could be avoided. As James Leasor wrote recently in *The Daily Telegraph Magazine*:

> "More and more accidents, most quite unnecessary, seem inevitable ... when there are too many people with too much time and money and too little sense to learn something of the art of seamanship ... the father from some industrial city who suddenly takes his young son and daughter fishing in a rowing boat. He means the outing well, but he knows nothing of currents and tides and winds ..."

You can drown a few yards from shore in six feet of water, an inch or two out of your depth, just as surely as you can in sixty fathoms, sixty miles from land. And a lot of people do.

Most of these accidents happen because of some elementary mistake. The fatalities are due to panic bred from ignorance of how to behave in emergency.

More than once in my life I have been plunged fully clothed and booted into deep water: a fall from the rigging of a topsail schooner; a swamped duck-punt in a winter gale; an injudicious step on a bank overhanging a river in spate; a boat sunk by a huge wave several miles from shore. . . . I am still alive because I knew what to do, and did it.

Once, many years ago in one of my television programmes, I demonstrated how to behave if you fall into deep, freezing water, fully clothed, wearing long waders and holding a rod. It was similar to the photographic sequence on pp. 136–139. Months later a man wrote to say that because of what he had seen in the programme his life had been saved.

Since then I have made dozens of vastly more successful films—but I always think of that one as being the most important.* It occurs to me that if one accident is prevented because of what I have written here and in Chapter IV, the whole of this book will have been worthwhile.

Many of the boats that anglers take with them on trailers and roof-racks for their holiday fishing are unsuitable. Although most hired boats are sound and reliable and most gillies are good boatmen, some are not.

---

*In a more recent film, *Salmo the Leaper* (1977), I included a similar sequence. To date (1981), no fewer than eight lives have been saved by this demonstration. It illllustrates the value of being "forewarned" and I urge my reader to study *Emergency*, pp 134–140.

An angler's safety is his first responsibility—if only to his family! He should always take a boating trip seriously; be prepared for emergencies; take nothing for granted. If he has had no experience of boats he should learn the rudiments of boat handling before going afloat by himself. And even if he goes out with a professional boatman, let him always have an eye for safety.

For the benefit of the novice, here are some "*don'ts*".

Don't step on the gunwale or on one of the seats or thwarts, or on the bare planking between the ribs, when you get into a boat. Always step on to the floorboards as near to the middle of the boat as possible. Having stepped into the boat, *sit down*.

Don't go out in any boat that is not provided with a baler; a spare oar and spare rowlocks or thole-pins (whichever are used).

Don't set off in a rowing boat unless the rowlocks are tied down with lanyards. Without a safety lanyard a rowlock is easily jerked out and lost overboard when an oar is shipped. This so-easily-avoided accident happens with monotonous frequency—and not only to novices!

Don't rely solely on an outboard engine, make sure the boat also carries oars. Don't relax this rule however calm the day. Engines can fail. Weather can change very rapidly. From dead calm a big lake can quickly become a sheet of white water. Very dangerous, especially when the wind is whipping down between clefts in the mountains. It may seem unlikely that anyone would go afloat without the insurance of a pair of oars, but it happens. I recently had to assist an innocent who was drifting oarless in a high wind straight for the rocks—having dropped his outboard motor overboard! Which prompts another "don't".

Don't use an outboard without:

1. A safety line that secures the motor to the boat's transom.
2. Making sure the tank contains sufficient fuel.
3. Tools.
4. A spare plug.
5. A spare pull-cord (if old type).
6. Spare propellor-spring and split-pins.

Don't go afloat without some sort of safety gear. An inflated rubber ring makes a comfortable (and dry) seat, and provides buoyancy for someone in the water.

Don't stand up in a boat, either to cast or to pee, without warning the other occupant or occupants. If you are inexperienced don't stand up at all.

403

Don't attempt to change places with a companion without first planning exactly, move by move, where each of you is going to position himself.

Don't throw a rope to a person in difficulties in the water without first tying a Bowline in it (see diagram). An exhausted man may have numbed fingers, or be on the verge of collapse and quite unable to tie the knot himself—even if he knows how to do it. Without a loop in it the rope is virtually useless. A Bowline is a loop that does not slip. Remember: the man in the water must be able to get his arms and shoulders through the loop—so don't tie it too small!

Don't shout out and wave your arms if for whatever reason you are suddenly plunged into the water. Keep your mouth shut and your arms down—otherwise you will sink. When you are floating on your back you can start shouting for help. (See also River Safety, p. 132.)

Don't try to pull yourself out of the water into a small boat by clambering over the *side* of the boat. Pull yourself over the stern (the blunt end).

BOWLINE

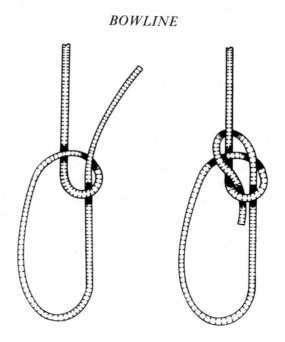

Although little used in angling, the Bowline is a knot every angler should know. Apart from being the best knot for tying a boat's painter to a ring-bolt, this non-slip loop is a life-saver. It should be used whenever a rope is thrown to a person in difficulties.

Don't panic if the boat is suddenly swamped or overturned. If the water is cold you must decide very quickly whether to swim for the shore or stay where you are and wait for help. If you know or think that help is coming you will naturally cling to the oars or the water-logged hull or any other item of life-saving equipment and wait to be picked up. But the colder the water the sooner you will lose consciousness. When this happens (unless you are wearing a life-jacket that keeps the head upright) your face will go underwater and you will drown. So, if there is no help forthcoming, the sooner you start swimming the better.

Don't undress if you have only a short distance to swim. For a time the air trapped in your clothes will help to keep you afloat. *But* if you have far to go, strip off your clothes as quickly as possible. As I know from experience, undressing in the water is made much easier if you have something buoyant to support you while you are struggling to get things undone: a petrol tin, rubber ring, oars or the hull of the boat.

Don't flop down and lie inert when you reach the shore, however tired you may be. Force yourself to keep moving until you get help. If you become unconscious you may die of exposure. It is the cold you are really up against.

The following notes are included in this chapter for convenience. They apply to boat handling in saltwater (see Chapter XIV).

The sea is potentially more dangerous than the lake if only because of its currents. But the more obvious and dramatic accidents at sea are not necessarily the most dangerous. A boat may be swept out to sea due to the loss of an oar, a motor breakdown or a change of wind (and every year this happens to hundreds of people), but so long as the boat remains afloat the occupants have a chance of survival—they can be rescued by helicopters or fishing boats or other pleasure craft. Although there is always danger when a small boat is adrift in a strong current, there can be even greater danger when the boat is at anchor. One example will suffice.

An angler, we will imagine, is fishing a sea voe from a dinghy anchored in a narrow channel. At low spring tide (when he anchored) the water was slack. As the tide rose the strength of the current increased. Now, at half to three-quarters flood the tide is running through the channel like a mill-race, and the angler decides to move.

But this is not so easy. The boat is being held against the current by the straining anchor rope and water is piled up against the bows. (This is similar in effect to water piled up against the body waders of an angler in a fast-running river. See pp. 132–135.) It is a highly dangerous situation.

1. Angler anchors boat at slack water.

2. Tide flowing strongly. Water piled up against bows.

3. If angler moves forward too quickly towards anchor rope, bows may be dragged under.

4. Anchor tripping line and buoy.

If the angler's weight is suddenly moved too far forward—as it may be when he goes to pull up the anchor—the boat will be swamped.

If you ever find yourself in this situation remember to edge towards the bows very carefully, a foot at a time. If it is doubtful whether you can reach the anchor rope without the bows going under, stay where you are and wait for the tide to slacken. That is, if you are able to do so. You may be forced to move by a rising wind and sea. In which case there is no time to lose. Tie your knife to the loom of an oar or the handle of the landing net, crane forward and cut the rope. In these circumstances the loss of an anchor is of no account.

> *Note.* An angler anticipating this situation would buoy his anchor in advance (see diagram). In emergency he could let it slip—and recover it later, at slack water.

If you do manage to reach the anchor rope make sure it is running through a fairlead on the bows as you pull it up. Keep your hands low as you pull. If the rope comes out of the fairlead the boat will swing broadside to the current and unless you instantly let go of the rope the boat may capsize. If the released rope catches in a rowlock that has been left in position a capsize is almost certain. So—*don't* leave rowlocks in position when not in use. Make a habit of it. Wherever you happen to be, when you ship the oars always ship the rowlocks.

I write from experience. My own dinghy capsized in this way when I was a boy. A few years later the same thing happened to my father—as anyone who has read the last chapter of my book *The Stolen Years* may remember. We were both lucky to escape. Not so an angler who made the same mistake recently while fishing in a Scottish sea loch—and was drowned.

In describing this accident I have tried to point out the danger that can arise from a seemingly simple situation and to emphasize the need for taking sensible precautions. It is certainly not my intention to dissuade anyone from going to sea. On the contrary, there are splendid chances of sport with sea trout in saltwater, both from a boat and from the shore. To help my reader to take advantage of them is the object of the next chapter.

A good angler (and I do not necessarily mean a man who can cast X yards) is almost always a good amateur naturalist. He need not know Latin names for wild creatures, flowers or insects, but he needs to know about otters and elvers and why insect-feeding birds feed here and not there, why some types of vegetation grow in some waters and on some shores and not in other places. He must be able to smell weather, to have an eye for wind and cloud and light and most of all perhaps have the ability, understanding currents in loch as in river, to visualize the life of the fish in relation to its environment.

Sidney Spencer, *Salmon and Sea Trout in Wild Places* (1968)

XIV
Saltwater Fishing

Due to the rising demand for sport (resulting from a general increase in affluence and leisure) recent years have shown a dramatic leap in the cost of game fishing. But today, even for the well-to-do angler, it is difficult to find good fishing and uncrowded water. There must also be many anglers of limited means who would like to try their hands at sea trout fishing but cannot afford it. Because of this I find it puzzling that so few anglers take advantage of the exciting and inexpensive sport available in saltwater. At many places round the coasts of Great Britain and Ireland—particularly in the north-west—there is sea trout fishing of exceptional quality, much of which is entirely free.

It occurs to me that there may be freshwater fishermen who are quite unaware of the opportunities existing in the sea; who think of "sea fishing" only in terms of surf casting, or the pier head, or day trips in boats whose richly-scented bilges betray bygone hauls of cod and conger. Even some of those anglers who are aware may feel they have too slight a knowledge of sea trout saltwater fishing to justify spending much time in search of it. If this is so, a few pages on the subject may be helpful. Hence this chapter.

Sea trout behaviour varies from one stretch of coastline to another, as indeed it does from river to river and lake to lake, and I cannot hope to give a comprehensive coverage of saltwater chances all over the British Isles. Like previous chapters, this is written only from my own experience of fishing in certain places, and these represent only a fraction of the available coastline. Nevertheless, I have no reason to suppose that the lures and methods described will not work equally well elsewhere—provided sea trout are present and willing to take.

Even in the sea, sea trout show a marked difference in their willingness to take a lure. I know of adjoining rivers that have runs of sea trout; fish will take well in the estuary of one river, but not in that of the other. Similarly, although angling can be good on some stretches of coast well away from a river mouth, on other stretches (although taken in shore nets) sea trout are seldom if ever taken on rod and line.

It seems strange that sea trout will take well in some estuaries but not in others. I have never heard a convincing explanation of this, but it seems not impossible that the non-takers are fish that (like salmon) have stopped feeding some time before running into the rivers in which they are destined to spawn.

Most migratory fishes return to their parent rivers. It is likely that those rivers in which (on their return) the fish do little feeding—most probably because there is little to feed on—breed others of similar kind. These fish (I believe) do little or no feeding in their local estuaries. These estuaries, therefore, offer the sea trout angler few chances of sport.

This I feel sure must be true of an estuary where my friends and I often fish for bass. A great number of sea trout run through this water in the summer months. We fish for bass with the identical lures that catch sea trout in the river. In the saltwater these lures catch many bass, but never a sea trout—although we have had them jump over our lines often enough! The same day in the river, if it is in spate (or that night, if it is not), we may catch sea trout on the very same lures. It is significant that, almost without exception, sea trout caught in this river, fresh from sea, carrying female sea lice as evidence of their freshness, have empty stomachs.

I am well aware that sea trout tend to take more food items in fresh-water than salmon do, but the behaviour of these two migratory species has a closer similarity than many anglers seem to think. Much closer, for instance, than that of the migratory (sea) trout and the non-migratory (brown) trout.

The sea trout's choice of sea food undoubtedly depends on seasonal availability. They are known to take young herring, pollack, whiting, haddock, coalfish, as well as sparling, sandeels and elvers; various marine worms; prawns and shrimps and other crustacea, and a host of inverte-brates. From my own experience of catching sea trout when they are feeding in saltwater, their diet has consisted almost entirely of sparling, sandeels and whitebait. On this evidence I based my approach: a silver spoon, or a "fly" designed to simulate a small fish.

I have found such lures to be very successful both by day and by night. Day fishing can be very good. But night fishing is better. Sea trout will feed at any time, but most avidly when darkness falls.

There is a multiplicity of lures that will attract sea trout in saltwater.

Indeed when sea trout are feeding almost anything will catch them, from a mackerel spinner to a strip of wash leather—which includes a range of flies, minnows, spoons, artificial sandeels, and plugs. My own preference is always for something that resembles a little fish; for instance, the Medicine and the Sunk Lure (both of which I brought from saltwater to freshwater with equal success).

There is little doubt that when small fish are present (e.g. young herrings, sprats, sandeels, sparling), they are preferred to other food.

For daylight fishing when the sea is calm and clear, spinning fine and far off usually produces the best results. This is not because sea trout prefer a spinner to a feathered lure, but because in calm conditions a spinner can be presented with less disturbance than a fly. Fish will be taken on fine spinning tackle that will not be caught on fly tackle.

From my experience of spinning in clear water, a $1\frac{5}{8}$ inch Norwegian "Bergen" spoon is probably the best of a rather poor lot. The hooking quality of spoons is not good. Of all the spoons I have tried, the Toby is the best attractor, but the worst hooker. The Mepps is a good all-rounder, but the treble is suspect. Of all the minnows, I prefer the Quill Minnow, but without the flying trebles that are often provided with this lure. Some of my friends speak highly of a new type of plug that has recently come on the market. I have had no experience of it, but can affirm that plugs will certainly catch sea trout. Where there is a good tide running, a mackerel spinner will do as well as most other lures, especially if it trails a thin strip of belly skin. If anything, its hooking quality is better than that of spoons. A single-hooked artificial sandeel hooks well. But of all the lures mentioned, my choice is still the "Bergen" spoon, even though it fails to hold on to a lot of the fish it hooks. This preference is probably due to sentimentality: it was the first lure I ever used as a boy. It caught me my first salmon and sea trout.

When conditions are suitable I prefer to use the fly rod—both for pleasure and results. Fly fishes well when the water is broken or there is sufficient ripple. I have made good catches on fly even in bright sunlight when there has been a bit of lop on the water; the sun, I need hardly add, being neither behind the rod nor shining in the fishes' eyes. Of all "flies", the Sunk Lure has given the best results. As in the river, when it comes to hanging on to a hooked sea trout this lure is way out ahead of any other.

But is there no time when small flies are used in saltwater? Indeed there is. Large numbers of sea trout often come close inshore, together with shoals of mullet, and mill about inside a sea pool, or an inlet where a tiny stream enters the sea.

If these sea trout are chasing small fish, all well and good, the lures already described will catch them. But often they may be feeding only on invertebrates. Spinners, spoons, large lures and flies are ignored. Even a conventional size of sea trout fly is refused. Only a very small lure will be taken. Try the size 12 or 14 double described on p. 62. If that is ignored, go down in size still further and use the longest, lightest leader you can fish with safety.

Strangely, sea trout coming into the same inlet the same evening on the night tide will often take large lures—although on the day tide anything larger than the "tiniest fly in the box" was ignored.

PLAN VIEW

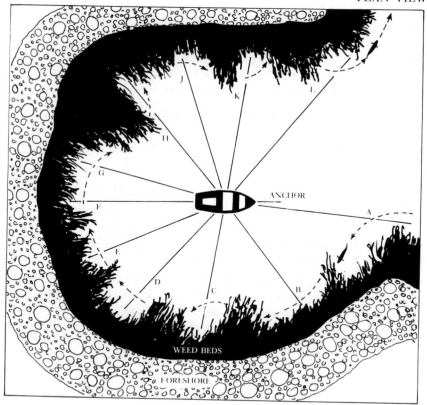

Although much depends on the prevailing weather conditions and the type of water to be fished, there are times when a boat can be very useful. This is particularly so in daylight when sea trout are on the move, feeding along a shore with the flood tide among weed beds in calm, shallow water. The angler can fish fine and far off, keeping his distance in deeper water well away from the fish. The boat enables him to position himself advantageously in relation to weed, wind and light (whether from sun or moon). It also makes it easy for him to follow the fish as they move along the shore or to the other side of a channel. When sport tails off the boat is paddled quietly to the next inlet. Feeding sea trout can usually be spotted by the surface swirls as they take their prey.

> *Note.* When watching for sea trout on the feed it is easy to be fooled by the swirls of mullet—the two species often come in with the tide together. Indeed I call the mullet the "fool's sea trout". But I am not trying to be superior. I have been fooled often enough myself!

The diagram shows a very productive little sea trout bay typical of many I have fished by boat, both in daylight and darkness, part of a complex of Irish sea loughs. Fish come in with the tide and feed their way round the shallows among the weed beds (see dotted line).

The boat is moored in the centre of the bay for two reasons:

1. By fishing round-the-clock as indicated by the alphabetical lines A to L, and casting a long line, all the water likely to be holding sea trout can be quickly covered. This is very important on the flood. Sea trout will not hang about for long in one place when the rising tide brings them in over shallow flats.

2. Casting towards the shore means that a hooked fish can be played away from the weed into open water—in the way of the pike fisherman who fishes his bait close to a reed bed from a boat lying well clear. To moor close to a weed bed is asking for trouble. Any fish being brought to the boat will unfailingly dive into the weed.

If the water is rippled and you have a boatman there is of course no need to anchor as shown in the diagram. But I find it pays to do so in these small bays simply because there is less chance of disturbance. The splash of an oar; the shadow of a moving boat; these can only help to scare fish. In shallow water, weights dropped fore and aft will keep the boat steady. One important point: *stealth is just as important afloat as it is ashore.* Don't tread heavily on the floorboards. Don't rattle things about. Keep still and keep quiet.

413

Note on tackle care. Seawater plays the devil with fishing tackle. As soon as you get home rinse everything in freshwater: landing nets, rods, reels, lines, hooks, lures and lure cases. Then dry them thoroughly. Like cleaning a gun immediately after use, this has always been my inflexible rule. Results have justified it. The built-cane Hardy rods and "Perfect" reels I first used in saltwater over thirty years ago are still just as sound today.

Generally speaking the ebb tide provides better sport than the flood. When the tide is coming in, sea trout seldom stay for long in one place—unless they are in a sea pool. They tend to keep on the move, going from bay to bay, routing about in shallow water among the weed beds.

When the tide turns their behaviour changes. Instead of hunting actively, they lie in ambush behind some weedy reef or group of rocks, waiting for food to be swept to them by the ebbing tide. In this, they are very similar to bass. I have made good catches of bass drifting in a dinghy with the flood tide. But on the ebb, my best catches have been made when anchored close to some feature: a reef of rocks, weedy stakes, or the ribs of a sunken hulk. One such feature that has given me particularly good fishing is the downstream end of an old salmon trap.

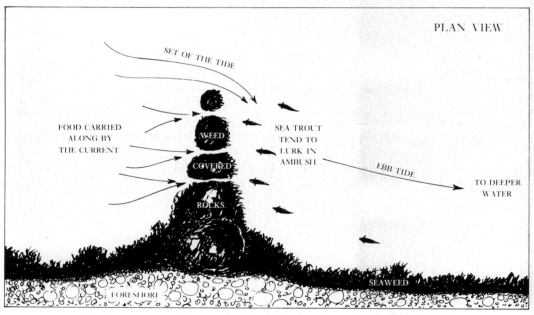

Small promontory of scattered rocks. A foreshore feature likely to attract sea trout.

Rarely have I caught bass there on the flood tide. When the ebb gathers strength, however, bass congregate just below the trap's slatted tail, feeding on sandeels and brit that are swept through the slats by the current. There they will stay until little more than a foot or so of water remains. In certain places sea trout will behave in the same way.

As I soon discovered when first starting to fish for sea trout in salt-water, there is much more to it than going to the water's edge at random and chucking out. Just as we can develop water-sense and learn to "read" a river, so we can learn to "read" a shoreline. Sea trout tend to con-centrate at certain times in certain places because of certain features that help them to get a meal. When I tumbled to the fact that some-times when these features are absent one can *create them*, and so attract sea trout to places within comfortable casting range, a whole new sport opened up in front of me. In this I was fortunate to have the opportunity of devoting a lot of time to it. . .

Sunrise over a lonely shore.

415

For a while as a young man I lived in a cottage perched above an Irish sea lough. The Lough of the Shadows they called it. A lonely place, remote and beautiful. In the winter, when wigeon whistled along the shore and an Atlantic wind came whining from the north, the lough was ridged with steel and fishing only a dream. But from the Atlantic, in the ever changing lights of early summer, came the sea trout.

It was a morning after rain, a day or two following my arrival. The distant hills were like turf smoke and the lough all violet and blue, with the flood tide creaming in curly-edged across the sands. Work was impossible. I had heard stories of sea trout seen swirling at dusk. . .

I left my typewriter and went down to the shore.

There was a little bridge over a stream that ran from inland fields under the road and out among beds of seaweed on the shore of the lough. I leaned over the parapet. The tide was high and there were several feet of seawater piled up under the bridge. A flood gate stopped it going any further inland.

The water was very clear. A fish suddenly appeared, hung for a moment just below me its nose almost touching the gate, then darted into a clump of seaweed. A fish of about 2 lb. I had only a glimpse of it, but it looked very like a sea trout.

I felt a surge of excitement. It seemed to me that if sea trout came inshore in daylight right up to the flood gate—presumably attracted by the freshwater from the stream—they would certainly do so on the night tide. Under cover of darkness there would be an infinitely better chance of doing business with them in such clear, shallow water. I had a sudden vision of twilight, and a hooked sea trout's flashing beauty.

But *was* it a sea trout I had seen? I waited hopefully, while the tide began to ebb. Surely where there was one there would be others. I watched the weed beds eagerly. But nothing moved.

An angling rustic of slight acquaintance came pedalling past. I stopped him.

Were there, I asked, white trout on that shore?

He dismounted with slow deliberation.

"Oh, indeed there are", he said. "Oh, indeed. But there's little hope of catching them at all."

"Why not?"

"It's the weed you understand. If you hook one it's gone in the weed at once. Oh I know. You'll land divil a one."

"Oh", I said. "Then why not clear the weed away?"

He gave me the dazed half-frightened look of a man who has come face to face with an idiot.

"Ah, sure, sure. . . ." he said, mounting his bike. "Indeed and why not? There'd be nothing to it. No trouble at all."

He stepped on a pedal and was gone—off round a bend in the road. As he went out of sight he gave a furtive glance back over his shoulder.

Although at the time I did not fully appreciate the point, his startled reaction to my suggestion would certainly have been shared by all other local anglers. And perhaps by anglers farther afield. It is a strange fact that although most people who have written about sea trout fishing in saltwater mention the troubles caused by seaweed, both while one is casting to and playing a fish, none that I have ever read has suggested clearing it away.

When I was young I had read very little about fishing for sea trout and nothing at all about fishing for them in the sea. I started from scratch, and that was no bad thing. As earlier chapters of this book indicate, I had no preconceived notions about the sport. And in the present instance, clearing seaweed to create a fishing space seemed the natural thing to do.

I pass all this on merely to give heart to any reader who finds himself confronted with similar problems. It does not seem to be generally realized that all fisheries demand a considerable amount of upkeep. And a saltwater fishery, of whatever sort, is no exception. In the same way that weed may need to be cleared from a river bed, so weed may need to be cleared from the sea bed—where this is possible. And it is always possible if the tide goes out far enough. It is only a question of removing your coat and rolling up your sleeves.

As I learned later with amusement, my conversation with the old Irish angler on the bridge caused heads to be shaken in the village. But by then I had astounded him with my success. At the time, I had simply learned what I wanted to know, and my vision of sea trout at dusk took on more than a tinge of reality.

The tide drained from the shore. Soon the sand was high and dry, the stream itself only a trickle. I went to work on the seaweed beds.

It was tedious, and hard on the back. But I was strong and fit. By early evening, with only a break for tea, I had cleared a fishable space. At dusk when the night tide was lapping the flood gate I hooked a three-pounder on a fly just downstream of the bridge. A beautiful fish, silver and lilac, firm as a rock and covered with sea lice.

The next day I started to roll rocks down the shore and build a dam between the outlying horns of the two rocky outcrops.

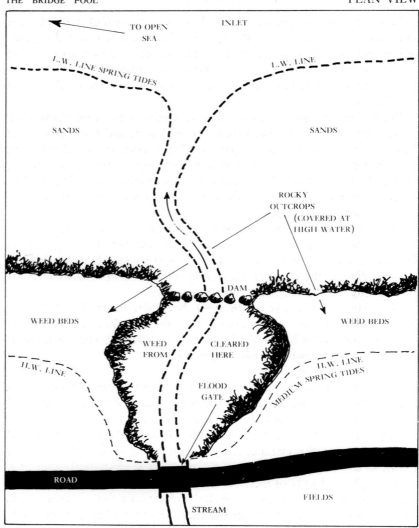

There were three fishing spots in what I called the "bridge" pool.

1. As the tide began to build up, fish would nose about in the seaweed beds just below the dam.

2. At the top of the tide they would be just below the bridge.

3. During the early part of the ebb, before the tide dropped too far, fish would hang about behind the stones of the dam, feeding on sandeels. The falling tide washed sandeels between the stones of the dam and the waiting sea trout snapped them up. They snapped up my fly too, sometimes. I would wade out in body waders and fish from the edge of the rocky outcrop on the righthand side of the stream.

418

This ploy, too, proved successful. For a few more nights I had some splendid fishing. After that the spring tides slackened and the neaps began, and the tide no longer reached the bridge. I knew then that until the next spring tides the sea trout would go elsewhere.

For me, this would have meant "back to work"—if I hadn't discovered the "Channel".

The channel in question was about a couple of hundred yards long. It ran between two small sea loughs (Inner No. 1, and Inner No. 2, see diagram on p. 421, themselves part of a larger complex of inlets). Both these loughs and the channel between them were empty at low water, indeed the tide was out of the channel at about two thirds ebb. So that, roughly speaking, a potential fishing period lasted from half-flood to half-ebb—about six hours.

The sea trout came in with the tide. Some toured Lough No. 1. Others came through the channel and spent their time in Lough No. 2. As I noticed on my first visit, however, on the ebb tide a few fish did some feeding in the channel. Obviously, there was the chance of some good fishing—if I could make room to do it in.

The channel was choked with weed, both bladderwrack and kelp of one sort and another. Apart from a few small patches of open water, there was nowhere a lure could be thrown without it getting snagged at every cast. Fishing was virtually impossible.

I set about rectifying this.

Bit by bit I cleared the centre of the channel. Then the curtain of bladderwrack for fifty or sixty yards along one shore, the shore I had elected to fish from. This enabled me to start fishing.

I should explain that when the tide came in there was a current running through the channel from Lough No. 1 to Lough No. 2 (as shown in the diagram). This current would vary in strength according to the height and state of the tide. Sluggish on the neaps. Strong on the springs. It was like a river, and had all the charm of a river. To start with, on the incoming tide, I would be fishing from the left bank. At high tide there would be a period of slack water for about half an hour. Then, when the tide turned and flowed the other way I would automatically find myself on the right bank. The variation was rather fun. During one fishing session, without moving position, I could cast (as it were) from both sides of a river, in all speeds of current—from dead slow to very fast—and varying in depth from a few inches to nine or ten feet.

Once the weed clearance was done there was open water for a lure to swing, and a clean bank to cast from and land a fish. But that was only the start.

Stretching across the channel from side to side was a jumbled line of big flat rocks—once, perhaps, a shepherd's causeway long fallen into desuetude. These formed a low weir behind which a shallow pool had formed. I noticed that as the tide began to ebb and the current increase in strength, sea trout stopped foraging in the inner loughs and took up station behind these rocks—at least, some of them did. There would be the occasional swirl as a feeding fish snapped up food washed over by the tide.

Remembering the behaviour of the fish below the little bridge, it seemed to me that I might be able to improve these "lies"—and perhaps construct some new ones. Building materials presented no problems. There were plenty of boulders lying about on the shore and the moorland above. It was just a question of moving them. In the end, with infinite labour, much patience and the aid of a lever, I managed to tumble some of them down the shore and into position. Some were used to build up the weir; some were planted out in the middle of the channel in groups to form extra "lies" (see A, B, and C).

It all took a long time to complete, much longer than the fishing spot below the bridge. But it was a labour of love and I was obsessed. Day after day over a period of neap tides I worked away, while the typewriter stood idle in the cottage and a mound of cleared seaweed grew beside the channel, stinking in the hot summer sun.

I was quite alone, and supremely happy. No other anglers seemed to have found that lonely shore. It was my own little fishery. There were no distractions; no sound, except the wind and the seabirds' crying.

The results exceeded all my dreams. During the time I fished it regularly, that channel between the sea loughs gave me some wonderful fishing. Even now, on those occasions when I make a pilgrimage to fish it, I stagger away bemused by my good luck.

One rather strange anomaly may be worth mentioning. Some of the sea trout I have caught on that Irish coast are bigger than any I have heard of being caught in neighbouring rivers. There are several explanations of this. But one that occurs to me has particular appeal. For reasons unknown, larger sea trout run up British rivers than Irish rivers. Is it not possible that during May and June after visiting the northern area of the Atlantic Shelf (which I believe is what they do) some of these fish are eating their way back towards the Irish Sea? If so, and I like to think it is so, then perhaps an occasional fish I see lying in my little Cumbrian river in July or August is a fish I have seen before, earlier that summer—swirling under the stars by the seaweed-covered stones of that lonely sea lough.

420

PLAN VIEW

Connecting channel between sea loughs.

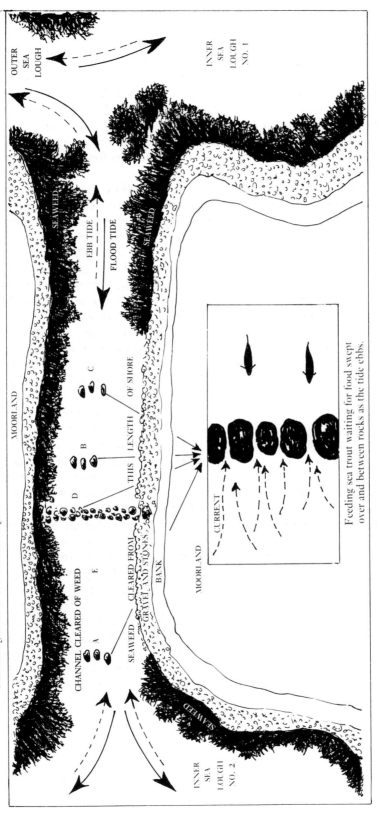

OUTER SEA LOUGH

INNER SEA LOUGH NO. 1

EBB TIDE

FLOOD TIDE

SEAWEED

SEAWEED

MOORLAND

THIS LENGTH OF SHORE

CHANNEL CLEARED OF WEED

SEAWEED CLEARED FROM GRAVEL AND STONES

BANK

MOORLAND

CURRENT

Feeding sea trout waiting for food swept over and between rocks as the tide ebbs.

SEAWEED

INNER SEA LOUGH NO. 2

A
B } Constructed "lies".
C
D Rocky barrier built up with boulders to form a 3 ft. weir.
E Natural pool.

Sport in saltwater is better on spring tides than neaps. Certainly at night. When half-flood on a spring tide is at dusk; high water at, say, one o'clock in the morning, and half-ebb at daybreak, in a place you know to be visited regularly by feeding sea trout, good sport is almost certain. This is so predictable that when you know your water, something about the behaviour of the local sea trout, and the run of the tides, you can plan a night's fishing a month (or even a year) hence, with only an Almanac to help you. And it will all work out exactly as planned.

This I have often proved when planning an expedition to the Irish sea loughs, choosing a week of high spring tides, preferably over the period of the new moon rather than the full. I have made good catches in bright moonlight but, given the choice, I would rather plan for dark nights.

A stretch of shore has been cleared of seaweed at low water. Now, with three rods set up ready, the author waits by a convenient grassy bank as the tide begins to flood.

A tide rip running through a channel in the weed beds that was cleared a few hours before. Sea trout are coming in with the tide and feeding along the edge of the weed.

A 3 lb. sea trout hooked on fly in the little channel is running for the open water beyond.

When fishing in saltwater one is not, of course, restricted to night fishing. Fish come in with the tide in daylight as well as darkness, it is simply that night fishing is more predictable. In the little channel I have described, sea trout can be caught at any hour—provided there is sufficient water. But the best sport is usually at night.

In this I am somewhat biased, since I am a night owl by nature and, as an old Irish fishing companion put it, would rather fish by night any day. Nevertheless, as in so many rivers, darkness offers the best chances—and when the spring tides are running, with high water somewhere between 11.0 p.m. and 2.0 a.m., night fishing in the channel is very exciting.

The incoming tide gradually builds up on the upstream side of the weir. Then it starts to sluice between the boulders, and finally cascades over the top. While this is happening, a few sea trout can be taken on fly in the deepening water above the weir. After which, a spoon fished for a time in the fast broken water below the weir brings results. Then, when the rising tide has smoothed out this turbulence, fly fishes well in the pool.

At high tide most of the fish are in Lough No. 2. You can hear them swirling out there in the darkness. While slack water lasts, I fish with a spinning rod, casting a Surface Lure as far as possible in the direction of the swirling fish, and reeling it quickly back again. The lure is made of wood, which casts well from a fixed-spool reel and accounts for some good fish from time to time. One advantage of the floating lure at high tide is that it swims over the top of the weed beds.

With the ebbing tide, sea trout drop back from the inner lough and lie below the weir and the various groups of rocks (A, B, C), the boulders I rolled into position. (Their success was most gratifying. Never was hard labour so well rewarded.) These "lies" provide a chance of catching fish at any time during the ebb, until the tide finally leaves the channel.

But although fish can be caught at any hour of the night, it seemed to me years ago that there was a distinct pattern of feeding behaviour. This consisted of three periods, during which most of my fish were caught. At dusk; for a time after midnight, and again at daybreak—when sea trout take very freely, sometimes until well after sunrise. It is during these periods that they seem to feed most avidly.

I have mentioned using a Surface Lure. That sea trout in the sea will take a floating lure dragged across the surface may come as a surprise. It certainly surprised me. But take it they will. And, as in the river, it will attract some of the biggest fish. It was in the channel that I dis-

424

Sea trout feeding grounds—a great mass of bladderwrack. The bay seems to be choked with the weed, but there is plenty of swimming room underneath the surface blanket, among the weed stems.

Fishing the flood tide from a rocky outcrop. A spinner is cast well out and brought back along the fringe of seaweed. Here, in water of 2–5 ft. deep, the sea trout are chasing shrimps and small fish.

425

covered how well this lure serves in saltwater. I had never heard of such a method being used in the sea, but one evening when fishing fly on greased line in the late dusk without success, I put on a three-inch quill Surface Lure as an experiment—and immediately hooked a fish.

It was a very exciting moment. Although alone, I shouted aloud in sheer exultation—a predatory crow of triumph that found a strange echo on another occasion when, in an emergency, a made-on-the-spot floating lure consisting of a roughly-trimmed beer cork with a hook whipped to it caught me the biggest sea trout I have ever hooked in saltwater.

The sea trout food in the saltwater loughs I fish consists mainly of sparling (an example is shown on p. 44). It is possibly the action of these little fish in the shallow water that makes the Surface Lure so attractive. Sparling often dart along with their backs just breaking surface, leaving a tiny wake. Judging by their swirls, feeding sea trout are in the habit of taking these little fish at or near the surface—certainly at night in the comparatively shallow water I have described.

In the night fishing section of this book, for the sake of convenience, I recommend the use of two rods. When fishing in the sea, either from a boat or when movement along the shore is restricted, I use three. These consist of one spinning rod and two fly rods: one with floating line, the other with sinking line—as for the river. In years gone by, of course, I used greased or ungreased silk lines.

When fishing the channel I tackle-up before the tide comes in, and lean the rods against a convenient bank ready for instant use. Conditions change rapidly when the tide is flowing fast. It is essential to lose no time when changing methods.

Nothing special is needed in the way of tackle. It is the same as one uses in freshwater. Fly rod No. 1 (floating line) starts off with a Medicine. Fly rod No. 2 (sinking line) has a Sunk Lure. On the spinning rod, a Norwegian spoon—or perhaps some experimental lure.

The water is usually gin clear. At dusk, when the tide starts to flow up the channel bringing the first sea trout with it, a Medicine is fished on a long line.

Then, a spoon can be tried in the broken water behind the weir.

After that, a Medicine in the pool below.

By now it is dark. The water is much deeper, the current pretty strong. Having put a Surface Lure on the first rod in place of the Medicine, I would try the Sunk Lure on sinking line, most likely continuing with it until high water.

426

In the period of slack water at the top of the tide, the best chance of a fish is in Lough No. 2, on a wooden lure cast with the spinning rod.

On the ebb tide, when fish are feeding behind the rocks, I would try Sunk Lure and Surface Lure in turn. Both are good for hooking big fish, and the use of two fly rods set up ready with different lines is very handy.

At daybreak—a particularly good time for "taking" fish—I would give the Medicine another try if the morning is calm and there is little water left, but the Sunk Lure will stay on as long as fish are prepared to show an interest in it.

Well—this, roughly, is the programme of a night's fishing in one particular place on the shore. It gives an indication of the sort of methods that can be used, whatever the setting. Feeding sea trout are obviously potential "takers", and provided a suitable lure is fished attractively, there is no real difficulty in catching fish. When sea trout come in on the tide a blank night is very rare.

The tide is starting to ebb from the rocky shore seen in foreground. A tiny stream runs under the little bridge and out into the sea through beds of seaweed. Attracted by the freshwater, sea trout swim in and out with the tide and can be caught just downstream of the bridge. Here, a fish of 3–4 lb. jumped a few seconds before this picture was taken.

427

Needless to say, sea trout do not always appear. This is probably due to a chain reaction: a shifting drift of plankton will be followed by the small fish and fry, and these in turn will be followed by the sea trout. Nor are weather conditions always favourable. Sea trout when in the sea are less affected by weather than they are in the river, but thunder will put them off the "take" just as it will in freshwater. In the same way as it is in the river, however, fishing can be very good once the storm breaks, more particularly during the intervals between periods of heavy rain. As on the river, if you can knock up some sort of rain shelter, so much the better. There is little in the way of cover on most shores, and getting soaked never helped anyone to catch fish. But to sit out a thunderstorm is very worthwhile. When the fish "come on", and they usually do, they come with a bang.

As I have already suggested, stealth and concealment are as important in a boat or on the shore as they are on river or lake. The effects of shadow are the same wherever one fishes. Feeding sea trout will take well however bright the sun or moon, but the light must never be behind the rod.

And where will you fish in saltwater? That you must find out for yourself. I shall certainly not describe the whereabouts of my enchanted channel. Find it if you can. If you can't, you will not be disappointed, your search will bring you to many other places just as good—that is, if you care to do some work on them. My channel and the place below the bridge fished well only because of the weed clearance, and the "lies" that were improved and made. There are thousands of other places along the shores of Britain where sea trout feed. Find them, and you have some of the most exciting fishing in the world.

Finally, the approach to sea trout night fly-fishing described in the earlier chapters of this book works equally well in saltwater. It was, after all, largely on the pattern of the sea trout's feeding times, and the tendency of the bigger fish to take late at night, that my night fly-fishing philosophy was based. Whether my reasons were valid I leave future anglers to decide. But one thing I know for certain: they give very good results!

* * *

As this book goes to press I have stumbled on a splendid way of preparing small sea trout for the table. The result is as good as the finest smoked salmon.

SCANDINAVIAN SEA TROUT

You need:

1 herling or small sea trout ($\frac{3}{4}$ lb.–$1\frac{1}{2}$ lb.). Sea salt. Castor sugar. Fresh ground black pepper. Fresh dill if in season. If not, used dried dill or dried thyme. I prefer thyme.

To prepare:

1. Clean the fish. Split it in half down the back. *Bone it completely.* (It is worth taking some trouble over this.)
2. Lay one side flat, skin downwards, and sprinkle evenly with salt on flesh side only.
3. On top of the salt sprinkle a tablespoonful of sugar.
4. Sprinkle with black pepper to taste.
5. Sprinkle with half a teaspoonful of dried dill or dried thyme. If using fresh dill just lay two or three fronds along the fish.
6. Place the other half of the fish on top of this lot, skin uppermost, and press gently into place.
7. Place the whole fish on a dish, making sure it is lying flat.
8. Place another dish on top of the fish, and on top of that place a heavy weight—say, 10–12 lb.
9. Place the whole lot in the refrigerator.
10. Leave it there for 12 hours.
11. Remove weights and top dish, and without disturbing the fish pour away the juice that has been pressed out of the fish into the bottom dish.
12. Very carefully, turn the fish over. Replace the upper dish and weights. Return to the refrigerator for another 12 hours.
13. The fish is now ready to eat. Remove dill (if fresh) and wipe off any traces of salt or dried herbs. Slice off the flesh as thinly as possible with a sharp knife—like smoked salmon. Serve with red or black pepper and lemon juice on brown bread and butter, or on hot buttered toast. Delicious!

Note. In cold weather the use of a refrigerator is unnecessary, it can all be done on a stone floor. At Cragg we have used fish from the deep freeze in winter with excellent results. We find that mackerel, either fresh or deep frozen, is also delicious prepared in this way.

But where are the snows of yesteryear?
François Villon (b. 1431), *Le Grand Testament* . . .

XV
Past and Future

We have reached the end of the book. In it is most of what I know and think about the sport of sea trout fishing. But it is based largely on the experience of days and nights long past—when rivers seemed to sing more sweetly and time moved softly by and the pools were blue with fish. It is not the same today. In the rivers I fish regularly the numbers of migratory fishes are only a fraction of what they were eight or ten years ago. Now, in pools where during the "First-Half" alone I could hook a dozen fish, I have to work hard all night to kill two brace. On my own river the decline has been dramatic.

In one sense I do not mind this. Success, after all, is relative. And in terms of skill the bags I make today are as satisfying as those bigger bags of yesterday. But what of the future? There is no satisfaction in the thought of diminishing runs of fish and barren pools. This unhappy change of recent years has caused some observers to suggest that sport as we knew it a decade or so ago may never return; that between them, UDN, pollution and commercial fishing have written the beginning of the end for salmon and sea trout.

They may be right. Estuary netting continues unabated, and doubtless will continue to do so until the final fish is caught. The spectre of disease still lurks. For all our policies of conservation and re-stocking, the ghosts that shriek and squeal about the streets may indeed be real: the warnings and portents and evils imminent may all come true.

The outbreak of the "Salmon Disease" (Ulcerative Dermal Necrosis) is of particular importance to the future of the sport. First reported from south-west Ireland in 1964, it became established in some English, Welsh and Scottish rivers by the autumn of 1966, and has persisted ever since. The disease is not restricted to salmon. Sea trout, brown trout, charr and grayling can also become infected.

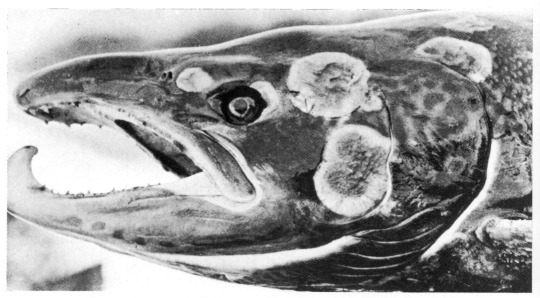

Over seventy years ago. Early stages of fungal growth on the head of a 7 lb. male grilse. Picture (taken in December, 1905) is from P. D. Malloch's *Life-History and Habits of The Salmon, Sea Trout, and other Freshwater Fish* (1910).

For the following points, I am grateful to Dr L. G. Willoughby of the Freshwater Biological Association, Windermere.

    1. Three forms of this disease have been observed (see diagrams).

        I   1st stage: Ulcer.

                  2nd stage: Ulcer. (No fungal growth.)

                  Fish have been known to recover from this form of UDN.

       II   1st stage: Ulcer.

                  2nd stage: Fungal growth on ulcer.

                  No recoveries known.

      III 1st stage: Fungus.

                  2nd stage: Fungus.

                  No recoveries known.

    Note. Strictly speaking the term "UDN" covers only fish without fungal. growth (see diagram I). By common consent, however, this has been expanded to cover fish *with* fungus (see diagrams II and III).

    2. The current disease shows extraordinary parallels with the distribution of a previous outbreak of what is believed to have been the same disease. This began in 1877 and continued until the turn of the century.

    3. The fungus (*Saprolegnia*) is found only in freshwater (or in estuarine water with a very low saline content). It grows on the fish very quickly— within twenty-four hours.

432

THREE FORMS OF U.D.N.

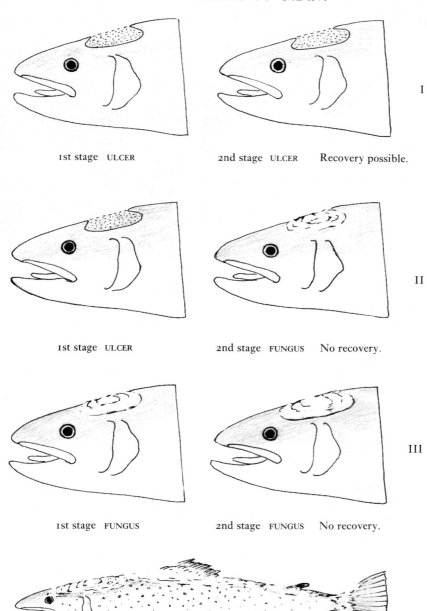

1st stage ULCER 2nd stage ULCER Recovery possible. I

1st stage ULCER 2nd stage FUNGUS No recovery. II

1st stage FUNGUS 2nd stage FUNGUS No recovery. III

The back of the head, dorsal fin, adipose fin and tail fin are the places most likely to become infected.

4. The cause of death has been controversial. From research done at Windermere by Dr Alan Pickering, it seems that one probable cause is the upset of the fish's osmotic process—which results in loss of body salts.

5. The eggs from diseased fish are viable. If a diseased fish survives long enough to spawn, the eggs will hatch normally.

Walter Caddy

He looks pleased with himself. But he would probably have felt even more pleased had he realized what he'd caught. Examination of the picture under a low-power microscope reveals that this fish is unquestionably a sea trout. I estimate its weight as being between 14 and 15 lb. No record of such a magnificent sea trout is to be found in Walter's diaries. During the season in which I think this photograph was taken, he records a "salmon" of $14\frac{1}{2}$ lb. I feel sure this was the fish.

I like his hat.

434

But prolonged and violent fluctuations in runs of salmon and sea trout are not peculiar to the present time.

The note of doom has been rung before. Listen to the voice of Walter Caddy tolling away nearly a century ago.

You will not have heard of Walter Caddy. So far as I am aware he published nothing, nor has he himself received publicity. But, as you will soon appreciate, his words have a familiar ring.

That I seem to know Walter as well as I know my river bank is not surprising. Day in night out, he walked that bank during the whole of a long lifetime. He was a great character, an all-round sportsman and, above all, an angler of limitless enthusiasm. An engineer by profession, he seems fortunate to have been not over-burdened with work, and day after day, night after night, wet or fine, we find him with his big green-heart rod beside the river. He knew the beauty of my valley, and the cottage I live in. Season after season, summer and autumn, he fished the pools I fish today. And he wrote about it all in his many diaries with great gusto—and in the end a certain sadness.

Through the kindness of their present owner, Mr. R. B. Woodall, I have read these diaries. Walter's singleness of purpose, his consuming enthusiasm for the sport of angling, fill me with delight and a feeling of deep affinity. We have shared similar pleasures on the same river and the same pools in the valley that I love. He was upset, as I am upset, to think that what once was, might never come again.

And so now, a little of what he wrote shall be published—which I think would have pleased him, and certainly pleases me. I quote him partly from respect and partly because these brief extracts from his diaries may offer some hope for the future of migratory fishes—by dispelling the myth that everything was always so much better long ago!

We take up the story in 1891. Walter has had a good year on the river and, at the end of a volume that runs to 53 pages, he sums up his sport.

I have had the best season that I ever had both for salmon and sea trout. . . . Have still been unlucky in getting broken, but taking it all through have had a magnificent time.

This sounds fine. Just like mother made. These were "the good old days" we've been told about. But now read on. Volume by volume we follow the story intermittently until 1913 (after which the introduction of sheep-dipping tubs that emptied into the river caused further havoc).

For the uninitiated, I should explain that Smelt=Small=Herling. Mort=Big=Sea trout. (Both Cumbrian terms.)

1893   A bad salmon season—very. . . . Smelts took fairly well at night in summer, but we fished hard and they were never plentiful. . . . A bad salmon season in all rivers. No doubt the exceptionally fine summer had something to do with it.

1896   It has been a very bad season for morts and smelts. In fact smelts have been the scarcest ever known. We did very little night fishing. . . . They had the best season for netting [in the estuary] both among morts and salmon they have ever had. [How many times have I heard this!] Very few morts got up at all and most of the early salmon were got too, on account of the dry weather. With plenty of water the river might have been full of early salmon. . .

1897   The most aggravating and disappointing season I have ever had since I killed my first salmon. . . . Smelts have been as scarce as last year, more scarce if anything. It seems very curious what can have happened to them. . . . Morts were more plentiful than last year and I killed as many morts as smelts all but one. Still one should have killed far more morts, too, than I actually got.

1903   I have had a very poor season among morts and smelts both at night fishing and daytime. . .

1904   So has ended the worst salmon season since I commenced to fish the rivers. . . . No one else has done anything much. . . . There is no doubt salmon have been very scarce indeed, the dry summer most likely accounting for it. . . . A good season for night fishing.

1905   Salmon have been even scarcer than last year. . . . A really good sea trout season. All holes well filled with smelts . . . and a lot of good fish killed chiefly night fishing. Not so many morts as usual. I have had splendid sport with my new method of worm fishing in the daytime. Have great hopes for it in the future.

1906   The salmon fishing has again been a complete failure. . . . There have scarcely been any salmon in the river. . . . It seems there cannot be enough to spawn to keep up the stock. The new river course having spoiled all the holes and spawning ground. [Where has one heard this before! The familiar story of river-canalization that has done so much harm to the fishing—and almost nothing to improve the drainage!] It looks very doubtful whether there will ever again be salmon fishing of any account. . . . A fair mort season. . .

1907   A few salmon this year, but never anything like the old times. . . .
[Note that. The "old times" syndrome was in evidence even
then!] I have done well among smelts considering that they have
never been plentiful . . . never had the fish gathered in the holes
in any number. Did well with fly amongst them. Found my own
dressing of Red Cock hackle and Grey Mallard wing a killer.

Now comes an improvement.

1908   A real satisfactory season among morts and smelts . . . have had
some grand days with fine worm tackle, and grand evenings with
fly after dusk.

1909   It has been a splendid season for morts and smelts, particularly
smelts. Am glad smelts seem to be as plentiful as ever. . . .

Halcyon days indeed. But the "plentiful" herling runs of 1908 and
1909 seem to have had no effect on the sea trout runs during the years
to come.

1910   Often came home before dark, as no heart in trying with so few
fish in.

1911   Have had a very bad season among small fish on account of the
long dry summer . . . never were many up. . . . The less said
about this season the better.

1912   Can't help the feeling that salmon are getting scarcer and scarcer.
. . . Morts and smelts a complete failure. Scarcely a mort in the
river and any smelts there were mostly quite little ones. Very
discouraging, but hope for better years.

1913   This ends the fishing season for 1913. If it can be called a fishing
season. There have been no salmon in the river . . . and what is
more, no morts except little ones . . . and the smelts that seemed
to be coming about the end of August seemed to disappear. [I
know just what he means!] The long dry summer must have had
something to do with it, but I doubt they were never there to
come. . . . Quite out of heart. Unless there is a great change it
seems the fishing is about finished.

That was written a long time ago, about a river that in later years
provided some of the finest sea trout fishing of my life. And what of the
future?

Well—*Plus ça change . . .* !

I leave you with that faint note of hope.

"Come, Sir, let us be going: for the sun grows
low. . . ."
Izaak Walton

438

Bibliography

ANON, *The Arte of Angling*, 1577

BERNERS, Dame Juliana, *A Treatyse of Fysshynge wyth an Angle*, 1496.
BICKERDYKE, John, *The Book of the All Round Angler*, 1888.
BRIDGETT, R. C., *Sea-Trout Fishing*, 1929.
BULLER, Fred, and FALKUS, Hugh, *Falkus and Buller's Freshwater Fishing*, 1975.

CHETHAM, James, *The Angler's Vade-Mecum*, 1681.

DENNYS, John, *The Secrets of Angling*, 1613.

FALKUS, Hugh, *The Stolen Years*, second edition, 1979.

GRAY, L. R. N., *Torridge Fishery*, 1957.

KINGSMILL MOORE, T. C., *A Man May Fish*, second edition, 1979.

MALLOCH, P. D., *Life-History and Habits of the Salmon, Sea Trout, Trout and other Freshwater Fish*, 1910.
MARKHAM, Gervase, *The Pleasures of Princes*, 1614.
——, *The Whole Art of Angling*, fifth edition 1633.
McCLAREN, Charles C., *The Art of Sea Trout Fishing*, 1963.

NALL, G. H., *The Life of the Sea Trout*, 1930.

O'GORMAN, *The Practice of Angling*, two vols. 1845.

RANSOME, Arthur, *Mainly about Fishing*, 1959.
RATCLIFFE, William, *Fishing from the Earliest Times*, 1921.

SALTER, T. F., *The Angler's Guide*, eighth edition 1833.
SHERINGHAM, H. T., *Elements of Angling*, 1908.
SPENCER, Sidney, *Salmon and Seatrout in Wild Places*, 1968.
——, *Newly from the Sea*, 1969.
STEWART, W. C., *The Practical Angler*, 1857.
STUART, Hamish, *The Book of the Sea Trout*, c. 1917.

VENABLES, Robert, *The Experienc'd Angler*, 1662.
VOSS BARK, Conrad, *Fishing for Lake Trout*, 1972.

WALTON, Izaak, *The Compleat Angler*, 1653.
WHEELER, Alwyne, *The Fishes of the British Isles and North West Europe*, 1969.
WHITE, Gilbert, *Natural History and Antiquities of Selborne*, 1789.
WIGGIN, Maurice, *Troubled Waters*, 1960.

Index

440